THE MATTHEW 16 CONTROVERSY
Peter and the Rock

Other Resources Offered Through Christian Resources

Holy Scripture: The Ground and Pillar of Our Faith, Volume I, A Biblical Defense of the Reformation Principle of Sola Scriptura

Holy Scripture: The Ground and Pillar of Our Faith, Volume II, An Historical Defense of the Reformation Principle of Sola Scriptura

Holy Scripture: The Ground and Pillar of Our Faith, Volume III, The Writings of the Church Fathers Affirming the Reformation Principle of Sola Scriptura

The Church Of Rome At The Bar Of History

Salvation, The Bible and Roman Catholicism

The Christian: What It Means to Know and Follow Christ

Must Jesus Be Lord To Be Savior?

Saving Faith: How Does Rome Define It?

Roman Catholic Tradition: Claims and Contradictions

The Gospel of the Reformation

THE MATTHEW 16 CONTROVERSY
Peter and the Rock

An Examination of the Patristic Understanding of the Rock of Matthew 16 and of the Early Church's Relationship to the Bishops of Rome

William Webster

CHRISTIAN RESOURCES INC.

CHRISTIAN RESOURCES INC
1505 NW 4th Avenue
Battle Ground, WA 98604

Email: ChristianResources@christiantruth.com
Web Page: www.christiantruth.com

© *William Webster, 1996*
Second Printing, Revised 1999

ISBN 1-879737-25-6

Cover: St. Matthew from the Book of Kells

Cover Design by Michael Rotolo

Contents

Foreword by Dr. Tom J. Nettles   *9*
Introduction   *17*

Part I: The Historical Exegesis Of The Early Church

Chapter 1: The Father's Interpretation of the Rock
of Matthew 16 and the Role of Peter   *25*

Tertullian	*26, 343*
Origen	*29, 336*
Cyprian	*32, 137, 309*
Optatus of Milevis	*40*
Firmilian	*43, 319*
Eusebius	*45, 316*
Athanasius	*48, 288*
Didymus the Blind	*50, 314*
Augustine	*51, 138, 253*
Ambrose	*62, 279*
Hilary of Poitiers	*67, 325*
Jerome	*68, 328*
Ambrosiaster	*72, 138, 282*
Chrysostom	*74, 138, 295*
Theodoret	*86, 344*
Cyril of Alexandria	*89, 311*
Basil the Great	*93, 291*
Gregory of Nyssa	*96, 325*
James of Nisbis	*97, 328*
Cyril of Jerusalem	*98, 314*
John Cassian	*99, 293*
Epiphanius	*101, 315*
Aphraates	*103, 284*

Ephrem Syrus	*105, 316*
Palladius of Helenopolis	*106, 339*
Basil of Seleucia	*107, 291*
Nilus of Ancyra	*108, 336*
Asterius	*109, 286*
Paul of Emessa	*110, 340*
Isidore of Pelusium	*111, 327*
Cassiodorus	*111, 292*
Fulgentius of Ruspe	*113, 320*
Gregory the Great	*114, 321*
Maximus of Turin	*121, 332*
Peter Chrysologus	*126, 308*
Comments of 6th Century Eastern Clergy	*128, 346*
Isidore of Seville	*129, 327*
John of Damascus	*130, 331*
Bede	*133, 292*
Paschasius Radbertus	*135, 340*
Ignatius	*136, 326*
The Apostolical Constitutions	*138*

PART II: THE HISTORICAL PRACTICE OF THE EARLY Church

Chapter 2: The Historical Practice of the Early Church in Relation to the Bishops of Rome

The Church Councils	
Individual Fathers	*194*
The Papacy: A Process of Gradual Development	
Historical Summary	*228*

CONCLUSION *237*

Part III: Appendices

Appendix A: The Official Teaching of the Roman Catholic Church on Papal Primacy and Infallibility from Vatican I, Vatican II, and *The Catechism of the Catholic Church* — *241*

Appendix B: Documentation from the Writings of the Fathers from the 3rd through the 8th Centuries on the Meaning of the Rock of Matthew 16 and of Peter's Relationship to the Other Apostles — *251*

ENDNOTES — *349*

INDEX — *379*

Foreword

Recent years have seen an increase in serious attempts at achieving some reapproachment between Roman Catholics and Protestants. Tired of caricature and hostility, suspicion and misrepresentation, division and misunderstanding, Catholics and Protestants at many levels have sought to bridge chasms in relationships which have existed for years. Encumbered on the one hand by the emotional baggage engendered by such historical phenomena as the inquisition, the burnings at Smithfield under 'Bloody Mary', the ruthlessness of the Duke of Alva, and the massacre of St. Bartholomew's day, and, on the other hand, by the decades of political repression promoted by such Protestant groups as the 'Know Nothing' party, Christians within Catholicism and Protestantism desire to be shed of such heavy loads.

Impetus for the surge of interest in establishing new relationships has come from several quarters. Years of ecumenical discussion while achieving little unity have at least established a precedent of talking to each other. The popularity of John F. Kennedy as president removed many fears that Americanism and Catholicism were mutually exclusive. Now that two Southern Baptists have occupied the White House from the same political party and have expressed indebtedness to the leadership style of Kennedy, the anti-Catholic political incubus has seemingly been exorcised. Vatican II encouraged Bible study within Catholic communities and helped remove fear of, and even provoked some healthy curiosity about, Protestantism among Catholic lay people. The charismatic movement with its elevation of experience and minimizing of doctrine put Roman Catholics and Protestants in the same worship services, singing the same music, listening to the same speakers, and speaking in the same unknown tongues.

With all that as prelude, the current rapid breakdown in public morality has served as a fast-setting concrete poured into the cracks that still remain in the Catholic/Protestant relationship. The brutalizing of society through legalized abortion, the enormously horrific implications for aging of doctor–assisted suicide, the glamorization of the macabre by Hollywood, the normalizing of sexual perversion, and the floodtide of pornography combined with the mounting evidence that brutality is fueled by it, have given good reason for the idea that something must be done. As Pat Robertson has written:

> We have a moral imperative to join together in our efforts to oppose the killing of the unborn, the hostility toward and censorship of the Christian message, and the wholesale assault on the traditional family. The next seven years are crucial if we are going to make any inroads against the pressing darkness of our age. The lives of thirty–one million children alone, killed in the womb by legalized abortion, cry out for judgment. But, if we have any hope of turning the tide, we must come together in our efforts.[1]

The moral imperative of the case makes the reasoning of the call for coming together appear compelling. No Christian would oppose a show of strength and unity that can help bring into captivity the cult of death exalting itself against the divine prerogatives of life. Neighbors working together for the integrity of the moral climate in schools and communities often bring levels of respect, friendship, and admiration that transcend the religious tension of the past. These attempts at minimizing the ravages of sin conform to the apostolic injunction to resist evil wherever it appears.

Other issues, however, need to be considered and a more nuanced, multi–level approach to cooperation should be developed. Ignoring differences, even temporarily, does nothing for the cause of truth in the long run and, in fact, gradually erodes the very moral foundation necessary for cultural righteousness. Pushing aside important differences makes the church more energetic about a moralism focused on man than true piety focused on God. This in turn creates a pragmatism, and eventually a relativism, that will destroy the love of truth and with it the sense of oughtness that gives perserverance to righteous action.

Beyond that, however, lurks the subtle and deceitful, but often pleasing, temptation to labor for bread which perishes rather than that which endures to eternal life. As compelling as the moral issues we face are, if attention to them causes a blindness to the infinitely more serious issues of condemnation under the law and righteousness in Christ, then we have forsaken heaven for the world and the cross for the law. The hatred is so great that Satan has for the cross and the redemptive work done by the Son of God there, that he might rest somewhat satisfied with a 'righteous' union that is content to ignore the final satisfaction of Christ's work on the cross and the doctrine of justification. The dangerous beauty of this temptation is seen in Pat Robertson's concept that '...we lay aside certain concerns over legitimate theological differences to join together and support things upon which we all agree, such as the sanctity of all human life.'[2] The poison in the apple is not that the groups 'join together;' it is in what they 'lay aside.'

What is being laid aside here? Nothing other than the doctrine of justification by faith. Instead of the doctrine of the imputed righteousness insisted on by Paul as the foundation of justification before God (Rom. 4:22–25), a doctrine of gradual conversion is substituted. Paul insisted that a man 'is justified by faith apart from observing the law' (Rom. 3:28). The justification occurs immediately and 'since we have been justified through faith, we have peace with God through our Lord Jesus Christ, through whom we have gained access by faith into this grace in which we now stand' (Rom. 5:1,2).

By faith, the grace of justification is a present reality, accomplished for us and outside us by the Lord Jesus Christ. It is complete and perfect the moment by grace through faith we enter into it. No development of holiness or righteousness in our lives will ever match the purity or perfection of Christ's righteousness imputed to us by God (Phil. 3:9).

Sanctification is gradual. This process of conversion may be defined in terms of conformity to the law. The Holy Spirit is the agent of change, the law is the rule of conformity, and increase of love is the proof of progress (Gal. 5:13–16). The increase of sanctification also confirms the reality of justifying faith so that one may say truly that a faith which will not result in sanctification does not suffice for justification. But the distinction between these two graces must be maintained: justification comes apart from observing the law; sanctification comes through personal conformity to the law. Justification is completed by Christ outside of us; sanctification develops through the work of the Holy Spirit within us.

When Keith Fournier explains what it means to be a 'Catholic Christian,' his first point concentrates on what he perceives as the 'evangelical moments' of his conversion:

> First, I am a Catholic Christian who can point to various times of deepening faith or conversion in my life, 'evangelical moments' as I call them, not just one experience. This is consonant with my understanding of what is involved in being transformed into the image of Christ. Conversion is a process, and individuals and the church itself are being continually renewed into His image.[3]

He is right in describing conversion as a process and in affirming God's purpose that we be renewed into Christ's image. None of that, however, will give a sinner right standing before God. In this life, such conformity to Christ will be substantial but will, nonetheless, remain incomplete. The highest degree of it cannot escape the deformity of the Spirit–opposing flesh and by itself would leave us under condemnation. Sinners must have an absolute spotless conformity to the law as the substance of their right standing before God. This is the burden of the Protestant (biblical!) doctrine of justification. Fournier has not a word about justification and in fact consciously avoids it. He knows that his description is distinctively Catholic. He may have a saving experience with Christ and be united with Him in His completed doing and dying in a way that is superior to his expression, or his undersatnding, of salvation. But the reality of his statement is that justification by faith can be omitted without significant loss. And Pat Robertson concedes this in considering it something that can be laid aside.

Fournier rests so steadfastly, and with such clear commitment, in that understanding because of his view of religious authority. 'I have committed myself to the teaching office of the Catholic Church and its leadership,' he says. 'I do this willingly and with conscious choice.' While he respects his many Protestant friends who consider themselves 'Bible–toting believers,' Fournier relishes the idea of being a 'magisterium-toting Catholic.'[4] For him, this gives moral clarity as well as a sure and tested voice in the confusing world of theological controversy.

Fournier's submission to the magisterium, and consequently its teaching on salvation, conforms perfectly to expected Catholic practice. This submission comes because Catholics are convinced that the teaching office of the church has been granted infallibly to the bishops under the leadership of Peter's successor, the Pope. The *Catechism of the Catholic Church* states:

> The mission of the Magisterium is linked to the definitive nature of the covenant established by God with his people in Christ. It is this Magisterium's task to preserve God's people from deviations and defections and to guarantee them the objective possibility of professing the true faith without error. Thus, the pastoral duty of the Magisterium is aimed at seeing to it that the People of God abides in truth that liberates. To fulfill this service, Christ endowed the Church's shepherds with the charism of infallibility in matters of faith and morals.[5]

On whom principally rests this infallibility? 'The Roman Pontiff...enjoys this infallibility in virtue of his office, when as supreme pastor and teacher of all the faithful...he proclaims by a definitive act a doctrine pertaining to faith or morals.' This may happen in conjunction with the body of Bishops in an Ecumenical Council. When such a teaching is issued it must be received as the teaching of Christ, must be adhered to with the obedience of faith and its infallibility 'extends as far as the deposit of divine Revelation itself.'[6]

With such infinitely important issues at stake in the assumption of this authority, one may legitimately ask, 'When was such authority granted to the Roman Pontiff? What evidence is there that the apostles and the early church understood this promise of charismatic authority? According to the *Catechism* the authority to 'absolve sins, to pronounce doctrinal judgments, and to make disciplinary decisions in the Church' was committed particularly to Peter, 'to whom he specifically entrusted the keys of the kingdom.'[7] In fact, 'The Lord made Simon alone...the "rock" of his Church' and the Pope, the 'Bishop of Rome and Peter's successor...by reason of his office as Vicar of Christ' has 'full, supreme, and universal power over the whole Church, a power which he can always exercise unhindered.'[8] According to the Catechism, Jesus granted this authority in Matthew 16:18–19.

At this point the present volume is imminently important. William Webster has gathered the most formidable body of data concerning the interpretation of the *locus classicus* of the authority of the Bishop of Rome to be found anywhere. In addition he has included the studied judgments of a large number of contemporary scholars, Protestant, Catholic, and Orthodox, concerning the historical treatment of the Matthew 16 passage. That the contemporary Roman Catholic interpretation had no place in the biblical understanding of the early church doctors cannot be disputed. Neither Jerome, Augustine, Chrysostom, Ambrose, Athanasius, nor a host of others gave any impetus to the false assumption of authority. It began as a small trickle from Rome itself probably more than two centuries after the time of Christ and was forced on the Western world through power, intrigue, and imposture. On the basis of such sad authority the doctrine of Justification by faith now is treated as something that must be laid aside so as not to offend the followers of the Roman Pontiff. It may be time, however, for many pious Catholics to become like the apostle Paul who 'opposed (Peter) to his face, because he was in the wrong' (Gal. 2:11), and for the same purpose, to uphold the integrity of Paul's gospel.

Though the point made here comes with conviction and is applied with unambiguous intent, the concern behind it is one of love for souls, humble gratitude for saving grace, and zeal for free access to the truth. The author himself is a former Roman Catholic who has come into the experience of the assurance of Christ's completed work. There may be other 'Magisterium-toting Catholics' who are hesitant to consider the reality of Justification by faith, who falsely assure themselves with a supposed gradual increase in holiness through obedient reception of the sacraments, simply because they think that in Matthew 16 Jesus committed to the Bishops of Rome through Peter the powers of absolution and dogmatic teaching. If this book can release one from such bondage and give freedom to search the Scriptures, William Webster's labor of years will have succeeded in their missionary purpose.

Dr. Tom J. Nettles
Professor of Historical Theology, Southern Baptist Theological Seminary, Louisville, KY. Formerly Professor and Chairman of the Department of Church History, Trinity Evangelical Divinity School, Deerfield, IL.

Introduction

One of the major issues in the ongoing debate between the Roman Catholic and the Orthodox and Protestant Churches is that of authority. The Roman Catholic Church has long claimed to be the one true Church with an infallible teaching and ruling authority given it by Christ. Inherent in the authority issue is the exclusive right to rule the Church universal, to formulate dogmas and to interpret scripture. The teachings of Vatican I[9] on the papacy can be summed up in the following propositions:

- Christ gave Peter the primacy of jurisdiction over the Church universal as well as the entire world.

- This right of jurisdiction is passed down to Peter's successors, the Bishops of Rome, for all time.

- The Roman Pontiff has absolute authority in himself, possesses authority over all Councils and his judgment cannot be questioned. He, himself, can be judged by no human tribunal.

- These teachings have always been held in the entire Church through all the ages and can be validated by the scriptures, the canons of general Councils and the unanimous consent of the fathers.

- It has at all times in the history of the Church been necessary that every Church throughout the world should agree with the Roman Church.

- When speaking *ex cathedra* the pope is endowed with the gift of infallibility.

As a basis for these claims Vatican I references two major areas of proof: scripture and history. Scripturally, it claims that its teachings can be supported by Matthew 16, Luke 22 and John 21. Historically, it claims that its teaching, and the scriptural interpretations upon which it is based, can be validated by the universal teaching of the fathers and the practice of the Church of the patristic age. Vatican I then goes on to state in unequivocal terms that it is necessary for salvation that individuals embrace its teachings on the papacy and that they submit themselves to the authority of the Roman Pontiff in all areas of faith, morals and discipline. It states that if anyone disagrees with these teachings and does not submit to them he cannot be saved and is anathematized:

> If any one, therefore, shall say that blessed Peter the Apostle was not appointed the Prince of all the Apostles and the visible Head of the whole Church militant; or that the same directly and immediately received from the same our Lord Jesus Christ a primacy of honor only, and not of true and proper jurisdiction: let him be anathema.
>
> If, then, any should deny that it is by institution of Christ the Lord, or by divine right, that blessed Peter should have a perpetual line of successors in the Primacy over the universal Church, or that the Roman Pontiff is the successor of blessed Peter in this primacy: let him be anathema.
>
> If, then, any shall say that the Roman Pontiff has the office merely of inspection or direction, and not full and supreme power of jurisdiction over the universal Church, not only in things which belong to faith and morals, but also in those which relate to the discipline and government of the Church spread throughout the world; or assert that he possesses merely the principal part, and not all the fulness of this supreme power; or that power which he enjoys is not ordinary and immediate, both over each and all the churches, and over each and all the pastors and the faithful: let him be anathema.
>
> This is the teaching of Catholic truth, from which no one can deviate without loss of faith and salvation.[10]
>
> Further, all those things are to be believed with divine and Catholic faith which are contained in the Word of God, written or handed down, and which the Church, either by a solemn judgment, or by her

ordinary and universal magisterium, proposes for belief as having been divinely revealed. And since, without faith, it is impossible to please God, and to attain to the fellowship of his children, therefore without faith no one has ever attained justification, nor will any one obtain eternal life unless he shall have persevered in faith unto the end.[11]

The Roman Catholic Church has authoritatively declared that its teachings and claims for the papacy are essential elements of saving faith. They must be believed in order to obtain eternal salvation. The Church of Rome claims for itself the gift of infallibility in the interpretation of Scripture. It has authoritatively decreed a gospel message which it says is binding upon all who would be saved. And part of that message is the need to embrace its teachings on the papacy. Many sincere individuals within Roman Catholicism implicitly accept the claims of the Church of Rome based on its interpretation of Matthew 16:18 relative to Peter and the rock. They believe that Christ established the Church upon Peter as the rock and through his supposed successors at Rome. Their presupposition is this: that the promises made to Peter are as relevant today as they were when Christ first made them to Peter. Consequently, these individuals accept whatever teaching the Roman Church promulgates, without question, believing that the Church cannot err because it is founded upon the rock. And many outside of Rome are being persuaded by these arguments. But are these arguments valid? Are the Roman Catholic claims true and can they be validated by the evidence appealed to by Vatican I?

Roman Catholic apologists, in an effort to substantiate the claims of Vatican I, make appeals to certain statements of Church fathers which they claim give unequivocal and unambiguous evidence of a belief in papal primacy in the early Church. Briefly, the arguments can be summarized as follows:

• The fathers often speak in lofty language when referring to the apostle Peter implying a personal primacy
• Numerous fathers interpret the rock of Matthew 16 as the person of Peter

- While some of the fathers interpret the rock to be Peter's confession of faith, they do not separate Peter's confession from his person
- The fathers refer to the bishops of Rome as successors of Peter.

Roman apologists historically have often resorted to the use of selected statements of major Church fathers, interpreting them as supportive of papal primacy. An excellent example of this type of argumentation is cited, for example, by Roman Catholic professor Robert Fastiggi in which he references the writings of Cyprian, Ambrose and Augustine:

> Now St. Cyprian of Carthage (d. 258 A.D.) in his letter to Cornelius of Rome (c. 251 A.D.) speaks of the Church of Rome as the 'chair of Peter (*cathedra Petri*)' and 'the principle Church in which sacerdotal unity has its source' (Ep. 59, 14). St Ambrose (d. 397 A.D.) states that 'where Peter is, there is the Church' (*Commen.. on the Psalms* 40, 30)...St. Augustine's recognition of the authority of the Pope is manifested by the famous words with which he welcomes the decision made by the Pope: *Roma locuta est; causa finita est*—Rome has spoken the case is concluded (*Sermon* 131, 6:10). Why does Augustine believe the Bishop of Rome has the final word? The answer is because the Pope is the successor of St. Peter—a fact clearly recognized by Augustine in his *Letter to Generosus* (c. 400 A.D.) in which he names all 34 of the bishops of Rome from Peter to Anastasius (*Letter* 53, 1,2).[12]

The above arguments are very common. They are precisely the same citations found in *The Faith of the Early Fathers* by the Roman Catholic patristics scholar William Jurgens as proof for the purported belief in papal primacy in the early Church. And Karl Keating uses the same reference to Augustine in his book *Catholicism and Fundamentalism*. But do the statements of these fathers actually support the claims of papal primacy? Is this what *they* meant by these statements? The facts do not support this contention. These statements are given completely out of context of the rest of the writings of these fathers thereby distorting the true meaning of their words. And in the case of Augustine, as we will see, his words are actually misquoted. All too frequently statements from the fathers are isolated and quoted without any proper interpretation, often giving the impression that a father taught a particular point of view when, in fact, he did not. But for those unfamiliar with the writings of the Church fathers such arguments can seem fairly convincing. An example of this kind of methodology is seen in a recent Roman Catholic work entitled *Jesus, Peter and the Keys*. This work is being touted by Roman Catholics as providing definitive evidence of the teaching of the Church fathers on the meaning of the rock of Matthew 16 and of Peter's role. But the actual references from the fathers cited in this work are very selective, often omitting important citations of their overall works that demonstrate a view contrary to that which is being proposed. This will become evident as we examine the writings of the Church fathers themselves. What we will discover, if we give the statements of the fathers in context and in correlation with their overall writings, is that their actual perspective is often the opposite of that claimed by these Roman apologists.

An objective examination of the historical record will reveal that the facts do not support the Roman Catholic point of view. In the following pages, we will examine the historical facts which Vatican I asserts will support its claims. In particular we will examine the interpretation of the rock of Matthew 16 by the fathers of the early Church to see if there is a unanimous consensus of the meaning of this passage. Is the Vatican I interpretation of this famous passage the same as that of the early Church fathers? In addition we will examine many of the commonly used Roman Catholic patristic arguments for papal primacy and infallibility to determine their validity. We will also look in detail at the practice of the early Church, especially as it is revealed in the canons of the early Councils, to see if it supports the teachings of Vatican I. Did the early Church, and especially the Eastern Church, hold to the Vatican I view of the papacy in its theology and practice? Finally, we will document the historical facts of the early Church from the statements of renowned Roman Catholic, Orthodox and Protestant historians. There will be lengthy quotations given from the writings of these men in order to thoroughly establish a consensus of opinion. I beg the reader's indulgence in this but I feel it is immensely important to establish the facts from a consensus to demonstrate that they are not simply personal opinion but the overall view of historians from these different communions. I ask the reader to examine this material with an open mind; to honestly assess the facts and allow truth to be the final arbiter. A full documentation of teaching of the fathers is found in Appendix B.

Part One

THE PATRISTIC INTERPRETATION OF THE ROCK OF MATTHEW 16

Chapter 1

The Patristic Interpretation of Peter and the Rock

Matthew 16:18 is *the* critical passage of Scripture for the establishment of the authority claims of the Roman Catholic Church. It is upon the interpretation of the rock and keys that the entire structure of the Church of Rome rests. And Vatican I plainly states that its interpretation of Matthew 16 is that which has been held by the Church from the very beginning. The Council asserted that its interpretation was grounded upon the unanimous consent of the fathers. In saying this Vatican I is claiming a two thousand year consensus for its interpretation and teaching. It specifically states that the Roman Catholic Church alone has authority to interpret scripture and that it is unlawful to interpret it in any way contrary to what it calls the *unanimous consent* of the fathers. This principle does not mean that every single father agrees on a particular interpretation of scripture, but it does mean that there is a general consensus of interpretation, and Vatican I claims to be consistent with that consensus. This is very important to establish because it has direct bearing on the Roman Church's claim, that of being the one true Church established by Christ, unchanged from the very beginning.

However, an examination of the historical exegesis of the rock of Matthew 16:18 provides a very different picture. The overwhelming patristic consensus on the meaning of Matthew 16:18 is one that is completely contrary to the Roman Catholic interpretation. In his book, *Catholicism and Fundamentalism,* Karl Keating states that the reformers had invented a novel exegesis of Matthew 16 in order to aid them in their rebellion against the papacy. This is a complete misrepresentation. As Oscar Cullmann points out, the view of the Reformers was not a novel interpretation invented by them but hearkened back to the patristic tradition: 'We thus see that the exegesis that the Reformers gave...was not first invented for their struggle against the papacy; it rests upon an older patristic tradition.'[13] As we examine the writings of the fathers we do find a consistent viewpoint expressed, but it is not that of the Roman Catholic Church, as the following detailed documentation of the major fathers of the East and West will demonstrate.

Tertullian (A.D. 155/160—240/250)

Tertullian was born in Carthage in North Africa and practiced law before his conversion to Christianity *ca.* A.D. 193. As a Christian he was a prolific writer and has been called the 'Father of Latin Christianity'. He was most likely a layman and his writings were widely read. He had a great influence upon the Church fathers of subsequent generations, especially Cyprian. He is the first of the Western fathers to comment on Matthew 16. In one of his writings Tertullian identifies the rock with the person of Peter on which the Church would be built:

> Was anything withheld from the knowledge of Peter, who is called the 'rock on which the church should be built' who also obtained 'the keys of the kingdom of heaven,' with the power of 'loosing and binding in heaven and earth?[14]

Though Tertullian states that Peter is the rock he does not mean it in a pro–papal sense. We know this because of other comments he has made. But if we isolate this one passage it would be easy to read a pro–Roman interpretation into it. However, in other comments on Matthew 16:18–19, Tertullian explains what he means when he says that Peter is the rock on which the Church would be built:

If, because the Lord has said to Peter, 'Upon this rock I will build My Church,' 'to thee have I given the keys of the heavenly kingdom;' or, 'Whatsoever thou shalt have bound or loosed in earth, shall be bound or loosed in the heavens,' you therefore presume that the power of binding and loosing has derived to you, that is, to every Church akin to Peter, what sort of man are you, subverting and wholly changing the manifest intention of the Lord, conferring (as that intention did) this (gift) personally upon Peter? 'On thee,' He says, 'will I build My church;' and, 'I will give thee the keys'...and, 'Whatsoever thou shalt have loosed or bound'...*In (Peter) himself the Church was reared; that is, through (Peter) himself,* (Peter) himself essayed the key; you see what key: 'Men of Israel, let what I say sink into your ears: Jesus the Nazarene, a man destined by God for you,' and so forth. (Peter) himself, therefore, was the first to unbar, in Christ's baptism, the entrance to the heavenly kingdom, in which kingdom are 'loosed' the sins that were beforetime 'bound;' and those which have not been 'loosed' are 'bound,' in accordance with true salvation...[15]

When Tertullian says that Peter is the rock and the Church is built upon him he means that the Church is built *through* him as he preaches the gospel. This preaching is how Tertullian explains the meaning of the keys. They are the declarative authority for the offer of forgiveness of sins through the preaching of the gospel. If men respond to the message they are loosed from their sins. If they reject it they remain bound in their sins. In the words just preceding this quote Tertullian explicitly denies that this promise can apply to anyone but Peter and therefore he does not in any way see a Petrine primacy in this verse with successors in the bishops of Rome. The patristic scholar, Karlfried Froehlich, states that even though Tertullian teaches that Peter is the rock he does not mean this in the same sense as the Roman Catholic Church: 'Tertullian regarded the Peter of Matthew 16:18–19 as the representative of the entire church or at least its 'spiritual' members.'[16]

It is a common practice of Roman Catholic apologists to omit part of the quotation given above by Tertullian in order to make it appear that he is a proponent of papal primacy. A prime example off this is found in a recently released Roman Catholic defense of the papacy entitled *Jesus, Peter and the Keys*. The authors give the following partial citation from Tertullian:

> I now inquire into your opinion, to see whence you usurp this right for the Church. Do you presume, because the Lord said to Peter, 'On this rock I will build my Church, I have given you the keys of the kingdom of heaven' [Matt. 16:18-19a] or 'whatever you shall have bound or loosed on earth will be bound or loosed in heaven' [Matt. 16:19b] that the power of binding and loosing has thereby been handed on to you, that is, to every church akin to Peter? What kind of man are you, subverting and changing what was the manifest intent of the Lord when he conferred this personally upon Peter? On you, he says, I will build my Church; and I will give to you the keys, not to the Church; and whatever you shall have bound or you shall have loosed, not what they shall have bound or they shall have loosed.[17]

The part of the quotation that is omitted defines what Tertullian means by the authority invested in Peter by Christ, when he states that Christ built his Church on Peter by building it *through* him as he preached the gospel. This is a meaning that is clearly contrary to the Roman Catholic perspective. To omit this is to distort the teaching of Tertullian and to give the impression that he taught something he did not teach.

So, though Tertullian states that Peter is the rock, he does not mean this in the same way the Roman Catholic Church does. Peter is the rock because he is the one given the privilege of being the first to open the kingdom of God to men. This is similar to the view expressed by Maximus of Tours when he says: 'For he is called a rock because he was the first to lay the foundations of the faith among the nations.'[18]

Not only do we see a clear denial of any belief in a papal primacy in Tertullian's exegesis of Matthew 16, but such a denial is also seen from his practice. In his later years Tertullian separated himself from the Catholic Church to become a Montanist. He clearly did not hold to the view espoused by Vatican I that communion with the Bishop of Rome was the ultimate criterion of orthodoxy and of inclusiveness in the Church of God.

Origen (A.D. 185—253/254)

Origen was head of the catechetical school at Alexandria during the first half of the third century. He was an individual of enormous intellect and was by far the most prolific writer of the patristic age. Eusebius states that his writings numbered in the neighborhood of six thousand. He has been called the greatest scholar of Christian antiquity. He had immense influence upon fathers in both the East and West in subsequent centuries.

Origen is the first father to give a detailed exposition of the meaning of the rock of Matthew 16:18. His interpretation became normative for the Eastern fathers and for many in the West. Apart from the specific passage of Matthew 16 he states that Peter is the rock:

> Look at the great foundation of that Church and at the very solid rock upon which Christ has founded the Church. Wherefore the Lord says: 'Ye of little faith, why have you doubted?'[19]

But, like Tertullian, he does not mean this in the Roman Catholic sense. Often, Origen is cited as a proponent of papal primacy because he says that Peter is the rock. Quotes such as the one given above are isolated from his other statements about Peter and his actual interpretation of Matthew 16:18 thereby inferring that he taught something which he did not teach. In his mind Peter is simply representative of all true believers and what was promised to Peter is given to all believers who truly follow Christ. They all become what Peter is. This is the view expressed in the following comments:

> *And if we too have said like Peter*, 'Thou art the Christ, the Son of the living God,' not as if flesh and blood had revealed it unto us, but by the light from the Father in heaven having shone in our heart, *we become a Peter, and to us there might be said by the Word, 'Thou art Peter,'* etc. *For a rock is every disciple of Christ* of whom those drank who drank of the spiritual rock which followed them, and upon every such rock is built every word of the Church, and the polity in accordance with it; for in each of the perfect, who have the combination of words

and deeds and thoughts which fill up the blessedness, is the church built by God.

But if you suppose that upon the one Peter only the whole church is built by God, what would you say about John the son of thunder or each one of the Apostles? Shall we otherwise dare to say, that against Peter in particular the gates of Hades shall not prevail, but that they shall prevail against the other Apostles and the perfect? Does not the saying previously made, 'The gates of Hades shall not prevail against it,' hold in regard to all and in the case of each of them? And also the saying, 'Upon this rock I will build My Church?' *Are the keys of the kingdom of heaven given by the Lord to Peter only, and will no other of the blessed receive them?* But if this promise, 'I will give unto thee the keys of the kingdom of heaven,' be common to others, how shall not all things previously spoken of, and the things which are subjoined as having been addressed to Peter, be common to them?

'Thou art the Christ, the Son of the living God.' If any one says this to Him...he will obtain the things that were spoken according to the letter of the Gospel to that Peter, but, as the spirit of the Gospel teaches to every one who becomes such as that Peter was. For all bear the surname 'rock' who are the imitators of Christ, that is, of the spiritual rock which followed those who are being saved, that they may drink from it the spiritual draught. *But these bear the surname of rock just as Christ does. But also as members of Christ deriving their surname from Him they are called Christians, and from the rock, Peters...And to all such the saying of the Savior might be spoken, 'Thou art Peter' etc., down to the words, 'prevail against it.'* But what is the it? Is it the rock upon which Christ builds the Church, or is it the Church? For the phrase is ambiguous. *Or is it as if the rock and the Church were one and the same?* This I think to be true; for neither against the rock on which Christ builds His Church, nor against the Church will the gates of Hades prevail. *Now, if the gates of Hades prevail against any one, such an one cannot be a rock upon which the Christ builds the Church, nor the Church built by Jesus upon the rock.*[20]

This is one of the most important passages in all the writings of Origen for an understanding of his view of the rock of Matthew 16.

The Patristic Interpretation 31

Yet this passage is not included in those referenced by the authors of *Jesus, Peter and the Keys*. This is a glaring omission given the importance of the passage and the fact that it is easily accessible in the work the *Ante-Nicene Fathers*. One can only conclude that the authors purposefully omitted the passage because it is antithetical to the position they are seeking to establish.

John Meyendorff was a world renowned and highly respected Orthodox theologian, historian and patristics scholar. He was dean of St. Vladimir's Orthodox Theological Seminary and Professor of Church History and Patristics. He gives the following explanation of Origen's interpretation and of his influence on subsequent fathers in the East and West:

> Origen, the common source of patristic exegetical tradition, commenting on Matthew 16:18, interprets the famous *logion* as Jesus' answer to Peter's confession: Simon became the 'rock' on which the Church is founded because he expressed the true belief in the divinity of Christ. Origen continues: 'If we also say "Thou art the Christ, the Son of the living God," then we also become Peter...for whoever assimilates to Christ, becomes rock. Does Christ give the keys of the kingdom to Peter alone, whereas other blessed people cannot receive them?' According to Origen, therefore, Peter is no more than the first 'believer,' and the keys he received opened the gates of heaven to him alone: if others want to follow, they can 'imitate' Peter and receive the same keys. Thus the words of Christ have a soteriological, but not an institutional, significance. They only affirm that the Christian faith is the faith expressed by Peter on the road to Caesarea Philippi. In the whole body of patristic exegesis, this is the prevailing understanding of the 'Petrie' *logia*, and it remains valid in Byzantine literature...Thus, when he spoke to Peter, Jesus was underlining the *meaning of the faith* as the foundation of the Church, rather than organizing the Church as guardian of the faith.[21]

James McCue in Lutherans and Catholics in Dialogue affirms these views of Origen in these statements:

> When Origen is commenting directly on Matthew 16:18f, he carefully

puts aside any interpretation of the passage that would make Peter anything other than what every Christian should be...(His) is the earliest extant detailed commentary on Matthew 16:18f. and interestingly sees the event described as a lesson about the life to be lived by every Christian, and not information about office or hierarchy or authority in the Church.²²

Origen and Tertullian are the first fathers, from the East and West respectively, to give an exposition on the meaning of the rock of Matthew 16 and the role and position of Peter. Their views are foundational for the interpretation of this important passage for the centuries following. Strands of their teaching will appear in the views of the fathers throughout the East and West. It is important to point out that the first Eastern and Western fathers to give an exegesis of Matthew 16 do not interpret the passage in a pro–Roman sense.

Cyprian (A.D. 200–210—*ca.* 258)

Cyprian was a bishop of Carthage in North Africa in the mid–third century. He was one of the most influential theologians and bishops of the Church of his day and gave his life in martydom for his faith. He was greatly influenced by the writings of Tertullian, the North African father who preceded him. He is often cited by Roman Catholic apologists as a witness for papal primacy. In his treatise *On the Unity of the Church* Cyprian gives the following interpretation of the rock of Matthew 16:

> The Lord saith unto Peter, I say unto thee, (saith He,) that thou art Peter, and upon this rock I will build My Church, and the gates of Hell shall not prevail against it. And I will give unto thee the keys of the kingdom of heaven, and whatsoever thou shalt bind on earth, shall be bound in heaven, and whatsoever thou shalt loose on earth, shall be loosed in heaven (Matt. 16:18–19). To him again, after His resurrection, He says, Feed My sheep. Upon him being one He builds His Church; and although He gives to all the Apostles an equal power, and says, As My Father sent Me, even so I send you; receive ye the Holy

The Patristic Interpretation 33

Ghost: whosoever sins ye remit, they shall be remitted to him, and whosoever sins ye shall retain, they shall be retained (John 20:21);—yet in order to manifest unity, He has by His own authority so placed the source of the same unity, as to begin from one.[23]

Cyprian clearly says that Peter is the rock. If his comments were restricted to the above citation it would lend credence to the idea that he was a proponent of papal primacy. However Cyprian's comments continue on from the statements given above. His additional statements prove conclusively that although he states that Peter is the rock he does not mean this in a pro–Roman sense. His view is that Peter is a symbol of unity, a figurative representative of the bishops of the Church. Cyprian viewed all the apostles as being equal with one another. He believed the words to Peter in Matthew 16 to be representative of the ordination of all Bishops so that the Church is founded, not upon one Bishop in one see, but upon all equally in collegiality. Peter, then, is a representative figure of the episcopate as a whole. His view is clearly stated in these words:

> *Certainly the other Apostles also were what Peter was, endued with an equal fellowship both of honour and power; but a commencement is made from unity, that the Church may be set before as one*; which one Church, in the Song of Songs, doth the Holy Spirit design and name in the Person of our Lord: My dove, My spotless one, is but one; she is the only one of her mother, elect of her that bare her (Cant. 9:6).[24]

Our Lord whose precepts and warnings we ought to observe, determining the honour of a Bishop and the ordering of His own Church, speaks in the Gospel and says to Peter, I say unto thee, that *thou art Peter, and on this rock I will build My Church*; and the gates of hell shall not prevail against it. And I will give unto thee the keys of the kingdom of heaven: and whatsoever thou shalt bind on earth shall be bound in heaven. *Thence the ordination of Bishops, and the ordering of the Church*, runs down along the course of time and line of succession, so that *the Church is settled upon her Bishops*; and every act of the Church is regulated by these same Prelates.[25]

Cyprian, like Tertullian, states that Peter is the rock. But such a statement must be qualified. He definitely does not mean this in the same way the Church of Rome does. In his treatise, *On the Unity of the Church,* Cyprian teaches that Peter alone is *not* the rock or foundation on which the Church is built, but rather, he is an example of the principle of unity. He is representative of the Church as a whole. The entire episcopate, according to Cyprian, is the foundation, though Christ is himself the true Rock. The bishops of Rome are not endowed with divine authority to rule the Church. All of the bishops together constitute the Church and rule over their individual areas of responsibility as co–equals. If Cyprian meant to say that the Church was built upon Peter and he who resists the bishop of Rome resists the Church (cutting himself off from the Church), then he completely contradicts himself, for, as we will see in Part II, he opposed Stephen, the bishop of Rome in his interpretation of Matthew 16 as well as on theological and jurisdictional issues. His actions prove that his comments about Peter could not coincide with the Roman Catholic interpretation of his words. To do so is a distortion of his true meaning. Historically there has been some confusion on the interpretation of Cyprian's teaching because there are two versions of his treatise, *The Unity of the Church.* In the first Cyprian speaks of the chair of Peter in which he equates the true Church with that chair. He states that there is only one Church and one chair and a primacy given to Peter. In the second, the references to a Petrine primacy are softened to give greater emphasis to the theme of unity and co–equality of bishops. Most Roman Catholic and Protestant scholars now agree that Cyprian is the author of both versions. He wrote the second in order to offset a pro–Roman interpretation which was being attached to his words which he never intended. The episcopate is to him the principle of unity within the Church and representative of it. The 'chair of Peter' is a figurative expression which applies to every bishop in his own see, not just the bishops of Rome. The bishop of Rome holds a primacy of honor but he does not have universal jurisdiction over the entire Church for Cyprian expressly states that all the apostles received the same authority and status as Peter and the Church is built upon all the bishops and not just Peter alone.

Some object to these conclusions about Cyprian citing his statements about the chair of Peter. As pointed out previously, Professor Fastiggi mentions this fact. He would lead us to believe that Cyprian's comments refer *exclusively* to the bishops of Rome and that they therefore possess special authority as the successors of Peter. The Roman Catholic historian, Robert Eno, repudiates this point of view as a misrepresentation of Cyprian's view:

> Cyprian makes considerable use of the image of Peter's *cathedra* or chair. Note however that it is important in his theology of the local church: 'God is one and Christ is one: there is one Church and one chair founded, by the Lord's authority, upon Peter. It is not possible that another altar can be set up, or that a new priesthood can be appointed, over and above this one altar and this one priesthood' (Ep. 43.5).

The *cathedri Petri* symbolism has been the source of much misunderstanding and dispute. Perhaps it can be understood more easily by looking at the special treatise he wrote to defend both his own position as sole lawful bishop of Carthage and that of Cornelius against Novatian, namely, the *De unitate ecclesiae*, or, as it was known in the Middle Ages, On the Simplicity of Prelates. The chapter of most interest is the fourth. Controversy has dogged this work because two versions of this chapter exist. Since the Reformation, acceptance of one version or the other has usually followed denominational lines.

Much of this has subsided in recent decades especially with the work of Fr. Maurice Bevenot, an English Jesuit, who devoted most of his scholarly life to this text. He championed the suggestion of the English Benedictine, John Chapman, that what we are dealing with here are two versions of a text, both of which were authored by Cyprian. This view has gained wide acceptance in recent decades. Not only did Cyprian write both but his theology of the Church is unchanged from the first to the second. He made textual changes because his earlier version was being misused.

The theology of the controverted passage sees in Peter the symbol of unity, not from his being given greater authority by Christ for, as he says in both versions, '...a like power is given to all the Apostles' and '...No doubt the others were all that Peter was.' Yet Peter was given the power first: 'Thus it is made clear that there is but one Church and one chair.' The Chair of Peter then belongs to each lawful bishop in his own see. Cyprian holds the Chair of Peter in Carthage and Cornelius in Rome over against Novatian the would-be usurper. You must hold to this unity if you are to remain in the Church.

Cyprian wants unity in the local church around the lawful bishop and unity among the bishops of the world who are 'glued together' (Ep. 66.8).

Apart from his good relations and harmony with Bishop Cornelius over the matter of the lapsed, what was Cyprian's basic view of the role, not of Peter as symbol of unity, but of Rome in the contemporary Church? Given what we have said above, it is clear that he did not see the bishop of Rome as his superior, except by way of honor, even though the lawful bishop of Rome also held the chair of Peter in an historical sense (Ep. 52.2). Another term frequently used by the Africans in speaking of the Church was 'the root' (*radix*). Cyprian sometimes used the term in connection with Rome, leading some to assert that he regarded the Roman church as the 'root.' But in fact, in Cyprian's teaching, the Catholic Church as a whole is the root. So when he bade farewell to some Catholics travelling to Rome, he instructed them to be very careful about which group of Christians they contacted after their arrival in Rome. They must avoid schismatic groups like that of Novation. They should contact and join the Church presided over by Cornelius because it alone is the Catholic Church in Rome. In other words, Cyprian exhorted '...them to discern the womb and root...of the Catholic Church and to cleave to it' (Ep. 48.3).

It is clear that in Cyprian's mind...one theological conclusion he does not draw is that the bishop of Rome has authority which is superior to that of the African bishops.'[26]

As Charles Gore has pointed out, Cyprian used the phrase, the Chair of Peter' in his Epistle 43, which Fastiggi cites in defense of an exclusive Roman primacy, to refer to his own see of Carthage, not the see of Rome. This is confirmed as a general consensus of Protestant, Orthodox and Roman Catholic historians. James McCue, writing

The Patristic Interpretation

for Lutherans and Catholics in Dialogue, in the work *Papal Primacy and the Universal Church*, affirms this interpretation of Cyprian's view in the following comments:

> According to Cyprian's interpretation of Matthew 16:18, Jesus first conferred upon Peter the authority with which he subsequently endowed all the apostles. This, according to Cyprian, was to make clear the unity of the power that was being conferred and of the church that was being established. Cyprian frequently speaks of Peter as the foundation of the church, and his meaning seems to be that it was in Peter that Jesus first established all the church-building powers and responsibilities that would subsequently also be given to the other apostles and to the bishops.
>
> Peter is the source of the church's unity only in an exemplary or symbolic way...Peter himself seems, in Cyprian's thought, to have had no authority over the other apostles, and consequently the church of Peter cannot reasonably claim to have any authority over the other churches.[27]

This judgment is further affirmed by the Roman Catholic historian, Michael Winter:

> Cyprian used the Petrine text of Matthew to defend episcopal authority, but many later theologians, influenced by the papal connexions of the text, have interpreted Cyprian in a propapal sense which was alien to his thought...Cyprian would have used Matthew 16 to defend the authority of any bishop, but since he happened to employ it for the sake of the Bishop of Rome, it created the impression that he understood it as referring to papal authority...Catholics as well as Protestants are now generally agreed that Cyprian did not attribute a superior authority to Peter.[28]

This Roman Catholic historian insists that it is a misrepresentation of Cyprian's true teaching to assert that he is a father who supports the Roman Catholic interpretation of Matthew 16. And he says that both Protestant and Roman Catholic scholars are now agreed on this. Once again, Roman Catholic historians specifically repudiate what some Roman apologists often teach about Cyprian and his comments on the 'Chair of Peter'. Karlfried Froehlich states:

> Cyprian understood the biblical Peter as representative of the unified episcopate, not of the bishop of Rome...He understood him as symbolizing the unity of all bishops, the privileged officers of penance...For (Cyprian), the one Peter, the first to receive the penitential keys which all other bishops also exercise, was the biblical type of the one episcopate, which in turn guaranteed the unity of the church. The one Peter equaled the one body of bishops.[29]

John Meyendorff explains the meaning of Cyprian's use of the phrase 'chair of Peter' and sums up the Cyprianic ecclesiology which was normative for the East as a whole:

> The early Christian concept, best expressed in the third century by Cyprian of Carthage, according to which the 'see of Peter' belongs, in each local church, to the bishop, remains the longstanding and obvious pattern for the Byzantines. Gregory of Nyssa, for example, can write that Jesus 'through Peter gave to the bishops the keys of heavenly honors.' Pseudo–Dionysius when he mentions the 'hierarchs'—i.e., the bishops of the early Church—refers immediately to the image of Peter....Peter succession is seen wherever the right faith is preserved, and, as such, it cannot be localized geographically or monopolized by a single church or individual.[30]
>
> Cyprian's view of Peter's 'chair' (*cathedri Petri*) was that it belonged not only to the bishop of Rome but to every bishop within each community. Thus Cyprian used not the argument of Roman primacy but that of *his own* authority as 'successor of Peter' in Carthage...For Cyprian, the 'chair of Peter', was a sacramental concept, necessarily present in each local church: Peter was the example and model of each local bishop, who, within his community, presides over the Eucharist and possesses 'the power of the keys' to remit sins. And since the model is unique, unique also is the episcopate (*episcopatus unus est*) shared, in equal fullness (*in solidum*) by all bishops.[31]

The Patristic Interpretation

And finally, Reinhold Seeberg explains Cyprian's interpretation of Matthew 16 and his ecclesiology in these words:

> According to Matt. 16:18f., the church is founded upon the bishop and its direction devolves upon him: 'Hence through the changes of times and dynasties the ordination of bishops and the order of the church moves on, so that the church is constituted of bishops, and every act of the church is controlled by these leaders' (Epistle 33.1)...The bishops constitute a college (*collegium*), the episcopate (*episcopatus*). The councils developed this conception. In them the bishops practically represented the unity of the church, as Cyprian now theoretically formulated it. Upon their unity rests the unity of the church...This unity is manifest in the fact that the Lord in the first instance bestowed apostolic authority upon Peter: 'Hence the other apostles were also, to a certain extent, what Peter was, endowed with an equal share of both honor and power; but the beginning proceeds from unity, in order that the church of Christ may be shown to be one' (de un. eccl. 4)...In reality all the bishops—regarded dogmatically—stand upon the same level, and hence he maintained, in opposition to Stephanus of Rome, his right of independent opinion and action...[32]

The above quotations from world renowned Roman Catholic, Protestant and Orthodox historians reveal a consensus of scholarly opinion on Cyprian's teaching effectively demonstrating the incompatibility of Cyprian's views with those espoused by Vatican I. This consensus also reveals the danger of taking the statements of Church fathers at face value without regard for the context of those statements or for seeking a proper interpretation of the meaning of the terms they use. It is easy to import preconceived meanings into their statements resulting in misrepresentation of their teaching. The above example of Professor Fastiggi is indicative of this. The authors of *Jesus Peter and the Keys* are likewise guilty of the same thing. They list quotations from Cyprian in total disregard of the true facts as they have been enumerated by the above historians giving the impression that Cyprian believed in papal primacy when in fact he did not. Their point of view and that of Professor Fasteggi is thoroughly repudiated even by conservative Roman Catholic historians. Cyprian is an excellent example of a father who states that Peter is the rock but who does not mean this in a Roman Catholic sense. But without giving the proper historical context and understanding of his writings it would be quite easy to mislead the unintiated by investing Cyprian's words with the doctrinal development of a later age thereby misrepresenting his actual position.

Optatus of Milevis (A.D. 320—385)

Optatus was a Bishop of Milevis in Numedia in Africa. Little is known of him save for one extant writing, *The Schism of the Donatists*, in which he defends the orthodox Church against the schismatic Donatists. He is a father who is often referenced as a proponent of papal primacy because, like Cyprian, he also employs the phrase 'the Chair of Peter' in referring to the Church of Rome. The Donatists had set up a rival Bishop in Rome and he writes to refute their claim to be in a genuine apostolic succession. He uses the argument of the 'chair of Peter' in this context. He makes the following statements:

> I see that you are ignorant that the schism at Carthage was begun by your chiefs. Search out the origin of these things, and you will find that in associating heretics with schismatics, you have pronounced judgment against yourselves. For it was not Caecilian who went forth from Majorinus, your father's father, but it was Majorinus who deserted Caecilian; nor was it Caecilian who separated himself *from the chair of Peter or of Cyprian*, but Majorinus, on whose chair you sit, which had no existence before Majorinus himself.
> So we have proved that the Catholic Church is the Church which is diffused throughout the world. We must now mention its ornaments...For one who knows, to err is sin; those who do not know

may sometimes be pardoned. You cannot deny that you know that upon Peter first in the city of Rome was conferred the episcopal chair, on which sat Peter, the head of all the apostles, whence he was called Cephas, that in this one chair unity should be preserved by all, lest the other apostles might uphold each for himself separate chairs, so that he who should set up a second chair, against the unique chair, would already be a schismatic and a sinner.

Well, then, on the one chair, which is the first of the endowments, Peter first sat, to whom succeeded Linus; to Linus succeeded Clement, Anacletus, Evaristus, Sixtus, Telesphorus, Iginus, Anicetus, Pius, Soter, Victor, Zephyrinus, Calixtus, Urban, Pontian, Anterus, Fabian, Cornelius, Lucius, Stephen, Sixtus, Dionysius, Felix, Marcellinus, Eusebius, Miltiades, Silvester, Mark, Julius, Liberius, Damasus; to Damasus Siricius, who today is our colleague, and he, with the whole world, agrees with us in one bond of communion through the intercourse of letters of peace. Now do you show the origin of your chair, you who wish to claim the holy Church for yourselves.

But you say that you too have some sort of a party in the city of Rome. It is a branch of your error growing out of a lie, not from the root of truth...So, of the aforesaid endowments, the chair is, as we have said, the first, which we have proved to be ours, through Peter, and which draws to itself the angelus, unless perchance you, claiming him for yourselves, have him shut up in a little place. Send him out if you can, and let him exclude the seven angeli who are amongst our colleagues in Asia, to whose churches writes John the apostle, churches with which it is proved that you have no intercourse of communion. Whence is your angelus; who amongst you is able to move the waters, or to be numbered with the other endowments of the Church? Whatever is outside the seven churches is alien. Supposing then that you really had even one, through that one you would be in communion with the other angeli too, and through the angeli with the above-mentioned churches, and through these churches with us.[33]

Optatus is using the phrase 'Chair of Peter' similarly to Cyprian. He is dealing with a Western schism and seeks to demonstrate from the supreme see in the West the lawful succession of bishops demonstrating that the Donatists were cut off from the true Church. He does not exalt the see of Rome as alone possessing the chair of Peter. He refers to Cyprian's chair in the same sentence with the chair of Peter and equates the two. He says Cyprian and all other legitimate bishops, be they in Rome, Carthage or the East possess the chair of Peter and are part of the true Church. The see of Rome certainly possesses great authority, as Optatus acknowledges, but he does not point to Rome as having universal headship over the Church. His comments about the seven Churches of Asia demonstrate that the Church of Rome was just one standard of communion by which orthodoxy was measured. However, as with Cyprian, Optatus' comments have often been misinterpreted. Robert Eno clarifies his views in these comments:

> Cyprian's theology of the Church was largely concerned with the local church. This was no longer adequate because it was now a question of a regional schism. The North African system was not one of geographically extensive dioceses. Here every little village had a bishop. And in this time of schism, the fourth century, almost every little village had its Catholic and Donatist bishops.
>
> In this new situation, Optatus' theology needed to put forward a revised argument for unity and, of course, it had to extend, not only beyond the local church, but beyond the region as well...Optatus' appeal (and Augustine's after him) must be to a geographic catholicity of the Church beyond Africa...The test of such geographic catholicity was: is your church in communion with the rest of the Church? For Westerners that meant: Are you in communion with the Roman church?...But Rome was not the sole criterion of communion. He asked if they were in communion with the Eastern churches to which Paul had written. What about the churches in Asia Minor to which John wrote at the beginning of the Apocalypse?
>
> Cyprian's use of 'Chair of Peter'...was largely symbolic. Optatus still began his argument with the same mindset. In Book I.10, in arguing over who was responsible for the initial schism, Optatus stated: 'Nor was it Caecilian who separated himself from the chair of

Peter or from the chair of Cyprian...' Catholic commentators have usually interpreted this as referring to two distinct separations, from Rome (Chair of Peter) and from Carthage (Chair of Cyprian). They called attention to the fact that the 'Chair of Peter' was named first. In fact, I believe, here Optatus is using Cyprianic terminology. The Chair of Peter and Chair of Cyprian are one and the same, to be occupied only by the lawful bishop of Carthage who is, of course, Caecilian, not Majorinus.[34]

From the examples of Origen, Tertullian, Cyprian and Optatus there is a principle that emerges which should be carefully observed whenever interpreting certain statements of the Church fathers. Out of concern for truth, we must be careful to interpret their statements within their immediate context and within the context of their overall writings. Just because a father uses terms such as the rock when referring to Peter, or the *chair of Peter* when referring to the see of Rome, it does not mean that they mean he is using these terms in a Roman Catholic sense.

Firmilian (Died *ca.* A.D. 268)

Firmilian was a leading Bishop of Caesarea in Cappadocia in the mid–third century. He was a contemporary of Cyprian and one of the most important theologians of his day. Firmilian is an important witness to the ecclesiology of the early Church and its interpretation of Matthew 16. He is one of the most important of the early fathers in this regard for he expresses his opinion in the context of a dispute with Stephen, the bishop of Rome, and his claims to a unique Petrine primacy. This was the same dispute involving Cyprian in which Firmilian wrote to give him moral support. It is from this letter that we learn indirectly the primacy claims that were beginning to be taught by the bishop of Rome in the mid–third century. This is the first piece of historical evidence that such claims were being formulated by the Roman bishops on the basis of a particular interpretation of the rock of Matthew 16. As we saw with Cyprian, Stephen most likely applied Cyprian's interpretation of Matthew 16 to himself in a way that was completely unacceptable to Cyprian and to Eastern fathers such as Firmilian since they both completely repudiate his claims. Firmilian makes the following comments about Stephen and his interpretation of Matthew 16:

> But how great his error, how exceeding his (Stephen's) blindness, who says, that remission of sins can be given in the synagogues of heretics, and abideth not on the foundation of the one Church which was once fixed by Christ on a rock, may be hence learnt, that Christ said to Peter alone, Whatsoever thou shalt bind on earth shall be bound in heaven; and whatsoever thou shalt loose on earth shall be loosed in heaven: and again in the Gospel, when Christ breathed on the Apostles only, saying, Receive ye the Holy Ghost: whose soever sins ye remit, they are remitted unto them; and whose soever sins ye retain, they are retained. The power then of remitting sins was given to the Apostles, and the Churches which they, sent by Christ, established, and to the Bishops who succeeded them by vicarious ordination.
>
> And herein I am justly indignant at such open and manifest folly in Stephen, that he who boasts of the seat of his episcopate, and contends that he holds the succession from Peter, on whom the foundations of the Church were laid, introduces many other *rocks*, and *buildeth* anew many Churches, in that by his authority he maintains baptism among them...Nor does he perceive that he who thus betrays and abandons unity, casts into the shade, and in a manner effaces, the truth of the Christian *Rock*...Stephen, who proclaims that he occupies by succession the chair of Peter, is roused by no zeal against heretics...He who concedes and assigns to heretics such great and heavenly privileges of the Church, what else does he than hold communion with them, for whom he maintains and claims so much grace?...But as to the refutation of the argument from custom, which they seem to oppose to the truth, who so foolish as to prefer custom to truth, or not to leave darkness, when he sees light?...And this you of Africa may say in answer to Stephen, that on discovering the truth you abandoned the error of custom. But we join custom to truth, and to the custom of the Romans we oppose custom, but that of truth; from the beginning holding that which was delivered by Christ and by His Apostles.[35]

The Patristic Interpretation 45

Firmilian expresses a view here of the overall government of the Church which is directly opposed to Vatican I. He states that the keys given to Peter are representative of the Church universal. They were subsequently given to all the Apostles and passed on to every legitimate succeeding bishop. In his mind all bishops are on an equal footing. He mocks Stephen's claim to superiority based upon the supposed possession of a unique Petrine succession. According to Firmilian, all bishops possess the chair of Peter and are built upon the rock. This is not the exclusive and unique possession of the bishops of Rome. And if, as Firmilian claims was true of Stephen, they depart from the unity of the Church which is expressed in the collegiality of its bishops, they separate themselves from the rock and foundation of the Church. His views are closely aligned with those of Cyprian and are not supportive in the least of a Roman primacy.

Eusebius (A.D. 263—340)

Eusebius was born in Caesarea in Palestine around the year 263 A.D. He took the name Eusebius Pamphilus after his mentor and teacher Pamphilus. He was consecrated bishop of Caesarea in 313 A.D. and was a participant at the Council of Nicaea. He is known as the father of ecclesiastical history for his work on the history of the Church. He has very clearly expressed his views on the meaning of the rock of Matthew 16:

> 'And he sent out arrows, and scattered them; he flashed forth lightnings, and routed them. Then the channels of the sea were seen, and the foundations of the world were laid bear, at thy rebuke, O Lord, at the blast of thy nostrils' (Ps. 18.14)...By 'the foundations of the world,' we shall understand the strength of God's wisdom, by which, first, the order of the universe was established, and then, the world itself was founded—a world which will not be shaken. Yet you will not in any way err from the scope of the truth if you suppose that 'the world' is actually *the Church of God, and that its 'foundation' is in the first place, that unspeakably solid rock on which it is founded, as Scripture says: 'Upon this rock I will build my Church, and the gates of hell shall not prevail against it'; and elsewhere: 'The rock, moreover, was*

Christ.' For, as the Apostle indicates with these words: 'No other foundation can anyone lay than that which is laid, which is Christ Jesus.' Then, too, after the Savior himself, you may rightly judge the foundations of the Church to be the words of the prophets and apostles, in accordance with the statement of the Apostle: 'Built upon the foundation of the apostles and the prophets, Christ Jesus himself being the cornerstone.' These foundations of the world have been laid bare because the enemies of God, who once darkened the eyes of our mind, lest we gaze upon divine things, have been routed and put to flight—scattered by the arrows sent from God and put to flight by the rebuke of the Lord and by the blast from his nostrils. As a result, having been saved from these enemies and having received the use of our eyes, we have seen the channels of the sea and have looked upon the foundations of the world. This has happened in our lifetime in many parts of the world.[36]

Eusebius unambiguously teaches that the rock is Christ. He correlates this interpretation with the parallel rock and foundation statements of 1 Corinthians 10:4 and 3:11. He goes on to say that there is a subsidiary foundation, from Ephesians 2:20, of the apostles and prophets, the Church also built upon them, but the cornerstone is Christ. However he interprets this to mean that the Church is to be built upon the words or teachings of the apostles and prophets as opposed to their persons. It is in this sense that it can be said that the Church is built upon Peter and the other apostles. It is clear that Christ alone is the true foundation and rock of the Church and that Eusebius sees no peculiar Petrine primacy associated with Christ's statements in Matthew 16. Peter is simply one of a number of the apostles who is a foundation of the Church. This has nothing to do with his person, but everything to do with his words—his confession. This helps us to properly understand other references of Eusebius to Peter. For example, when he says: 'But Peter, upon whom the Church of Christ is built, against which the gates of hell shall not prevail, has left one epistle undisputed,'[37] he does not mean that Christ established a papal office in Peter and that the Church is built upon him in a personal sense and through him upon his supposed successors. The Church is built upon Peter by being built upon his confession of faith. In light of his comments from his *Commentary on the Psalms* we can conclude that Eusebius did not interpret Matthew 16:18 in agreement with the Roman Catholic Church. It is Christ and Christ alone that fills Eusebius' vision from this passage. However, one will search in vain for the above quotation from Eusebius in the Roman Catholic work *Peter, Jesus and the Keys*. This work purports to give a definitive patristic perspective on the rock of Matthew 16. But the failure to give a full documentation of what this father has actually written on the subject once again leaves the authors open to the charge of a biased and manipulative presentation of the facts.

The interpretation of Eusebius, along with that of Origen, had an immense influence upon the Eastern and Western fathers. Over and over again, as we will see, we find the fathers of subsequent generations interpreting this rock passage with the focus on the person of Christ. The corresponding passages of 1 Corinthians 3:11 and 10:4 are used as justification for the interpretation. Michael Winter describes Eusebius' point of view and influence:

> In the *Ecclesiastical History* he says without any explanation or qualification: 'Peter upon whom the church of Christ is built, against which the gates of hell shall not prevail...' Elsewhere he speaks of Christ as the foundation of the church in such a way as to exclude St. Peter. For instance in his commentary on the Psalms the reference to the foundation of the earth in Psalm 17 leads him to consider the foundation of the church. Using Matthew 16, he declares that this foundation is a rock, which is then identified as Christ on authority of 1 Cor. 10:4. This interpretation of the text of Matthew which seems so strange to the modern reader indicates a problem which perplexed quite a number of the early fathers. Their theology of the church was, thanks to Paul, so thoroughly Christocentric that it was difficult for them to envisage a foundation other than Christ...The third opinion which Eusebius put forward was an interpretation of Matthew 16 which envisaged the rock of the church neither as Christ nor precisely Peter himself, but as the faith which he manifested in his

acknowledgment of Christ. This latter view of Eusebius, together with his other innovation, namely that the rock was Christ, had considerable influence on the later exegesis of the text in question, both in the Eastern and Western church.[38]

Athanasius (A.D. 295—373)

Athanasius succeeded Alexander of Alexandria as bishop in 328 A.D. He is remembered as the indomitable champion of Nicene orthodoxy and was the principal theologian responsible for the formulation of the Nicene doctrine of the Trinity. He is one of the most important bishops and theologians of the fourth century. The following are his comments on the nature of the foundation of the Church and the meaning of the rock of Matthew 16:

> I know moreover that not only this thing saddens you, but also the fact that while others have obtained the churches by violence, you are meanwhile cast out from your places. *For they hold the places, but you the Apostolic Faith.* They are, it is true, in the places, but outside of *the true Faith*; while you are outside the places indeed, but the Faith, within you...But ye are blessed, who by faith are in the Church, dwell upon *the foundations of the faith*, and have full satisfaction, even the highest degree of faith which remains among you unshaken. For it has come down to you from Apostolic tradition, and frequently has accursed envy wished to unsettle it, but has not been able. On the contrary, they have rather been cut off from their attempts to do so. *For thus it is written, 'Thou art the Son of the Living God,' Peter confessing it by revelation of the Father,* and being told, 'Blessed art thou Simon Barjona, for flesh and blood did not reveal it to thee, but 'My Father Who is in heaven,' and the rest. *No one therefore will ever prevail against your Faith, most beloved brethren.*[39]
>
> *Wisdom Itself is founded for us, that It may become beginning and foundation of our new creation and renewal.* Accordingly here as before, He says not, 'Before the world He has made me Word or Son,' lest there should be as it were a beginning of His making. *For this we*

The Patristic Interpretation 49

must seek before all things, whether He is Son, and on this point specially search the Scriptures; for this it was, when the Apostles were questioned that Peter answered, saying, 'Thou art the Christ, the Son of the Living God.' This also the father of the Arian heresy asked as one of his first questions; 'If Thou be *the Son of God;*' for he knew that *this is the truth and the sovereign principle of our faith;*

For He says not, 'Before the world He founded me as Word or Son,' but simply, 'He founded me,' to shew again, as I have said, *that not for His own sake but for those that are built upon Him* does He here also speak, after the way of proverbs. For this knowing, *the Apostle also writes, 'Other foundation can no man lay than that is laid, which is Jesus Christ;* but let every man take heed how he buildeth thereupon.' And it must be that the foundation should be such as the things built on it, that they may admit of being well compacted together. Being then the Word, He has not, as Word, any such as Himself, who may be compacted with Him; for He is Only-begotten; but having become man, He has the like of Him, those namely the likeness of whose flesh He has put on. *Therefore according to His manhood He is founded, that we, as precious stones, may admit of building upon Him,* and may become a temple of the Holy Ghost who dwelleth in us. *And as He is a foundation, and we stones built upon Him...*

Now what is founded is founded for the sake of the stones which are raised upon it...For so He is founded for our sakes, taking on Him what is ours, that we, as incorporated and compacted and bound together in Him...the Lord who 'before the world' was founded for this purpose; that we, as built upon Him, might partake as well-compacted stones, the life and grace which is from Him?[40]

And so the works of the Jews are undone, for they were a shadow; *but the Church is firmly established; it is founded on the rock, and the gates of hell shall not prevail against it.* Theirs it was to say, Why dost Thou, being a man, make Thyself God? and their disciple is the Samosatene; whence to his followers with reason does he teach his heresy. But we have not so learned Christ, if so be that we have heard Him, and have learned from Him.[41]

In Thy saints, who in every age have been well pleasing to Thee, is truly Thy faith; for Thou hast founded the world on Thy faith, and the gates of hell shall not prevail against it.[42]

But what is also to the point, let us note that the very tradition, teaching and *faith* of the Catholic Church from the beginning, which the Lord gave, was preached by the Apostles, and was preserved by the Fathers. *On this was the Church founded*; and if anyone departs from this, he neither is nor any longer ought to be called a Christian. ...And because this is *the faith of the Church*, let them somehow understand that the Lord sent out the Apostles and commanded them *to make this the foundation of the Church...*[43]

For Athanasius, faith in Christ as the Son of the living God is the rock and foundation of the Church against which the gates of hell will not prevail. The constant focus of Athanasius is not upon men but upon the person of Christ. In his reference to the Matthew 16 passage, the rock is not the person of Peter, but Peter's confession of faith that Christ is the Son of God, pointing ultimately to Christ himself as the true rock. He consistently states that believers, as living stones, are built upon the foundation—Christ himself. The Church therefore is built upon Christ, not Peter.

Didymus the Blind (A.D. 313—398)

Didymus was born in Alexandria and appointed head of the catechetical school at Alexandria by Athanasius. He was blind from the age of four, but renowned as a man of great learning and spirituality. Jerome was one of his students. He gives the following exposition of Matthew 16:18-19:

> *How powerful is Peter's faith and his confession that Christ is the only–begotten God, the word, the true Son of God, and not merely a creature.* Though he saw God on earth clothed in flesh and blood, Peter did not doubt, for he was willing to receive what 'flesh and blood have not revealed to you.' Moreover he recognized the consubstantial and coeternal branch of God, thereby glorifying that uncreated root,

that root without beginning which had revealed the truth to him. Peter believed that Christ was one and the same deity with the Father; and so he was called blessed by him who alone is the blessed Lord. *Upon this rock the Church was built, the Church which the gates of hell—that is, the arguments of heretics—will not overcome.* The keys to the kingdom of heaven were given to Peter in order that, 'baptizing them in the name of the Father, and Son, and the Holy Spirit,' he might open the gates of God's kingdom to those whose faith agreed both with his own confession and with those things which he and the other apostles heard from Christ. To those, however, who do not, *by like confession,* offer a hymn of praise, Peter shuts the most blessed and hoped for entrance.[44]

There are some who would suggest that the rock here refers to Peter and that Didymus teaches that the Church was built upon him in a way that is consistent with the Roman Catholic point of view. However, this interpretation does not do justice to his words or the historical context in which Didymus lived. It is clear from Didymus' statements that his main emphasis is on the faith of Peter. He is from the see of Alexandria which boasts Origen and Athanasius, neither of whom interpreted the rock of Matthew 16 in a pro–Roman sense. There is no reason to suppose that Didymus would express an interpretation that was contradictory to that of his own bishop or that expressed by the Eastern church as a whole. In referring to the rock upon which the Church would be built Didymus is referring to Peter's confession of faith.

Augustine (A.D. 354—430)

Augustine is considered by many the most important theologian in the history of the Church for the first twelve hundred years. No other Church father has had such far reaching influence upon the theology of the Church. His authority throughout the patristic and middle ages is unsurpassed. He was the bishop of Hippo in North Africa from the end of the fourth century and on into the first quarter of the fifth, until his death in 430. William Jurgens makes these comments about his importance:

If we were faced with the unlikely proposition of having to destroy completely either the works of Augustine or the works of all the other Fathers and Writers, I have little doubt that all the others would have to be sacrificed. Augustine must remain. Of all the Fathers it is Augustine who is the most erudite, who has the most remarkable theological insights, and who is effectively most prolific.[45]

He was a prolific writer and he has made numerous comments which relate directly to the issue of the interpretation of the rock of Matthew 16:18. In fact, Augustine made more comments upon this passage than any other Church father. At the end of his life, Augustine wrote his *Retractations* where he corrects statements in his earlier writings which he says were erroneous. One of these had to do with the interpretation of the rock in Matthew 16. At the beginning of his ministry Augustine had written that the rock was Peter. However he later changed his position and throughout most of his ministry he adopted the view that the rock was not Peter but Christ. The following are statements from his *Retractations* which refer to his interpretation of the rock of Matthew 16:

> In a passage in this book, I said about the Apostle Peter: 'On him as on a rock the Church was built'...But I know that very frequently at a later time, I so explained what the Lord said: *'Thou art Peter, and upon this rock I will build my Church,' that it be understood as built upon Him whom Peter confessed saying: 'Thou art the Christ, the Son of the living God,' and so Peter, called after this rock, represented the person of the Church which is built upon this rock, and has received 'the keys of the kingdom of heaven.'* For, 'Thou art Peter' and not 'Thou art the rock' was said to him. *But 'the rock was Christ,' in confessing whom, as also the whole Church confesses, Simon was called Peter.* But let the reader decide which of these two opinions is the more probable.[46]

Clearly Augustine is repudiating a previously held position, adopting the view that the rock was Christ and not Peter. This

The Patristic Interpretation 53

became his consistent position. He does leave the interpretation open for individual readers to decide which was the more probable interpretation but it is clear what he has concluded the interpretation should be and that he believes the view that the rock is Christ is the correct one. The fact that he would even suggest that individual readers could take a different position is evidence of the fact that after four hundred years of church history there was no official authoritative Church interpretation of this passage as Vatican One has stated. Can the reader imagine a bishop of the Roman Catholic Church today suggesting that it would be appropriate for individuals to use private interpretation and come to their own conclusion as to the proper meaning of the rock of Matthew 16? But that is precisely what Augustine does, although he leaves us in no doubt as to what he, as a leading bishop and theologian of the Church, personally believes. And his view was not a novel interpretation, come to at the end of his life, but his consistent teaching throughout his ministry. Nor was it an interpretation that ran counter to the prevailing opinion of his day. The following quotation is representative of the overall view espoused by this great teacher and theologian:

> And I tell you...'You are Peter, Rocky, and on this rock I shall build my Church, and the gates of the underworld will not conquer her. To you shall I give the keys of the kingdom. Whatever you bind on earth shall also be bound in heaven; whatever you loose on earth shall also be loosed in heaven' (Mt 16:15-19). In Peter, Rocky, we see our attention drawn to the rock. Now the apostle Paul says about the former people, 'They drank from the spiritual rock that was following them; but *the rock was Christ*' (1 Cor 10:4). *So this disciple is called Rocky from the rock, like Christian from Christ*...Why have I wanted to make this little introduction? In order to suggest to you that in Peter the Church is to be recognized. ***Christ, you see, built his Church not on a man but on Peter's confession. What is Peter's confession? 'You are the Christ, the Son of the living God.' There's the rock for you, there's the foundation, there's where the Church has been built, which the gates of the underworld cannot conquer.***[47]

Augustine could not be clearer in his interpretation of the rock of Matthew 16. In his view, Peter is representative of the whole Church. The rock is not the person of Peter but Christ himself. In fact, in the above statements, in exegeting Matthew 16, *he explicitly says that Christ did not build his Church on a man, referring specifically to Peter.* If Christ did not build his Church on a man then he did not establish a papal office with successors to Peter in the bishops of Rome. Again, if one examines the documentation from the writings of Augustine that are provided in *Jesus, Peter and the Keys*, this particular reference will not be found. Clearly, the authors neglected to provide such documentation because it completely undermines their position. The following extensive documentation reveals that Augustine taught that Peter was simply a figurative representative of the Church, not its ruler—a view reminiscent of Cyprian:

> But whom say ye that I am? Peter answered, 'Thou art the Christ, The Son of the living God.' One for many gave the answer, Unity in many. Then said the Lord to him, 'Blessed art thou, Simon Barjonas: for flesh and blood hath not revealed it unto thee, but My Father which is in heaven.' Then He added, 'and I say unto thee.' As if He had said, 'Because thou hast said unto Me, "Thou art the Christ the Son of the living God;" I also say unto thee, "Thou art Peter."' For before he was called Simon. *Now this name of Peter was given him by the Lord, and in a figure, that he should signify the Church. For seeing that Christ is the rock (Petra), Peter is the Christian people. For the rock (Petra) is the original name. Therefore Peter is so called from the rock; not the rock from Peter; as Christ is not called Christ from the Christian, but the Christian from Christ.* 'Therefore,' he saith, 'Thou art Peter; and upon this Rock' which Thou hast confessed, upon this rock which Thou hast acknowledged, saying, 'Thou art the Christ, the Son of the living God, will I build My Church;' that is upon Myself, the Son of the living God, 'will I build My Church.' I will build thee upon Myself, not Myself upon Thee.
>
> For men who wished to be built upon men, said, 'I am of Paul; and I of Apollos; and I of Cephas,' who is Peter. *But others who did not wish to built upon Peter, but upon the Rock, said, 'But I am of Christ.'* And

The Patristic Interpretation

when the Apostle Paul ascertained that he was chosen, and Christ despised, he said, 'Is Christ divided? was Paul crucified for you? or were ye baptized in the name of Paul?' And, as not in the name of Paul, so neither in the name of Peter; *but in the name of Christ: that Peter might be built upon the Rock, not the Rock upon Peter.* This same Peter therefore who had been by the Rock pronounced 'blessed,' *bearing the figure of the Church.*[48]

And this Church, symbolized in its generality, was personified in the Apostle Peter, on account of the primacy of his apostleship. For, as regards his proper personality, he was by nature one man, by grace one Christian, by still more abounding grace one, and yet also, the first apostle; but when it was said to him, 'I will give unto thee the keys of the kingdom of heaven, and whatsoever thou shalt bind on earth, shall be bound in heaven; and whatsoever thou shalt loose on earth, shall be loosed in heaven,' *he represented the universal Church, which in this world is shaken* by divers temptations, that come upon it like torrents of rain, floods and tempests, *and falleth not, because it is founded upon a rock (petra), from which Peter received his name. For petra (rock) is not derived from Peter, but Peter from petra; just as Christ is not called so from the Christian, but the Christian from Christ. For on this very account the Lord said, 'On this rock will I build my Church,' because Peter had said, 'Thou art the Christ, the Son of the living God.' On this rock, therefore, He said, which thou hast confessed, I will build my Church. For the Rock (Petra) was Christ; and on this foundation was Peter himself built. For other foundation can no man lay than that is laid, which is Christ Jesus.* The Church, therefore, which is founded in Christ received from Him the keys of the kingdom of heaven in the person of Peter, that is to say, the power of binding and loosing sins. *For what the Church is essentially in Christ, such representatively is Peter in the rock (petra); and in this representation Christ is to be understood as the Rock, Peter as the Church.*[49]

Before his passion the Lord Jesus, as you know, chose those disciples of his, whom he called apostles. Among these it was only *Peter who almost everywhere was given the privilege of representing the whole Church. It was in the person of the whole Church, which he alone represented, that he was privileged to hear, 'To you will I give the keys of the kingdom of heaven' (Mt 16:19). After all, it isn't just one man that received these keys, but the Church in its unity.* So this is the reason for Peter's acknowledged pre-eminence, that he stood for the Church's universality and unity, when he was told, 'To you I am entrusting,' what has in fact been entrusted to all.

I mean, to show you that it is the Church which has received the keys of the kingdom of heaven, listen to what the Lord says in another place to all his apostles: 'Receive the Holy Spirit;' and straightway, 'Whose sins you forgive, they will be forgiven them; whose sins you retain, they will be retained' (Jn 20:22-23). *This refers to the keys, about which it is said, 'whatever you loose on earth shall be loosed in heaven, and whatever you bind on earth shall be bound in heaven' (Mt 16:19). But that was said to Peter. To show you that Peter at that time stood for the universal Church,* listen to what is said to him, what is said to all the faithful, the saints: 'If your brother sins against you, correct him between you and himself alone.'[50]

According to Augustine the Apostles are equal in all respects. Each receives the authority of the keys, not Peter alone. But some object, doesn't Augustine accord a primacy to the apostle Peter? Does he not call Peter the first of the apostles, holding the chief place in the Apostleship? Don't such statements prove papal primacy? While it is true that Augustine has some very exalted things to say about Peter, as do many of the fathers, it does not follow that either he or they held to the Roman Catholic view of papal primacy. This is because their comments apply to Peter alone. They have absolutely nothing to do with the bishops of Rome. How do we know this? Because Augustine and the fathers do not make that application in their comments. They do not state that their descriptions of Peter apply to the bishops of Rome. The common mistake made by Roman Catholic apologists is the assumption that because some of the fathers make certain comments about Peter—for example, that he is chief of the apostles or head of the apostolic choir—that they also have in mind the bishop of Rome in an exclusive sense. *But they do not state this in their writings.* This is a preconceived theology that is

The Patristic Interpretation

read into their writings. Did they view the bishops of Rome as being successors of Peter? Yes. Did they view the bishops of Rome as being the *exclusive* successors of Peter? No. In the view of Augustine and the early fathers *all* the bishops of the Church in the East and West were the successors of Peter. They all possess the chair of Peter. So when they speak in exalted terms about Peter they do not apply those terms to the bishops of Rome. Therefore, when a father refers to Peter as the rock, the 'coryphaeus,' the first of the disciples, or something similar, this does not mean that he is expressing agreement with the current Roman Catholic interpretation. This view is clearly validated from the following statements of Augustine:

> This same Peter therefore who had been by the Rock pronounced 'blessed,' bearing the figure of the Church, *holding the chief place in the Apostleship* (Sermon 26).

> The blessed Peter, *the first of the apostles* (Sermon 295)

> Before his passion *the Lord Jesus*, as you know, *chose those disciples of his, whom he called apostles. Among these* it was *only Peter* who almost everywhere *was given the privilege of representing the whole Church.* It was in the person of the whole Church, which he alone represented, that he was privileged to hear, 'To you will I give the keys of the kingdom of heaven' (Mt 16:19). After all, *it isn't just one man that received these keys*, but the Church in its unity. *So* this *is the reason for Peter's acknowledged preeminence, that he stood for the Church's universality and unity*, when he was told, 'To you I am entrusting,' what has in fact been entrusted to all (Sermon 295).

> Previously, of course, he was called Simon; *this name of Peter was bestowed on him by the Lord, and that with the symbolic intention of his representing the Church. Because Christ, you see, is the petra or rock; Peter, or Rocky, is the Christian people* (Sermon 76).

> So then, this self–same Peter, blessed by being surnamed Rocky from the rock, representing the person of the Church, *holding chief place in the apostolic ranks* (Sermon 76).

For as some things are said which seem peculiarly to apply to the Apostle Peter, and yet are not clear in their meaning, unless when referred to *the Church*, whom *he* is acknowledged to have *figuratively represented, on account of the primacy which he bore among the Disciples*; as it is written, 'I will give unto thee the keys of the kingdom of heaven,' and other passages of like purport: so Judas doth represent those Jews who were enemies of Christ (Exposition on the Book of Psalms, Psalm 119).

You will remember that the apostle Peter, *the first of all the apostles*, was thrown completely of balance during the Lord's passion (Sermon 147).

Christ, you see, built his Church not on a man but on Peter's confession. What is Peter's confession? 'You are the Christ, the Son of the living God.' There's the rock for you, there's the foundation, there's where the Church has been built, which the gates of the underworld cannot conquer. (Sermon 229).

And this Church, symbolized in its generality, was personified in the Apostle Peter, *on account of the primacy of his apostleship*. For, as regards his proper personality, he was by nature one man, by grace one Christian, by still more abounding grace one, and yet also, *the first apostle*; but when it was said to him, I will give unto thee the keys of the kingdom of heaven, and whatsoever thou shalt bind on earth, shall be bound in heaven; and whatsoever thou shalt loose on earth, shall be loosed in heaven,' he represented *the universal Church*, which in this world is shaken by divers temptations, that come upon it like torrents of rain, floods and tempests, and *falleth not, because it is founded upon a rock (petra), from which Peter received his name*. For petra (rock) is not derived from Peter, but Peter from petra; just as Christ is not called so from the Christian, but the Christian from Christ. For on this very account the Lord said, 'On this rock will I build my Church,' because Peter had said, 'Thou art the Christ, the Son of the living God.' *On this rock, therefore, He said, which thou hast confessed, I will build my Church. For the Rock (Petra) was Christ; and on this foundation was*

Peter himself built. For other foundation can no man lay than that is laid, which is Christ Jesus. The Church, therefore, which is founded in Christ received from Him the keys of the kingdom of heaven in the person of Peter, that is to say, the power of binding and loosing sins. *For what the Church is essentially in Christ, such representatively is Peter in the rock (petra); and in this representation Christ is to be understood as the Rock, Peter as the Church* (Commentary on the Gospel of John, Tractate 124.5).

Augustine states that Peter is the first and head of the apostles and that he holds a primacy. However he does not interpret that primacy in a Roman Catholic sense. He believes that Peter's primacy is figurative in that he represents the universal Church. Again, *he explicitly states that Christ did not build his Church upon a man but on Peter's confession of faith.* Peter is built on Christ the rock and as a figurative representative of the Church he shows how each believer is built on Christ. In Augustine's view, Peter holds a primacy or preeminence, but none of this applies to him in a jurisdictional sense, because he says that 'Christ did not build his Church upon a man.' We can not get a clearer illustration that the fathers did indeed separate Peter's confession of faith from Peter's person. In commenting on one of Augustine's references to Peter and the rock, John Rotelle, the editor of the Roman Catholic series on the Sermons of Augustine, makes these observations:

> 'There was Peter, and he hadn't yet been confirmed in the rock': That is, in Christ, as participating in his 'rockiness' by faith. It does not mean confirmed as the rock, because *Augustine never thinks of Peter as the rock.* Jesus, after all, did not in fact call him the rock...but 'Rocky.' The rock on which he would build his Church was, for Augustine, both Christ himself and Peter's faith, representing the faith of the Church (emphasis mine).[51]

Augustine does not endorse the Roman Catholic interpretation. Again and again he states that the rock is Christ, not Peter. Augustine claims no exclusive Petrine succession in the Roman bishops and no papal office. Karlfried Froehlich sums up

Augustine's views on Peter and the rock of Matthew 16 in these comments:

> Augustine's formulation (of Matthew 16:18-19), informed by a traditional North African concern for the unity of the church, that in Peter *unus pro omnibus* (one for all) had answered and received the reward, did not suggest more than a figurative reading of Peter as an image of the true church. In light of Peter's subsequent fall and denial, the name itself was regularly declared to be derived from Christ, the true rock. Augustine, who followed Origen in this assumption, was fascinated by the dialectic of the 'blessed' Peter (Matt. 16:17) being addressed as 'Satan' a few verses later (v. 23). In Peter, weak in himself and strong only in his connection with Christ, the church could see the image of its own total dependence on God's grace.
>
> Augustine rigorously separated the name-giving from its explanation: Christ did not say to Peter: 'you are the rock,' but 'you are Peter.' The church is not built upon Peter but upon the only true rock, Christ. Augustine and the medieval exegetes after him found the warrant for this interpretation in 1 Cor. 10:4. The allegorical key of this verse had already been applied to numerous biblical rock passages in the earlier African *testimonia* tradition. Matt. 16:18 was no exception. If the metaphor of the rock did not refer to a negative category of 'hard' rocks, it had to be read christologically.[52]

Karl Morrison sums up Augustine's views of ecclesiology in these words:

> Peter was said to have received the power of the keys, not in his own right, but as the representative of the entire Church. Without contesting Rome's primacy of honor, St. Augustine held that all the Apostles, and all their successors, the bishops, shared equally in the powers which Christ granted St. Peter.[53]

Reinhold Seeberg, the Protestant Church historian, makes these comments on Augustine's interpretation of Peter pointing out that it reflects the view of Cyprian:

The Patristic Interpretation 61

The idea of the Roman Primacy likewise receives no special elucidation at the hands of Augustine. We find a general acknowledgment of the 'primacy of the apostolic chair,' but Augustine knows nothing of any special authority vested in Peter or his successors. Peter is a 'figure of the church' or of 'good pastors,' and represents the unity of the church (serm. 295.2; 147.2). In this consists the significance of his position and that of his successors...As all bishops (in contradistinction from the Scriptures) may err (unit. eccl. II.28), so also the Roman bishop. This view is plainly manifest from the bearing of Augustine and his colleagues in the Pelagian controversy...Dogmatically, there had been no advance from the position of Cyprian. The Africans, in their relations with Rome, played somewhat the role of the Gallicanism of a later period.[54]

W.H.C. Frend affirms the above consensus of Augustine's ecclesiology and his interpretation of Peter's commission:

> Augustine...rejected the idea that 'the power of the keys' had been entrusted to Peter alone. His primacy was simply a matter of personal privilege and not an office. Similarly, he never reproached the Donatists for not being in communion with Rome, but with lack of communion with the apostolic Sees as a whole. His view of Church government was that less important questions should be settled by provincial councils, greater matters at general councils.[55]

Augustine is the greatest Church father and theologian of the patristic age writing after 400 years of Church history. The constitution of the Church should have been a firmly settled issue, especially since Vatican I claims that its papal teachings and interpretation of Matthew 16 upon which they rest have been the belief and teaching of the Church from the very beginning. Yet Augustine interprets Matthew 16 in a Protestant and Orthodox way, explicitly repudiating the Roman Catholic interpretation of Vatican I. How are we to explain this? Vatican I states the rock of Matthew 16 is the person of Peter and has been the unanimous opinion of the Church fathers. Then why did Augustine hold a contrary view to that which was supposedly the universal opinion of the Church of his day and in all preceding Church history? According to Rome, this passage holds the key to the constitution of the Church given by Christ himself which was fully recognized from the very beginning. If this was so, why would Augustine purposefully contradict the universal interpretation of so fundamental and important a passage? The answer, quite simply, is that the fathers did not interpret the rock of Matthew 16 the way Vatican I does. Augustine is merely a prominent representative of the opinion of the Church as a whole.

The authors of *Jesus, Peter and the Keys* suggest that Augustine invented a novel interpretation of the rock of Matthew 16 in stating that the rock is Christ. Specifically they state: 'St. Augustine invented a new exegesis (of Matthew 16:18-19)—that the rock is Christ.'[56]

This is a completely misinformed statement. As we have seen this interpretation was utilized by Eusebius in the fourth century, many years before Augustine.

Ambrose (*ca.* A.D. 333—397)

Ambrose was bishop of the see of Milan in the latter part of the fourth century. He was one of the greatest fathers of the Western Church, the mentor of St. Augustine, and universally recognized as one of the greatest theologians of the patristic age. He is one of a handful of Western fathers who would be recognized theologically by the Roman Catholic Church as a doctor of the Church. He was the leading theologian and outstanding bishop of the Western Church. He is a father who is often cited in support of the present day Roman Catholic interpretation of Matthew 16:18. Robert Fastiggi references the quotation that is most often given in support of this view:

> It is to Peter himself that He says: 'You are Peter, and upon this rock I will build My Church.' Where Peter is, there is the Church.[57]

The Patristic Interpretation 63

The impression given by Fastiggi and others is that in these comments Ambrose supports the Roman Catholic interpretation of Matthew 16. They apply the following logic to his statement: The above quote seems to suggest that Peter's person is the rock. And since the bishops of Rome are the successors to Peter they are, therefore, by succession, the rocks of the Church. Therefore, according to Ambrose, the Church is founded upon the universal rule of the bishops of Rome. To be in communion with Rome is to be in the Church. To be out of communion with Rome is to be out of the Church for where Peter (that is, the bishop of Rome) is, there is the Church. Is this what Ambrose meant? If we divorce this one sentence from its context and from the rest of his comments on Peter in other writings, we could certainly lean towards that interpretation. However, Ambrose made other comments on Peter and Matthew 16 which explain exactly what he meant when he said that Peter is the rock. Unfortunately, these other comments are often neglected in discussions by Roman Catholic apologists. Often a quote like this is given out of the context. The result is that an interpretation is given the words of Ambrose that is completely foreign to his true meaning. This becomes clear upon examination of his other statements:

> He, then, who before was silent, to teach us that we ought not to repeat the words of the impious, this one, I say, when he heard, 'But who do you say I am,' immediately, not unmindful of his station, *exercised his primacy, that is, the primacy of confession, not of honor; the primacy of belief, not of rank.*
>
> This, then, is Peter, who has replied for the rest of the Apostles; rather, before the rest of men. And so he is called the foundation, because he knows how to preserve not only his own but the common foundation...*Faith, then, is the foundation of the Church, for it was not said of Peter's flesh, but of his faith, that 'the gates of hell shall not prevail against it.'* But his confession of faith conquered hell. And this confession did not shut out one heresy, for, since the Church like a good ship is often buffeted by many waves, the foundation of the Church should prevail against all heresies.[58]

Jesus said to them: Who do men say that I am? Simon Peter answering said, The Christ of God (Lk. ix.20). If it is enough for Paul 'to know nothing but Christ Jesus and Him crucified,' (1 Cor. ii.2), what more is to be desired by me than to know Christ? For in this one name is the expression of His Divinity and Incarnation, and faith in His Passion. And accordingly though the other apostles knew, yet Peter answers before the rest, 'Thou art the Christ the Son of God'...Believe, therefore, as Peter believed, that thou also mayest be blessed, and that thou also mayest deserve to hear, 'Because flesh and blood hath not revealed it to thee, but My Father who is in heaven'...Peter therefore did not wait for the opinion of the people, but produced his own, saying, 'Thou art the Christ the Son of the living God': Who ever is, began not to be, nor ceases to be. Great is the grace of Christ, who has imparted almost all His own names to His disciples. 'I am,' said He, 'the light of the world,' and yet with that very name in which He glories, He favored His disciples, saying, 'Ye are the light of the world.' 'I am the living bread'; and 'we all are one bread' (1 Cor. x.17)...Christ is the rock, for 'they drank of the same spiritual rock that followed them, and the rock was Christ' (1 Cor. x.4); also He denied not to His disciple the grace of this name; that he should be Peter, because he has from the rock (petra) the solidity of constancy, the firmness of faith. *Make an effort, therefore, to be a rock! Do not seek the rock outside of yourself, but within yourself! Your rock is your deed, your rock is your mind. Upon this rock your house is built. Your rock is your faith, and faith is the foundation of the Church. If you are a rock, you will be in the Church, because the Church is on a rock. If you are in the Church the gates of hell will not prevail against you*...He who has conquered the flesh is a foundation of the Church; and if he cannot equal Peter, he can imitate him.[59]

What does Ambrose mean when he says that Peter is the foundation? In the sense that he was the first to openly confess faith in Christ as the Messiah and Son of God. The rock is not Peter himself but Peter's *confession of faith*! It is this faith which is the foundation of the Church. Peter possesses a primacy, but he explains that primacy

The Patristic Interpretation 65

as one of confession and faith and not of rank in the sense of ruling over the other apostles. Thus, when Ambrose says that 'where Peter is there is the Church,' he means that where Peter's *confession* is, there is the Church. He does not mean the bishop of Rome at all. He goes on to give an exposition of the rock reminiscent of the interpretation of Origen who says that all believers are rocks. As Robert Eno points out, when the overall context of Ambrose's statement is taken into account, it demonstrates that the interpretation given by Fastiggi and others is a complete misrepresentation of Ambrose's statement since his statement has nothing to do with ecclesiology and papal authority. Robert Eno gives the following explanation:

> There is no question then that Ambrose honored the Roman see, but there are other texts which seem to establish a certain distance and independence as well. He commented, for example, that Peter's primacy was a primacy of confession, not of honor; a primacy of faith, not rank...Finally, one further text should be mentioned in connection with Ambrose since it is a text which like *Roma locuta est* has become something of a shibboleth or slogan. This is the brief phrase from his commentary on the fortieth Psalm: *Ubi Petrus, ibi ecclesia* (where Peter is, there is the Church)...As Roger Gryson has shown, in his study on Ambrose and the priesthood, the context of such a statement has nothing to do with any treatise on ecclesiology. It is but one statement in a long chain of allegorical exegesis starting with the line from Ps. 41:9: 'Even my bosom friend in whom I trusted...has lifted his heel against me.' This is not to deny the fairly common association of Peter as the symbol of the Church, the *figura ecclesiae* we have seen in Augustine. But it says little that is new and nothing at all about papal authority.[60]

In the view of the fathers, as seen in the examples of Cyprian, Ambrose and Augustine, the Church is not embodied in one individual but in a confession of right faith. Where you have that right confession you have Peter. This is explicitly stated for example by Chrysostom. Like Ambrose, he says that where Peter is there is the

Church in the sense of Peter's confession and he applies it not to Rome but to Antioch: 'Though we do not retain the body of Peter, we do retain the faith of Peter, and retaining the faith of Peter we have Peter.'[61] It is important to note also that Ambrose, like Augustine, separates Peter's confession of faith from the person of Peter himself: 'Faith, then, is the foundation of the Church, for *it was not said of Peter's flesh, but of his faith*, that "the gates of hell shall not prevail against it".' This conclusively demonstrates the spuriousness of some Roman apologists' claims that the fathers did not separate the confession of Peter from the person of Peter. Ambrose did this as did Augustine, and other fathers as well, as we will see. These fathers did not believe that the Church was built on the person of Peter but on Christ alone or on Peter's confession of faith in a secondary sense. And generally speaking, when the fathers state that the Church is built on Peter, they mean it is built upon his faith. Karlfried Froehlich makes this very point in his comments on the patristic exegesis of the rock of Matthew 16:18:

> Most of the Eastern exegetes, especially after the doctrinal controversies of the fourth century, read v. 18 as the culmination of vv. 16-17: 'upon this rock' meant 'upon the orthodox faith which you have just confessed.' Introduced in the West by Ambrose and the translation of the Antiochene exegetes, this *Petra=fides* equation maintained an important place alongside the christological alternative, or as its more precise explanation: the rock of the church was Christ who was the content of Peter's confession.[62]

As Froehlich mentions this can be seen, in particular, from the example of Ambrose himself. In other passages he refers to Christ and Peter's confession as the rock:

> 'They sucked honey out of the firm rock,' (Deut. xxxii.13): for the flesh of Christ is a rock, which redeemed heaven and the whole world (1 Cor. x.4).[63]

> The Lord said to Peter: on this rock I will build My Church...On this catholic confession of faith he establishes the faithful in life.[64]

The Patristic Interpretation 67

For Ambrose, then, the rock is not Peter but his confession of faith. It points to the person of Christ as the ultimate rock. So it is possible to make it appear that Ambrose holds a particular view when in fact he does not, by not presenting his complete teaching on this subject.

Hilary of Poitiers (A.D. 315—368)

Hilary was consecrated bishop of Poitiers in 350 A.D. He is known as the Athanasius of the West due to his staunch stand for Nicene orthodoxy in opposition to Arianism. He died in 367–368 A.D. and was declared a doctor of the Church by pope Pius IX. His views on the rock of Matthew 16 are consistent with those of Augustine and Ambrose:

> A belief that the Son of God is Son in name only, and not in nature, is not the faith of the Gospels and of the Apostles...whence I ask, was it that the blessed Simon Bar–Jona confessed to Him, Thou art the Christ, the Son of the living God?...*And this is the rock of confession whereon the Church is built*...that Christ must be not only named, but believed, the Son of God.
> *This faith is that which is the foundation of the Church; through this faith the gates of hell cannot prevail against her. This is the faith which has the keys of the kingdom of heaven. Whatsoever this faith shall have loosed or bound on earth shall be loosed or bound in heaven*...The very reason why he is blessed is that he confessed the Son of God. This is the Father's revelation, *this the foundation of the Church*, this the assurance of her permanence. Hence has she the keys of the kingdom of heaven, hence judgment in heaven and judgment on earth.... *Thus our one immovable foundation, our one blissful rock of faith, is the confession from Peter's mouth, Thou art the Son of the living God*...Matthew also, chosen to proclaim the whole mystery of the Gospel, first a publican, then an Apostle, and John, the Lord's familiar friend, and therefore worthy to reveal the deepest secrets of heaven, and *blessed Simon, who after his confession of the mystery was set to be the foundation-stone of the Church*, and received the keys of

the kingdom of heaven, and all his companions who spoke by the Holy Ghost, and Paul, the chosen vessel, changed from persecutor into Apostle, who, as a living man, abode under the deep sea and ascended into the third heaven, who was in paradise before his martydom, whose martydom was the perfect offering of a flawless faith...[65]

The Church, according to Hilary, is built upon Peter's confession of faith. This is the rock and foundation of the Church, not the person of Peter. He does mention that Peter is set as the foundation–stone of the Church but he means this in regard to his confession. It is the confession of Peter that is the true foundation upon which the Church is built.

Jerome (A.D. 347—420)

Jerome is the great biblical scholar of the Western Church of the patristics age. He spent time in both the East and West and was a master of three languages: Latin, Greek and Hebrew. Along with Origen, he is considered the only true biblical scholar of the entire patristic age. He was ordained to the priesthood in 379 A.D. and died around 420 A.D. He had been the personal secretary of pope Damasus and spent the last thirty–five years of his life in the Holy Land in Bethlehem. In 375 A.D. Jerome wrote some personal correspondence to pope Damasus from Antioch. At the time there was great confusion due to a schism which had erupted in the East and Jerome writes two letters to pope Damasus seeking his counsel with respect to the situation. Jerome makes reference to the pope as being identified with the chair of Peter, which is the rock upon which the Church is built:

> Away with all that is overweening; let the state of Roman majesty withdraw. My words are spoken to the successor of the fisherman, to the disciple of the cross. As I follow no leader save Christ, so I communicate with none but your blessedness, that is, with the chair of Peter. For this I know, is the rock on which the church is built![66]

The Patristic Interpretation 69

This statement would seem to indicate a very strong papal view by Jerome. But if his other writings are taken into account we find that the view he expresses in the above statement is greatly modified. Did Jerome believe that the bishop of Rome was the successor of Peter, who possessed the chair of Peter, which is the rock on which the Church was built? Yes. Did he believe this of the bishop of Rome in an exclusive sense? No. First of all, Jerome states that Christ is the only true foundation and rock on which the Church was built:

> *The one foundation which the apostolic architect laid is our Lord Jesus Christ. Upon this stable and firm foundation, which has itself been laid on solid ground, the Church of Christ is built...For the Church was founded upon a rock...upon this rock the Lord established his Church; and the apostle Peter received his name from this rock* (Mt. 16.18).[67]

> *She, that with a firm root is founded upon the rock, Christ, the Catholic Church*, is the one dove; she stands the perfect one, and near to His right hand, and has nothing sinister in her.[68]

> *The rock is Christ, Who gave to His apostles, that they also should be called rocks, 'Thou art Peter, and upon this rock I will build My Church.'*[69]

> Was there no other province in the whole world to receive the gospel of pleasure, and into which the serpent might insinuate itself, except *that which was founded by the teaching of Peter upon the rock Christ.*[70]

Secondly, Jerome states that while Christ is the ultimate foundation of the Church, the other apostles share this status with him in a secondary sense—the Church is built upon their teaching. He states that all the apostles are what Peter was. They have all been given the keys and they all share an equal authority. All lawful bishops are successors of the apostles. The Church is built upon the foundation of the apostles and prophets and Peter is only one of the foundations. Just as the Church is built upon Peter, it is built upon all the apostles. While the bishop of Rome does sit upon the chair of Peter, this is not an exclusive possession of the bishop of Rome, as we saw in the use of this term by Cyprian and Optatus of Milevis:

> This mountain is in the house of the Lord, which the prophet sighs after, saying, 'One thing I have asked of the Lord, this will I seek after, that I may dwell in the house of the Lord all the days of my life' (Ps. xvii.4), and concerning which Paul writes to Timothy, 'But if I tarry long, that thou mayest know how thou oughtest to behave thyself in the house of God, which is the Church of the living God, the pillar and ground of the truth' (1 Tim. iii.15). *This house is built upon the foundation of the apostles and prophets*, as imitators of Christ. Of this house, Jerusalem, the Psalmist cries out saying, 'They that trust in the Lord shall be as Mount Sion; he shall not be moved for ever that dwelleth in Jerusalem. Mountains are round about it; and the Lord is round about His people' (Ps. cxxiv.1). *Whence also upon one of the mountains Christ founds the Church, and says to him, 'Thou art Peter, and upon this rock I will build My Church, and the gates of hell shall not prevail against it.*[71]

> 'You are Peter and upon this rock I shall build my Church.' Just as Christ himself gave light to the apostles, in order that they might be called the light of the world, so other names were derived from the Lord: for example, *Simon, who believed in the rock, Christ, was given the name 'Peter.'* And in accordance with the metaphor of the rock, Jesus rightly said to him: 'I shall build my Church upon you. And the gates of hell shall not prevail against it.'[72]

> 'Built upon the foundation of the apostles and prophets'...For if those who are no longer strangers and sojourners, but fellow citizens with the saints and *members of God's household have been built upon the foundation of the apostles and the prophets, Christ himself being the cornerstone*—in whom the whole building has been joined together into a temple holy in the Lord, in whom the Ephesians are built into a temple of God in the spirit: if this is so, then there is one God of one building and temple which is built upon the foundation of the apostles and prophets. Now if a universal building is joined together and is growing into a temple holy in the Lord, then we must strive

with every effort to become the sorts of stones about which it is written: 'holy stones are rolled upon the earth.'[73]

Though, he says, the Lord had with Him the apostles Peter and John; and they saw Him transfigured on the mount, and upon them the foundation of the Church is placed...[74]

When subsequently one presbyter was chosen to preside over the rest, this was done to remedy schism and to prevent each individual from rending the church of Christ by drawing it to himself. For even at Alexandria from the time of Mark the Evangelist until the episcopates of Heraclas and Dionysius the presbyters always named as bishop one of their own number chosen by themselves...For what function, excepting ordination, belongs to a bishop that does not also belong to a presbyter? *It is not the case that there is one church at Rome and another in all the world beside. Gaul and Britain, Africa and Persia, India and the East all worship one Christ and observe one rule of truth. If you ask for authority, the world outweighs its capital. Wherever there is a bishop, whether it be at Rome or at Engubium, whether it be at Constantinople or at Rhegium, whether it be at Alexandria or at Zoan, his dignity is one and his priesthood is one. Neither the command of wealth nor the lowliness of poverty makes him more of a bishop or less a bishop. All alike are successors of the apostles.*[75]

But you say, the Church was founded upon Peter: although elsewhere the same is attributed to all the Apostles, and they all receive the keys of the kingdom of heaven, and the strength of the Church depends upon them all alike, yet one among the twelve is chosen so that when a head has been appointed, there may be no occasion for schism.[76]

Finally, in one of his letters Jerome makes reference to pope Anastasius and the extent of his jurisdiction. He states that he ruled the *Roman* Church, not the Church universal.

I have all but passed over the most important point of all. While you were still quite small, bishop Anastasius of holy and blessed memory ruled the *Roman* church.[77]

The views expressed by Jerome are consistent with many of the fathers of the Eastern Church as we will see.

The Ambrosiaster (Latter 4th Century)

Ambrosiaster is a set of commentaries by an unknown author in Rome during the latter part of the fourth century, probably around the time of pope Damasus. In this work, the author, in exegeting Matthew 16:18, states that the rock and foundation of the Church is Peter's confession of faith. He places Paul on an equal footing with Peter in authority, saying that they both share an equal primacy. This work is important, originating as it does from Rome:

> By the apostles who were somewhat distinguished among their colleagues, whom also he, *Paul,* because of their constancy calls 'pillars,' and who had always been intimate with the Lord, even beholding his glory on the mount, by them he (Paul) says the gift which he received from God was approved; *so that he would be worthy to have primacy in preaching to the Gentiles, even as Peter had the primacy in preaching to the circumcision.* And even as he gives colleagues to Peter, outstanding men among the apostles, so he also joins to himself Barnabas, who was associated with him by divine choice; *yet he claims the privilege of primacy granted by God for himself alone, even as it was granted to Peter alone among the apostles,* in such a way that the apostles of the circumcision stretched out their right hands to the apostles of the Gentiles to manifest a harmony of fellowship, that both parties, knowing that they had received from the Lord a spirit of completeness in the imparting of the gospel, might show that they were in no way appointing one another.[78]

(Ephesians 2:20): 'Built upon the foundation of the apostles and prophets, Christ Jesus himself being the cornerstone.' The above puts together New and Old Testaments. For the apostles proclaimed what the prophets said would be, although Paul says to the Corinthians: 'God placed the apostles first, the prophets second' (1 Cor. 12.28). But this refers to other prophets, for in 1 Cor. Paul writes about

The Patristic Interpretation

ecclesiastical orders; *here he is concerned with the foundation of the Church. The prophets prepared, the apostles laid the foundations. Wherefore the Lord says to Peter: 'Upon this rock I shall build my Church,' that is, upon this confession of the catholic faith I shall establish the faithful in life.*[79]

After the concord of fellowship and the honor which each accorded to the other in the matter of the privilege of founding churches, now, because some matter of neglect or error has intervened, the apostles seem to differ among themselves—not in a personal concern, but in a concern of the Church. 'To his face,' Paul says, '*I opposed him.' What does this mean, except that Paul contradicted Peter in his presence?* And Paul has added the reason: '*Because he stood condemned.' Condemned assuredly by evangelical truth which Peter's act (of separating himself from the circumcision) opposed. For who dared to contradict Peter, the chief apostle to whom the Lord had given the keys of the kingdom of Heaven, except such another who in the assurance of his election knew that he was not unequal, and so could firmly disavow what Peter had thoughtlessly done.*[80]

Worthy it was that Paul desired to see Peter, since Peter was chief among the apostles, to whom the Savior had entrusted the care of the Church. Not, to be sure, that Paul could learn anything from him, since he had already been taught by that same authority by whom Peter himself had been instructed: but on account of the disposition of the apostolic office, *so that Peter might know that this office which he himself had received had been given also to Paul.* Coming, therefore, to Peter, Paul was warmly received, and he remained with Peter for 15 days, as co-apostle in harmony with him. Paul makes these things known, in order to show that he possessed the agreement of the apostles and that they in no way dissented, as certain pseudo–apostles were murmuring about him.[81]

Michael Winter makes these comments about Ambrosiaster:

To a certain extent his views tend to weaken the position of St. Peter.

In the first place he bestows the title of 'primacy' (*primatum*) on St. Paul in a sense which would seem somewhat prejudicial to Peter. Moreover, the 'rock' in the Petrine promise is for him simply faith: 'The Lord said to Peter: On this rock I will build my church; that is: in this confession of catholic faith I will consolidate the faithful for eternal life.[82]

John Chrysostom (A.D. 344/354—407)

John Chrysostom was an Eastern father who lived during the second half of the fourth century. He was a priest of Antioch, bishop of Constantinople and contemporary of some of the greatest Church fathers in the history of the Church (such as Epiphanius, Ambrose, Augustine and Jerome). He was the most prolific writer of the Eastern fathers and is considered by many to be the greatest preacher, commentator and theologian to grace the Eastern Church. He was known as the golden–mouthed preacher for his eloquence. He died in exile in 407 A.D. William Jurgens makes these comments about him:

> Some will say that John Chrysostom is unparalleled anywhere, while others will say that he is matched only by Augustine...No one else among the Greek Fathers has so large a body of extant writings as has Chrysostom.[83]

What was Chrysostom's view of Peter and his interpretation of the rock of Matthew 16? Does it coincide with the teaching of papal primacy espoused by the Church of Rome? The answer is no. Chrysostom's views are very similar to those of Augustine. As we have seen Augustine held a very high view of Peter. He called him the chief and first of the apostles and yet stated that the rock was not Peter but Christ. A very similar picture presents itself in the writings of Chrysostom. In his book *Studies in the Early Papacy*, the Roman Catholic apologist Dom Chapman has referenced approximately ninety citations from Chrysostom's writings which he claims as proof of a clear and unambiguous affirmation of a Petrine and thereby a papal primacy. But Dom Chapman has committed a

The Patristic Interpretation 75

primary error of historiography—that of reading back into the writings of a previous age the presuppositions and conclusions of a later age. He assumes that because a particular father makes certain statements about Peter that he must have a primacy of jurisdiction in mind and that this applies in his thinking to the bishop of Rome in an exclusive sense as well. But as we have seen with Augustine this is not the case. A close examination of the comments of Chrysostom demonstrates this to be true in his case as well. Like Augustine, Chrysostom makes some very exalted statements about Peter:

> *Peter, that chief of the apostles, first in the Church, the friend of Christ* who did not receive revelation from man but from the Father, as the Lord bore witness to him saying: 'Blessed are you, Simon Bar–Jonah, for flesh and blood has not revealed this to you but my Father who is in heaven': this same Peter (*when I say 'Peter,' I name an unbreakable rock, an immovable ridge, a great apostle, the first of the disciples, the first called and the first obeying*), this same Peter, I say, did not perpetrate a minor misdeed but a very great one. He denied the Lord. I say this, not accusing a just man, but offering to you the opportunity of repentance. Peter denied the Lord and governor of the world himself, the savior of all...[84]

> Peter, *the coryphaeus of the choir of apostles, the mouth of the disciples, the foundation of the faith, the base of the confession, the fisherman of the world*, who brought back our race from the depth of error to heaven, he who is everywhere fervent and full of boldness, or rather of love than boldness.[85]

These are exalted titles but in using them Chrysostom does not mean that Peter possesses a primacy of jurisdiction in the Church or that he is the rock upon which the Church is built. Again, we have already seen this in Augustine. He uses similar language in describing Peter but without its having a Roman Catholic meaning. We know this is also true for Chrysostom because he applies similar titles to the other apostles and did not interpret the rock of Matthew 16 to be Peter.

The term *coryphaeus*, for example, was a general title applied by Chrysostom to several of the apostles, not to Peter exclusively. It carries the idea of leadership but implies no jurisdiction. Chrysostom uses this term to describe Peter, James, John, Andrew and Paul. He states that just as Peter received the charge of the world, so did the apostles Paul and John. Just as Peter was appointed teacher of the world, so was Paul. Just as Peter was a holder of the keys of heaven, so was the apostle John. He places the apostles on an equal footing relative to authority:

> He took *the coryphaei* and led them up into a high mountain apart...Why does He take these three alone? Because they excelled the others. Peter showed his excellence by his great love of Him, John by being greatly loved, James by the answer...'We are able to drink the chalice.'[86]...Do you not see that *the headship was in the hands of these three*, especially of Peter and James? This was the chief cause of their condemnation by Herod.[87]...*The coryphaei, Peter the foundation of the Church, Paul the vessel of election.*[88]
>
> *And if any should say 'How then did James receive the chair at Jerusalem?' I would make this reply, that He appointed Peter teacher not of the chair, but of the world*...And this He did to withdraw them (*Peter and John*) from their unseasonable sympathy for each other; *for since they were about to receive the charge of the world*, it was necessary that they should no longer be closely associated together[89]...*For the Son of thunder, the beloved of Christ, the pillar of the Churches throughout the world, who holds the keys of heaven*, who drank the cup of Christ, and was baptized with His baptism, who lay upon his Master's bosom, with much confidence, this man now comes forward to us now[90]...The merciful God is wont to give this honor to his servants, that by their grace others may acquire salvation; as was agreed by *the blessed Paul, that teacher of the world* who emitted the rays of his teaching everywhere.[91]

It is clear from these statements that Chrysostom, while certainly granting a large leadership role to Peter, does not consider him to have been made the supreme ruler of the Church. These passages demonstrate that the exalted titles applied to Peter were not *exclusively* applied to Peter. But these passages are completely absent from the work *Jesus, Peter and the Keys*. The passage in which Chrysostom exegetes the rock of Matthew 16 explaining that it is Peter's confession of faith is also not included. How can the authors of this work claim to give a truthful and balanced presentation of Chrysostom's perspective when they are guilty of such blatant and purposeful disregard of his writings?

There is one passage in which Chrysostom does state that Peter received authority over the Church:

> For he who then did not dare to question Jesus, but committed the office to another, was even *entrusted with the chief authority over the brethren.*[92]

This would seem to indicate that Chrysostom taught that Peter was the supreme ruler of the Church. However in the passage cited above Chrysostom speaks of the apostle John as also receiving the charge of the whole world and the keys equally with Peter:

> And this He did to withdraw them (***Peter and John***) from their unseasonable sympathy for each other; *for since they were about to receive the charge of the world*, it was necessary that they should no longer be closely associated together[93]...*For the Son of thunder, the beloved of Christ, the pillar of the Churches throughout the world, who holds the keys of heaven*...[94]

He goes on to speak of Paul as being on an equal footing with Peter:

> Where the Cherubim sing the glory, where the Seraphim are flying, there shall we see *Paul, with Peter, and as chief and leader of the choir of the saints*, and shall enjoy his generous love....I love Rome even for this, although indeed one has other grounds for praising it...Not so bright is the heaven, when the sun sends forth his rays, as is the city of Rome, sending out *these two lights* into all parts of the world. From thence will ***Paul*** be caught up, thence ***Peter***. Just bethink you, and shudder, at the thought of what a sight Rome will see, when ***Paul ariseth suddenly from that deposit, together with Peter***, and is lifted up to meet the Lord. What a rose will Rome send up to Christ!...what two

crowns will the city have about it! what golden chains will she be girded with! what fountains possess! Therefore I admire the city, not for the much gold, nor for the columns, not for the other display there, but for *these pillars of the Church* (1 Cor. 15:38).[95]

Further, Chrysostom speaks of James, and not Peter, as possessing the chief rule and authority in Jerusalem and over the Jerusalem Council:

> This (James) was bishop, as they say, and therefore he speaks last..There was no arrogance in the Church. After Peter Paul speaks, and none silences him: James waits patiently; not starts up (for the next word). No word speaks John here, no word the other Apostles, but held their peace, for *James was invested with the chief rule*, and think it no hardship. So clean was their soul from love of glory. Peter indeed spoke more strongly, but James here more mildly: for thus it behooves one in high authority, to leave what is unpleasant for others to say, while he himself appears in the milder part.[96]

Dom Chapman interprets these statements in a limited sense this way:

> Obviously, it is James who has the 'rule' and the 'great power' as bishop of those believing Pharisees who had initiated the discussion. But the idea that he had (rule) over Peter is, of course, ludicrous, and the notion that he could possibly be the president of the council certainly never occurred to Chrysostom's mind.[97]

The problem with what Chapman says is that this is not what Chrysostom says. Chrysostom says nothing about the chief rule of James being limited to that of the believing Pharisees. There is not one word said about Pharisees. His reference to the chief rule is of the overall Council over which James presided. When all of his statements about Peter, Paul, James and John are taken together, it becomes clear that in the mind of Chrysostom, all the apostles together held the care of the world and headship of the Church universally. Peter did not hold a primacy of jurisdiction but of teaching, which he says is equally true of John and Paul:

And if anyone would say 'How did James receive the chair of Jerusalem?' I would reply that he appointed Peter a *teacher* not of the chair, but of the world.[98]

Chrysostom interprets the keys given to Peter as a declarative authority to teach and preach the gospel and to extend the kingdom of God, not a primacy of jurisdiction over the other apostles:

> For the Father gave to Peter the revelation of the Son; but *the Son gave him to sow that of the Father and that of Himself in every part of the world*; and to mortal man He entrusted the authority over all things in Heaven, giving him *the keys; who extended the Church to every part of the world*, and declared it to be stronger than heaven.[99]

This authority was shared equally by all the apostles. Chrysostom states, for example, that John also held the authority of the keys and, like Peter, he held a universal teaching authority over the Churches throughout the world:

> *For the Son of thunder, the beloved of Christ, the pillar of the Churches throughout the world, who holds the keys of heaven...*[100]

It is also evident from Chrysostom's exegesis of Matthew 16 that he did not teach that Peter was made supreme ruler of the Church. He did not interpret the rock of Matthew 16 to be the person of Peter, but his confession of faith, pointing to Christ himself as the rock and only foundation of the Church:

> 'And I say unto thee, Thou art Peter, and *upon this rock I will build my Church'; that is, on the faith of his confession.* Hereby He signifies that many were on the point of believing, and raises his spirit, and makes him a shepherd...*For the Father gave to Peter the revelation of the Son; but the Son gave him to sow that of the Father and that of Himself in every part of the world; and to mortal man He entrusted the authority over all things in Heaven, giving him the keys; who extended the church to every part of the world, and declared it to be stronger than heaven.*[101]

He speaks from this time lowly things, on his way to His passion, that He might show His humanity. *For He that hath built His church upon Peter's confession*, and has so fortified it, that ten thousand dangers and deaths are not to prevail over it...[102]

'For other foundation can no man lay than that is laid, which is Jesus Christ.' I say, no man can lay it so long as he is a master–builder; but if he lay it...he ceases to be a master–builder. See how even from men's common notions he proves the whole of his proposition. His meaning is this: 'I have preached Christ, I have delivered unto you the foundation. Take heed how you build thereon, lest haply it be in vainglory, lest haply so as to draw away the disciples unto men.' Let us not then give heed unto the heresies. 'For other foundation can no man lay than that which is laid.' *Upon this then let us build, and as a foundation let us cleave to it, as a branch to a vine; and let there be no interval between us and Christ*...For the branch by its adherence draws in the fatness, and the building stands because it is cemented together. Since, if it stand apart it perishes, having nothing whereon to support itself. Let us not then merely keep hold of Christ, but let us be cemented to Him, for if we stand apart, we perish...And accordingly, there are many images whereby He brings us into union. Thus, if you mark it, *He is the 'Head', we are 'the body': can there be any empty interval between the head and the body? He is a 'Foundation', we are a 'building': He a 'Vine', we 'branches': He the 'Bridegroom', we the 'bride': He is the 'Shepherd', we the 'sheep'.* He is the 'Way', we 'they who walk therein.' Again, we are a 'temple,' He the 'Indweller': He the 'First–Begotten,' we the 'brethren': He the 'Heir,' we the 'heirs together with Him': He the 'Life,' we the 'living': He the 'Resurrection,' we 'those who rise again': He the 'Light,' we the 'enlightened.' All these things indicate unity; and they allow no void interval, not even the smallest.[103]

Chrysostom argues that the rock is not Peter but Peter's confession of faith in Christ as the Son of God. Even Dom Chapman is forced to admit that Chrysostom consistently interpreted the rock to be Peter's confession of faith: 'The rock on which the Church is to be built is regularly taken by St. Chrysostom to be the confession of

The Patristic Interpretation

Peter, or the faith which prompted this confession.'[104] It is Peter's confession that is the foundation of the Church. Peter is not the foundation. According to Chrysostom that position belongs to Christ alone. Dom Chapman objects to this claiming that in Chrysostom's mind, the rock is not only Peter's faith but also Peter's person. He cites a quote where Chrysostom speaks of Peter as being strengthened by Christ to stand as a rock against a hostile world:

> For those things which are peculiar to God alone, (both to absolve from sins, and to make the church incapable of overthrow in such assailing waves, and to exhibit a man that is a fisher more solid than any rock, while all the world is at war with him), these He promises Himself to give; as the Father, speaking to Jeremiah, said, He would make him as 'a brazen pillar, and as a wall;' but him to one nation only, this man in every part of the world.[105]

In light of these statements Chapman says:

> I think this statement alone would have made it clear that the Rock is Peter, in St. Chrysostom's view, as well as, and because of, the firmness of his confession. He has no idea of the two notions, 'Peter is the Rock' and 'his faith is the Rock' being mutually exclusive, as, in fact, they are not.[106]

But this statement is a complete misrepresentation. In exegeting the rock of Matthew 16, just prior to the above statements, Chrysostom states that Peter is *not* the rock. In the quotes given by Chapman, what Chrysostom is saying is that just as the Lord strengthened Jeremiah for his calling so he would strengthen Peter. He says he will be *like* a rock, not that he is the rock of Matthew 16. This is very similar to Augustine's position on Peter:

> So is it the case that Peter is now true, or that Christ is true in Peter? When the Lord Jesus Christ wished, he left Peter to himself, and Peter was found to be a man; and when it so pleased the Lord Jesus Christ, he

filled Peter, and Peter was found to be true. The Rock had made Rocky Peter true, for the Rock was Christ.[107]

According to Augustine, the rock is Christ and Christ made Peter a rock of strength in his faith. But Peter is not the rock of Matthew 16. He simply derives strength to be a rock from *the* rock, Christ Jesus himself. And what is true for Peter becomes true for all Christians because Peter is a figurative representative of the Church. In contradistinction to Chapman's assertions the fathers do in fact separate Peter's faith from Peter's confession, making them mutually exclusive, as we have seen with Augustine and Ambrose. While it is true that it is the person of Peter who makes the confession, the focus of Chrysostom is not on Peter's person but on Peter's faith. Chrysostom holds a similar view to that of Ambrose which we referenced earlier. Ambrose says that where Peter is (his confession), there is the Church. Chrysostom affirms the same point when he says: 'For though we do not retain the body of Peter, we do retain the faith of Peter, and retaining the faith of Peter we have Peter.'[108]

While holding a very high view of the status of the apostle Peter, Chrysostom, like Augustine, did not transfer this status to the bishops of Rome. In his thinking, along with Cyprian, Augustine, Jerome and Ambrose, all bishops are successors of Peter. There is no supreme authority of one bishop over another. In all his remarks about Peter, where does Chrysostom apply them to the bishops of Rome in an exclusive sense? He never does that. He never personally makes that application in his statements and it is historically dishonest to assert that is what he *meant* when he personally never said it. In similar fashion to Cyprian, Chrysostom refers to the chair of Peter, stating that the bishop of Antioch possesses that chair, demonstrating that in his mind all legitimate bishops are successors of Peter and not just the bishop of Rome:

> In speaking of S. Peter, the recollection of another Peter has come to me, the common father and teacher, who has inherited his prowess,

The Patristic Interpretation 83

and also *obtained his chair*. For this is the one great privilege of our city, Antioch, that it received the leader of the apostles as its teacher in the beginning. For it was right that she who was first adorned with the name of Christians, before the whole world, should receive the first of the apostles as her pastor. But though we received him as teacher, we did not retain him to the end, but gave him up to royal Rome. Or rather we did retain him to the end, *for though we do not retain the body of Peter, we do retain the faith of Peter, and retaining the faith of Peter we have Peter.* [109]

In his book, *The Eastern Churches and the Papacy*, Herbert Scott makes the assertion that John Chrysostom held to the view of papal primacy because he expressed exalted views about the apostle Peter. He makes the assumption that because Chrysostom speaks of Peter in exalted terms that such statements apply to the bishops of Rome in an exclusive sense. But when pressed by the question as to whether Chrysostom actually makes this application himself, Scott is forced to this significant admission:

> Granted that Chrysostom reiterates that Peter is the *coryphaeus*, 'the universal shepherd,' etc., what evidence is there, it is asked, that he recognised these claims in the Bishop of Rome? Is there anything in his writings to that effect?...If it be held that all this labouring by Chrysostom of the honour and powers of Peter does not of itself demand the exalted position of his successors as its explanation, it must be conceded that there is little or nothing in his writings which explicitly and incontestably affirms that the Bishop of Rome is the successor of S. Peter in his primacy.[110]

In other words, there is no evidence in any of the writings of Chrysostom that he applied his statements about Peter to the bishops of Rome. Nevertheless, Scott goes on to suggest that Chrysostom's statements *imply* a papal interpretation to his words. As Scott puts it:

> Surely, however, if Peter is the *foundation* of the Church as

Chrysostom constantly affirms, and if the Church is eternal as the Founder made it, he must last as long as the building, the Church, which is erected upon him.[111]

The logic employed here by Scott is flawed. Chrysostom never makes such a statement. He has in fact explained what he means when he says that Peter is the foundation. There is no reason to suppose that Chrysostom envisioned a papal office when he speaks of Peter as the foundation of the Church. We have seen quite clearly from Chrysostom's statements that he taught that the Church was built on Peter's confession of faith. It can be said to be built on Peter only in the sense that it is built on his confession. Chrysostom's comments given above on Antioch demonstrate that he teaches that the Church's foundation is preserved throughout history as Peter's confession of faith is preserved. It is not preserved by being built upon the bishops of Rome as supposed exclusive successors of Peter, but upon Peter's confession. As Chrysostom put it, 'Where you have Peter's confession there you have Peter: '*for though we do not retain the body of Peter, we do retain the faith of Peter, and retaining the faith of Peter we have Peter.*'[112] Nevertheless, Scott goes on to offer what he considers incontrovertible proof of the expression of papal primacy from Chrysostom's writings:

> There is indeed one passage which may be a categorical affirmation of the primacy of the pope: *De Sacerdotio* 53: 'Why did Christ shed His Blood? To purchase the sheep which *He confided to Peter and those who came after him.*'
>
> It may be urged that S. Chrysostom means no more by this than all those who have the care of souls. On the other hand, there may be a reference to Peter only and to his personal commission: 'Feed my sheep'; and Chrysostom soon afterwards actually quotes these words. And when one recalls his comments on them given above, as meaning Peter's 'government' and 'ruling the brethren,' it is at least likely that here is a reference to Peter's successors in the see of Rome.[113]

These assertions are refuted by Dom Chrysostom Baur, the Roman Catholic biographer on the life of John Chrysostom. He points out

The Patristic Interpretation 85

that Chrysostom's writings contain no allusion to a papal primacy and that the supposed evidence as that appealed to by Scott twists his writings to say what one wants them to say. It is to read a preconceived theology into his writings that Chrysostom himself never expressed. Baur comments:

> A more important question is whether Chrysostom considered the primacy of Peter as only personal, or as an *official primacy*, hence a permanent arrangement of the Church, and whether he correspondingly attributed the primacy of jurisdiction in the Church also to the Bishops of Rome...Chrysostom never made in his works any questionable deductions, never passed sentence with clear words on the jurisdiction of the Pope. Even P. Jugie admits this frankly. N. Marini, who later became a Cardinal, published a book on this question. In this he seeks, with the help...of a number of quotations from Chrysostom, to prove that this must pass for unqualified evidence of the jurisdictional primacy of the successors of Peter in Rome. His first argument is borrowed from the Treatise on the Priesthood. In Book 2.1 Chrysostom asks: 'Why did Christ shed His blood? In order to ransom His sheep, which He entrusted to Peter and to those after him.' Marioni translates here 'Peter and his successors,' which naturally facilitates his proof. But Chrysostom actually expressed himself in a more general way, and means by 'those after him' all the pastors generally, to whom the sheep of Christ had been entrusted after Peter.
>
> So it is not practicable to interpret this passage so narrowly as Marini has done. Still less convincing is Marini's second piece of evidence. In a letter which Chrysostom addressed to Pope Innocent from his exile, he says that he would gladly assist in putting an end to the great evil, 'for the strife has spread over almost the *entire world.*' So then, one concludes, Chrysostom ascribes to the Pope authority *over the whole world.* Then Chrysostom writes once more, to the Bishop of Thessalomki: 'Do not grow weary of doing that which contributes to the *general* improvement of the Church,' and he praises Bishop Aurelius of Carthage, because he put forth so much effort and struggle *for the churches of the whole world.* It would not occur to anyone to wish to construe from this a possible proof of the primacy of the bishops of Saloniki or of Carthage.[114]

86 THE MATTHEW 16 CONTROVERSY

Clearly, Chrysostom cannot be cited as a proponent of a Petrine or papal primacy in the Roman Catholic sense any more than Augustine. Michael Winter candidly admits that Chrysostom's views, especially his interpretation of the rock of Matthew 16, were antithetical to those of Rome and greatly influenced the Eastern fathers who followed him. He states that such Eastern fathers as Theodore of Mopsuestia, Palladius of Helenopolis, Theodore of Ancyra, Basil of Seleucia and Nilus of Ancyra held to an opinion that was unfavourable to the superiority of Peter, an opinion that was widespread in the East in the first half of the fifth century:

> The antipathy to Rome which finds its echo even in the works of St. John Chrysostom became more pronounced as the Eastern Church came more and more under the control of the emperor and effected eventually their estimate of St. Peter. Although they were not influenced by the Eusebian idea that the 'rock' of the church was Christ, the lesser Antiocheans betray an unwillingness to admit that Peter was the rock. Theodore of Mopsuestia, who died a quarter of a century after Chrysostom, declared that the rock on which the church was built was Peter's confession of faith. The same opinion is repeated by Palladius of Helenopolis in his *Dialogues on the life of St. John Chrysostom*. Without any elaboration he states that the rock in Matthew 16 is Peter's confession. The complete absence of reasons or arguments in support of the contention is an indication of how widely the view was accepted at that date. Such an opinion was, in fact, held also by Theodore of Ancyra, Basil of Seleucia, and Nilus of Ancyra, in the first half of the fifth century...The opinion unfavourable to the superiority of St. Peter gained a considerable following in the East under the influence of the school of Antioch...[115]

Theodoret of Cyr (A.D. 393—466)

Theodoret was the leading theologian of Antioch in the fifth century. In interpreting the rock passage of Matthew 16 he shares the opinion of the Eastern fathers, especially that of Chrysostom. The 'opinion unfavourable to the superiority of St. Peter' in the school of Antioch mentioned by Winter in the above quote finds representative expression in the following comments of Theodoret:

> Let no one then foolishly suppose that the Christ is any other than the only begotten Son. Let us not imagine ourselves wiser than the gift of the Spirit. Let us hear the words of the great Peter, 'Thou art the Christ, the Son of the living God.' *Let us hear the Lord Christ confirming this confession, for 'On this rock,' He says, 'I will build my church and the gates of Hell shall not prevail against it.' Wherefore too the wise Paul, most excellent master builder of the churches, fixed no other foundation than this. 'I,' he says, 'as a wise master builder have laid the foundation, and another buildeth thereon. But let every man take heed how he buildeth thereon. For other foundation can no man lay than that is laid, which is Jesus Christ.'* How then can they think of any other foundation, when they are bidden not to fix a foundation, but to build on that which is laid? The divine writer *recognises Christ as the foundation*, and glories in this title.[116]

Other foundation no man can lay but that which is laid, which is Christ Jesus (1 Cor. iii.11). It is necessary to build upon, not to lay foundations. For it is impossible for him who wishes to build wisely to lay another foundation. The blessed Peter also laid this foundation, or rather the Lord Himself. *For Peter having said, 'Thou art the Christ, the Son of the living God;' the Lord said, 'Upon this rock I will build My Church.' Therefore call not yourselves after men's names, for Christ is the foundation.*[117]

Surely he is calling pious faith and true confession a 'rock.' For when the Lord asked his disciples who the people said he was, blessed Peter spoke up, saying 'You are Christ, the Son of the living God.' To which the Lord answered: 'Truly, truly I say to you, you are Peter and *upon this rock I shall build my Church, and the gates of hell shall not prevail against it.'*[118]

'Its foundations are on the holy mountains.' The 'foundations' of piety are divine precepts, while the 'holy mountains' upon which these foundations are laid are the apostles of our Saviour. Blessed Paul says concerning these foundations: 'You have been built upon the foundation of the apostles and prophets whose cornerstone is Christ Jesus.' And again he says: 'Peter, James and John who are perceived to be pillars.' And after Peter had made that true and divine confession, Christ said to him: 'You are Peter, and upon this rock I shall build my Church; and the gates of hell shall not prevail against it.' And elsewhere Christ says: 'You are the light of the world, and a city set on a hill cannot be hid.' *Upon these holy mountains Christ the Lord laid the foundations of piety.*[119]

Wherefore our Lord Jesus Christ permitted *the first of the apostles, whose confession He had fixed as a kind of groundwork and foundation of the Church*, to waver to and fro, and to deny Him, and then raised him up again.[120]

According to Theodoret the rock is Peter's confession of faith in Christ which points to Christ as the foundation of the Church. The main cornerstone is Jesus Christ and the subsidiary foundation includes all the apostles equally in their teachings and faith. He does refer to Peter personally as the foundation:

For if they say that these things happened before baptism, let them learn that *the great foundation of the Church was shaken, and confirmed by divine grace.* For the great Peter, having denied thrice, remained first; cured by his own tears. And the Lord commanded him to apply the same cure to the brethren, 'And thou,' He says, 'converted, confirm thy brethren' (Luke xxii.32).[121]

Peter is called the foundation because of his confession of faith. It is his confession which is the rock of the Church. The rock and foundation is Jesus Christ alone. Theodoret does state that Peter is first among the apostles and the *coryphaeus* but, like Chrysostom and Augustine, these titles carry no unique jurisdictional primacy in a Roman Catholic sense. All the apostles are equal in authority and all bishops are successors of Peter. In a statement reminiscent of

The Patristic Interpretation 89

Cyprian and Chrysostom, Theodoret speaks of the bishop of Antioch as possessing the throne and authority of Peter demonstrating that this was not something unique to the see of Rome:

> Dioscurus, however, refuses to abide by these decisions; he is turning the see of the blessed Mark upside down; and these things he does though he perfectly well knows that *the Antiochean metropolis possesses the throne of the great Peter, who was the teacher of the blessed Mark, and first and coryphaeus of the apostles.*[122]

In *Jesus, Peter and the Keys*, the authors list only one very short passage from Theodoret omitting completely all the others that have been listed here. That passage is the one referred to above where Peter is spoken of as 'the great foundation of the Church.' As we have seen Theodoret's understanding of Peter as a foundation must be interpreted in the light of his other comments about Peter and his confession of faith. This is consistent with the prevailing patristic view of the East in that day as we have seen represented by Chrysostom and in the West by Ambrose and Augustine. But one can easily mislead people if one chooses to disregard the other references and to cite only that one which superficially seems to support one's position because it speaks of Peter as a foundation. Without a proper reading of this one passage in the context of Theodoret's other writings one cannot possibly fairly and objectively represent what he actually taught. By citing only this one passage, in isolation from the others, the authors of *Jesus, Peter and the Keys* impose a preconceived papal theology onto Theodoret's words which was not true to his own thought. They have misrepresented the writings of this Church father and they are at odds with their own historians. The Roman Catholic historian, Michael Winter, demonstrates this to be the case when he sums up Theodoret's views this way:

> He declared at one time that the rock foundation of the church was faith, and at another that it was Christ. Elsewhere he applies the notion

to all the Apostles...It is evident that he did not acknowledge the primacy of St. Peter.[123]

Cyril of Alexandria (Died A.D. 444)

Cyril is one of the most important and influential theologians of the Eastern Church. He was bishop of Alexandria in the first half of the fifth century from 412 A.D to 444 A.D. He presided over the Council of Ephesus and is considered the great defender of the orthodox faith against Nestorius. His views on the rock of Matthew 16 and the foundation of the Church are unambiguously presented in his writings:

> For that reason divine Scripture says that Peter, that exceptional figure among the apostles, was called blessed. For when the Savior was in that part of Caesarea which is called Philippi, he asked who the people thought he was, or what rumor about him had been spread throughout Judea and the town bordering Judea. And in response Peter, having abandoned the childish and abused opinions of the people, wisely and expertly exclaimed: 'You are Christ, Son of the living God.' Now when Christ heard this true opinion of him, he repaid Peter by saying: 'Blessed are you Simon Bar–Jonah, for flesh and blood have not revealed this to you but my Father who is in heaven. And I tell you, you are Peter, and upon this rock I will build my Church, and the gates of hell shall not prevail against it.' *The surname, I believe, calls nothing other than the unshakable and very firm faith of the disciple 'a rock,' upon which the Church was founded and made firm and remains continually impregnable even with respect to the very gates of Hell.* But Peter's faith in the Son was not easily attained, nor did it flow from human apprehension; rather it was derived from the ineffable instruction from above; since God the Father clearly shows his own Son and causes a sure persuasion of him in the minds of his people. For Christ was in no way deceptive when he said, 'Flesh and blood has not revealed this to you, but my Father in heaven.' If, therefore, blessed Peter, having confessed Christ to be the Son of the living God, are those not very wretched and abandoned who rashly rail

The Patristic Interpretation

at the will and undoubtedly true teaching of God, who drag down the one who proceeds from God's own substance and make him a creature, who foolishly reckon the coeternal author of life to be among those things which have derived their life from another source? Are such people not at any rate very ignorant?[124]

But why do we say that they are 'foundations of the earth'? *For Christ is the foundation and unshakable base of all things*—Christ who restrains and holds together all things, that they may be very firm. Upon him also we all are built, a spiritual household, put together by the Holy Spirit into a holy temple in which he himself dwells; for by our faith he lives in our hearts. *But the next foundations, those nearer to us, can be understood to be the apostles and evangelists, those eyewitnesses and ministers of the word who have arisen for the strengthening of the faith.* For when we recognize that their own traditions must be followed, we serve a faith which is true and does not deviate from Christ. For when he wisely and blamelessly confessed his faith to Jesus saying, 'You are Christ, Son of the living God,' Jesus said to divine Peter: 'You are Peter and upon this rock I will build my Church.' *Now by the word 'rock', Jesus indicated, I think, the immoveable faith of the disciple.* Likewise, the psalmist says: 'Its foundations are the holy mountains.' Very truly should the holy apostles and evangelists be compared to holy mountains for their understanding was laid down like a foundation for posterity, so that those who had been caught in their nets would not fall into a false faith.[125]

The Church is unshaken, and 'the gates of hell shall not prevail against it,' according to the voice of the Saviour, for it has Him for a foundation.[126]

It is likely that by these words (Is. 33:16) our Lord Jesus Christ is called a rock, in Whom, as some cave or sheepfold, the Church is conceived as having a safe and unshaken abiding place for its well-being; 'For thou art Peter,' the Saviour says, 'and upon this rock I will build My Church.'[127]

Cyril's views are very similar to those of Chrysostom. He identifies the rock of the Church to be Peter's confession of faith and not the person of Peter himself. He separates Peter's faith from Peter's person, just as Augustine, Chrysostom and Ambrose did. All of the apostles according to Cyril are Shepherds and foundations. It is their teaching on Christ which is foundational and points to Christ as the true rock and only foundation upon which the Church is built. He interprets the rock of Matthew 16 to be Christ as well as Peter's confession of faith. This amounts to the same thing as Peter's confession points to the person of Christ. Cyril's views are completely antithetical to those of the Roman Catholic Church. He is no proponent of the teaching of papal primacy. Michael Winter summarizes Cyril's views in the following statements:

> Cyril of Alexandria's theology on the question of St. Peter resembles closely that of the Antiochean fathers. The life work of St. Cyril, for which he is renowned in the church, was his upholding of the orthodox faith against Nestorius, principally at the Council of Ephesus in 431. This preoccupation with Christological questions influenced his exegesis of the text of Matthew 16 in a manner which is reminiscent of the earliest fathers who were writing against Gnosticism. Although he alludes frequently to the text, it is the Christological application which interests him and the resultant picture of St. Peter is inconclusive. For instance when, commenting on the passage he writes: 'Then he also names another honour: "Upon this rock I will build my church; and to thee will I give the keys of the kingdom of heaven." Observe how he summarily manifests Himself Lord of heaven and earth for. . . He promises to found the church, assigning immovableness to it, as He is the Lord of strength, and over this He sets Peter as shepherd. Then He says, "And I will give thee the keys of the kingdom of heaven." Neither an angel nor any other spiritual being is able to speak thus.'
>
> The application to Peter of the title 'shepherd' is deceptive, since he applies it elsewhere to all the Apostles and it cannot therefore indicate a peculiar authority for Peter. It seems to have been his

consistent opinion that the 'rock–foundation' of the church was Peter's immovable faith. Although it seems a small matter to distinguish Peter's faith from his person in the function of being the foundation of the church, it does appear that Cyril did, in fact, isolate St. Peter himself for that role and in this respect he is at one with the later Antiocheans...The school of Antioch (and those who were influenced by it) presents a conflicting set of opinions. St Chrysostom and some followers uphold the primacy of St. Peter, while St. Cyril of Alexandria and others deny it.[128]

It is significant that this Roman Catholic historian is forced by the evidence of Cyril's writings to conclude that his use of the word shepherd as applied to Peter did not imply any peculiar authority to him and that he was not a proponent of Petrine primacy. In fact, that he actually denied it. He deals honestly with the facts. This cannot be said of the authors of *Jesus, Peter and the Keys*. They give selective quotations from this father, purposefully omitting those that are unfavorable to their position. There is no attempt at an honest assessment of what Cyril actually meant by the words that he used leading the reader to conclude that Cyril taught that Peter was the rock and was a supporter of a primacy of Peter in a pro-papal sense, neither of which is true. Cyril's views are consistent with those of the other major fathers of the East and West which we have examined. Peter's faith is the rock and foundation of the Church. It points to the person of Christ as the true rock and only foundation.

Basil the Great (A.D. 330—379)

Basil was an Eastern father of great renown during the fourth century. He is one of the three great Cappadocean fathers, the other two being Gregory of Nyssa, brother of Basil, and Gregory of Nazianzan. He became bishop of Caesarea in 370 A.D. and was one of the great defenders of the orthodox faith against Arianism and one of the greatest of the Eastern theologians. William Jurgens describes his importance:

> Basil is accounted the founder of Eastern monasticism; and with St.

John Chrysostom, he is one of the two pillars of the Oriental Church. Other pillars there may be in other contexts; but in the presence of Basil and Chrysostom they become mere pilasters.[129]

What were Basil's views of the rock of Matthew 16? They are very similar to those of the other Eastern fathers such as Origen, Chrysostom and Theodoret. There are statements Basil has made which would seem to support a papal interpretation. An example of this is seen in the following comments by Michael Winter:

> St. Basil the Great, who died in 379, makes the formal identification between St. Peter and the foundation of the church, in terms which indicate that he must have had in mind the text of Matthew 16: 'Peter upon which rock the Lord promised that he would build his church'.[130]
>
> The role which his faith played is indicated quite naturally in his treatise *Against Eunimius*, where he says that it was Peter, 'who on account of the pre-eminence of his faith, received on himself the building of the church.'[131]

The above statements are given without reference to their context. As a result they are interpreted by Winter in a way that actually contradicts the overall intent of Basil. Winter cites the first quote above as if it were a complete sentence on its own. But this is not the case. He neglects to give the complete sentence and has excised and isolated this statement from its overall context. In so doing he has attempted to give a pro–papal interpretation to it which is not there. If we compare the above statement to the actual context in which it is found a very different picture emerges. The following comments are taken from the paragraph out of which the statement above is referenced:

> And the house of God, located on the peaks of the mountains, is the Church according to the opinion of the Apostle. For he says that one must know 'how to behave in the household of God. *'Now the foundations of this Church are on the holy mountains, since it is built upon the foundation of the apostles and prophets. One of these*

mountains was indeed Peter, upon which rock the Lord promised to build his Church. Truly indeed and by highest right are sublime and elevated souls, souls which raise themselves above earthly things, called 'mountains.' *The soul of the blessed Peter was called a lofty rock because he had a strong mooring in the faith* and bore constantly and bravely the blows inflicted by temptations. All, therefore, who have acquired an understanding of the godhead—on account of the breadth of mind and of those actions which proceed from it—are the peaks of mountains, and *upon them the house of God is built.*[132]

Basil states that the Church is built upon all the apostles and prophets equally, not just upon Peter. All of them are the foundation of the Church. He states that Peter is only one of the foundations. He follows Origen in this point of view. He also follows Origen in teaching that all who confess Christ as the Son of God are rocks and the Church is built upon them. All true believers then are rocks equally with Peter. Peter is simply one example of a rock, a title which he received because of his confession of faith and his faithfulness. In no way does Basil believe that the title given to Peter meant that the Church is built upon him in an exclusive and papal sense. It can be said to be built on Peter in that it is built on Peter's faith, as opposed to a primacy of jurisdiction. The same is true for the other apostles as foundations. The Church is built upon them in the sense of its being built upon their teaching. This is his overall teaching and ecclesiology. It is right in line with the predominant Eastern understanding of the Matthew 16 passage. But if one isolates certain comments of Basil from their context it is possible to imply that he has taught something he did not teach. This concept of the Church being built upon Christ as the principle rock or foundation and upon Peter and the other apostles as secondary foundations is explained by George Salmon in this way:

> It is undoubtedly the doctrine of Scripture that Christ is the only foundation: 'other foundation can no man lay than that is laid, which is Jesus Christ' (1 Cor. Iii.11). Yet we must remember that the same metaphor may be used to illustrate different truths, and so, according to circumstances may have different significations. The same Paul who has called Christ the only foundation, tells his Ephesian converts

(ii.20): 'Ye are built upon the foundation of the Apostles and Prophets, Jesus Christ himself being the chief corner-stone.'...How is it that there can be no other foundation but Christ, and yet that the Apostles are spoken of as foundations? Plainly because the metaphor is used with different applications. Christ alone is that foundation, from being joined to which the whole building of the Church derives its unity and stability, and gains strength to defy all assaults of hell. But, in the same manner as any human institution is said to be founded by those men to whom it owes its origin, so we may call those men the foundation of the Church whom God honoured by using them as His instruments in the establishment of it; who were themselves laid as the first living stones in that holy temple, and on whom the other stones of that temple were laid; for it was on their testimony that others received the truth, so that our faith rests on theirs.[133]

These thoughts are expressed very cogently by two other Eastern fathers: Gregory of Nyssa, the brother and contemporary of Basil the Great, and James of Nisbis.

Gregory of Nyssa (A.D. 335—394)

Gregory was educated primarily by his brother Basil the Great and was consecrated by him as Bishop of Nyssa in A.D. 371. His views on Peter and the rock are similar to those expressed by his brother, Basil:

> *These men (i.e., Peter, James, & John) are the foundations of the Church, and the pillars and mainstays of truth.* They are the perpetual founts of salvation, from whom the copious waters of divine doctrine flow. The prophet bids us go to them when he writes: 'With joy you will draw water from the founts of the Saviour.' We celebrate the memory of *Peter, who is the chief of the apostles*, and together with him the other members of the Church are glorified; for upon him the Church of God is established. Indeed *this man*, in accordance with the title conferred upon him by the Lord, *is the firm and very solid rock upon which the Saviour has built his Church.* Finally we celebrate the memory of James and John.

But what effort is required of us to exert ourselves in such a way that our commemoration may be worthy of the virtue of the apostles? *The warmth of our praises does not extend to Simon insofar as he was a catcher of fish; rather it extends to his firm faith, which is at the same time the foundation of the whole Church.*[134]

According to Gregory, Peter, James and John are all foundations of the Church. This is the same teaching as Basil. And like Basil, Gregory singles out Peter as the rock of Matthew 16 upon whom the Church would be built. However he goes on to explain what he means by that statement. Peter is a rock *because* of his confession of faith. This confession has become the foundation of the whole Church. Peter is often referred to, for example, as 'the rock of faith.' The Church is built upon Peter, James and John as foundations in that it is built upon their teaching and faith.

James of Nisbis (4th Century)

James was an Eastern father, the bishop of Nisbis and teacher of Ephraim. He was present at the Council of Nicaea. He gives an interpretation of Matthew 16 which mirrors that of Athanasius, Eusebius and Basil:

> Faith is composed and compacted of many things. It is like a building, because it is constructed and completed in much hope. You are not ignorant that large stones are placed in the foundations of a building, and then all that is built thereon has the stones joined together, and so raised till the completion of the work. *So, of all our faith, our Lord Jesus Christ is the firm and true foundation; and upon this rock our faith is established. Therefore, when any one has come to faith, he is set upon a firm rock, which is our Lord Jesus Christ. And, calling Christ a rock, I say nothing of my own, for the prophets have before called Him a rock*...And our Lord, the bestower of life, to all those who come to Him to be healed, said, 'Be it done unto thee according to thy faith.' Thus, when the blind man came to Jesus, He says to him, 'Dost thou believe that I can cure thee?' And he answered, 'Yea, Lord, I believe.' (Matt. ix.28)...*And Simon, who was called a rock, was deservedly called a rock because of his faith.*[135]

And *Simon, the head of the apostles,* who denied Christ, saying, 'I saw Him not,' and cursed and swore that 'he knew Him not,' as soon as he offered unto God contrition and penitence, and washed his sins in the tears of his sorrow, *our Lord received him, and made him the foundation, and called him a rock, of the building of His Church.*[136]

Josue arranged and set stones as a testimony to Israel; and *Jesus, our Saviour, called Simon the rock of faith, and placed him as a faithful testimony amongst the Gentiles.*[137]

James, like Eusebius and Augustine, states that the rock of the Church is Christ. He alone is the true and unique foundation. However, Peter is also called a rock and foundation of the Church but only because of his faith. The Church is built upon Christ as the foundation, not upon Peter. It can be said to be built upon Peter only in the sense that it is built upon his faith which points to Christ.

Cyril of Jerusalem (A.D. 315—386)

Cyril was consecrated bishop of the eminent see of Jerusalem in 348. His most important work was his *Catechetical Lectures* which he delivered around 350. These are a series of lectures instructing catechumens in the essentials of the Christian faith. Cyril himself states that in these lectures he is passing on to them everything that is necessary for salvation and a complete exposition of the tradition of the Catholic Church—the 'whole knowledge of godliness' (*Lectures* 5.12). In other words, he has omitted nothing of major importance. Surely then, if what Vatican I states is true, that the early Church in its doctrine and practice, is a continual witness to its teachings on papal primacy and infallibility, we should find some hint of that in such an important document as the *Catechetical Lectures,* especially since Vatican I states that it is necessary for salvation that these teachings be acknowledged and embraced. Surely if this is so, Cyril could not overlook so essential a doctrine for it would have direct application for the faith of these catechumens. And yet Cyril does not say one word about a papal primacy or infallibility. He does make mention of Peter, referring to him as many of the fathers did, for example, as 'chief and first of the apostles.' He mentions Peter as the one who had received the keys of the kingdom of heaven, and as an example of the power of repentance and of faith. But when he refers to the Matthew 16 passage and Peter's confession, he emphasizes the supernatural enlightenment of Peter by God but completely omits any reference to Peter and the rock, focusing rather upon the person of Christ:

> And when all were silent...Peter, the leader of the Apostles, and chief herald of the Church, uttering no refinement of his own, nor persuaded by man's reasoning, but having his mind enlightened from the Father, says to Him; *Thou art the Christ*; nor only so, but *the Son of the living God*. And a blessing follows the speech, (for in truth it was above man), and what he had said received this seal, that the Father had revealed it to him. For the Saviour says, *Blessed art thou, Simon Barjona, for flesh and blood hath not revealed it unto thee, but My Father which is in heaven*. He therefore who acknowledges our Lord Jesus Christ, the Son of God, partakes of this blessedness; but he who denies the Son of God, is a poor miserable man.[138]

Imagine a bishop of the Church, in instructing catechumens on the essentials of the faith, failing to expound for them the meaning of the rock of Matthew 16 when referring to the passage? There is only one other reference to the passage in the entirety of his writings which comprise over 270 pages in the Oxford edition, that being in Lecture 18.25. Here he quotes the rock passage but does not expound upon its importance for the constitution of the Church or make any reference to Peter at all. The obvious reason is that in Cyril's day, the Roman Catholic interpretation of Matthew 16 as espoused by Vatican I, was not that of the Church of Jerusalem, the Church from which Christianity itself originated. Cyril did not see a Petrine primacy in this passage and certainly inferred no papal primacy from it. In fact, Cyril places Paul on an equal footing with Peter in authority:

As the delusion was extending, *Peter and Paul,* a noble pair, *chief rulers of the Church,* arrived and set the error right...[139]

John Cassian (A.D. 360—435)

John Cassian was a native of Southern Gaul and was ordained to the diaconate by John Chrysostom in 405. He founded two monastaries which he ruled as Abbott. He gives the following interpretation to the rock of Matthew 16:

> Tell us then, O Evangelist, tell us the confession: tell us the faith of the chief Apostle...'Thou art,' he says, 'the Christ the Son of the living God'...Is there anything puzzling or obscure in this? It is nothing but a plain and open confession: he proclaims Christ to be the Son of God. But what are the other words which follow that saying of the Lord's, with which He commends Peter? *'And I,' said He, 'say unto thee, that thou art Peter and upon this rock I will build My Church.' Do you see how the saying of Peter is the faith of the Church? He then must of course be outside the Church, who does not hold the faith of the Church.* 'And to thee,' saith the Lord, 'I will give the keys of the kingdom of heaven.' This faith deserved heaven: this faith received the keys of the heavenly kingdom. See what awaits you. You cannot enter the gate to which this key belongs, if you have denied the faith of this key. 'And the gate,' He adds, 'of hell shall not prevail against thee.' The gates of hell are the belief or rather the misbelief of heretics. For widely as hell is separated from heaven, so widely is he who denies from him who confessed that Christ is God. 'Whatsoever,' He proceeds, 'thou shalt bind on earth, shalt be bound in heaven, and whatsoever thou shalt loose on earth, shalt be loosed also in heaven.' *The perfect faith of the Apostle* somehow is given the power of Deity, that what it should bind or loose on earth, might be bound or loosed in heaven. For you then, who come against the Apostle's faith, as you see that already you are bound on earth, it only remains that you should know that you are bound also in heaven.[140]

Cassian states that the rock is Peter's confession of faith upon which the Church is built. As we have seen, this was the common

The Patristic Interpretation 101

interpretation prevalent in the Eastern and Western Church of that day. Michael Winter affirms that this was Cassian's point of view when he says: 'The emphasis which Ambrose placed on the faith of St. Peter commanded some following. His influence can be seen in Cassian and Maximus of Turin. The former interprets the 'rock' of Matthew 16 quite simply as the faith of the Church.'[141]

Epiphanius (A.D. 315—403)

Epiphanius was born in Palestine and was bishop of Salamis on Cyprus. He was an ardent defender of Nicene orthodoxy. He gives an interpretation of the rock of Matthew 16 that is consistent with the overall Eastern exegesis:

> Those too who have fallen away through persecution, if they show full repentance, sit in sackcloth and ashes and weep before the Lord—the Benefactor has the power to show mercy even to them. No ill can come of repentance. Thus the Lord and his church accept the penitent, as Manasseh the son of Hezekiah returned and was accepted by the Lord—and the *chief of the apostles, St. Peter,* who denied for a time and still *became our truly solid rock* which supports the Lord's faith, and *on which the church is in every way founded.* This is, first of all, because *he confessed that 'Christ' is 'the Son of the living God,'* and was told, '*On this rock of sure faith will I build my church*'—for he plainly confessed that Christ is true Son. For when he said, 'Son of the living God,' with the additional phrase, 'the living,' he showed that Christ is God's true Son, as I have said in nearly every Sect. Peter also makes us certain of the Holy Spirit by saying to Ananias, 'Why hast Satan tempted you to lie to the holy Ghost? Ye have not lied unto man, but unto God,' for the Spirit is of God and not different from God. And *Peter also became the solid rock of the building and foundation of God's house, because, after denying, turning again, and being found by the Lord, he was privileged to hear, 'Feed my lambs and feed my sheep.'* For with these words Christ led us to the turning of repentance, so that our well founded faith might be rebuilt in him—a faith that forbids the salvation of no one alive who truly repents, and amends his faults in this world.[142]

The first of the Apostles, that firm rock upon which the church of God is built, so that the gates of hell, that is to say the heresies and heresiarchs, will not prevail against it. For in every way was the faith confirmed in him who received the key of heaven, in him who looses on earth and binds in heaven. For in him are found all the subtle questions of faith.[143]

Epiphanius interprets the rock as Peter's confession of faith in Christ. He adds also that Peter is a rock because of his faith and his restoration by Christ as a teacher of the Church. The Church is built upon Peter because it is built upon his faith. The focus of Epiphanius when interpreting the rock of Matthew 16 is upon the person of Christ, the content of Peter's confession. From time to time in polemical literature one encounters the assertion that Epiphanius interpreted the rock of Matthew 16 in a pro–Roman sense. For example, Michael Winter, in quoting the above citations from Epiphanius, makes these comments:

> His (Epiphanius') writings about St. Peter show how smoothly the notions of 'faith' and 'primacy' complement each other in the minds of these fathers. In his *Ancoratus* he describes St. Peter thus: 'The first of the Apostles, that firm rock upon which the church of God is built, so that the gates of hell, that is to say the heresies and heresiarchs, will not prevail against it. For in every way was the faith confirmed in him who received the key of heaven, in him who looses on earth and binds in heaven. For in him are found all the subtle questions of faith.' The same ideas are to be found elsewhere in the *Ancoratus* and also in his apologetical work the *Panarion*, better known as *Adversus Haereses*, which contain the passage: 'Peter, who was the very chief of the Apostles, who became for us a truly firm rock, founding the faith of the Lord, upon which the church was in every way built...'[144]

It is important to note that in referencing the quotation from *Adversus Haereses* Winter neglects to give the complete quote as it is found above. By isolating certain phrases as he does, Winter leads us to think that when interpreting Matthew 16 Epiphanius believes Peter to be the rock, when in fact, he states that the rock is Peter's

The Patristic Interpretation

confession, and that the Church is built upon this confession. Specifically, Epiphanius says that Peter founded *the faith* of the Lord, and it is upon *that faith* that the Church is built. The complete quote in context states: 'the chief of the apostles, St. Peter, who denied for a time and still became our truly solid rock which supports *the Lord's faith,* and *on which the church is in every way founded.* This is, first of all, because *he confessed that 'Christ' is 'the Son of the living God,'* and was told, *'On this rock of sure faith will I build my church'*—for he plainly confessed that Christ is true Son.' Thus, when Epiphanius' statements are given in complete context it is clear that his point of view is consistent with the Eastern Church and are not supportive of the interpretation adopted by the Church of Rome.

Aphraates (A.D. 280—345)

Aphraates is one of the most important fathers of the Syrian Church. The following are his comments on the foundation of the Church:

> But before all things I desire that thou wouldst write and instruct me concerning this that straitens me, namely concerning our faith; how it is, and what its foundation is, and on what structure it rises, and on what it rests, and in what way is its fulfilment and consummation, and what are the works required for it.
> Faith...is like a building that is built up of many pieces of workmanship and so its edifice rises to the top. And know, my beloved, that in the foundations of the building stones are laid, and so resting upon stones the whole edifice rises until it is perfected. *Thus also the true Stone, our Lord Jesus Christ is the foundation of all faith. And on Him, on (this) Stone faith is based. And resting on faith all the structure rises until it is completed. For it is the foundation that is the beginning of all the building. For when anyone is brought nigh unto faith, it is laid for him upon the Stone, that is our Lord Jesus Christ.* And His building cannot be shaken by the waves, nor can it be injured by the winds. By the stormy blasts it does not fall, *because its structure is reared upon the rock of the true Stone. And in that I have called Christ the Stone,* I have not spoken my own thought, but the Prophets

beforehand called Him the Stone.

And now hear concerning faith that is based upon the Stone, and concerning the structure that is reared up upon the Stone...So also let the man, who becomes a house, yea, a dwelling place, for Christ take heed to what is needed for the service of Christ, Who lodges in him, and with what things he may please Him. For first he builds his building on the Stone, which is Christ. On Him, on the Stone, is faith built...All these things doth the faith demand that is based on the rock of the true Stone, that is Christ.

And if perchance thou shouldest say: If Christ is set for the foundation, how does Christ also dwell in the building when it is completed? For both these things did the blessed Apostle say. For he said: 'I as a wise architect have laid the foundation.' *And there he defined the foundation and made it clear, for he said as follows: 'No man can lay other foundation than that which is laid, which is Christ Jesus'*...And therefore that word is accomplished, that Christ dwells in men, namely, in those who believe on Him, and *He is the foundation on which is reared up the whole building.*

But I must proceed to my former statement *that Christ is called the Stone in the Prophets.* For in ancient times David said concerning Him: 'The stone which the builders rejected has become the head of the building.' And how did the builders reject this Stone which is Christ? How else than that they so rejected Him before Pilate and said: 'This man shall not be King over us'...By these things they *rejected the Stone which is Christ.*

And furthermore Isaiah also prophesied beforehand with regard to this stone. For he said: Thus saith the Lord, Behold I lay in Zion a chosen stone in the precious corner, the head of the wall of the foundation. And he said again there: Every one that believeth on it shall not fear. And whosoever falleth on that stone shall be broken, and everyone on whom it shall fall, it will crush. For the people of the house of Israel fell upon Him, and He became their destruction for ever. And again: it shall fall on the image and crush it. And the Gentiles believed on it and do not fear. And he shows thus with regard to that stone that it was laid as head of the wall and foundation.

And again *Daniel also spoke concerning this stone which is Christ.* For he said: The stone was cut out from the mountain, not by hands, and it smote the image, and the whole earth was filled with it. This he showed beforehand with regard to Christ that the whole earth shall be filled with Him. For lo! by the faith of Christ are all the ends of the earth filled, as David said: The sound of the Gospel of Christ has gone forth into all the earth. And again when He sent forth His apostles He spake thus to them: Go forth, make disciples of all nations and they will believe on Me. And again the *Prophet Zechariah also prophesied about the stone which is Christ.* For he said: I saw a chief stone of equality and of love.

And again the Apostle has commented for us upon this building and upon the foundation; for he said thus: 'No man can lay another foundation than that which is laid, which is Jesus Christ'...And he showed with regard to faith that first it is laid on a sure foundation... *These then are the works of faith which is based on the true Stone which is Christ, on Whom the whole building is reared up.*[145]

According to Aphraates the rock, stone and foundation of the Church is the person of the Lord Jesus Christ. In his mind, according to 1 Corinthians 3:11, there is only one foundation that can be laid, Christ himself.

Ephrem the Syrian (A.D. 306—376)

Ephrem was born in Nisbis and was a student of James, the bishop of Nisbis. He has been called the greatest poet of the patristic age. He was ordained to the diaconate around 338 A.D. and remained a deacon until his death. He teaches that the rock is Christ upon whom the Church is built:

> In the tenth year let Mount Sinai give glory, which melted - before its Lord! It saw against its Lord—stones taken up: but He took stones— *to build the Church upon the Rock*; blessed be His building![146]

> Shadowed forth in thy beauty is *the beauty of the Son*, Who clothed Himself with suffering when the nails passed through Him. The awl passed in thee since they handled thee roughly, as they did His hands; and because He suffered He reigned, as by thy sufferings thy beauty

increased. And if they showed no pity upon thee, neither did they love thee: still suffer as thou mightest, thou hast come to reign! *Simon Peter showed pity on the Rock*; whoso hath smitten it, is himself thereby overcome; it is by reason of Its suffering that Its beauty hath adorned the height and the depth.[147]

Other Eastern fathers who interpret the rock of Matthew 16 consistent with the prevailing view of the Eastern Church are Palladius of Helenopolis, Basil of Seleucia and Nilus of Ancyra.

Palladius of Helenopolis (A.D. 363—431)

Palladius was a fourth century monk, bishop and writer from Galatia. He was consecrated bishop of Helenopolis by John Chrysostom. His comments on the rock passage reflect the perspective of Chrysostom:

> 'You, however, who do you say I am?' Not all responded, but Peter only, interpreting the mind of all: 'You are Christ, Son of the living God.' The Saviour, approving the correctness of this response, spoke, saying: *'You are Peter, and upon this rock'—that is, upon this confession—'I shall build my Church, and the gates of Hell shall not prevail against it.'* Now with respect to this confession you will find...among all men both censure and praise. Thus at one time the Ephesians spoke ill of Christ and the apostles, crying: 'They turn the world upside down' (Acts 17.6). Now, however, they have ceased speaking ill, they themselves having been glorified...They are swine and dogs who say, 'He deceived the world'; but they are disciples who seek after him, saying: 'You are Christ, the Son of the living God.'[148]

The following observations by Michael Winter are significant in underscoring the fact that this particular interpretation was a point of view widely held within the Church:

> The lesser Antiocheans betray an unwillingness to admit that Peter was the rock. Theodore of Mopsuestia, who died a quarter of a century after Chrysostom, declared that the rock on which the church was

The Patristic Interpretation 107

built was Peter's confession of faith. The same opinion is repeated by Palladius of Helenopolis in his *Dialogues on the life of St. John Chrysostom*. Without any elaboration he states that the rock in Matthew 16 is Peter's confession. The complete absence of reasons or arguments in support of the contention is an indication of how widely the view was accepted at that date. Such an opinion was, in fact, held also by Theodore of Ancyra, Basil of Seleucia, and Nilus of Ancyra, in the first half of the fifth century...The opinion unfavourable to the superiority of St. Peter gained a considerable following in the East under the influence of the school of Antioch...[149]

Basil of Seleucia (Died—A.D. 468)

Basil was a fifth century Eastern bishop of Seleucia in Isauria. He took part in the Council of Chalcedon in 451. He was influenced by the Antiochean school as represented by Chrysostom and Theodoret. This is evident in his comments on Peter and the rock:

'You, however, who do you say I am?' And silence held them all suspended, for not all knew. But when Jesus asked, acknowledged ignorance in some divine way suggested a response to Peter, and towards a response he was spontaneously moved, like a lyre endowed with reason and roused by action of invisible hands. In obedience the tongue of Peter sought employment and though ignorant of doctrine, supplied a response: 'You are Christ, Son of the living God.' Jesus confirmed this statement with his approbation, thereby instructing all: 'Blessed are you Simon Bar–Jonah, for flesh and blood have not revealed this to you, but my Father who is in Heaven.' He called Peter blessed, so that Peter might join faith to his statement, just as he praised the response because of its meaning...*Now Christ called this confession a rock, and he named the one who confessed it 'Peter,' perceiving the appellation which was suitable to the author of this confession. For this is the solemn rock of religion, this the basis of salvation, this the wall of faith and the foundation of truth: 'For no other foundation can anyone lay than that which is laid, which is Christ Jesus.'* To whom be glory and power forever.[150]

Peter, the Coryphaeus of the apostles, The chief of the disciples of Christ, the accurate expositor of the revelations from the Father, he who walked on the sea, &c.[151]

We find in Basil, as in other fathers we have examined, a great respect and admiration for Peter. He is accorded the appellations of primacy (coryphaeus; first of the disciples) that are repeated throughout the writings of the Church fathers in the East and West. But when it comes to interpreting the foundation passage of Matthew 16, he interprets the rock to mean Peter's confession of faith, correlating this passage with that of 1 Corinthians 3:11. He is trying to demonstrate that there is only one rock and foundation of the Church, the person of Christ. The Church is built upon Peter's confession of faith which points to Christ as the only foundation. Therefore, even though he applies exalted titles to Peter, he does not apply these titles to the bishops of Rome as Peter's successors. He does not interpret the rock of Matthew 16 in a pro–Roman sense.

Nilus of Ancyra (Died—A.D. 430)

Nilus was a fifth century abbott who was a friend of John Chrysostom. His comments on the rock reflect the point of view of Chrysostom:

> If, moreover, a man of the Lord is meant, the first to be compared to gold would be *Cephas, whose name is interpreted 'rock.' This is the highest of the apostles, Peter, also called Cephas, who furnished in his confession of faith the foundation for the building of the Church.*[152]

Nilus informs us that Peter's name means rock. But he emphasizes Peter's confession when he speaks of the foundation upon which the Church would be built. As we have seen, the fathers often state that the Church is built upon Peter, meaning by this that it is built upon his faith, and not upon his person in the sense of an establishment of some kind of papal office. They separate his faith from his person. We have seen this clearly enunciated in the teaching of Augustine.

The Patristic Interpretation

This emphasis is also found in a quotation from the patristic age which was falsely ascribed to Victor of Antioch. *The Encyclopedia of the Early Church* gives the background to this writing in its comments on Victor of Antioch:

> Presbyter (AD 500), wrongly known as author of a commentary on Mark; this text is part of a catena, whose main sources are homilies on Matthew by John Chrysostom, Origen, Cyril of Alexandria, Titus of Bostra and Theodore of Heraclea.[153]

Even though the precise author is unknown, the thought expressed is drawn from the writings of the major Eastern fathers mentioned above:

> Christ the Lord was about to *build His Church on Peter, that is, on the unbroken and sound doctrine of Peter, and his unshaken faith*, therefore in prophetic spirit does He call him Peter.[154]

This particular understanding of the meaning of the Church being built on Peter in that it is built on Peter's faith became normative for the fathers of the East.

Asterius (A.D. 350—410)

Asterius was bishop of Amasea in the late fourth and early fifth centuries. He was born in Cappadocia and was greatly influenced by the great Cappadocian fathers: Basil the Great, Gregory of Nyssa and Gregory of Nazianzen. We see this influence in his thoughts on the foundation of the Church:

> Aptly indeed Isaiah says prophetically that *the Father was laying the Son as a cornerstone, doubtless signifying that the whole structure of the world was borne upon that foundation and base*. No doubt at another time, as has been written in the holy books of the Gospel, *the only Begotten calls Peter the foundation of the Church, saying: 'You are Peter and upon this rock I shall build my Church.' Now this chief, as it were, great and hard stone, Christ*, was set into the excavated hollow

of this world, into this vale of tears, as David says, *in order that he might bear all Christians founded upon him aloft into the domicile of our hope. 'For no other foundation can anyone lay than that which is laid, which is Christ Jesus.'* But our Saviour did give Peter a like appellation, thereby teaching that his chief disciple ought to be honored, calling him a *rock of faith*. Through Peter, therefore who was made a true and faithful teacher of piety, *a stable and inflexible foundation for the Church exists*. Moreover, having struck root in this foundation we stand complete, who are Christians all over the world. To be sure from the time of the announcement of the Gospel, many temptations have sprung up, and innumerable tyrants with their chief, the devil, have tried to destroy the foundations and to turn us from our moorings. Rivers have run like torrents, say the saving and holy Scriptures; the violent winds of diabolical spirits have rushed; the plentiful and harsh showers of persecution have poured down forcefully upon Christians. Yet nothing has proved more powerful than the divine ramparts, because doubtless *the foundation of faith* was raised by the holy hands of that chief apostle. These things, I think, needed to be said in response to that word of blessing from him who called the evangelist and holy preacher a rock. Moreover we may see, if we please, the method by which Peter built—not with stones and walls, or other earthly materials, but with words and deeds which he performed at the instigation of the Holy Spirit.[155]

Asterius is yet another example of a father who speaks of Peter as being the rock but not in the Roman Catholic meaning. We have seen this previously with such fathers as Origen, Tertullian, Cyprian and Basil the Great. He mentions that Christ is the foundation as well as Peter. Peter is called the rock but only from the standpoint that the Church is built upon his confession of faith in Christ. He is called the rock of *faith*, the foundation of *faith*. What is emphasized is not Peter the person, but Peter's faith. He is much like Chrysostom in his point of view. The only person upon which the Church is built is Christ. Peter is a Shepherd who is given responsibility for the Church as a whole but this is also true of all the apostles. The Church is built by Peter through his preaching and teaching and therefore it is built *through* him. Asterius states that Peter built the Church through his words and deeds.

Paul of Emesa (Died—*ca.* A.D. 444)

Paul was consecrated bishop of Emesa just after 410 A.D. He took part in the Council of Ephesus and was ambassador for John of Antioch in his talks of reconciliation with Cyril of Alexandria. He interprets the rock and foundation of the Church to be Peter's confession of faith:

> *Upon this faith the Church of God has been founded. With this expectation, upon this rock the Lord God placed the foundations of the Church.* When then the Lord Christ was going to Jerusalem, He asked the disciples, saying, 'Whom do men say that the Son of Man is?' The apostles say, 'Some Elias, others Jeremias, or one of the prophets.' And He says, but you, that is, My elect, you who have followed Me for three years, and have seen My power, and miracles, and beheld Me walking on the sea, who have shared My table, '*Whom do you say that I am?*' *Instantly, the Coryphaeus of the apostles, the mouth of the disciples, Peter, 'Thou art the Christ, the Son of the living God.'*[156]

Isidore of Pelusium (Died *ca.* A.D. 435)

Isidore was an Eastern monk of Pelusium in Egypt. It is believed he did his studies at Alexandria and became a devout disciple of John Chrysostom. In the following comments he states that Christ is the ultimate rock and therefore Peter's confession of faith in Christ is the rock of Matthew 16. It is therefore the foundation upon which the Church is built:

> Christ, who searcheth the hearts, did not ask His disciples, 'Whom

do men say that I, the Son of Man, am? Because He did not know the varying opinion of men concerning Himself, but was desirous, of teaching all that same *confession which Peter*, inspired by Him, *laid as the basis and foundation, on which the Lord built His Church.*[157]

Christ is the Rock, abiding unshaken, when He was incarnate.[158]

Cassiodorus (A.D. 490—583)

Cassiodorus was an influential Italian scholar and educator. At the age of 50 he moved to Constantinople to pursue religious studies. He returned fifteen years later to pursue monastic life at a monastery he had founded at his place of birth. He is best known as a Christian writer and commentator. In his commentary on the Psalms, Cassiodorus repeats the familiar and common patristic interpretation of the rock in his identification of the rock with Christ:

> 'It will not be moved' is said about the Church to which alone that promise has been given: '*You are Peter and upon this rock I shall build my Church and the gates of Hell shall not prevail against it.*' *For the Church cannot be moved because it is known to have been founded on that most solid rock, namely, Christ the Lord...*[159]

> *The Church's foundation is Christ the Lord*, who thus holds his Church together, so that it can by no shaking collapse, just as the Apostle says: '*For no other foundation can any one lay than that which is laid, which is Christ Jesus*' (1 Cor. 3:11)...Moreover, the words 'on the holy mountains' signify the apostles and the prophets who are called mountains because of the firmness of their faith and the excellence of their righteousness. Deservedly have they been called by such a name upon whom the true Church of God has been established.[160]

> Psalm 103.5: 'Who established the earth on its foundation so that it will never be shaken.' It does not seem this verse can be construed literally; for since we have read that the earth must be changed, how can it happen that it should never be shaken? But here when we read

The Patristic Interpretation

'established earth,' let us rather understand the strengthened Church, which can be called 'earth' insofar as it is composed of earthly men, as we read in another place: 'The earth is the Lord's and the fulness thereof.' *From this 'foundation,' Christ is rightly inferred, who is an immovable foundation and an inviolable rock. Concerning this the Apostle says: 'For no other foundation can any man lay than that which is already laid, which is Christ Jesus' (1 Cor. 3.11).* If we abide continually upon Christ we will in no way be shaken.[161]

In Cassiodorus' view, like so many of the Eastern and Western fathers that we have studied, the rock and foundation of the Church is Christ. He correlates the key foundation passage of 1 Corinthians 3:11 with the rock passage of Matthew 16 and interprets the rock to be the person of Christ.

Fulgentius of Ruspe (A.D. 467—553)

Fulgentius was consecrated bishop of Ruspe in 502 A.D. He was a devoted student of Augustine and was greatly influenced by his writings. He was considered to be one of the greatest theologians of his age, certainly the greatest Western theologian of the sixth century. We see the influence of Augustine in his comments on Peter and the keys:

> For the Saviour and judge of men has ordained, that only in this life would anyone's sins be remitted by him...Wherefore human vanity should not pointlessly hope to hear (at some future time after death) what divine truth has or has not promised. It is for this reason that *Christ has assigned on earth the power of binding and loosing to Peter—that is, to his Church*—in order that we may recognise during this life the free mercy offered in the forgiveness of sins and in the future the just wages which are repaid to all for the quality of their deeds.[162]

Supplication for the pardon of one's sins would never have been ordained for the sinner, if forgiveness were not truly offered to the suppliant. But repentance will indeed benefit the sinner, provided the catholic Church oversees it. *For God ascribed to the Church in the person of blessed Peter the power to bind and to loose, saying: 'Whatever you bind on earth shall be bound in heaven, and whatever you loose on earth shall be loosed in heaven' (Mt. 16.19).* At whatever age, therefore, a man should make true repentance of his sins and by the direction of God should correct his life, he will not be deprived of the reward of forgiveness, since God, as he says through the prophet, does not wish the death of a sinner; but let the sinner turn from his way and let his soul live (Ez. 33.11).[163]

Fulgentius was greatly influenced by Augustine. Like his mentor before him, in interpreting the Matthew 16 passage he teaches that Peter is a figurative representative of the Church. Since his views are so thoroughly Augustinian it would follow that he also held to the view that the Church is not built upon Peter personally but upon his confession of faith.

Gregory the Great (Reigned as Pope from A.D. 590—604)

Gregory I is considered by the Roman Catholic Church to be one of the great theologians of the patristic age. He was born in Rome and spent a number of years in the East in Constantinople as an ambassador of pope Pelagius II. He and Leo I are the only two popes who have been given the title 'the great.' Gregory is a pivotal figure in the history of the papacy. He was a great administrator and pastor with a heart for missions. He was also a great admirer of Augustine and his views on the rock and Peter, and his overall ecclesiology reflect an Augustinian and Eastern influence:

> For since the truth shines forth from the Church Catholic alone, the Lord says that there is a place by Him, from which He is to be seen. Moses is placed on a rock, to behold the form of God, because if any one maintains not *the firmness of Faith*, he discerns not the Divine presence. *Of which firmness* the Lord says, *'Upon this rock I shall build my Church.'*[164]

In these comments Gregory states that the rock of Matthew 16 is the faith of Peter. Gregory had a very high estimate of the office he possessed as bishop of Rome as the successor of Peter. On one occasion Gregory interpreted the rock of Matthew 16 as the person of Peter in support of a Petrine primacy and of a subsequent papal primacy in the Church. But this primacy was not interpreted in terms of a single universal jurisdiction but as a shared authority between the major patriarchates in collegiality. Certainly, within the Western Church Gregory viewed himself as the supreme authority in the West. But in the Church as a whole his ecclesiology was not monarchial but collegial. He made the point that the apostle Peter had been in Antioch and Alexandria and therefore these sees share the primacy with him given to Peter. His view was clearly articulated by him in his conflict with John, the bishop of Constantinople, over the use of the title 'universal patriarch'. John had applied this title to himself and Gregory strenuously objected, claiming it was an unlawful title, which reversed the ancient rule of collegiality within the Church by placing one bishop as supreme head over all others. This, he stated emphatically, is nothing less than Satanic pride and the spirit of Antichrist. The following are excerpts from his personal letter to John. Let the reader ask, Could the individual who wrote these words actually be singled out as a proponent of the kind of papal primacy promulgated by Vatican I?:

> *Gregory to John, Bishop of Constantinople*: At the time when your Fraternity was advanced to Sacredotal dignity, you remember what peace and concord of the churches you found. But, with what daring or with what swelling of pride I know not, you have attempted to seize upon a new name, whereby the hearts of all your brethren might have come to take offence. I wonder exceedingly at this, since I remember how thou wouldest fain have fled from the episcopal office rather than attain it. And yet, now that thou hast got it, thou desirest so to exercise it as if thou hadst run to it with ambitious intent. For, having confessed thyself unworthy to be called a bishop, thou hast at length been brought to such a pass as, despising thy brethren, to covet to be named the only bishop...I have taken care to address your Fraternity, not indeed in writing, but by word of mouth, desiring you to restrain

yourself from such presumption...I beg you, I beseech you, and with all the sweetness in my power demand of you, that your Fraternity gainsay all who flatter you and offer you this name of error, nor foolishly consent to be called by the proud title.

Consider, I pray thee, that in this rash presumption the peace of the whole Church is disturbed, and that it is in contradiction to the grace that is poured out on all in common...And thou wilt become by so much the greater as thou restrainest thyself from the usurpation of a proud and foolish title: and thou wilt make advance in proportion as thou art not bent on arrogation by derogation of thy brethren. Wherefore, dearest brother, with all thy heart love humility, through which the concord of all the brethren and the unity of the holy universal Church may be preserved.

Certainly the apostle Paul, when he heard some say, I am of Paul, I of Apollos, but I of Christ (1 Cor. 1:13), regarded with the utmost horror such dilaceration of the Lord's body, whereby they were joining themselves, as it were, to other heads, and exclaimed, saying, Was Paul crucified for you? or were ye baptized in the name of Paul (ib.)? If then he shunned the subjecting of the members of Christ partially to certain heads, as if beside Christ, though this were to the apostles themselves, *what wilt thou say to Christ, who is the Head of the universal Church, in the scrutiny of the last judgment, having attempted to put all his members under thyself by the appellation of Universal?* Who, I ask, is proposed for imitation in his wrongful title but he who, despising the legions of angels constituted socially with himself, attempted to start up to an eminence of singularity, that he might seem to be under none and to be alone above all? Who even said, I will ascend into heaven, I will exalt my throne above the stars of heaven; I will sit upon the mount of the testament, in the sides of the North: I will ascend above the heights of the clouds; I will be like the most High (Isai. xiv.13).

For what are all thy brethren, the bishops of the universal Church, but stars of heaven, whose life and discourse shine together amid the sins and errors of men, as if amid the shades of night? *And when thou desirest to put thyself above them by this proud title, and to tread down their name in comparison with thine, what else dost thou say but I will ascend into heaven; I will exalt my throne above the stars of heaven?*

The Patristic Interpretation 117

Are not all the bishops together clouds, who both rain in the words of preaching, and glitter in the light of good works? And when your Fraternity despises them, and you would fain press them down under yourself, what else say you but what is said by the ancient foe, I will ascend above the heights of the clouds?

This most holy man the lord John, of so great abstinence and humility, has, through the seduction of familiar tongues, broken out into such a pitch of pride as to attempt, in his coveting of that wrongful name, to be like him who, while proudly wishing to be like God, lost even the grace of the likeness granted him, and because he sought false glory, thereby forfeited true blessedness...

Certainly Peter, the first of the apostles, himself a member of the holy and universal Church, Paul, Andrew, John—what were they but heads of particular communities? And yet all were members under one Head. And (to bind all together in a short girth of speech) the saints before the law, the saints under the law, the saints under grace, all these making up the Lord's Body, were constituted as members of the Church, and not one of them has wished himself to be called universal. Now let your Holiness acknowledge to what extent you swell within yourself in desiring to be called by that name by which no one presumed to be called who was truly holy...

Was it not the case, as your Fraternity knows, that the prelates of this Apostolic See, which by the providence of God I serve, had the honour offered them of being called universal by the venerable Council of Chalcedon. But yet not one of them has ever wished to be called by such a title, or seized upon this ill-advised name, lest if, in virtue of the rank of the pontificate, he took to himself the glory of singularity, he might seem to have denied it to all his brethren...What, then, can we bishops say for ourselves, who have received a place of honour from the humility of our Redeemer, and yet imitate the pride of the enemy himself?...What, then, dearest brother, wilt thou say in that terrible scrutiny of the coming judgment, if thou covetest to be called in the world not only father, but even general father?...Lo, by reason of this execrable title of pride the Church is rent asunder, the hearts of all the brethren are provoked to offence...And thou attemptest to take the honour away from all which thou desirest unlawfully to usurp to thyself singularly...

I therefore have once and again through my representatives taken care to reprove in humble words this sin against the whole Church; and now I write myself.[165]

Note what Gregory says about the apostle Peter. He is not head over the other apostles such as Paul, John and Andrew, but shares an equal authority with them. All under one head, the Lord Jesus Christ. The overall thrust of this letter and admonition is a complete repudiation of the idea that in the Church universal the Lord Jesus Christ had established one bishop who would exercise universal rule over all. In his correspondence with his friend, Eulogius, the bishop of Alexandria, he made it clear that all the bishops of the major sees were all Petrine sees and shared equally in a Petrine authority:

> *To Eulogius, Bishop of Alexandria*: In position you are my brethren...And lo, in the preface of the epistle which you have addressed to myself who forbade it, you have thought it fit to make use of a proud appellation, calling me Universal Pope. But I beg your most sweet Holiness to do this no more, since what is given to another beyond what reason demands is subtracted from yourself. For as for me, I do not seek to be prospered by words but by my conduct. Nor do I regard that as an honour whereby I know that my brethren lose their honour. For my honour is the honour of the universal Church...Then am I truly honoured when the honour due to all and each is not denied them. For if your Holiness calls me Universal Pope, you deny that you are yourself what you call me universally. But far be this from us. Away with words that inflate vanity and wound charity.[166]

> *To Eulogius, Bishop of Alexandria*: Your most sweet Holiness has spoken much in your letter to me about the chair of Saint Peter, Prince of the apostles, saying that he himself now sits on it in the persons of his successors...*He has spoken to me about Peter's chair who occupies Peter's chair*...I greatly rejoiced because you, most holy ones, have given to yourselves what you have bestowed upon me. For who can be ignorant that holy Church has been made firm in the solidity of the

Prince of the apostles, who derived his name from the firmness of his mind, so as *to be called Petrus from petra.* And to him it is said by the voice of Truth, To thee I will give the keys of the kingdom of heaven (Matt. xvi.19). And again it is said to him, And when thou art converted, strengthen thy brethren (xxii.32). And once more, Simon, son of Jonas, lovest thou Me? Feed My sheep (Joh. xxi.17). Wherefore though there are many apostles, yet with regard to the principality itself of *the See of the Prince of the apostles alone has grown strong in authority, which in three places is the See of one.* For he himself exalted the See in which he deigned even to rest and end the present life. He himself adorned the See to which he sent his disciple as evangelist. He himself stablished the See in which, though he was to leave it, he sat for seven years. *Since then it is the See of one, and one See, over which by divine authority three bishops now preside, whatever good I hear of you, this I impute to myself...We are one in Him...*[167]

Given the contradictory opinions so often surrounding the true meaning of Gregory's views we will support the above contentions with the statements of world renowned historians. After stating that Gregory objected to the title 'universal bishop', John Meyendorff gives the following background and summation of Gregory's views:

> In letters addressed to John the Faster himself, to emperor Maurice and to empress Constantina, St. Gregory shows a surprising misunderstanding of the title's true significance. Used previously by patriarchs of Alexandria, Constantinople, and other sees, as well Rome, the title 'ecumenical'...affirmed a certain authority within the framework of the *oikoumene,* the 'inhabited earth.' It was *de facto* applied primarily to the bishop of Constantinople. In the mind of the Byzantines, it certainly did not imply any challenge to the 'apostolic' and moral authority of Old Rome, since the title was readily used in the case of the bishop of Rome as well...St. Gregory gave the issue an ecclesiological dimension which proves, on the one hand, even after his long sojourn in Constantinople, the exaggerated use of titles by the Byzantines remained foreign to his straightforward Latin mind, and, on the other

hand, that he understood all primacies, including his own, in a way which excluded the existence of a 'universal' bishop.

The episode provided St. Gregory with the clear opportunity to express an ecclesiology and a theology of the episcopate, which were precisely those maintained by the Orthodox East against the papal claims in the later period of church history...The incipient papal ecclesiology, expressed in the *Decretum Gelasianum* was foreign to St. Gregory the Great. Like all the popes of the period, he viewed himself as a successor of Peter, and he saw Peter, as the source (*origio*) of episcopal power, but he did not consider that this power was communicated to other bishops from Rome only. He is, therefore, a major witness to 'the ecclesiology of communion' which kept the East and West together during the first millenium of Christian history.[168]

Karl Morrison states:

Though Gregory cherished the precedence of his see, he did not judge its pre-eminence, absolute in administrative and juridical offices, as the unifying element of the entire Church. His emphasis on the Petrine commission in the conventional Roman sense was qualified by the eastern understanding that the rock upon which the Church was built was not Peter, but Christ Himself. In his mind, the oecumenical councils held a similar position—'for on them as on a four-square stone, the structure of the holy faith rises'—'because they have been established by universal consent.'...The great popes of the fifth century had argued vehemently that the canons of the Council of Nicaea and of other eminent synods confirmed Rome's administrative headship of all churches, and they had entered this assertion particularly against the claims of the eastern patriarchates to autonomy. Gregory, however, advanced no such doctrines, and towards the great eastern sees, he maintained a 'collegiate' rather than a 'monarchic' policy.

Much the same collegial concept was in Gregory's mind when he denounced John the Faster for assuming the title 'oecumenical patriarch.'...The full force of Gregory's argument struck in the protest that there could be no 'universal patriarch,' no 'universal pope,' no

The Patristic Interpretation 121

'general Father' of the universal Church. Rome declined the offensive title in Gregory's mind for the same reason John should have shunned it: it deprived the other patriarchs of their titles and rights; it denied the glory of the episcopate to all other bishops. For, he argued, if there was one universal bishop, there could be no other bishops, and the 'absurd' or 'demented' position must be maintained that the universal Church stood or fell in the person of one man.[169]

R.A. Markus makes the following observations:

Whatever he thought the title ('ecumenical patriarch') meant, it was something that could not be claimed for the Roman Church any more than it could be claimed for Constantinople. Gregory tells us this in the explanation he repeatedly gives of the grounds of his objection, most emphatically in a reply to a letter from the patriarch of Alexandria. He had been an old friend and supporter of Gregory's in his conflict with John the Faster, and had received the pope's recent request for support. In his reply he had called the pope, of all things, 'ecumenical patriarch.' Evidently he had been anxious to please Gregory and to give him moral support, while, perhaps, less than painstaking in his efforts to understand what the dispute was all about...At any rate, he was willing to oblige the pope by denying it to the patriarch of Constantinople, and—with supreme indifference to the pope's abhorrence—to apply it to the pope himself. His well-meant *faux pas* gave Gregory the occasion for his clearest exposition of the reason for his detestation of the title. The claim to universal bishophood implied in it undermines the proper standing of each and every bishop in his own church. What the Constantinopolitan claim injures is not, in the first place, Rome's *principatus,* but the status of each individual bishop—and that would be equally injured if Rome were to claim the offending title. Whatever it was that the patriarch was claiming for Constantinople, or rather, whatever it was Gregory took him to be claiming, it was something that Gregory rejected on behalf of Rome. What he was defending in this controversy, based as it was on ancient misunderstanding and a certain inflation of trivialities, was the honour and the rightful status of each and every bishop, not the Roman *principatus*.[170]

Maximus of Turin (Died—*ca.* A.D. 412)

Maximus was born in the mid fourth century and was bishop of Turin. He was greatly influenced by the writings of Augustine and Ambrose. Maximus has a great deal to say about Peter and the rock. He first of all states that the rock of Matthew 16 is Peter although Christ is the rock in the ultimate sense:

> This is Peter to whom Christ the Lord freely conceded participation in his name. For as the Apostle teaches, *Christ is the rock; and by Christ Peter was made a rock when the Lord said to him: 'You are Peter and upon this rock I shall build my Church.'* For just as water flowed from the rock when God's people were thirsting in the desert, so when the whole world was languishing in drought the *spring of a saving confession flowed from the mouth of Peter.* This is Peter to whom Christ entrusted the feeding of his sheep and lambs just before he ascended to the Father. As Christ had redeemed these by the compassion of his obedient service, so Peter served them by virtue of his faith. And rightly did that witness of mysteries, the Son of God, commit the feeding and tending of sheep to Peter whom he knew would not desist in his enthusiasm and faithfulness in nourishing the Lord's flock...[171]

> We have frequently said that *Peter was called a rock by the Lord.* Thus: 'Thou are Peter, and upon this rock I will build my Church.' *If, then, Peter is the rock upon whom the Church is built, rightly does he first heal feet, so that as he maintains the foundations of the Church's faith he also strengthens the foundations of a person's limbs.* Rightly, I say, does he first heal a Christian's feet so that he can walk upon the rock of the Church not as one who is fearful and weak but as one who is robust and strong. And where are the words of Paul the apostle not read? Where are they not written down, kept in the heart, and preserved in speech? This *Paul was called a vessel of election by the Lord.* A good

vessel, in which the precious precepts of Christ's commandments are treasured! A good vessel, from whose fulness the substance of life is always poured forth for the peoples, and still it is full. *Rock and vessel— most appropriate names for the apostles, and necessary instruments for the house of the Savior! For a strong house is built of rock and rendered useful by vessels. A rock provides the peoples with something firm lest they waver, while a vessel shelters Christians lest they be tempted.*[172]

In what sense does Maximus mean that Peter is a rock and that the Church is built upon him? He tells us in these statements:

Last Sunday we showed that Saint Peter proceeded along his erring ways during the Savior's suffering and that after he denied the Lord he was better. For he became more faithful after he wept over the faith that he had lost, and for that reason he gained back a greater grace than he lost: like a good shepherd he accepted the charge of protecting the sheep, so that he who had previously been weak to himself would now become the foundation for all, and the very person who had faltered when tested by questioning would strengthen others with the unwavering character of his faith. *On account of the firmness of his faithfulness he is called the rock of the churches, as the Lord says: You are Peter, and upon this rock I will build my Church. He is called a rock because he will be the first to lay the foundations of faith among the nations and so that, like an immovable stone, he might hold fast the fabric and structure of the whole Christian endeavor. Because of his faithfulness, therefore, Peter is called a rock, as the apostle says: And they drank from the spiritual rock, and the rock was Christ. Rightly does he who merits fellowship in deed merit fellowship also in name, for in the same house Peter laid the foundation and Peter does the planting, and the Lord gives the increase and the Lord provides the watering.*[173]

On account of his faithfulness Peter is told: Blessed are you, Simon bar Jonah, because flesh and blood have not revealed this to you but my Father who is in heaven. And I say to you: You are Peter, and upon this rock I will build my Church. Although he used to be called Simon, then, he is named Peter on account of his faithfulness. We read what the Apostle says of the Lord Himself: *They drank from the spiritual rock, but the rock was Christ. Rightly, then, inasmuch as Christ is a rock, is Simon named Peter, in order that he who shared with the Lord in faith might be at one with the Lord as well in the Lord's name—that just as a Christian is so called from Christ, the apostle Peter would similarly receive his name from Christ the rock.*[174]

The true rock foundation of the Church is Christ, according to Maximus. He also calls Peter the rock because of his faithfulness and his ministry in which he would establish the foundations of the faith among the Gentiles through his preaching. Therefore the Church is built upon him in that it is built *through* him by his preaching. The keys are interpreted by Maximus as Peter's faith and the means whereby heaven is opened to men:

It is necessary, however, to inquire how closed heavens are to be opened. I think that they cannot be opened otherwise than by taking up the keys of the apostle Peter—the keys which the Lord bestowed on him when he said: 'To you I give the keys of the kingdom of heaven.' Indeed let us ask Peter, that as a good gate keeper of the heavenly palace, he may open to us. Moreover, let us diligently ask what these keys may be. I say that Peter's key is Peter's faith, by which he opened heaven, by which, secure, he penetrated hades, by which, fearless, he walked on water. For so great is the power of apostolic faith, that all elements lie open to it: the angelic gates are not closed to it, nor do the gates of Hell prevail against it, nor do floods of water sink it. That key itself, which we call faith, let us see how firm and solid it is. I judge that it was produced by the work of 12 artisans; for the holy faith was comprehended in the creed of the 12 apostles, who, like skilled artisans working in concert, produced the key by their understanding. For *I call the creed itself the key*, which causes the shades of the devil to draw back, that the light of Christ may come. The hidden sins of conscience are brought into the open so that the clear works of justification may shine. Therefore this key must be shown to our brothers in order that they also as followers of Peter may learn to unlock hades and to open heaven.[175]

Peter is called a rock because through his preaching he would be the first to open the kingdom of God to the Gentiles, not because Christ would establish some kind of papal office in him. Maximus emphasizes over and over again that the rock was Christ and Peter gets his name, rock, only in a derivative sense from him. He makes it clear in the following statements that the true foundation of the Church is not Peter's person but Peter's confession of faith:

> But let us see what Simon Peter's boat is, which the Lord judged the more fitting of the two to teach from and which keeps the Savior safe from harm and brings the words of faith to the people. For we have discovered that the Lord previously set sail in another boat and was provoked by serious wrongs. For He sailed with Moses in the Red Sea when he led the people of Israel through the waters, but He was hurt by serious wrongs, as He himself says to the Jews in the Gospel: If you believe Moses you would also believe Me. The wrong inflicted upon the Savior is the Synagogue's disbelief. *Therefore He chooses Peter's boat and forsakes Moses*; that is to say, *He spurns the faithless Synagogue and takes the faithful Church*. For the two were appointed by God as boats, so to speak, which would fish for the salvation of humankind in this world as in a sea, as the Lord says to the apostles: Come, I will make you fishers of men.
>
> Of these two boats, then, one is left useless and empty on the shore, while the other is led out heavily laden and full to the deep. It is the Synagogue that is left empty at the shore because it has rejected Christ as well as the oracles of the prophets, but it is *the Church that is taken heavily laden out to the deep because it has received Christ with the teaching of the apostles*. The Synagogue, I say, stays close to the land as if clinging to earthly deeds. The Church, however, is called out into the deep, delving, as it were, into the profound mysteries of the heavens, into that depth concerning which the Apostle says: O the depth of the riches of the wisdom and knowledge of God. For this reason it is said to Peter: Put out into the deep—that is to say, into the depths of reflection upon the divine generation. *For what is so profound as what Peter said to the Lord: You are the Christ, the Son of the living God?* What is so trivial as what the Jews said about the Lord: Is this not the son of Joseph the carpenter? For the one, by a higher counsel, assented

in divine fashion to the birth of Christ, while the others, with a viper's mind, considered His heavenly generation in fleshly wise. Hence the Savior says to Peter: because flesh and blood has not revealed this to you but my Father who is in heaven. But to the Pharisees he says: How are you able to speak good things when you are evil?

The Lord, then, gets only into this boat of the Church, in which Peter has been proclaimed pilot by the Lord's own words: Upon this rock I will build my Church. This boat so sails upon the deeps of this world that, when the earth is destroyed, it will preserve unharmed all whom it has taken in. Its foreshadowing we see already in the Old Testament. For as Noah's ark preserved alive everyone whom it had taken in when the world was going under, so also Peter's Church will bring back unhurt everyone whom it embraces when the world goes up in flames. And as a dove brought the sign of peace to Noah's ark when the flood was over, so also Christ will bring the joy of peace to *Peter's Church* when the judgment is over, since He Himself is dove and peace, as He promised when He said: I shall see you again and your heart will rejoice.

But since we read in Matthew that this same boat of Peter, from which the Lord is now drawing forth the sacraments of His heavenly teaching, was so shaken about by violent winds as the Lord was sleeping in it that all the apostles feared for their lives, let us see why in one and the same boat at one time He teaches the people in tranquility and at another He inflicts the fear of death upon the disciples in stormy weather, especially inasmuch as Simon Peter was there with the other apostles. This was the reason for the danger: Simon Peter was there, but the betrayer Judas was also there. *For although the faith of the one was the foundation of the boat*, still the faithlessness of the other shook it. *Tranquility exists when Peter alone pilots*, stormy weather when Judas comes aboard.[176]

Maximus likens the Church to a boat with a pilot. The true Church, he says, is piloted by Peter. But what exactly does he mean by this? He is emphasizing Peter's confession of faith in Christ as the Son of God. He is saying that the Church has Peter for a pilot when it has Peter's faith. It is this faith which is the foundation of the boat and therefore of the Church. This hearkens back to Ambrose's statement

The Patristic Interpretation

that 'where Peter is there is the Church'—meaning his confession of faith—and to Chrysostom's statement that the see of Antioch retains the person of Peter when it remains faithful to the faith of Peter. Maximus is saying that Peter will establish the Church among the Gentiles and that the Church is built upon him in the sense that it is built upon his faith. Peter's faith is the foundation of the Church.

Peter Chrysologus (A.D. 380—450)

Peter Chrysologus was archbishop of Ravenna, a powerful and eloquent preacher who has been declared a Doctor of the Church. He makes these comments on Peter:

> For though to be called Peter is elsewhere merely to receive a name, in this place (the Church) it is a sign of strength. Truly, blessed *Peter, that immovable foundation of salvation*, showed himself to be such in the priestly office as they who desire the priesthood would wish to see...*Peter is the guardian of the faith, the rock of the Church*, and the gate keeper of heaven. He was chosen to be an apostolic fisher and with the hook of sanctity he brought to himself crowds submerged in waves of error, while by the nets of his teaching he brought from the multitude an abundance of men. Moreover, he was a most blessed and apostolic bird catcher, who reached the souls of youths flying through the air with the rod of the divine word.[177]

> Just as *Peter received his name from the rock, because he was the first to deserve to establish the Church, by reason of his steadfastness of faith*, so also Stephen was named from a crown...the first who deserved to bear witness with his blood. *Let Peter hold his ancient primacy of the apostolic choir. Let him open to those who enter the kingdom of heaven.* Let him bind the guilty with his power and absolve the penitent in kindness.[178]

Chrysologus describes the apostle Peter as the rock and immovable foundation of salvation, the guardian of the Church and gatekeeper of heaven. But in what sense does he interpret these terms? In a similar way to Augustine. He says first of all that Christ is the rock of the Church from whom Peter received his name. He then interprets Peter's primacy in terms of preaching, teaching and evangelism. Peter is called a rock by Christ because of the steadfastness of his faith and because he would be the first to establish the Church through his preaching for he was 'chosen to be an apostolic fisher.' These thoughts are similar to those of Maximus of Turin.

Comments of 6th Century Eastern Clerics (Palestine and Syria) from a Letter Written to the Emperor Justin

In a letter addressed to Pope Hormisdas, the Emperor Justin urges the Pope to adopt a conciliatory and lenient attitude toward those Eastern churches which were reluctant to condemn the names of certain deceased bishops who had leaned towards or embraced monophysite doctrines. To indicate how orthodox these churches were, Justin enclosed a letter that he had received from the Palestinian and Syriac clergy. The following is an excerpt from that letter in which these clerics make mention of the rock and Peter's confession in Matthew 16:

> With joy you will draw water from the springs of salvation (Isa. 12). Springs of salvation, says the prophet, meaning obviously *the preaching of evangelical truth*, from which spring the blessed apostles and their followers who were disciples through ordination and the wise teachers of the Church drew the saving water of faith, then irrigated *the holy Church of God* which, *fixed on the rock of that greatest of apostles, defends the true and inflexible confession, and faithfully in every age exclaims with him (i.e. Peter) to the only Son of God: You are the Christ, the Son of the living God.* Receiving this saving confession from the four holy synods which are honored for their evangelical teachings, we have never, by the grace of Christ, deviated from the true dogmas handed down to us; as an examination of the matter proves and as the constancy of our faith in times of necessity demonstrates. Since, therefore, as Christians we share in the doctrines of faith, and since,

most reverend lord (i.e. Justinian), we press for common peace and unity, we hereby make the faith, which we have acknowledged, from the beginning, open to your goodness through this our apology.[179]

This letter from the Eastern clergy of the 6th century is representative of the overall Eastern interpretation of the rock of Matthew 16. They state that the Church of God is fixed on the rock of the greatest of the apostles, Peter. But how did they mean this? They mean that the Church is built on Peter when it is built on Peter's confession of faith. The foundation upon which the Church is erected is faith, not that of a papal office. In commenting on the differences that existed between the Roman bishops and those of Constantinople in their understanding of the meaning of Christ's words to Peter in Matthew 16 in the 6th century, Karl Morrison makes the following observations regarding this letter and its meaning:

> Neither John nor Epiphanius were of one mind with Hormisdas in understanding Christ's commission to St. Peter. They understood the critical verse of St. Matthew in the general fashion implicit in a letter of Syriac and Palestinian clergy to Justin, the fashion long before conventional among eastern exegetes. For them, St. Peter was the representative and first spokesman of the Church's true confession, not the first bishop of one particular see.[180]

Isidore of Seville (A.D. 560—636)

Isidore is considered to be the last Church father of the Western Church. He succeeded his brother as Archbishop of Seville and was declared a Doctor of the Church by Pope Innocent XIII. Theologically he was known as a great synthesizer of the teachings of earlier fathers. William Jurgens makes these observations about him: 'There is no great originality to Isidore; but he was perhaps the most learned and broadly educated man of his age, and he excelled in synthesizing knowledge and information of the most diverse kinds.'[181] Isidore gives the following comments on the foundation of the Church and the relationship of the apostles to one another:

> Peter bears the character of the Church, which has the power to forgive sins and to lead men from Hades to the heavenly kingdom...*All the apostles also bear the type of the whole Church, since they also have received a like power of forgiving sins.* They bear also the character of the patriarchs, who by the word of preaching spiritually brought forth God's people in the whole world...*The wise man who built his house upon the rock signifies the faithful teacher, who has established the foundations of his doctrine and life upon Christ.*[182]
> Moreover, *Christ is called a 'foundation' because faith is established in him, and because the catholic Church is built upon him.*[183]

> Thus far we have spoken of priestly origins in the Old Testament. But in the New Testament after Christ the priestly order arises from Peter; for to him the first priestly office in the Church of Christ was given. Thus the Lord says to him: 'You are Peter and upon this rock I shall build my Church, and the gates of Hell shall not prevail against it; and I shall give you the keys of the kingdom of Heaven.' *So Peter first received the power of binding and loosing, and he first led people to faith by the power of his preaching. Still, the other apostles have been made equal with Peter in a fellowship of honor and power. They also, having been sent out into all the world, preached the Gospel. Having descended from these apostles, the bishops have succeeded them, and through all the world they have been established in the seats of the apostles.*[184]

Isidore states that the rock and foundation of the Church is the person of Christ. It is upon Christ that the Catholic Church is built and not upon a particular apostle. He reproduces the Augustinian thought that Peter is a figurative representative of the Church and that all the apostles are of equal honor and authority. In almost all respects Isidore mirrors the teachings of Augustine. Michael Winter confirms this in these statements:

The later reaction to Augustine was not so independent, and tended to follow the great doctor almost slavishly...The climax of this tendency to imitate Augustine is to be seen in the writings of Isidore of Seville...In his *Allegories* and *Etymologies* he reproduces Augustine's theory of St. Peter in detail.[185]

John of Damascus (Died *ca.* A.D. 749)

The death of John of Damascus (around 749 A.D.) is considered to be the close of the patristic age. He was an Eastern father with a reputation as a great preacher and prolific writer. In his writings he clearly identifies the rock of the Church as the person of Christ or Peter's faith which points to Christ:

> At Caesarea Philippi...where his disciples were assembled, on the spur of the moment *the Rock of Life himself* excavated a seat from a certain rock. Then he asked his disciples who the people were saying the Son of Man was. He did not seek this information because he was unaware of the ignorance of men; for Jesus requires no investigation. But he wanted to dispel by the light of knowledge the fog which lay upon the disciple's spiritual eyes. The disciples responded that some called Jesus John the Baptist, others Elijah, still others Jeremiah or one of the prophets...In order to erase this suspicion and to give to the ignorant the most excellent gift possible, namely, a true confession, what did Jesus do, he for whom nothing was impossible? As a man he posed a probing question, but as God he brought him out of the dark who first had been called and first had followed. This was the man whom Christ in his foreknowledge had predestined to be a worthy overseer of the Church. As God, Jesus inspired this man and spoke through him. What was the question? 'But who do you say I am?' And Peter, fired by a burning zeal and prompted by the Holy Spirit replied: 'You are Christ, Son of the living God.' Oh blessed mouth! Perfectly, blessed lips! Oh theological soul! Mind filled by God and made worthy by divine instruction! Oh divine organ through which Peter spoke! Rightly are you blessed, Simon son of Jonah...because neither flesh nor blood nor human mind, but my Father in heaven has revealed

this divine and mysterious truth to you. For no one knows the Son, save he who is known by him...*This is that firm and immovable faith upon which, as upon the rock whose surname you bear, the Church is founded. Against this the gates of hell, the mouths of heretics, the machines of demons—for they will attack—will not prevail. They will take up arms but they will not conquer.*[186]

This rock was Christ, the incarnate Word of God, the Lord, for Paul clearly teaches us: 'The rock was Christ' (1 Cor. 10:4).[187]

Moreover, that Christ is one—one person and hypostasis—is evident. He asks: 'Who do people say that I am?'...Peter replied, saying: '*You are Christ, Son of the living God*'...Wherefore, indeed, he heard: 'Blessed are you Simon Bar-Jonah since neither flesh nor blood has revealed this to you, but my Father who is in heaven. You are Peter'—*and upon this rock the Church was firmly established*—'*and the gates of hell*'—*that is, the mouths of heretics*—'*shall not prevail against it*.'[188]

John Damascene's interpretation is consistent with that of the rest of the Eastern Church, as represented by such fathers as Chrysostom and Theodoret. John does state in places that the rock is Peter's confession and therefore the Church is built upon him. However, as we have seen with many of the Eastern fathers, they do not mean this in the same way that a Roman Catholic would mean it. When the fathers speak of the Church being founded on Peter they interpret this to mean it is founded on his confession of faith. It is common for Roman Catholic apologists to assert that while the fathers would often speak of the Church being founded upon Peter's confession, they did not separate Peter's confession from Peter's person. Such an assertion is found in *Jesus, Peter and the Keys* in the discussion of John of Damascus. The authors quote a statement from the French Roman Catholic scholar Martin Jugie as he comments on John of Damasacus' interpretation that the rock of Matthew 16 is Peter's confession of faith. He says:

'Peter's faith is undoubtedly the unshakable rock upon which the

Church rests, but this faith is not separable from Peter's person: it is indeed Peter who is the rock.'[189]

The problem with such a statement is that John of Damascus does not mean this in the same way that Martin Jugie means it. And, in fact, his statement that one cannot separate Peter's confession from Peter's person is simply not true. That is precisely what John of Damascus does and as we have seen is also the view of Ambrose, Chrysostom, Augustine, and Cyril of Alexandria. The great twelfth–century Eastern theologian, Theophylact of Bulgaria, in his comments on Matthew 16:18, follows the patristic tradition and demonstrates how the East could speak of the Church being founded upon Peter and yet not mean this in a pro–Roman papal sense:

> The Lord favors Peter, giving him a great reward, because he built the church upon him. For since Peter had confessed Jesus son of God, Jesus said that this confession which Peter uttered would be the foundation of future believers, just as every man should be about to raise up the house of faith and should be about to lay this foundation. For even if we put together innumerable virtues, we, however, may not have the foundation—a proper confession, and we build in vain. Moreover since Jesus said my church, he showed himself to be the lord of creation: for all realities serve God...Therefore if we shall have been confirmed in the confession of Christ, the gates of hell, that is, sins, will not prevail against us.[190]

This is reminiscent of Cyprian who could speak of Peter as the rock and not mean it in a Roman Catholic sense. The examples of two prominent Western theologians who flourished just subsequent to the patristic age demonstrate the overall influence of the Augustinian exegesis of Matthew 16. They are Bede and Paschasius Radbertus.

Bede (A.D. 672—735)

The Venerable Bede was born in England and has been declared a

Doctor of the Church. He was devoted to monastic life, was a prolific writer and biblical commentator, and considered to be the most learned man of his day. The two main theological influences in his life were Augustine and Isidore. He makes the following comments on Peter and the rock which demonstrate an Augustinian influence:

> He commends the great perfection of faith to us (Mt. 16.16), equally he demonstrates the great strength of this perfected and completed faith against all temptation (Mt. 16.18!).[191]

> You are Peter and *on this rock from which you have taken your name, that is, on myself, I will build my Church, upon that perfection of faith which you confessed I will build my Church* by whose society of confession should anyone deviate although in himself he seems to do great things he does not belong to the building of my Church...*Metaphorically it is said to him on this rock, that is, the Saviour which you confessed, the Church is to be built,* who granted participation to the faithful confessor of his name.[192]

> Moreover he is called Peter because of the vigour of his mind which clung fast to that most solid rock, Christ.[193]

> Peter, who before was called Simon, received from the Lord the name 'Peter' because of the strength of his faith and the firmness of his confession; for Peter clung with a firm and sturdy heart to him about whom it is written: 'the rock, moreover, was Christ.'[194]

> *And upon this rock, that is, upon the Lord and Saviour who gave participation in his name to the one who in faith recognized, loved, and confessed him, so that Peter might be called by the name of the rock: upon this rock the Church is built,* so that one does not attain to eternal life and the share of the elect except by faith in and love of Christ, by partaking of Christ's sacraments, and by observing his commandments.[195]

Repeatedly, Bede states that the rock upon which the Church is

The Patristic Interpretation 135

built is the person of Christ. Jaroslav Pelikan affirms these facts about Bede and states that his exegesis and that of many other Western fathers was in fundamental agreement with the Eastern interpretation:

> In his description of Peter, Bede likewise made use of traditional prerogatives. He called Peter 'the patron of the entire church' and 'the first pastor of the church,' as well as 'the prince of the apostles.' He acknowledged that the command of Christ to Peter, 'Feed my sheep,' had been spoken not only to him, but to all the disciples. This meant that 'the other apostles were the same as what Peter was, but the primacy was given to Peter for the purpose of commending the unity of the church.' All the apostles and their successors were shepherds, but there was to be only one flock, whose unity was represented by Peter. Elsewhere Bede could take the commission to Peter to mean that 'the Lord commanded Saint Peter to take care of his entire flock, that is, of the church,' adding that Peter had in turn conveyed this order to the pastors of the church who followed him in the government of the flock.
> But when he came to identify the 'rock' on which Christ had promised to build his church, Bede, together with other Latin theologians of the period, seemed to come closer to the Eastern exegesis of Matthew 16:18-19 than to the Western; for he spoke of the church as being founded 'on the rock of faith, from which Peter received his name,' and he stated that 'upon this rock' meant 'upon the Lord, the Savior, who conferred upon his knowing and loving confessor a participation in his name' by calling him 'Peter.' In this interpretation of the 'rock,' Bede was joined by biblical interpreters of his own and of later periods; for the most astonishing fact is that in the specifically exegetical literature of the entire Middle Ages one looks in vain for the equation 'petra=Petrus,' which was so prominent in the polemical and canonical literature.[196]

Paschasius Radbertus (A.D. 785—860)

Paschasius was abbott of the Benedictine Abbey at Corbie. He was one of the leading theologians of his day and was responsible for writing the first monograph on the eucharist. He gives the following interpretation of the Matthew 16 passage:

> *There is one response of all upon which the Church is founded and against which the gates of hell will not prevail...Such a great faith does not arise except from the revelation of God the Father and inspiration of the Holy Spirit so that anyone that has faith, like firm stone, is called Peter*...It should be noted that anyone of the faithful is rock as far as he is an imitator of Christ and is light as far as he is illuminated by light and by this the Church of Christ is founded upon those as far as they are strengthened by Christ. *So not on Peter alone but on all the apostles and the successors of the apostles the Church of God is built.* But these mountains are first built on the mountain Christ who is elevated above all mountains and hills.[197]

> One heavenly house in the heavens has been established, through the foundation of faith, upon him who is rightly called 'a rock.'[198]

> For the name, derived equally in Latin from the 'rock' (petra) which is Christ, designates the firmness of his faith.[199]

> *This is indeed the true and inviolable faith given to Peter* from God the Father, which affirms that if there had not always been a son there would not always have been a Father, *upon which faith the whole Church is both founded and remains firm,* believing that God is the Son of God.[200]

Paschasius states that the rock is Christ and that the Church is founded upon him by being founded upon Peter's confession.

The Patristic Interpretation of Luke 22:32

The evidence presented on the history of the patristic exegesis of Matthew 16 is similar for Luke 22:32 and John 21:15–17. This evidence reveals that the fathers did not interpret these passages in favor of Roman primacy and infallibility. There are very few references made to Luke 22:32 in the ante-Nicene period. The following comments by Ignatius in the early second century and by Cyprian in the third sum up the opinion of the ante-Nicene fathers:

Ignatius

> They are ashamed of the cross; they mock at the passion; they make a jest of the resurrection. *They are the offspring of that spirit who is the author of all evil*, who led Adam, by means of his wife, to transgress the commandment, who slew Abel by the hands of Cain, who fought against Job, who was the accuser of Joshua, the son of Josedech, *who sought to 'sift the faith' of the apostles*, who stirred up the multitude of the Jews against the Lord, who also now 'worketh in the children of disobedience;' from whom *the Lord Jesus Christ will deliver us, who prayed that the faith of the apostles might not fail*, not because He was not able of Himself to preserve it, but because He rejoiced in the pre-eminence of the Father.[201]

Cyprian

> For Apostolic men also ceased not to pray day and night; and our Lord Himself also, the Author of our rule of life, and the Way of our example, prayed often and with watching, as we read in the Gospel, He went out into a mountain to pray, and continued all night in prayer to God: and we may be assured that when he prayed, *He prayed for us*, since He Himself was not a sinner, but bore the sins of others. *But so truly did He pray for us, that we read in another place, And the Lord said to Peter, Behold, Satan hath desired to have you, that he might sift you as wheat, but I have prayed for thee that thy faith fail not.*[202]

> *The Lord offered petition, not for Himself (for what should He, the Innocent, ask for on His own account?) But for our sins, as Himself makes known when He says to Peter, Behold, Satan hath desired that he might sift you as wheat, but I have prayed for thee, that thy faith fail not.* And afterwards He entreats the Father for all, saying, Neither pray I for these alone, but for them also that shall believe on Me, through

their word; that they all may be one, as Thou, Father, art in Me, and I in Thee, that they also may be one in us.[203]

There is no mention in Ignatius or Cyprian of a charism of infallibility being bestowed upon Peter and subsequently through him to the bishops of Rome. Peter is presented by these two fathers as a representative of the Church as a whole. Therefore, when Christ prayed for Peter he was praying for the Church universal or for all the apostles. We also see this line of thought in the comments of the fathers in the centuries succeeding the Council of Nicaea. The following fathers are representative of the patristic viewpoint:

Augustine

> Listen to the Lord, when He says, 'I have prayed for thee, Peter, that thy faith fail not;' that we may never think of our
> faith as so lying in our free will that it has no need of the divine assistance.[204]

Chrysostom

> And that thou mayest learn, that this denial (arose) not so much from sloth, as from his being forsaken of God, who was teaching him to know the measures of man and not to contradict the sayings of the Master, nor to be more high–minded than the rest, but to know that nothing can be done without God, and that 'Except the Lord build the house, they labor in vain who build it' (Ps. cxxvii.1): therefore also Christ said to him alone, 'Satan desired to sift thee as wheat,' and I allowed it not, 'that thy faith may not fail' (Luke xxii.31, 32). For since it was likely that he would be high–minded, being conscious to himself that he loved Christ more than they all, therefore 'he wept bitterly'...[205]

Ambrosiaster

> Clearly, in Peter all are contained: praying for Peter, (Jesus) is understood to have prayed for all. It is always the people who are

rebuked or praised in a leader. This is why He also says elsewhere: 'I pray for those whom you have given me' (John 17:9).²⁰⁶

The Apostolical Constitutions

> For on this account *the devil himself* is very angry at the holy Church of God: he is removed to you, and has raised against you adversities, seditions, and reproaches, schisms and heresies. For he had before subdued that people to himself, by their slaying of Christ. But you who have left his vanities, he tempts in different ways, as he did the blessed Job. For indeed he opposed that great high priest Joshua the son of Josedek; and *he often times sought to sift us, that our faith might fail...He will say now, as He said formerly of us when we were assembled together, 'I have prayed that your faith may not fail.'*²⁰⁷

Karlfried Froehlich gives the following summation of the patristic understanding of Luke 22:32:

> We find the same distance from themes of Petrine primacy in the exegetical tradition about Luke 22:31-32. Modern theologians have issues of indefectibility and infallibility on their minds when they consider these verses...Medieval exegetes found very different contexts for the interpretation of these words. They took their cue from the patristic tradition.
> In the Middle Ages...the exegetical mainstream followed (Jerome) and Augustine. As we noted in connection with Matt. 16, the Bishop of Hippo was fascinated by the stark contrast between beatitude and curse, strength and weakness, fall and exaltation on the part of a Peter in whom he saw the *figura* (figure) of the church as well as of every believer. Peter had already been given first place; now he fell back behind even the weakest martyr who had stood up for Christ. There would have been no return for him had the Lord not intervened with his forgiveness and his prayer. Following Augustine, medieval exegetes rarely tried to soften the denial but explained it as part of God's providential pedagogy. The psychological need of a special lesson for the all too impulsive Peter had been emphasized by Eastern fathers, especially Chrysostom whose interpretation became quite popular in

the West in the later Middle Ages. Ambrose found in the incident a more general admonition to strengthen ascetic awareness among all prelates, while constantly stressing Peter's tears as the proper fruit of his divinely endorsed trial: 'Beware of pride! Beware of the world!'

In Matt. 16:16, Augustine laid stress on the confessing Peter as *figura ecclesiae* (figure of the church), speaking *pro omnibus* (for all). The same interpretation applied to Luke 22:32 in much of the exegetical tradition. Already before Augustine, the Ambrosiaster refused to change the accent on the disciples in v. 31 to an accent on Peter alone in v. 32: 'Clearly in Peter all are contained; praying for Peter, Jesus is understood to have prayed for all. It is always the people who are rebuked or praised in a leader. This is why he also says elsewhere: "I pray for those whom you have given me" (John 17:9).'[208] Augustine was equally clear about this point. For medieval exegetes, various verses from John 17 continued to provide biblical warrant for the extension of Jesus' prayer in Luke 22:32 far beyond Peter. All Christians, they concluded, are warned here how easily their faith can fail, but they also receive encouragement by the assurance of Christ's intercession for them. In the general stream of normative exegesis, the Peter who was upheld by Christ's prayer and whose faith was tempted yet did not finally succumb clearly remained *figura ecclesiae*; for most exegetes, this meant in the first instance: type of the universal church and of every individual believer.[209]

Froehlich goes on to confirm that Luke 22, beginning in the fifth century with Leo I, also had a papal application. But he points out that in the papal interpretation this verse was never interpreted to mean papal infallibility. In commenting on Gregory VII's *Dictatus papae*, from the 11th century, where he speaks of the inerrant faith of the Roman Church, Froehlich makes this important point:

> We should note, however, that even in the formulation of the *Dictatus papae* the church for whose faith Christ prayed in the person of Peter remained a collective *ecclesia Romana*, not the person or the office of Peter's successor himself.[210]

Brian Tierney is a world renowned medieval scholar. He gives the

The Patristic Interpretation

following analysis of the medieval interpretation of Luke 22 which was grounded in the patristic interpretation as documented by Froehlich. He demonstrates that the doctrine of papal infallibility was unknown in the patristic and medieval ages:

> The scriptural text most commonly cited in favor of papal infallibility is Luke 22.32. *There is no lack of patristic commentary on the text. None of the Fathers interpreted it as meaning that Peter's successors were infallible.* No convincing argument has ever been put forward explaining why they should not have stated that the text implied a doctrine of papal infallibility if that is what they understood it to mean. Again, it is difficult for us to know exactly what men of the sixth and seventh centuries understood by formulas like those of Hormisdas and Agatho. But we do know that the general council which accepted Agatho's formula also anathematized Agatho's predecessor, Pope Honorius, on the ground that he 'followed the views of the heretic Sergius and confirmed his impious dogmas.' Agatho's successor, Pope Leo II, in confirming the decrees of the council, added that Honorius 'did not illuminate the apostolic see by teaching the apostolic tradition but, by an act of treachery strove to subvert its immaculate faith.' Whatever the council fathers may have meant by the formula they accepted concerning the unfailing faith of the apostolic see, their meaning can have had little connection with the modern doctrine of papal infallibility.[211]

Luis Bermejo is a Spanish Jesuit who has taught theology at the Pontifical Athenaeum at Puna, India for the last thirty years. In a recently published book (1992), he makes the following compelling argument in confirmation of Brian Tierney's historical research:

> To my knowledge, nobody seems to have challenged Tierney's contention that the entire first millenium is entirely silent on papal infallibility and that, therefore, Vatican I's contention concerning the early roots of the doctrine is difficult to maintain. Practically the only objection of some substance raised against Tierney seems to be his interpretation of the twelfth century decretists: is the future dogma of Vatican I implicitly contained in them? Even after granting for the sake

of argument that it is—something that Tierney does not concede in any way—the formidable obstacle of the first millenium remains untouched. In my opinion his critics have fired their guns on a secondary target (the medieval decretists and theologians) leaving the disturbing silence of the first millenium out of consideration. Nobody seems to have been able to adduce any documentary proof to show that this long silence was illusory, that the doctrine was—at least implicitly—already known and held in the early centuries. It is not easy to see how a given doctrine can be maintained to be of apostolic origin when a thousand years of tradition do not echo it in any way.[212]

The patristic exegesis of Luke 22:32 did not follow that proposed by Vatican I with respect to papal infallibility. The fathers do not interpret this passage to mean that a personal infallibility had been granted to Peter or through him to his successors, the bishops of Rome. Such an interpretation is nonexistent in the patristic literature. And the same can be said historically for Matthew 16 regarding the concept of infallibility. The patristic exegetes, as documented by Froehlich, saw Christ's prayer for Peter as a guarantee that Peter's faith would not ultimately fail, not that he would be infallible. It also saw Peter as a figure of the Church as a whole, assuring us that Christ will not allow the Church ultimately to fall away. In interpreting Luke 22, the whole view of the Church, whether it was to Peter personally, or to the Church as represented in Peter, was one of indefectibility as opposed to infallibility. This patristic interpretation was inherited by the theologians and canonists of the middle ages.

The Patristic Interpretation of John 21:15–17

When we turn to the patristic exegesis of John 21:15-17, we find a similar situation to that documented on Mt. 16 and Lk. 22. We do not find the interpretation to be that espoused by the Roman Catholic Church. In the patristic interpretation of John 21 Peter is viewed as an example to all Christians of the meaning of true discipleship or as the representative or figure of all pastors in the Church. The fathers did not interpret this passage to mean a Petrine

The Patristic Interpretation 143

primacy passed on to his successors, the bishops of Rome. The following comments by Augustine reveal the fathers' view of Peter as a representative of the whole Church. In this view Peter is not set apart by Christ as a supreme ruler of the Church but is a figurative representative of the Church as a whole:

> For Peter in many places of the Scriptures appears to represent the Church; especially in that place where it was said, I give unto thee the keys of the kingdom of heaven. Whatsoever thou shalt bind on earth, shall be bound in heaven; and whatsoever thou shalt loose on earth, shall be loosed in heaven. What! did Peter receive these keys, and Paul not receive them? Did Peter receive them, and John, and James, and the rest of the Apostles, not receive them? Or are not these keys in the Church, in which sins are daily remitted? But since in figure Peter represented the Church, what was given to him singly, was given to the Church. Peter then represented the Church, the Church is the Body of Christ.[213]

> But what now? The Lord asketh him as ye heard when the Gospel was being read, and saith to him, Simon, son of John, lovest thou Me more than these? He answered and said, Yea, Lord, Thou knowest that I love Thee. And again the Lord asked this question, and a third time He asked it. And when he asserted in reply his love, He commended to him the flock. For each several time the Lord said to Peter, as he said, I love thee; Feed My lambs, feed My little sheep. In this one Peter was figured the unity of all pastors, of good pastors, that is, who know that they feed Christ's sheep for Christ, not for themselves.[214]

> One wicked man represents the whole body of the wicked; in the same way as Peter, the whole body of the good, yea, the body of the Church, but in respect to the good. For if in Peter's case there were no sacramental symbol of the Church, the Lord would not have said to him, 'I will give unto thee the keys of the kingdom of heaven: whatsoever thou shalt loose on earth shall be loosed in heaven; and whatsoever thou shalt bind on earth shall be bound in heaven.' If this was said only to Peter, it gives no ground of action to the Church. But if such is the case also in the Church, that what is bound on earth is

bound in heaven, and what is loosed on earth is loosed in heaven—for when the Church excommunicates, the excommunicated person is bound in heaven; when one is reconciled by the Church, the person so reconciled is loosed in heaven—if such, then, is the case in the Church, Peter, in receiving the keys, represented the holy Church.[215]

The Unanimous Consent of the Fathers

Vatican I has claimed that its papal teachings, based primarily on a particular interpretation of Matthew 16:18, find support historically from what it calls the 'unanimous consent of the fathers.' But the forgoing historical evidence reveals that there is no patristic consensus to support the Vatican I papal interpretation of Matthew 16:18–19. The Roman Catholic Church's appeal to the 'universal consent of the fathers' to support its exegesis of Matthew 16 is fallacious. Such a consensus does not exist. The quotations we have cited document the comments of the major fathers of the patristic age from both the East and West up through the eighth century. Their interpretation of Matthew 16:18 demonstrates that the overwhelming majority view of the Church historically is not that of the Roman Catholic Church today.

This whole issue of 'unanimous consent' has direct bearing upon the Roman Church's claims to authority and to infalliblity as an interpreter of scripture. This is a principle which was promulgated by the Council of Trent and later reaffirmed by Vatican I. Trent states:

> Furthermore, in order to restrain petulant spirits, it decrees, that no one, relying on his own skill, shall, in matters of faith, and of morals pertaining to the edification of the Christian doctrine, wresting the sacred Scripture to his own senses, presume to interpret the said sacred Scripture contrary to that sense which holy mother Church, whose it is to judge of the true sense and interpretation of the Holy Scriptures, hath held and doth hold; or even contrary to the unanimous consent of the Fathers.[216]

What the Council is saying, and Vatican I later reaffirmed, is that the Roman Catholic Church alone has the right to interpret scripture and that its interpretation is consistent with the overall interpretation (unanimous consent) of the fathers. It is making the point that the teaching of the Church has not changed over time—that there is a consensus of interpretation that can be traced back through the fathers to the apostles and ultimately to Christ himself. It is not suggesting that there are two levels of authority in interpretation, that of the fathers and that of the Church in a later age. Trent teaches that the Church of the 16th century is consistent in its interpretation with the fathers of earlier centuries. This is why it states that the interpretation of scripture which is contrary to what the Church *holds* or *has held*, or even contrary to the unanimous consent of the fathers is unlawful. That this is the proper interpretation of the Council's teaching is seen from the *Profession of the Tridentine Faith*, issued by Pius IV in 1564 which was required of all priests. Regarding the scriptures all priests were to take the following oath: 'Neither will I ever take and interpret them otherwise than according to the unanimous consent of the Fathers.'[217] Historically the Church has always claimed patristic consensus for its tradition as an affirmation of the continuity of its teaching. Even Vatican I affirms this principle when it states that its teachings on papal rule and infallibility have been the *practice* of the Church from the very beginning.

The Council of Trent laid down this principle of interpretation. It is not the Protestant Church but the Roman Catholic which has enunciated it. This does not mean that every single father has interpreted scripture in precisely the same way but that there is an overall consensus of meaning which the Church upholds. It should be evident then, since this is a formal principle enunciated by Trent, that there cannot be an authoritative interpretation of scripture that fundamentally contradicts what has been clearly promulgated by the fathers. This would be especially true of the fundamentals of the faith. Vatican I states that papal rule and infallibility and submission to it, must be embraced to obtain salvation. It then uses the Petrine texts (Mt. 16, Lk. 22, Jn 21) as the basis for its teaching and gives these passages a papal interpretation.

Vatican I teaches that the Church has held these particular views

146 THE MATTHEW 16 CONTROVERSY

from the very beginning. So it is only right to ask the question: Is there a unanimous consent of the fathers in the interpretation of Mt. 16, Lk. 22 and Jn. 21? Does it conform to that given by Vatican I? Has the Church from the very beginning always believed and practiced the views of Vatican I on papal rule and infallibility? The answer to these questions is a decided No!

It is clear that the Roman Catholic Church of later centuries interprets the rock of Matthew 16 differently from the overall patristic consensus, so how can it claim to be an infallible interpreter of scripture?

Summary Statements of Historians

The following section provides excerpts from the writings of major Roman Catholic, Orthodox and Protestant historians which summarize the patristic understanding of the person of Peter and the rock of Matthew 16.

Jaroslav Pelikan

Pelikan provides this overview of the Eastern Church's understanding of the rock and Peter in Matthew 16:16–19:

> The identification of the gates of hell with the great heresies of the second, third, and fourth centuries was generally accepted. Against these gates of hell not only the apostle Peter, but all the apostles, especially John, had successfully contended with the authority of the word of God. Indeed, the power of the keys conferred upon Peter by Christ in Matthew 16:19 was not restricted either to him or to his successors on the throne of Old Rome; all the faithful bishops of the church were imitators and successors of Peter. They had this status as orthodox adherents of the confession of Peter in Matthew 16:16: 'You are the Christ, the Son of the living God.' By attaching the promise in the following verses to that confession it was possible to admonish orthodox believers to 'run to the faith...of this immovable rock...and let us believe that Christ is both God and man.' The unshakable

foundation of the church was the rock that was Christ, but at the same time Peter could be called 'the foundation and support of our faith.' He was this, however, principally because of his confession, which was repeated by all true believers. It was a polemical extension of this general Greek tendency when a later treatise, falsely ascribed to Photius, stated flatly that the rock in Christ's promise was the confession of Peter rather than his person.

Thus Peter was the foundation of the church, so that whoever believed as he believed would not go astray. But for most Greek theologians Peter was above all 'the chief of the theologians' because of his confession. All the titles of primacy, such as foundation and basis and 'president of the disciples,' pertained to him as trinitarian theologian. The church was to be built on the rock, on Christ the cornerstone, on which Peter, as coryphaeus of the disciples of the Logos, had also been built—'built that is by the Holy and divine dogmas.' Primacy belonged to Peter on account of his confession, and those who confessed Christ to be the Son of the living God, as he had, were the beneficiaries of the promise that the gates of hell would not prevail against the church built on the rock.[218]

Johann Joseph Ignaz von Döllinger

Döllinger taught Church history as a Roman Catholic for 47 years in the 19th century and was one of the greatest and most influential historians in the Church of his day. He sums up the Eastern and Western understanding of Matthew 16 in the patristic period:

> In the first three centuries, St. Irenaeus is the only writer who connects the superiority of the Roman Church with doctrine; but he places this superiority, rightly understood, only in its antiquity, its double apostolical origin, and in the circumstance of the pure tradition being guarded and maintained there through the constant concourse of the faithful from all countries. Tertullian, Cyprian, Lactantius, know nothing of special Papal prerogative, or of any higher or supreme right of deciding in matter of doctrine. In the writings of the Greek doctors, Eusebius, St. Athanasius, St. Basil the Great, the two Gregories, and St.

Epiphanius, there is not one word of any prerogatives of the Roman bishop. The most copious of the Greek Fathers, St. Chrysostom, is wholly silent on the subject, and so are the two Cyrils; equally silent are the Latins, Hilary, Pacian, Zeno, Lucifer, Sulpicius, and St. Ambrose.

St. Augustine has written more on the Church, its unity and authority, than all the other Fathers put together. Yet, from all his numerous works, filling ten folios, only one sentence, in one letter, can be quoted, where he says that the principality of the Apostolic Chair has always been in Rome—which could, of course, be said then with equal truth of Antioch, Jerusalem, and Alexandria. Any reader of his Pastoral Letter to the separated Donatists on the Unity of the Church, must find it inexplicable...that in these seventy–five chapters there is not a single word on the necessity of communion with Rome as the centre of unity. He urges all sorts of arguments to show that the Donatists are bound to return to the Church, but of the Papal Chair, as one of them, he says not a word.

We have a copious literature on the Christian sects and heresies of the first six centuries—Irenaeus, Hippolytus, Epiphanius, Philastrius, St. Augustine, and, later, Leontius and Timotheus—have left us accounts of them to the number of eighty, but not a single one is reproached with rejecting the Pope's authority in matters of faith.

All this is intelligible enough, if we look at the patristic interpretation of the words of Christ to St. Peter. Of all the Fathers who interpret these passages in the Gospels (Matt. xvi.18, John xxi.17), not a single one applies them to the Roman bishops as Peter's successors. How many Fathers have busied themselves with these texts, yet not one of them whose commentaries we possess—Origen, Chrysostom, Hilary, Augustine, Cyril, Theodoret, and those whose interpretations are collected in catenas—has dropped the faintest hint that the primacy of Rome is the consequence of the commission and promise to Peter! Not one of them has explained the rock or foundation on which Christ would build His Church of the office given to Peter to be transmitted to his successors, but they understood by it either Christ Himself, or Peter's confession of faith in Christ; often both together. Or else they thought Peter was the foundation equally with all the other Apostles, the twelve being together the foundation–stones of the Church (Apoc. xxi.14). The Fathers could the less recognize in the power of the keys, and the power of binding and loosing, any special prerogative or lordship of the Roman bishop, inasmuch as—what is obvious to any one at first sight—they did not regard a power first given to Peter, and afterwards conferred in precisely the same words on all the Apostles, as anything peculiar to him, or hereditary in the line of Roman bishops, and they held the symbol of the keys as meaning just the same as the figurative expression of binding and loosing.[219]

Michael Winter

As we have seen, Michael Winter, the Roman Catholic historian, affirms that such major fathers as Origen, Eusebius, Theodoret, Ambrosiaster, Cyril of Alexandria, Augustine, Isidore of Seville, John of Damascus and many others do not hold to the Roman Catholic interpretation. In summing up the early fathers' interpretation of Matthew 16, Winter is forced by the evidence to these conclusions:

> Their theology of the church was, thanks to St. Paul, so thoroughly Christocentric that it was difficult for them to envisage a foundation other than Christ.[220]

Winter concludes his analysis of the Eastern Church's point of view and its antipathy to the Roman Catholic interpretation with these remarkable words:

> The subjection of the church to the state in the government of Constantine and his successors was such that it was virtually incompatible with an independent church and a papacy. The Eastern Church tacitly acquiesced in this system in practice, chiefly because they had no adequate theological understanding of the nature of the visible church.[221]

To actually suggest that the Eastern Church, which held the greatest theologians of the early Church—those responsible for standing victorious against the great heresies which threatened the Church of those centuries—did not have an adequate theological understanding of the nature of the visible Church is incredibly arrogant. They had a very clear understanding but one which did not correspond to the papal view that gradually developed over the centuries. What is interesting is that the view of the Western Church for centuries corresponded to the Eastern view and was not that of papal primacy. That was a much later historical development. But it is interesting that Winter found it necessary to propound some kind of theory because of the weight of the Eastern patristic evidence which so overwhelmingly contradicts Roman Catholic ecclesiology.

What Winter says about the interpretation of the Eastern fathers on the rock of Matthew 16 is worth reemphasizing: 'Their theology of the church was, thanks to St. Paul, so thoroughly Christocentric that it was difficult for them to envisage a foundation other than Christ.' In other words the early Church did not teach that the Church was founded upon a man but upon the person of the Lord Jesus Christ. It is he who is the rock and foundation of the Church.

Karlfried Froehlich

Karlfried Froehlich, one of the foremost medieval and patristic scholars living today, wrote his PhD. dissertation on the history of the patristic and medieval exegesis of Matthew 16. He affirms the above facts in discussing the history of the exegesis of the Petrine texts, demonstrating how the medieval theologians interpreted Matthew 16 in harmony with a clear patristic tradition contrary to the Roman Catholic point of view:

> Three biblical texts have traditionally been cited as the religious foundation of papal primacy: Matt. 16:18–19; Luke 22:32; and John 21:15–17...The combination of the three passages in support of the primatial argument reaches far back in the history of the Roman papacy. Leo I and Gelasius I seem to have been the first to use it...However, it would be a mistake to assume that the papal interpretation was the standard exegesis everywhere...Quite on the

contrary, the understanding of these Petrine texts by biblical exegetes in the mainstream of the tradition was universally nonprimatial before Innocent III.

Perhaps the most instructive case is that of Matt. 16:18–19. It is quite clear to modern exegetes that all three parts of the passage, the name–giving, its interpretation by Jesus' word about the founding of the church on the rock, and the promise of the keys, speak about the person of Peter, even if the nature of his prerogative and the application to any successors is set aside. The medieval interpretation shows a very different picture. The name–giving (v. 18a) was generally regarded as Jesus' answer to Peter's confession which, as the context suggested to medieval exegetes, Peter had uttered *pro omnibus* (for all). Following Origen, Chrysostom, and Jerome, exegetes widely assumed that in Peter the reward for the correct confession of Christ, the Son of God was given to all true believers; all Christians deserved to be called *petrae*. Even Augustine's formulation, informed by a traditional North African concern for the unity of the church, that in Peter *unus pro omnibus* (one for all) had answered and received the reward, did not suggest more than a figurative reading of Peter as an image of the true church. In light of Peter's subsequent fall and denial, the name itself was regularly declared to be derived from Christ, the true rock. Augustine, who followed Origen in this assumption, was fascinated by the dialectic of the 'blessed' Peter (Matt. 16:17) being addressed as 'Satan' a few verses later (v. 23). In Peter, weak in himself and strong only in his connection with Christ, the church could see the image of its own total dependence on God's grace.

Augustine rigorously separated the name-giving from its explanation: Christ did not say to Peter: 'you are the rock,' but 'you are Peter.' The church is not built upon Peter but upon the only true rock, Christ. Augustine and the medieval exegetes after him found the warrant for this interpretation in 1 Cor. 10:4. The allegorical key of this verse had already been applied to numerous biblical rock passages in the earlier African *testimonia* tradition. Matt. 16:18 was no exception. If the metaphor of the rock did not refer to a negative category of 'hard' rocks, it had to be read christologically.

The same result was obtained when exegetes focused on the image of 'the building of the church.' The rock metaphor in Matt. 16:18 stressed the firmness of the church's foundation. But the foundation image itself, *fundamentum ecclesiae*, was clearly explained in another key passage of the New Testament: 'Another foundation can no one lay except the one that is laid, which is Christ Jesus' (1 Cor. 3:11). The same interpretation of the 'firm foundation' being Christ seemed inevitable when exegetes associated Matt. 16:18 with Jesus' parable of Matt. 7:24 which spoke of the building of a house on firm ground. The exegetical tradition since Origen and the *Opus imperfectum in Matthaeum* identified the house with the church so that the wise master builder had to be Christ who builds the church upon the firm rock, himself. Even in a secondary moral interpretation which explained the master builder as the virtuous Christian, the image of the strong foundation was invariably christologized, often with direct reference to 1 Cor. 3:11 and 10:4, or even Matt. 16:18. A good Christian must build the house of his life on Christ. Applied to the imagery of Matt. 16:18, the final scope of Jesus' parable again reinforced a christological reading: the house of the wise master builder, Jesus taught, stands firm against all assaults of wind, flood, and weather. The parallel to Matt. 16:18c was very obvious to the interpreter: if the *portae inferi* (gates of hell) cannot prevail against it, the church must indeed be built on the one rock that cannot be moved, Christ.

The logic of these parallel texts must have seemed inevitable to medieval exegetes. In none of the biblical building and foundation passages which were understood as referring to the church was Matt. 16:18 used as a hermeneutical key that would suggest Peter as the foundation. On the contrary, the clear Petrine meaning of the verse was silenced by the weight of the christological parallels. In medieval exegesis these keys governed not only all references to the building of the church in the New Testament but also its Old Testament prefigurations: Christ was the foundation of the church prefigured in Solomon's temple (1 Kings 5ff), in the house which Wisdom built for herself (Prov. 9), and in the cosmological foundation images of

The Patristic Interpretation 153

the Psalms (Ps. 76:69; 86:1; 101:26; 103:5 etc.).

Most of the Eastern exegetes, especially after the doctrinal controversies of the fourth century, read v. 18 as the culmination of vv. 16–17: 'upon this rock' meant 'upon the orthodox faith which you have just confessed.' Introduced in the West by Ambrose and the translation of the Antiochene exegetes, this *petra=fides* equation maintained an important place alongside the christological alternative, or as its more precise explanation: the rock of the church was Christ who was the content of Peter's confession.

The North African catechetical tradition, on the other hand, understood the word about Peter, the rock of the church, as the preface to v. 19: Peter was the rock, because he received the keys of the kingdom, which signified the church's exercise of penitential discipline. Tertullian, nevertheless, regarded the Peter of Matt. 16:18-19 as the representative of the entire church or at least its 'spiritual' members. Cyprian understood him as symbolizing the unity of all bishops, the privileged officers of penance.

A basic lack of the primatial context also characterizes the exegetical tradition about the 'keys of the kingdom of heaven' (Matt. 16:19). Again, the major reason may have to be sought in the influence of biblical parallels. In the patristic commentaries, the keys were understood as penitential authority, primarily the priestly power of excommunication and reconciliation. This understanding was nourished by the parallel passages of Matt. 18:18...and especially John 20:23, where binding and loosing seemed to be explained as the retaining and forgiving of sins. Both texts, however, extended this power beyond the one Peter to all apostles. Thus, the exegetes were faced with the fact that 'what was bestowed on Peter, was also given to all apostles.'

We can now summarize our findings. The earlier exegetical history of Matt. 16:18–19, Luke 22:32, and John 21:15–17 was largely out of step with the primatial interpretation of these passages which had itself a long history among papal writers since the fifth, perhaps even the third century. The mainstream of exegesis followed an agenda set by patristic precedent, especially Augustine, but also other Western fathers. In the case of Matt. 16:18-19, the tradition was dominated by the christological interpretation of the 'rock' of the church, nourished by powerful biblical parallels such as 1 Cor. 10:4, Matt. 7:24–25, and 1 Cor. 3:11. For Luke 22:32, the tradition focused on the context of Jesus' passion and Peter's denial, applying the verse in tropological way to the theme of the 'humble prelate.' In the case of John 21:15–17, the traditional interpretation drew on the biblical imagery of flock and shepherds as a metaphor of the *cura pastoralis* in the church and saw in the text a lesson about the qualities of a 'good prelate.'[222]

Yves Congar

Yves Congar, the Roman Catholic historian and theologian, makes these comments:

> Many of the Eastern Fathers who are rightly acknowledged to be the greatest and most representative and are, moreover, so considered by the universal Church, do not offer us any more evidence of the primacy. Their writings show that they recognized the primacy of the Apostle Peter, that they regarded the See of Rome as the *prima sedes* playing a major part in the Catholic communion—we are recalling, for example, the writings of St. John Chrysostom and of St. Basil who addressed himself to Rome in the midst of the difficulties of the schism of Antioch—but they provide us with no theological statement on the universal primacy of Rome by divine right. The same can be said of St. Gregory Nazianzen, St. Gregory of Nyssa, St. Basil, St. John Chrysostom, St. John Damascene.[223]

> It does sometimes happen that some Fathers understood a passage in a way which does not agree with later Church teaching. One example: the interpretation of Peter's confession in Matthew 16:16–19. Except at Rome, this passage was not applied by the Fathers to the papal primacy; they worked out an exegesis at the level of their own ecclesiological thought, more anthropological and spiritual than juridical.[224]

Pierre Batiffol

Batiffol likewise affirms the fact that the Eastern Church, historically, has never embraced the ecclesiology of Roman primacy:

> I believe that the East had a very poor conception of the Roman primacy. The East did not see in it what Rome herself saw and what the West saw in Rome, that is to say, a continuation of the primacy of St. Peter. The bishop of Rome was more than the successor of Peter on his *cathedra,* he was Peter perpetuated, invested with Peter's responsibility and power. The East has never understood this perpetuity. St. Basil ignored it, as did St. Gregory Nazianzen and St. John Chrysostom. In the writings of the great Eastern Fathers, the authority of the Bishop of Rome is an authority of singular grandeur, but in these writings it is not considered so by divine right.[225]

John Meyendorff

John Meyendorff documents the overall Eastern exegesis of Matthew 16 and its view of ecclesiology:

> The reformed papacy of the eleventh century used a long-standing Western tradition of exegesis when it applied systematically and legalistically the passages on the role of Peter (especially Mt. 16:18, Lk. 22:32, and Jn. 21:15-17) to the bishop of Rome. *This tradition was not shared by the East.*[226]
>
> (After) the schism between East and West...Greek scholars and prelates continued the tradition of the Fathers without the slightest alteration...Origen is the common teacher of the Greek fathers in the field of biblical commentary. Origen gives an extensive explanation on Mt. 16:18. He rightly interprets the famous words of Christ as a consequence of the *confession* of Peter on the road of Caesarea Philippi: Simon became the Rock on which the Church is founded, because he expressed the true belief in the divinity of Christ. Thus, according to Origen, all those saved by faith in Jesus Christ receive also the keys of the Kingdom: in other words, the successors of Peter are *all* believers.

'If we also say,' he writes, 'Thou art the Christ, the Son of the living God, then we also become Peter...for whoever assimilates to Christ, becomes the Rock. Does Christ give the keys of the kingdom to Peter alone, whereas other blessed people cannot receive them?'

This same interpretation implicitly prevails in all the patristic texts dealing with Peter: the great Cappadocians, St. John Chrysostom and St. Augustine all concur in affirming that the *faith of Simon* made it possible for him to become the Rock on which the Church is founded and that in a certain sense all those who share the same faith are his successors. This same idea is to be found in later Byzantine writers. 'The Lord gives the keys to Peter,' says Theophanes Kerameus, a preacher of the twelfth century, 'and to all those who resemble him, so that the gates of the Kingdom of heaven remain closed for heretics, yet are easily accessible to the faithful.'

On the other hand, a very clear patristic tradition sees the succession of Peter in the episcopal ministry. The doctrine of St. Cyprian of Carthage on the 'See of Peter' as being present in every local church, and not only in Rome, is well known. It is also found in the East, among people who certainly never read *De unitate ecclesiae* of Cyprian, but who share its main idea, thus witnessing to it as a part of the catholic tradition of the Church...A careful analysis of Byzantine ecclesiastical literature...would certainly show that this tradition is a persistent one, and indeed it belongs to the essence of Orthodox ecclesiology to consider any local bishop to be the teacher of his flock and therefore to fulfil sacramentally, through the apostolic succession, the office of the first true believer, Peter.[227]

Conclusion

From the primary documentation of the writings of the fathers and the comments of Church historians we can summarize the patristic understanding of Peter and the rock from Matthew 16. Generally speaking, the fathers viewed the rock and foundation of the Church as the person of Christ, or Peter's confession of faith which pointed to Christ. Sometimes they speak of Peter as the rock or foundation in the sense that he is the example of true faith—that he exemplified faith. But they do not teach that he is representative of a papal office or that the Church was built upon him in a legalistic sense. They also viewed Peter figuratively as representative of the unity of the entire Church. What Christ spoke to Peter he spoke to the Church as a whole and what was given to Peter was given to all the apostles and through them to the entire Church. The keys are a declarative authority to teach truth, preach the gospel and exercise discipline in the Church.

Though the fathers spoke in very exalted terms about the apostle Peter, their comments were not applied in an exclusive sense to the bishop of Rome, nor did they view the Roman bishops as given universal jurisdiction over the Church. Although they saw the bishops of Rome as successors of Peter, they did not see them as the *exclusive* successors of Peter, nor as the universal rulers of the Church, nor the see of Rome as the only apostolic see. Roman Catholics assume that when a Church father speaks of Peter he is also talking about the bishops of Rome but this is not the case. That is to read a preconceived theology into their writings. The fathers teach that *all* bishops are successors of Peter. In their interpretation of Matthew 16, Luke 22 and John 21 we do not find any affirmation of the teaching of Vatican I on papal jurisdiction and infallibility.

This reveals two important points from both a theological and historical perspective. Theologically, there is no evidence of patristic consensus to support the papal interpretation of Matthew 16:18–19 equating the rock with the person of Peter, assigning to him and the Roman bishops the place of preeminence of rule in the Church through the authority of the keys. The fact is, apart from the popes themselves—beginning in the late fourth century—and with those who have an interest in promoting the papacy, the Roman interpretation of Matthew 16:18–19 has historically been universally rejected by the Church in both East and West. As we will see in Chapter two, it is clear from the history of the Church, in the attitudes and actions of the general Councils and with individual fathers in their dealings with the bishops of Rome that in the patristic age, the Church never operated on the basis of a universal Roman primacy or in the belief in papal infallibility.

The documentation from the writings of the church fathers and prominent Roman Catholic, Orthodox and Protetsant historians given in this chapter provides a devastating refutation of the assertions of Roman Catholic apologists and in particular the work *Jesus, Peter and the Keys*. Time and again it has been demonstrated that *Jesus, Peter and the Keys* is a glaring example of purposeful misrepresentation of the church fathers through selective quoting. The authors of this work consistently omit major portions of the writings of the fathers which have direct bearing on their interpretation of the rock of Matthew 16:18 and which completely undermine the Roman Catholic position. In addition, they make no attempt to provide a proper understanding for the interpretation of the words and terms employed by the fathers. They are guilty of reading their own preconceived theology into patristic statements, in utter disregard of the actual meaning of the terms as used by the fathers themselves. This is demonstrated conclusively by the fact that their conclusions and assertions regarding the teaching of the fathers are contradicted by their own Roman Catholic historians. These historians have affirmed the fact that the fathers can speak of Peter as the rock, and use exalted titles of Peter such as the *coryphaeus* and first of the apostles and make reference to the chair of Peter, and interpret these concepts in a way that is completely different from and contradictory to the present day Roman Catholic interpretation. The result is a distortion of historical truth and the promotion of an ecclesiology that is contradictory to that of the Church of the patristic age, all the while falsely claiming its support. *Jesus, Peter and the Keys* is a work that can easily mislead those who have no acquaintance with the facts of history and the writings of the church fathers. But when the true facts are presented with the appropriate scholarly consensus of Roman Catholic, Orthodox and Protestant historians this work can be seen for what it really is—an attempt to promote an agenda through the manipulation of the facts of history. Truth is the enemy of Roman Catholic claims and never so clearly seen as in the case of *Jesus, Peter and the Keys*.

Part Two

The Historical Practice Of The Early Church In Relation To The Bishops Of Rome

Chapter 2

The Practice Of The Early Church

Having demonstrated the claim of Vatican I to a patristic consensus for its exegesis of Matthew 16 to be invalid, we want to turn our attention now to the historical *practice* of the early Church. This is the second leg of the foundation upon which the Roman claims for the papacy rests. Vatican I has stated that its particular teaching on the papacy has been held from the very beginning and throughout the history of the Church. It claims that these assertions can be validated by the universal practice of the Church. In this section we will examine the legitimacy of this teaching by looking at a number of historical situations from the patristic age. We will begin with an examination of the Ecumenical Councils and then of individual Church fathers. The question is this: Do the actions of the Councils and the Church fathers reflect an ecclesiology consistent with the monarchial papal teachings of Vatican I?

The Ecumenical Councils

What was the attitude of the Ecumenical Councils towards the bishops of Rome? If Roman Catholic teaching is correct and has been accepted throughout the history of the Church as orthodox, then the popes should have always exercised supreme authority over the Church and all Church Councils. We should find this historically acknowledged by the Councils both in teaching and proceedings. But the facts reveal quite a different story. The Ecumenical Councils never viewed the position of the bishop of Rome as one of supreme authority over the Church. The Councils, in fact, always operated independently of Rome and with an authority derived, in their view, directly from the Holy Spirit, and not in any sense dependent on Roman approval. Contrary to seeing themselves under the authority of the Roman see, the Councils viewed the popes as subject to the authority of the Council itself, often refusing to submit to him. In the canons passed by these Councils we find that they saw the bishops of Rome as possessing a primacy of honor within the Church but on an equal footing with the other major sees in authority, exercising their authority of jurisdiction within well defined geographical limits. Döllinger makes these points about the relationship of the Councils to the bishops of Rome:

> (1) The Popes took no part in convoking Councils. All Great Councils, to which bishops came from different countries were convoked by the Emperors, nor were the Popes ever consulted about it beforehand.
>
> (2) They were not always allowed to preside, personally or by deputy, at the Great Councils, though no one denied them the first rank in the Church. At Nice, at the two Councils of Ephesus in 431 and 449, and at the Fifth Great Council in 553, others presided; only at Chalcedon in 451, and Constantinople in 680, did the Papal legates preside. And it is clear that the Popes did not claim this as their exclusive right.
>
> (3) Neither the dogmatic nor the disciplinary decisions of these Councils required Papal confirmation, for their force and authority depended on the consent of the Church, as expressed in the Synod, and afterwards in the fact of its being generally received. The confirmation of the Nicene Council by Pope Silvester was afterwards invented at Rome, because facts would not square with the newly devised theory.[228]

These Councils were responsible for passing a number of canons

The Practice of the Early Church 163

which dealt directly with the issue of jurisdiction within the Church and the authority of the Roman See. These would be found in particular in certain canons from Nicaea (325 A.D.), Constantinople (381) and Chalcedon (451). It is apparent from these Councils that Rome was given a primacy of honor in the Church because it was located in the capital city of the empire and had witnessed the martydom of Peter and Paul. But the canons of Constantinople and the 28th canon of Chalcedon elevate Constantinople, as the new capital of the empire, and give it a place of primacy next to Rome. These canons further specify that the sees of the different patriarchates were to hold equal authority within well defined limits. These canons make it clear that the early Church did not view the bishop of Rome as having a right of rule over the entire Church. These canons have provoked much controversy and discussion. But there is a consensus of scholarly opinion as to their meaning and intent. We will look at each of these canons individually to give some historical context in order to properly understand them.

The Council Of Nicaea

Nicaea was convoked by the emperor Constantine in 325 A.D. Canon 6 of this Council demonstrates that the church of Rome had a very limited jurisdiction which was not universal. The canon states:

> The ancient customs of Egypt, Libya and Pentapolis shall be maintained, according to which the bishop of Alexandria has authority over all these places, since a similar custom exists with reference to the bishop of Rome. Similarly in Antioch and the other provinces the prerogatives of the churches are to be preserved. In general the following principle is evident: if anyone is made bishop without the consent of the metropolitan, this great synod determines that such a one shall not be a bishop. If however two or three by reason of personal rivalry dissent from the common vote of all, provided it is reasonable and in accordance with the church's canon, the vote of the majority shall prevail.[229]

George Salmon makes the following observations about this canon:

> If we want to know the true tradition of the early Church, we have no better evidence than the general councils...(Note) the celebrated Nicene canon: 'Let the ancient customs prevail; with regard to Egypt, Libya, and Pentapolis, that the bishop of Alexandria should have authority over all these, since this is also customary to the bishop in Rome; and likewise in Antioch and the other provinces that the prerogatives of the Churches be preserved; so if any be made bishop without consent of the metropolitan, the council adjudges him to be no bishop.'
>
> It is evident that the council regarded the supremacy of Alexandria as then an old thing; and secondly, that the council treats this supremacy as quite parallel to that exercised elsewhere by the bishops of Rome and Antioch. There could not be a stronger implicit denial of the right of Rome to rule the whole Church, or to enjoy any exclusive privilege, than the use of such an argument as, The bishop of Rome has such and such powers in his neighborhood, therefore the bishop of Alexandria ought to have like in his. At the same time the right of Rome is acknowledged to rule the Churches in the immediate neighborhood.
>
> How far did that right extend? Rufinus, who translated these canons towards the end of the fourth century, says, Rome has the care of the suburbicarian Churches. Commentators differ as to what exactly this means. It is clear, however, that Rome had not patriarchal authority as yet over the whole West, as indeed is proved by the case of Apiarius.[230]

John Meyendorff gives the following summary:

> In the East, the canonical rights of all four patriarchates had been defined with some clarity by the councils. Thus, the highly centralized Alexandrian 'papacy' had been condoned, as a local 'ancient custom' by canon 6 of Nicaea, whereas the rights of Constantinople were clearly described both geographically and

The Practice of the Early Church 165

canonically in canon 28 of Chalcedon, as a right to consecrate metropolitans in the imperial dioceses of Thrace, Pontus and Asia. The canons also implied that Antioch and Jerusalem enjoyed similar rights within defined areas. In the case of Rome, there was only custom and a certain moral prestige, but no conciliar definitions on rights, territory, or jurisdiction. Rome itself never either exercised or claimed to exercise 'patriarchal' rights over the entire West. Such 'patriarchal' jurisdiction of Rome existed *de facto* over the so-called *suburbicarian* dioceses, which covered a relatively large territory—ten provinces—which were within the civil jurisdiction of the prefect of Rome. The power of the pope upon this territory was, in every way, comparable to the jurisdiction of Eastern patriarchs.[231]

James McCue states:

> Nicaea I, which took place during Sylvester's episcopate, is of interest...because of canon 6. It invoked ancient customs in assigning Egypt, Libya, and the Pentapolis to the bishop of Alexandria, affirming the customary jurisdiction of the bishop of Rome, and asserting the traditional authority of the bishop of Antioch and of the provincial metropolitans. The canon does not fix the boundaries of Roman regional power. But the expansion of the canon in Rufinus (345?–410) seems to limit Rome's authority to the suburbicarian sees. This may reflect the actual jurisdictional situation at the end of the fourth century...Nicaea presupposes a regional leadership of Rome, but indicates nothing more. Thus one concludes that down through the Council of Nicaea, a Roman universal primacy of jurisdiction exists neither as a theoretical construction nor as de facto practice awaiting theoretical interpretation.[232]

Peter L'Huillier, Adjunct Professor of Canon Law at St. Vladimir's Seminary, likewise confirms these judgments in these words:

> The object of canon 6 is the official recognition by the council of the

rights of the bishop of Alexandria over several civil provinces...To justify respecting the ancient customs giving the bishop of Alexandria jurisdiction over several provinces, the fathers of Nicea based themselves first and foremost on the example of Rome. Now we know with sufficient certitude that at that time the bishop of the capital exercised the authority of a metropolitan over all the civil territories dependent on the *vicarius urbis*, that is, over central and southern Italy as well as over Sicily, Sardinia and Corsica. Several ancient Latin translations in paraphrase of this canon highlight quite accurately that we are not dealing with a wider zone over which the see of Rome extended its influence and which later would correspond to the patriarchate of the West. In these translations, it is a matter of *loca suburbica*, of the *vicinae provinciae*, and of the *suburbicariae ecclesiae*.[233]

As the consensus of the above historians confirms, according to canon 6 of Nicaea, Rome had a *limited* jurisdiction in the Church. Some Roman apologists state that the original Roman version of canon 6 contained the words: 'Rome has always had the primacy.' This is used as supposed historical evidence for belief in and acceptance of papal primacy in the early Church. However, such an argument completely lacks historical validity. Canon 6 of Nicaea as quoted above is from the official Roman Catholic translation of the canons. This statement—Rome has always held the primacy—is nowhere mentioned. This is because it was never part of the original Nicene canons. At Chalcedon, the papal legates claimed this statement as part of canon 6 of Nicaea but they were repudiated by the Eastern bishops because the statement was not found in the original transcripts of the Council. As Robert Eno states:

> There was also circulating an interpolated western version of the sixth canon of Nicaea which stated flatly that the Roman church had always had the primacy. This had been presented at Chalcedon by the Roman representatives but had been rejected as inauthentic.[234]

Karl Morrison also confirms this in his comments on the proceedings of the Council of Chalcedon:

Every point of Leo's instructions was discarded. Contrary to his express demands, Dioscorus was admitted to the first session of the Council, the faith was discussed, and the order of primatial sees was changed to include Constantinople in the second place, after Rome. The Roman text of the Nicene Canon which, Leo argued, forbade this last measure, began, 'The Roman church has always had the primacy.' When Leo's legates read it, the imperial commissioners could not find that reading among the transcripts of Nicaea and barred it as inauthentic, recalling at the same time the pronouncement of the 'oecumenical' council of 381 in favor of Constantinople.[235]

The Arabic Canons

Another issue raised from time to time that relates to the Nicene canons is that of the so-called Arabic Canons. These are purported to be an Arabic collection of the canons of Nicaea but they do not correspond to the Latin and Greek versions. The Latin and Greek list twenty canons while the Arabic gives eighty. In addition, there are statements in the Arabic version which are very supportive of a papal primacy. Some Roman apologists have suggested that this discrepancy proves that the Latin and Greek canons are incomplete and that the Arabic canons are more reflective of the true extent of the canons as well as the overall ecclesiological mindset of the Eastern church of that day. However such reasoning is fallacious for these canons have proven to be spurious. They are the product of a later age. The *New Catholic Encyclopedia* confirms this when it says, 'Nicaea promulgated 20 disciplinary decrees...In later times certain Syriac and Arabic canons (*pseudonicaeni*) were falsely attributed to the Council.'[236] The true number of Nicene canons is that of the Greek and Latin Church, as listed in the official Roman Catholic translation, *The Ecumenical Councils*. Philip Schaff gives the following historical evidence supporting the number of Nicene canons as twenty in number, thereby repudiating the notion that the Arabic Canons are a legitimate reflection of Nicaea:

> Let us see first what is the testimony of those Greek and Latin authors

who lived about the time of the Council, concerning the number.

A. The first to be consulted among the Greek authors is the learned Theodoret, who lived about a century after the Council of Nicaea. He says in his *History of the Church*: 'After the condemnation of the Arians, the bishops assembled once more, and decreed twenty canons on ecclesiastical discipline.'

B. Twenty years later, Gelasius, Bishop of Cyzicus, after much research into the most ancient documents, wrote a history of the Nicene Council. Gelasius also says expressly that the Council decreed twenty canons; and, what is more important, he gives the original text of these canons exactly in the same order, and according to the tenor which we find elsewhere.

C. Rufinus is more ancient than these two historians. He was born near the period when the Council of Nicaea was held, and about a century after he wrote his celebrated history of the Church, in which he inserted a Latin translation of the Nicene canons. Rufinus also knew only these twenty canons; but as he has divided the sixth and the eighth into two parts, he has given twenty–two canons, which are exactly the same as the twenty furnished by the other historians.

D. The famous discussion between the African bishops and the Bishop of Rome, on the subject of appeals to Rome, give us a very important testimony on the true number of the Nicene canons. The presbyter Apiarius of Sicca in Africa, having been deposed for many crimes, appealed to Rome. Pope Zosimus (417–418) took the appeal into consideration, sent legates to Africa; and to prove that he had the right to act thus, he quoted a canon of the council of Nicaea, containing these words: 'When a bishop thinks he has been unjustly deposed by his colleagues he may appeal to Rome, and the Roman bishop shall have the business decided by the *judices in partibus*.' The canon quoted by the Pope does not belong to the Council of Nicaea, as he affirmed; it was the fifth canon of the Council of Sardica...What explains the error of Zosimus is that in the ancient copies of the canons of Nicaea and Sardica are written consecutively, with the same figures, and under the common title of the canons of the Council Nicaea; and Zosimus might *optima fide* fall into an error—which he shared with Greek authors, his contemporaries, who also mixed the canons of Nicaea with those of Sardica. The African bishops, not finding the

The Practice of the Early Church 169

canon quoted by the Pope either in their Greek or in their Latin copies, in vain consulted also the copy which Bishop Cecilian, who had himself been present at the Council of Nicaea, had brought to Carthage. The legates of the Pope then declared that they did not rely upon these copies, and they agreed to send to Alexandria and to Constantinople to ask the patriarchs of these two cities for authentic copies of the canons of the Council of Nicaea. The African bishops desired in their turn that Pope Boniface should take the same step (Pope Zosimus had died meanwhile in 418)—that he should ask for copies from the Archbishops of Constantinople, Alexandria, and Antioch. Cyril of Alexandria and Atticus of Constantinople, indeed, sent exact and faithful copies of the Creed and canons of Nicaea; and two learned men of Constantinople, Theilo and Thearistus, even translated these canons into Latin. Their translation has been preserved to us in the acts of the sixth Council of Carthage, and it contains only the twenty ordinary canons.

E. All the ancient collections of canons, either in the Latin or Greek, composed in the fourth, or quite certainly at least in the fifth century, agree in giving only these twenty canons to Nicaea. The most ancient of these collections were made in the Greek Church, and in the course of time a very great number of copies of them were written. Many of these copies have descended to us; many libraries possess copies...The Latin collections of the canons of the Councils also give the same result.

F. Among the later Eastern witnesses we may further mention Photius, Zonaras and Balsamon. Photius, in his *Collection of the Canons*, and in his *Namocanon*, as well as the two other writers in their commentaries upon the canons of the ancient Councils, quote only and know only twenty canons of Nicaea, and always those we possess.

G. The Latin canonists of the Middle Ages also acknowledge only these twenty canons of Nicaea. We have proof of this in the celebrated Spanish collection, which is generally but erroneously attributed to St. Isidore...and in that of Adrian (so called because it was offered to Charles the Great by Pope Adrian I). The celebrated Hincmar, Archbishop of Rheims, the first canonist of the ninth century, in his turn attributes only twenty canons of Nicaea, and even the pseudo–Isidore assigns it no more.[237]

The Council of 1 Constantinople

In 381 A.D. at Constantinople the emperors Gratian and Theodosius I convoked what has become known historically as the Council of I Constantinople or the Second Ecumenical Council. In canons 2 and 3 this Council dealt with the issue of authoritative jurisdiction within the Church and elevated the see of Constantinople to a position of primacy second only to Rome. These canons read as follows:

> Diocesan bishops are not to intrude in churches beyond their own boundaries, nor are they to confuse the churches: but in accordance with the canons, the bishop of Alexandria is to administer affairs in Egypt only; the bishops of the East are to manage the East alone (whilst safeguarding the privileges granted to the church of the Antiochenes in the Nicene canons); and the bishops of the Asian diocese are to manage only Asian affairs; and those in Pontus only the affairs of Pontus; and those in Thrace only Thracian affairs. Unless invited bishops are not to go outside their diocese to perform an ordination or any other ecclesiastical business. If the letter of the canon about dioceses is kept, it is clear that the provincial synod will manage affairs in each province, as was decreed at Nicaea. But the churches of God among barbarian peoples must be administered in accordance with the custom in force at the time of the fathers.
>
> Because it is new Rome, the bishop of Constantinople is to enjoy the privileges of honour after the bishop of Rome.[238]...The Bishop of Constantinople shall hold the first rank after the Bishop of Rome, because Constantinople is New Rome.[239]

W.H.C. Frend explains the significance of this canon:

> Between 378 and 398 one senses a major change in the manner in which papal authority was asserted. The pope now spoke as the mouthpiece of the apostle Peter, as *the* Apostolic See, superior to all others and even to church councils. The churches in Gaul and Spain, but not North Africa, were prepared to accept the situation. But as these claims were being made, and perhaps even provoking them, the

The Practice of the Early Church

Second Ecumenical Council in 381 had conferred on Constantinople equal status to Rome 'save in honour,' 'because Constantinople is New Rome.'...Determined that the see of Constantinople should not become the object of outside interference, particularly from Egypt, canon 2 forbade 'bishops outside a diocese to enter on churches beyond their borders,'...Then, almost as an afterthought, in an appendix to canon 2 it was asserted, 'However the Bishop of Constantinople shall have the primacy of honour after the Bishop of Rome, for Constantinople is New Rome' (canon 3). For the government at Constantinople the reasoning was impeccable, Rome was one, whether on the Tiber or the Bosporous, and its bishops were therefore coequal, but Rome as the older city could claim precedence.[240]

Francis Dvornik, the Roman Catholic historian, gives these insightful comments on the historical background of canon 3:

> In the West there was only one see—Rome—that could claim apostolic foundation...The see of Rome was left as the only city of the West that could boast apostolic origin: it had been founded by the first of the Apostles, Peter. But the question of the apostolic character of a see was viewed in quite different fashion in the East. There had been many important sees in the East which had been founded by an Apostle: this was the case for Jerusalem, Antioch, Alexandria and Ephesus. Apart from these great sees, there was a large number of less important ones in Asia Minor and in Greece which, according to both authentic and apocryphal writings, had at least been visited by an Apostle. For this reason the principle of apostolic origin never took very deep root in the ecclesiastical organization of the East and the principle of accomodation to the political divisions of the Empire remained always preponderant. It is in this light that we must examine Canon III of the Council of Constantinople, in 381, which gave the Bishop of Constantinople the second rank in the ecclesiastical hierarchy. For the Orientals this promotion was altogether natural granted the change that had taken place in the political organization of the Empire. The new capital of the Empire, the residence of the Emperor, could not remain

subordinate to the metropolitan of the diocese of Thrace, Heracleia. When Constantinople became the New Rome, it acquired the right of occupying a place immediately after Rome, the ancient capital of the Empire.[241]

George Salmon states:

> One of the Constantinopolitan canons forbids the bishops at the head of the great ecclesiastical divisions to meddle out of their own provinces, or to throw the Churches into confusion; but that according to the canons the bishop of Alexandria should alone administer the affairs of Egypt, the bishops of the East those of the East, and so on...What the council would be willing to grant to the bishop of Rome appears from what they granted to the bishop of Constantinople. They did not give him any right to meddle out of his own province, but they said that he should have precedency *of honour*...next after the bishop of Rome, 'because this city was new Rome.'[242]

Meyendorff observes:

> In the first years of his reign, emperor Theodosius I (379–395) presided over the liquidation of Arianism at the general council of the East—eventually to be recognized as the 'second ecumenical' council—in Constantinople (381). Canon 3 of that council gave the bishop of Constantinople 'an honorary seniority...after the bishop of Rome, because that city is the New Rome.' The text could easily be interpreted as implying that the primacy of 'old' Rome had become obsolete after the transfer of the imperial capital to Constantinople...The ancient tradition...recognized the bishop of Rome as the 'first bishop,' or 'primate' of the universal episcopate. However, the council of Constantinople, by attributing the second rank to the bishop of the new imperial capital could also be understood as implying that the pope had been honored for no other reason than the political position of 'older' Rome. This interpretation of canon 3 will be formally endorsed in 451 by the council of Chalcedon.[243]

The Practice of the Early Church 173

An additional significant fact about I Constantinople is that Meletius presided over the council while he was out of communion with Rome. This proves that communion with Rome was not a necessary prerequisite for being part of the communion of the Church as a whole. As Arthur Piepkorn affirms:

> The Meletian schism from 362 to 391 is a special and complex case...There is at least no explicit evidence that Meletius (died 381) was reconciled to the Roman see before his death. But Meletius presided over the Council of Constantinople in 381. Although it was convoked as an all–Eastern regional assembly without any Western bishops present, the bishops of Rome from the sixth century on recognized it as ecumenical. In the view of some, however, the primacy of the bishop of Rome is called into question if it is possible to preside over a Council like Constantinople I and not be in fellowship with the Roman see. It cannot be shown that this situation meant then what it would mean to Roman Catholics today.[244]

The Council of Chalcedon

It is clear from I Constantinople that the early councils granted *primacy* to certain cities due to their political importance within the empire. This is what Dvornik has called the principle of accomodation. This becomes even more evident from the 28th canon of Chalcedon in 451 A.D. This canon reads as follows:

> Following in every way the decrees of the holy fathers and recognising the canon which has recently been read out—the canon of the 150 most devout bishops who assembled in the time of the great Theodosius of pious memory, then emperor, in imperial Constantinople, new Rome—we issue the same decree and resolution concerning the prerogatives of the most holy church of the same Constantinople, new Rome. The fathers rightly accorded prerogatives to the see of older Rome, since that is an imperial city; and moved by the same purpose the 150 most devout bishops apportioned equal prerogatives to the most holy see of new Rome, reasonably judging that the city which is honoured by the imperial power and senate and

enjoying privileges equalling older imperial Rome, should also be elevated to her level in ecclesiastical affairs and take second place after her.[245]

This canon states that the see of Rome had been granted a certain primacy in the Church because it was located in the capital of the empire. Therefore, based upon this principle, the fathers at Chalcedon, in passing canon 28, reaffirmed canon 3 of 1 Constantinople granting Constantinople the second place of primacy next to Rome because Constantinople was new Rome. This reveals that the fathers of the early Church viewed the Roman primacy as primarily political in nature, not based on a Petrine succession. The following historians give the background and importance of Chalcedon and the significance of its 28th canon:

John Meyendorff says:

> The text makes two major points. First—reflecting the desire of the government of emperor Marcian and his wife Pulcheria to associate Rome and Constantinople, as the two 'imperial' centers of the Church against the pretensions of Alexandria—the text confirms the decision of 381 to give ecclesiastical 'New Rome' the second place of honor after the 'Old Rome.' It then goes further than the council of 381, by explicitly interpreting the primacy of both Romes in purely empirical or political terms, as determined by 'the presence of the emperor and the Senate.' The second point consists in formally establishing a 'patriarchate' of Constantinople (whose position, so far, had been purely honorary), and giving its bishop the right to consecrate the metropolitans in three imperial dioceses: Thrace, Pontus and Asia. The second point was of a purely practical and administrative nature, but the first consisted in a formal denial of the very basis of Leo's ecclesiology: the primacy of Rome was of a political nature, established 'by the Fathers,' and not a divine institution, or 'chair of Peter.'...The canon endorsed the principle of a purely political rationale for the existence of primacies: the older Rome itself, it proclaimed, was granted privileges 'by the fathers' because it was the imperial capital, not because it was founded by St. Peter. Logically,

The Practice of the Early Church

therefore, the new capital, although it had no 'apostolic' foundation, was entitled to the same status.[246]

W.H.C. Frend states:

> One hundred eighty-three of these assembled bishops signed the canon, but the Roman legates left in indignation. It was not, however, an unreasonable decision. The de facto seniority of Constantinople among the Eastern bishoprics had long been acknowledged...Moreover, in less than guarded moments the papal delegation had acknowledged Constantinople's precedence over the other Eastern patriarchs. The council also had settled other issues of ecclesiastical order. The boundaries of Antioch and Jerusalem had been established. Why, therefore, should not the vastly more important issue of authority of the see of Constantinople be decided? Henceforth, Christendom was to be divided into five patriarchates, whose bishops were supreme within the boundaries of their jurisdiction, and on whose harmony the peace of the church would rest. Rome's opposition to granting Constantinople the status agreed to at the Second Ecumenical Council in 381 served notice that harmony would be difficult to achieve.[247]

Karl Morrison emphasizes the following points regarding the validity of the council of Chalcedon and Leo's rejection of its 28th canon:

> The opposition to a canon of the very Council which he set on a level with Nicaea indicates the crux of Leo's thought on tradition, the dimensions of his conservatism and his revisionism. The decree to which he objected conformed entirely with his views on appropriate change in the administrative order of the Church. Since it was framed by an oecumenical council that had been summoned by imperial edict and papal assent, it expressed the consensus of the Fathers, the ratification of the universal Church, as much as did the approval of Leo's *Tome*. The criteria of episcopal agreement, conciliar approval, and universality urged its legitimacy. Against it, Leo advanced only the sixth canon of Nicaea in a sense which the East had steadfastly

repudiated for at least a century, and the warning that nothing could be firm apart from the rock of St. Peter.[248]

As Dvornik pointed out in the comments above on canon 3 of I Constantinople, the Petrine claims set forth by the bishops of Rome were of little significance to the East for, in their thinking, this was not the exclusive possession of the bishops of Rome. The East was home to numerous sees that could claim apostolic foundations of a Petrine character more ancient than Rome, most notably Antioch and Jerusalem. These facts are further confirmed by John Meyendorff:

> Three Churches are mentioned in Canon 6 (Nicaea) as enjoying *presbeia*: Rome, Alexandria, Antioch...Through what particular merit did these three cities acquire the authority which was now confirmed? Was it because of their apostolicity? This did not seem to be the case, at least as far as Alexandria was concerned. The tradition according to which the Church was established there by St. Mark would have been, by itself, insufficient for the Church of Alexandria to claim privileges similar to those of Rome: a very large number of Eastern Churches could claim a much more impressive apostolic foundation accredited by New Testament writings. In particular, this was the case for Antioch which was content with third place, after Rome and Alexandria. Moreover—and this has been pointed out several times by historians—a Church's apostolic origin was a far too common factor in the East to have had the importance it acquired in the West where the Roman See was the only apostolic see and the main center from which evangelization spread.[249]
>
> When the Council of Nicaea, in its famous Canon 6, vaguely mentioned the 'ancient customs' which recognized an exceptional prestige to the churches of Alexandria, Antioch, and Rome, the selection of these particular churches was determined not by their apostolic foundation, but by the fact that they were located in the most important cities of the empire. For if apostolicity were the criterion, as later Western interpretations insist, the position of Alexandria, purported to have been founded by a minor apostolic figure, Mark, could not be greater than Antioch's, where Peter's presence is attested by the New Testament.[250]

The Practice of the Early Church 177

The papal legates strenuously objected to the passage of canon 28 and Leo, the bishop of Rome, refused to accept it. However, the Council refused to acquiesce to papal demands and received the canon as valid, overriding the papal objections. As Meyendorff states:

> The commissioners bluntly declared the issue closed—'All was confirmed by the council,' they said—explicitly denying any papal right of veto.[251]

W.H.C. Frend comments:

> By Canon 28 not only were the decisions in favor of Constantinople as New Rome ratified, but its patriarchal jurisdiction extended into Thrace on the one hand, and Asia and Pontus in Asia Minor on the other. The legates were not deceived by the primacy of honor accorded to Rome. They protested loud and long. The Council, however, had decided, and the decision of the Council was superior to the wishes even of the Bishop of Rome.[252]

Even though Leo rejected this canon—and the Eastern bishops eagerly sought his approval— his nonacceptance did not affect the validity of the canon. As Robert Eno observes:

> The easterners seemed to attach a great deal of importance to obtaining Leo's approval of the canon, given the flattering terms in which they sought it. Even though they failed to obtain it, they regarded it as valid and canonical anyway.[253]

From a jurisdictional standpoint it is clear that Nicaea, I Constantinople and Chalcedon do not support the teaching of Vatican I on papal primacy. After pointing out that Chalcedon refused to submit to the demands of the Bishop of Rome, Frend sums up the historical reality of the ecclesiology of the patristic age with these observations:

> So ended Chalcedon. The Church was still the Church of the great patriarchates, maintaining an equilibrium in respect of each other,

whose differences could be solved, not by the edict of one against the other but by a council inspired and directed if no longer presided over by the Emperor. It was a system of Church government opposed to that of the papacy, but one which like its rival has stood the test of time.[254]

The fact that the Council fathers at Chalcedon received canon 28 as valid in direct opposition to papal demands demonstrates conclusively that papal primacy was not an historical reality at that time. Some have asserted, however, that because the Eastern bishops sought Leo's confirmation of the canon, this proves that they implicitly acknowledged the primacy of the Bishop of Rome. Herbert Scott, for example, states:

> Impartial examination of this celebrated XXVIIIth Canon of Chalcedon and its circumstances...shows that instead of depreciating papal claims it supports them...The Headship of Rome is shown and confessed in the very act of the bishops of this fragment of a council trying to obtain Leo's confirmation of their canon.[255]

While it is true that the Eastern bishops sought Leo's confirmation of canon 28, it is not true to assume their belief in papal primacy. This is demonstrated from a very simple historical reality: The bishops did not submit to papal demands. They sought Leo's confirmation, even using strongly primatial language in their appeals to him, but in the end they received the canon as valid despite his continuing opposition. The early Church greatly valued unity and sought it whenever possible. This was the desire of the bishops of Chalcedon in trying to obtain a unanimous decision regarding canon 28. However, the lack of confirmation by the Bishop of Rome did not prevent this canon from becoming ratified and received into the canon law of the Eastern Church and eventually that of the West as well. From a jurisdictional standpoint, therefore, it is clear that neither Nicaea, I Constantinople nor Chalcedon support the teaching of Vatican I on papal primacy.

It is sometimes claimed that Leo's role as theologian in the Christological controversy dealt with at Chalcedon proves that the Roman bishops were the ultimate standard of orthodoxy in the early Church and had the final say in theological disputes. However facts do not support this contention. Historically the popes, with the exception of Leo, were relatively uninvolved in the theological controversies of the early Church. Most of the theological controversies were settled by Eastern bishops. However, with Leo we find an exception. Leo wrote his *Tome*, his theological defense of the Trinity and the nature of Christ, which he presented to the Council of Chalcedon. In his mind it was a final and sufficient standard of orthodoxy to settle the issue before the council. He requested that it be received without debate. The Eastern bishops gave great praise to Leo's *Tome*, but they did not receive it uncritically. They were only willing to receive it when they were convinced that Leo's views were consistent with those of Cyril, the bishop of Alexandria. Leo's teaching was subjected to the standard of this Eastern bishop and theologian. Robert Eno makes the following observation:

> In the christological controversies of the fifth century...most of the theological discussion was carried on in the East, but in later stages Roman intervention was significant....The Roman outlook of Celestine and Leo implied very strongly that as far as they were concerned their decisions were the significant ones. The councils agreed with Rome. The Eastern view seemed to be rather that the conciliar decisions were the significant ones, and the Eastern bishops were pleased that the popes agreed with the councils. In general the Roman contribution to the theological elaboration of these doctrines was meager. Even the Tome of Leo was a summation of the relatively unsophisticated Western christological development rather than a 'doctrinal definition.' Looked at from the level of the universal church, it would be difficult to maintain that a Roman decision was the sole decisive factor in any theological dispute of the patristic age.[256]

Meyendorff amplifies these thoughts with these observations:

Leo did not participate personally in the council, but his legates at Chalcedon carried with them another remarkable letter addressed to the assembled fathers and expressing the pope's wish that 'the rights and honor of the most blessed apostle Peter be preserved'; that, not being able to come himself, the pope be allowed 'to preside'...at the council in the persons of his legates; and that no debate about the faith be actually held, since 'the orthodox and pure confession on the mystery of the Incarnation has been already manifested, in the fullest and clearest way, in his letter to bishop Flavian of blessed memory.' No wonder that his legates were not allowed to read this unrealistic and embarrassing letter before the end of the sixteenth session, at a time when acrimonious debates on the issue had already taken place! Obviously, no one in the East considered that a papal *fiat* was sufficient to have an issue closed. Furthermore, the debate showed clearly that the *Tome* of Leo to Flavian was accepted *on merits*, and not because it was issued by the pope. Upon the presentation of the text, in Greek translation, during the second session, part of the assembly greeted the reading with approval ('Peter has spoken through Leo!' they shouted), but the bishops from the Illyricum and Palestine fiercely objected against passages which they considered as incompatible with the teachings of St Cyril of Alexandria. It took several days of commission work, under the presidency of Anatolius of Constantinople, to convince them that Leo was not opposing Cyril. The episode clearly shows that it was Cyril, not Leo, who was considered at Chalcedon as the ultimate criterion of christological orthodoxy. Leo's views were under suspicion of Nestorianism as late as the fifth session, when the same Illyrians, still rejecting those who departed from Cyrillian terminology, shouted: 'The opponents are Nestorians, let them go to Rome!' The final formula approved by the council was anything but a simple acceptance of Leo's text. It was a compromise, which could be imposed on the Fathers when they were convinced that Leo and Cyril expressed the same truth, only using different expressions.[257]

Georg Kretschmar states it succinctly: 'The kind of questions that were asked in the trinitarian and christological controversies were determined wholly by Greek theology, and even the Latin formulas

The Practice of the Early Church 181

that were accepted at Nicaea and Chalcedon had first to undergo interpretation by Greek theologians.'[258] W.J. Sparrow–Simpson likewise affirms the fact that the history of Chalcedon proves that the early Church held to a view of Church government which was antithetical to that formulated by the Roman Bishops and Vatican I:

> What was the true relation of the Pope and the Council to each other? How was it understood in primitive times? Did the Collective Episcopate regard itself as subordinated, with no independent judgment of its own, to decisions of the Roman authority? Or was the Council conscious of possessing power to accept or refuse the papal utterances brought before it? Bossuet maintained that the treatment of Papal Letters by the early General Councils afforded convincing proof against their belief in any theory of papal in errancy. The famous letter of Leo to Flavia was laid before the Council of Chalcedon in the following terms: 'Let the Bishops say whether the teaching of the 318 Fathers (the Council of Nice) or that of the 150 (Constantinople) agrees with the letter of Leo.' Nor was Leo's letter accepted until its agreement with the standards of the former Ecumenical Councils had been ascertained. The very signatures of the subscribing Bishops bears this out—'The letter of Leo agrees,' says one, 'with the Creed of the 318 Fathers and of the 150 Fathers, and with the decisions at Ephesus under St Cyril. Wherefore I assent and willingly subscribe.' Thus the act of the Episcopate at Chalcedon was one of critical investigation and authoritative judgment, not of blind submission to an infallible voice.[259]

II Constantinople (The Fifth Ecumenical Council)

In 553 A.D. the emperor Justinian convened the Fifth Ecumenical Council at Constantinople without the assent of the pope. One of the chief objectives of the Council was to examine the orthodoxy of what has become known as the 'Three Chapters.' This refers to certain writings of Theodore of Mopsuestia, Theodoret of Cyrrhus, and Ibas of Edessa. Previous to the general Council Pope Vigilius had issued an official papal decree, known as the *Judicatum,* in which he opposed and anathematized these men and their writings. But the history of his involvement in the controversy, as well as the final outcome of the judgment of the Council reveal once again that history proves fatal to the dogma of papal primacy and infallibility. While the Council was in session, Vigilius reversed his first decree, and issued another entitled the *Constitutum,* in which he refused to condemn the authors of the Three Chapters, as he had previously done, stating that the letter of Ibas contained nothing worthy of condemnation. He then stated that the men themselves should not be condemned but left to the judgment of God since they were already dead and he decreed that the Council should drop the whole question of the Three Chapters. Hefele records the actual decrees of Vigilius:

> The *Constitutum* finally closes with the words: 'We ordain and decree that it be permitted to no one who stands in ecclesiastical order or office, to write or bring forward, or undertake, or teach anything contradictory to the contents of this *Constitutum* in regard to the three chapters, or, after this declaration, begin a new controversy about them. And if anything has already been done or spoken in regard of the three chapters in contradiction to this our ordinance, by any one whomsoever, this we declare void by the authority of the apostolic see.'[260]

The Council, however, far from acknowledging the supreme authority of the bishop of Rome, refused to submit to his decrees and 'infallible' judgment and condemned the Three Chapters. It anathematized the authors and any who refused to condemn them or who defended the writings of Ibas—which is a direct reference to Vigilius, though it does not mention him by name. This is precisely what he had done in his *Constitutum,* and so the Council is, in effect, anathematizing Vigilius and his papal decrees and theological judgments.

This is an amazing course of events given the persistent claims of Rome that the Church as a whole has always recognized papal infallibility and authority over Councils. The pope is not recognized here as infallible by the Council. It anathematized him. The Council did not submit to the papal decrees but on its own authority condemned what the pope had specifically sanctioned on issues directly related to doctrine. Since both the Ecumenical Councils and the pope are considered infallible in Roman Catholic theology there is a very real problem here. It becomes even bigger when, after the judgment of the ecumenical Council, Vigilius completely reversed himself again by submitting to the decrees of the Council, thereby repudiating his former declarations in his *Constitutum*, which itself had been a reversal of his decrees in his *Judicatum*. Here is irrefutable historical evidence of a pope officially contradicting himself on matters directly related to issues of doctrine. This new edict was issued in 554 A.D. and is known as the second *Constitutum*. Hefele gives the following description of Vigilius' actions after the Council had condemned the Three Chapters:

> That Pope Vigilius had given his assent to the fifth Synod sometime after its close, has long been known from Evagrius and Photius, and from the Acts of the sixth Ecumenical Synod, eighteenth session...More than seven months had passed since the end of the Synod when Vigilius arrived at his new resolve. Here he says: 'The enemy of the human race, who sows discord everywhere, had separated him from his colleagues, the bishops assembled in Constantinople. But Christ had removed the darkness again from his spirit, and had again united the Church of the whole world...There was no shame in confessing and recalling a previous error; this had been done by Augustine in his *Retractations*. He, too, following this and other examples, had never ceased to institute further inquiries on the matter of the three chapters in the writings of the Fathers. Thus he had found that Theodore of Mopsuestia had taught error, and therefore had been opposed in the writings of the Fathers...The whole Church must now know that he rightly ordained the following: We condemn and anathematise...Theodore, formerly bishop of Mopsuestia, and his impious writings; also that which Theodoret impiously wrote against the right faith.

Finally, we subject to the same anathema all who believe that the Three Chapters referred to could at any time be approved or defended, or who venture to oppose the present anathema...Whatever we ourselves or others have done in defence of the Three Chapters we declare invalid.'[261]

Thus, Pope Vigilius twice revokes his previous 'infallible' decrees and ultimately fully submits himself to the authority and judgment of the Council which had opposed him. The fact that he appealed to Augustine's *Retractations* is interesting. It seems to lend the weight of the authority of this eminent Church Father to his position. But it is one thing for Augustine, who was not infallible to write retractions, and quite another for a supposedly 'infallible' pope to do so. It would appear that though later Roman Catholic theology would promote the dogma of infallibility, it was not even believed by the popes of themselves, at least not by Vigilius, and obviously not by the Councils.

III Constantinople (The Sixth Ecumenical Council)

Pope Honorius reigned as bishop of Rome from 625 to 638 A.D. In a number of letters written to Sergius I, patriarch of Constantinople, and several other individuals, Honorius officially embraced the heresy of montheletism, which teaches that Christ had only one will, the divine. The orthodox position is that Christ, though one person, possesses two wills because he is divine and human. There is absolutely no doubt that he held to the teaching of one will in Christ. Jaroslav Pelikan makes these comments:

> In the controversy between East and West...the case of Honorius served as proof to Photius that the popes not only lacked authority over church councils, but were fallible in matters of dogma; for Honorius had embraced the heresy of the Monotheletes. The proponents of that heresy likewise cited the case of Honorius, not in opposition to the authority of the pope but in support of their own doctrine, urging that all teachers of the true faith had confessed it, including Sergius, the bishop of New Rome, and Honorius, the bishop of Old Rome.[262]

The Practice of the Early Church 185

There are many past and present Roman apologists who downplay the importance of Pope Honorius. It is typical in Roman Catholic writings to find the issue of Honorius dealt with in a very superficial way. For example the following comments by Karl Keating are representative:

> Actually, Honorius elected to teach nothing at all. Ronald Knox, in a letter to Arnold Lunn reprinted in their book *Difficulties*, put the matter like this: 'And Honorius, so far from pronouncing an infallible opinion in the Monothelite controversy, was "quite extraordinarily not" (as Gore used to say) pronouncing a decision at all. To the best of his human wisdom, he thought the controversy ought to be left unsettled, for the greater peace of the Church. In fact, he was an opportunist. We, wise after the event, say that he was wrong. But nobody, I think, has ever claimed that the Pope is infallible in *not* defining a doctrine.[263]

In one paragraph Keating dismisses this whole issue as trivial and Protestant objections as nothing more than misrepresentation of the true facts. But one thing Mr. Keating does not do is to give the judgment of the Council itself in its own words. He simply states that Honorius did not teach anything and is therefore not guilty of heresy. Is this how the Council understood the situation? Absolutely not! To allow the Council to speak for itself is enough to dispel Keating's and Knox's assertions. The facts speak for themselves. Honorius was personally condemned as a heretic by the Sixth Ecumenical Council. This was ratified by two succeeding Ecumenical Councils. He was also condemned by name by Pope Leo II, and by every pope up through the eleventh century who took the oath of papal office. In his classic and authoritative series on the history of the Councils, Hefele affirms this verdict in relating the following irrefutable facts regarding Honorius and the Sixth Ecumenical Council:

> It is in the highest degree startling, even scarcely credible, that an Ecumenical Council should punish with anathema a *Pope* as a

heretic!...That, however, the sixth Ecumenical Synod actually condemned Honorius on account of heresy, is clear beyond all doubt, when we consider the following collection of the sentences of the Synod against him.

1) At the entrance of the thirteenth session, on March 28, 681, the Synod says: 'After reading the doctrinal letter of Sergius of Constantinople to Cyrus of Phasis (afterwards of Alexandria) and to Pope Honorius, and also the letter of the latter to Sergius, we found that these documents were quite foreign...to the apostolic doctrines, and to the declarations of the holy Councils and all the Fathers of note, and follow the false doctrines of heretics. Therefore we reject them completely, and abhor...them as hurtful to the soul. But also the names of these men must be thrust out of the Church, namely, that of Sergius, the first who wrote on this impious doctrine. Further, that of Cyrus of Alexandria, of Pyrrhus, Paul, and Peter of Constantinople, and of Theodore of Pharan, all of whom also Pope Agatho rejected in his letter to the Emperor. We punish them all with anathema. But along with them, it is our universal decision that there shall also be shut out from the Church and anathematized the former Pope Honorius of Old Rome, because we found in his letter to Sergius, that in everything he followed his view and confirmed his impious doctrine.'

2) Towards the end of the same session the second letter of Pope Honorius to Sergius was presented for examination, and it was ordered that all the documents brought by George, the keeper of the archives in Constantinople, and among them the two letters of Honorius, should immediately be burnt, as hurtful to the soul.

3) Again, the sixth Ecumenical Council referred to Honorius in the sixteenth session, on August 9, 681, at the acclamations and exclamations with which the transactions of this day were closed. The bishops exclaimed: 'Anathema to the heretic Sergius, to the heretic Cyrus, to the heretic Honorius, to the heretic Pyrrhus...'

4) Still more important is that which took place at the eighteenth and last session, on September 16, 681. In the decree of the faith which was now published, and forms the principal document of the Synod, we read: 'The creeds (of the earlier Ecumenical Synods) would have sufficed for knowledge and confirmation of the orthodox faith.

The Practice of the Early Church 187

Because, however, the originator of all evil still always finds a helping serpent, by which he may diffuse his poison, and therewith finds fit tools for his will, we mean Theodore of Pharan, Sergius, Pyrrhus, Paul, Peter, former bishops of Constantinople, also Honorius, Pope of Old Rome, Cyrus of Alexandria, etc., so he failed not, by them, to cause trouble in the Church by the scattering of the heretical doctrine of one will and one energy of the two natures of the one Christ.'

5) After the papal legates, all the bishops, and the Emperor had received and subscribed this decree of the faith, the Synod published the usual (*logos prosphoneticos*), which, addressed to the Emperor, says, among other things: 'Therefore we punish with exclusion and anathema, Theodore of Pharan, Sergius, Paul, Pyrrhus, and Peter; also Cyrus, and with them Honorius, formerly bishop of Rome, as he followed them.'

6) In the same session the Synod also put forth a letter to Pope Agatho, and says therein: 'We have destroyed the effort of the heretics, and slain them with anathema, in accordance with the sentence spoken before in your holy letter, namely, Theodore of Pharan, Sergius, Honorius, Cyrus,' etc.

7) In closest connection with the Acts of the sixth Ecumenical Council stands the imperial decree confirming their resolutions. The Emperor writes: 'With this sickness (as it came out from Apollinaris, Eutyches, Themistius, etc.) did those unholy priests afterwards again infect the Church, who before our times falsely governed several churches. These are Theodore of Pharan, Sergius the former bishop of this chief city; also Honorius, the Pope of old Rome...the strengthener (confirmer) of the heresy who contradicted himself...We anathematise all heresy from Simon (Magus) to this present...besides, we anathematise and reject *the originators and patrons of the false and new doctrines*, namely, Theodore of Pharan, Sergius...also Honorius, who was Pope of Old Rome, who in everything agreed with them, went with them, and *strengthened the heresy*.'

It is clear that Pope Leo II also anathematized Honorius...in a letter to the Emperor, confirming the decrees of the sixth Ecumenical Council...in his letter to the Spanish bishops...and in his letter to the Spanish King Ervig.

Of the fact that Pope Honorius had been anathematized by the sixth Ecumenical Synod, mention is made by...the Trullan Synod, which was held only twelve years after...like testimony is also given repeatedly by the seventh Ecumenical Synod; especially does it declare, in its principal document, the decree of the faith: 'We declare at once two wills and energies according to the natures in Christ, just as the sixth Synod in Constantinople taught, condemning...Sergius, Honorius, Cyrus, etc.' The like is asserted by the Synod or its members in several other places...To the same effect the eighth Ecumenical Synod expresses itself.

In the *Liber Diurnus*, i.e. the Formulary of the Roman Chancery (from the fifth to the eleventh century), there is found the old formula for the papal oath...according to which every new Pope, on entering upon his office, had to swear that 'he recognised the sixth Ecumenical Council, which smote with eternal anathema the originators of the heresy (Monotheletism), Sergius, Pyrrhus, etc., together with Honorius.'[264]

The significance of these facts cannot be overstated. An Ecumenical Council, considered infallible by the Roman Catholic Church, and pope Leo II, who is also supposedly infallible, condemned and anathematized an 'infallible' pope for heresy. In light of the historical evidence the theory of papal infallibility as propounded by Vatican I is bankrupt. It is simply not true. Döllinger comments:

> This one fact—that a Great Council, universally received afterwards without hesitation throughout the Church, and presided over by Papal legates, pronounced the dogmatic decision of a Pope heretical, and anathematized him by name as a heretic—is a proof, clear as the sun at noonday, that the notion of any peculiar enlightenment or inerrancy of the Popes was then utterly unknown to the whole Church.[265]

Roman Catholic apologists generally attempt to salvage the dogma of papal infallibility from the case with Honorius by saying that he was not giving an *ex cathedra* statement but merely his opinion as a private theologian. Therefore he was not condemned in his official capacity as the pope. According to the Roman Catholic Church there are certain conditions which must be met for the teaching of the pope to fall within the overall guidelines of that which is considered to be *ex cathedra*. He must be teaching in his official capacity as the pope and he must be defining doctrine for the entire Church. The claim is made that Honorius did not meet these conditions. However, a careful reading of the official acts of the Council prove that it thought otherwise. The reader can judge for himself from the Council's own statements how the situation with Honorius was viewed and whether it would have agreed with the assertions of Keating and Knox that Honorius did not actively teach anything. The Council makes the following statements:

> Session XIII: The holy council said: After we had reconsidered, according to the promise which we had made to your highness, *the doctrinal letters of Sergius*, at one time patriarch of this royal God–protected city to Cyrus, who was then bishop of Phasius and *to Honorius some time Pope of Old Rome, as well as the letter of the latter to the same Sergius, we find that these documents are quite foreign to the apostolic dogmas, to the declarations of the holy Councils, and to all the accepted Fathers, and that they follow the false teachings of the heretics; therefore we entirely reject them, and execrate them as hurtful to the soul. But the names of those men whose doctrines we execrate must also be thrust forth from the holy Church of God, namely, that of Sergius* some time bishop of this God-preserved royal city who was the first to write on this impious doctrine; also that of *Cyrus of Alexandria, of Pyrrhus, Paul, and Peter,* who died bishops of this God–preserved city, and were like–minded with them; and that of *Theodore sometime bishop of Pharan*, all of whom the most holy and thrice blessed Agatho, Pope of Old Rome, in his suggestion to our most pious and God–preserved lord and mighty Emperor, rejected, because they were minded contrary to our orthodox faith, *all of whom we define are to be subject to anathema. And with these we define that there shall be expelled from the holy Church of God and anathematized Honorius who was some time Pope of Old Rome, because of what we found*

written by him to Sergius, that in all respects he followed his view and confirmed his impious doctrines.

Session XVI: To Theodore of Pharan, the heretic, anathema! To Sergius, the heretic, anathema! To Cyrus, the heretic, anathema! *To Honorius, the heretic, anathema!* To Pyrrhus, the heretic, anathema! To Paul, the heretic, anathema!...

Session XVIII: But *as the author of evil*, who, in the beginning, availed himself of the aid of the serpent, and by it brought the poison of death upon the human race, has not desisted, but in like manner now, *having found suitable instruments* for working out his will (*we mean* Theodorus, who was bishop of Pharan, Sergius, Pyrrhus...and moreover, *Honorius, who was Pope of the elder Rome...), has actively employed them in raising up for the whole Church* the stumbling blocks of one will and one operation in the two natures of Christ our true God, one of the Holy Trinity; *thus disseminating, in novel terms, amongst the orthodox people, an heresy similar to the mad and wicked doctrine of the impious Apollinaris.*[266]

The above statements prove that the condemnation of Honorius meets the basic criterion for *ex cathedra* statements. The following points show this to be the case:

- The Council condemns him specifically as a heretic and anathematized him in his official capacity as pope and not as a private theologian.

- He is condemned for following after and confirming the heresy of montheletism.

- He is condemned for actively disseminating and propagating heretical teachings in his official capacity as pope which affected the whole Church.

To suggest that the Sixth Ecumenical Council does not invalidate the teaching of papal infallibility because Honorius did not make an *ex cathedra* statement is historically absurd. This is to erect arbitrary

The Practice of the Early Church 191

conditions which were not existent at the time to save oneself the embarrassment of a historical fact which undermines one's position. The issue is not what does Karl Keating or Ronald Knox say, but what did the Sixth Ecumenical Council say. On what basis did it condemn Pope Honorius? By its own words it condemned him in his official capacity as the bishop of Rome, not as a private theologian, for advancing heretical teachings which it says were Satanically inspired and would affect the entire Church. It specifically states that Honorius advanced these teachings, approved of them, and in a positive sense was responsible for disseminating them. And it condemns him by name as a heretic, anathematizing him as such. We need to remember that an Ecumenical Council, according to official Roman teaching, is infallible. So an infallible Ecumenical Council has condemned as a heretic a bishop of Rome for teaching heresy. It is quite obvious that these Eastern fathers did not view the bishops of Rome as infallible.

John Meyendorff states that, contrary to the assertions of Keating and Knox, Honorius did in fact teach the doctrine of monotheletism in a positive sense and helped confirm Sergius in the heresy. Meyendorff gives this summary:

> This step into Monotheletism, which he was first to make, is the famous 'fall of Honorius,' for which the Sixth ecumenical council condemned him (681)—a condemnation which, until the early Middle Ages, would be repeated by all popes at their installation, since on such occasions they had to confess the faith of the ecumenical councils. It is understandable, therefore, that all the critics of the doctrine of papal infallibility in later centuries—Protestants, Orthodox and 'anti-infallibilists' at Vatican I in 1870—would refer to this case. Some Roman Catholic apologists try to show that the expressions used by Honorius could be understood in an orthodox way, and that there is no evidence that he deliberately wished to proclaim anything else than the traditional faith of the Church. They also point out—quite anachronistically—that the letter to Sergius was not a formal statement, issued by the pope ex cathedra, using his 'charisma of infallibility,' as if such a concept existed in the seventh century. Without denying the pope's good intentions—which can be

claimed in favor of any heresiarch of history—it is quite obvious that his confession of one will, at a crucial moment and as Sergius himself was somewhat backing out before the objections of Sophronius, not only condoned the mistakes of others, but actually coined a heretical formula—the beginning of a tragedy, from which the Church (including the orthodox successors of Honorius on the papal throne) would suffer greatly.[267]

The condemnation by Pope Leo II is significant. He affirmed the condemnation of Honorius as a heretic, confirming by this that Honorius had actively undermined the orthodox faith. W.J. Sparrow Simpson summarizes Leo's viewpoint in these comments:

> Leo accepted the decisions of Constantinople. He has carefully examined the Acts of the Council and found them in harmony with the declarations of faith of his predecessor, Agatho, and of the Synod of the Lateran. He anathematized all the heretics, including his predecessor, Honorius, 'who so far from aiding the Apostolic See with the doctrine of the Apostolic Tradition, attempted to subvert the faith by a profane betrayal.'[268]

It is significant that the letter of Honorius to Sergius was used in the East by the proponents of the Monothelite heresy as justification for their position. As Sparrow Simpson observes: 'This letter of Honorius was utilised in the East to justify the Monothelite heresy—the existence of one will in Christ.'[269]

The definition of what the Roman Catholic Church refers to as *ex cathedra* teaching was not enunciated and defined until 1870. One needs to keep this in mind when applying this test to the case of Honorius and the judgment of the Sixth Ecumenical Council. In the mind of this 'infallible' Council the pope was a heretic. In their official condemnation of him, he is judged on the basis of the criteria for *ex cathedra* statements which was defined some 1200 years later. One simply cannot avoid the historical facts. An 'infallible' Ecumenical Council has condemned an 'infallible' pope, in his official capacity, for heresy. No redefining of terms can erase the simple facts of history or the implications of those facts for the

The Practice of the Early Church 193

dogma of papal infallibility. This has direct bearing upon the issue of authority and jurisdiction. If an Ecumenical Council can excommunicate a bishop of Rome then the ultimate authority in the Church is not the bishop of Rome but the Council.

It is clear from this brief history of the Councils that the early Church did not view the bishops of Rome as possessing universal jurisdiction or supreme authority over the Church. We can summarize the historical reality in these comments by W.H.C. Frend:

> The Papacy had laid claim sporadically to the primacy of Christendom in earlier centuries, but these claims had either been denied or ignored by those to whom they had been addressed. The same was by and large to be true in the first half of the fifth century...In both East and West the decision of a council rather than the fiat of the Pope was the supreme instance of Church government. Against the Africans led by men like Augustine and Aurelius the popes were powerless. In the East they were confronted by a theory of Church government which had a place for episcopal authority, but none for Roman Primacy. 'Since when do the Orientals accept dictates from the West?' The question addressed to Pope Julius still had its relevance.[270]

This historical reality is further confirmed, as Frend implies, by the practice of individual Church fathers in their relations with the Bishops of Rome.

Individual Fathers

Cyprian and Pope Stephen

Cyprian was one of the most distinguished and important fathers of the patristic age. He was bishop of Carthage in North Africa in the mid–third century and died a martyr around 258 A.D. We have already noted that his exegesis of Matthew 16 is not supportive of a Roman primacy. We see the same opposition to such an ecclesiology in his relations with Stephen, the bishop of Rome. There are two highly significant historical incidents which underscore Cyprian's antipathy to the teachings of Vatican I. The first has to do with a major doctrinal conflict between Cyprian and Stephen over the rebaptizing of converted heretics. The second relates to an issue of discipline which bears directly upon the jurisdictional authority of the bishop of Rome. We will look at each of these in turn.

Heretical Baptism

The conflict regarding heretical baptism was over whether or not it was necessary to rebaptize those who had been baptized by Novationist groups—which baptized in the name of the Trinity—who were then later converted and sought membership in the orthodox Church. Cyprian and many Eastern bishops said yes, while Stephen said no. The controversy escalated to the point where Stephen demanded submission by Cyprian and the others to his point of view on pain of exclusion from communion with Rome upon refusal. Stephen went so far as to denounce Cyprian as a false prophet and deceitful worker. It is evident from Cyprian's correspondence that such a demand by Stephen was made on the basis of his application of Matthew 16 to himself as Peter's successor. In light of this, the response of Cyprian and the Eastern bishops is significant. Did they submit to Stephen?

They did not. In fact, Stephen's demand, his interpretation of scripture, and the ecclesiology which it represented, was unanimously repudiated by these bishops. Their response was a

North African Council in 256 A.D., attended by eighty–six Eastern and Western bishops. All agreed with Cyprian in rejecting not only Stephen's theology and practice on heretical baptism but also his claims to authority. In their opening remarks to the Council the bishops give the following remarks which clearly reflect their understanding of ecclesiology:

> It remains that we severally declare our opinion on this same subject, judging no one, nor depriving any one of his right of communion, if he differ from us. For no one setteth himself up as a Bishop of Bishops, or by tyrannical terror forceth his Colleagues to a necessity of obeying; inasmuch as every Bishop, in the free use of his liberty and power, has the right of forming his own judgment, and can no more be judged by another than he can himself judge another. But we must all await the judgment of our Lord Jesus Christ, Who alone has the power of both setting us in the government of His Church, and of judging of our acts therein.[271]

It is obvious from these comments that these bishops reject the notion that one particular bishop holds a position of authority over other bishops as head of the Church universal. No single bishop can legitimately claim to be 'Bishop of Bishops' as they put it. This is further illustrated by Firmilian, the leading bishop of Cappadocia, who completely supported Cyprian in his opposition to Stephen. In a personal letter to Cyprian he expressed his own personal opposition to Stephen by stating that Stephen had fallen into error and adopted a false ecclesiology by misinterpreting Matthew 16. He gives his point of view in the following words:

> But how great his error, how exceeding his blindness, who says, that remission of sins can be given in the synagogues of heretics, and abideth not on the foundation of the one Church which was once fixed by Christ on a rock, may be hence learnt, that Christ said to Peter alone, Whatsoever thou shalt bind on earth shall be bound in heaven; and whatsoever thou shalt loose on earth shall be loosed in heaven: and again in the Gospel, when Christ breathed on the Apostles only, saying, Receive ye the Holy Ghost: whose soever sins ye remit, they are

remitted unto them; and whose soever sins ye retain, they are retained. The power then of remitting sins was given to the Apostles, and the Churches which they, sent by Christ, established, and to the Bishops who succeeded them by vicarious ordination.

And herein I am justly indignant at such open and manifest folly in Stephen, that he who boasts of the seat of his episcopate, and contends that he holds the succession from Peter, on whom the foundations of the Church were laid, introduces many other *rocks*, and *buildeth* anew many Churches, in that by his authority he maintains baptism among them...Nor does he perceive that he who thus betrays and abandons unity, casts into the shade, and in a manner effaces, the truth of the Christian *Rock*...Stephen, who proclaims that he occupies by succession the chair of Peter, is roused by no zeal against heretics...He who concedes and assigns to heretics such great and heavenly privileges of the Church, what else does he than hold communion with them, for whom he maintains and claims so much grace?...But as to the refutation of the argument from custom, which they seem to oppose to the truth, who so foolish as to prefer custom to truth, or not to leave darkness, when he sees light?...And this you of Africa may say in answer to Stephen, that on discovering the truth you abandoned the error of custom. But we join custom to truth, and to the custom of the Romans we oppose custom, but that of truth; from the beginning holding that which was delivered by Christ and by His Apostles.[272]

Firmilian expresses a view of the overall government of the Church which is directly opposed to that of Vatican I. He states that the keys were given to Peter alone as a representative of the Church universal, but were subsequently given to all the Apostles who then passed them on to every legitimate succeeding bishop. In the mind of Firmilian, all bishops are on an equal footing. He mocks Stephen's claim of superiority to other bishops based on his possessing a unique Petrine succession. According to Firmilian all bishops possess the chair of Peter and are built upon the rock. This is not the exclusive and unique possession of the bishops of Rome. And if, as Firmilian claims Stephen did, they depart from the unity of the Church which is expressed in the collegiality of its bishops, they separate themselves from the rock and foundation of the Church. Because Stephen, in Firmilian's view, had departed from Apostolic truth, he was no longer in unity with Apostolic succession and the rock foundation of the Church. The Roman see itself was not inherently authoritative simply because it could claim a Petrine foundation and succession. This did not impress the Eastern bishops. The important thing to them, and to Cyprian as well, was conformity to Apostolic truth. Where Roman custom opposed what they considered to be truth, they felt obliged to oppose the bishop of Rome. These bishops did not submit to the bishop of Rome and Cyprian died out of communion with him. They clearly did not view the Roman bishop as the universal ruler of the Church, nor communion with him a necessary condition for membership in the Church universal. Cyprian could say, 'He who does not have the Church for his mother does not have God for his father,' but in so stating he did not mean submission to and communion with the bishop of Rome. Karl Morrison sums up the controversy between Stephen and Cyprian and the Eastern bishops in these words:

> Stephen had condemned Cyprian as 'false Christ, false apostle, and practicer of deceit,' because he advocated re-baptism; and the Bishop of Carthage reciprocated in kind. Since the headship which Stephen claimed was unwarranted, by the example of St. Peter, he could not force his brethren to accept his views. Even worse, his judgment opposed the authentic tradition of the Church. The bishop of Rome, wrote Cyprian, had confounded human tradition and divine precepts; he insisted on a practice which was mere custom, and 'custom without truth is the antiquity of error.' Whence came the 'tradition' on which Stephen insisted? Cyprian answered that it came from human presumption. Subverting the Church from within, Stephen wished the Church to follow the practices of heretics by accepting their baptisms, and to hold that those who were not born in the Church could be sons of God. And finally, Cyprian urged that bishops (Stephen was meant) lay aside the love of presumption and obstinacy which had led them to prefer custom to tradition and, abandoning their evil and false arguments, return to the divine precepts, to evangelical and apostolic

tradition, whence arose their order and their very origin.

In a letter to Cyprian, Firmilian endorsed everything the bishop of Carthage had said and added a few strokes of his own...Recalling the earlier dispute about the date of Easter, he upheld the practice of Asia Minor by commenting that, in the celebration of Easter and in many other matters, the Romans did not observe the practices established in the age of the Apostles, though they vainly claimed apostolic authority for their aberrant forms. The decree of Stephen was the most recent instance of such audacity, an instance so grave that Firmilian ranked Stephen among heretics and blasphemers and compared his doctrines and discipline with the perfidy of Judas. The Apostles did not command as Stephen commanded, Firmilian wrote, nor did Christ establish the primacy which he claimed...To the Roman custom, Firmilian, like Cyprian, opposed the custom of truth, 'holding from the beginning that which was delivered by Christ and the Apostles.' And, Firmilian argued, by his violence and obstinacy, Stephen had apostacized from the communion of ecclesiastical unity; far from cutting heretics off from his communion, he had cut himself off from the orthodox and made himself 'a stranger in all respects from his brethren, rebelling against the sacrament and the faith with the madness of contumacious discord. With such a man can there be one Spirit and one Body, in whom perhaps there is not even one mind, slippery, shifting, and uncertain as it is?'[273]

These facts are certainly no endorsement of the views promulgated by the First Vatican Council. The writings and practice of Cyprian reveal that he held an opinion directly opposing that of Vatican One on papal supremacy. William Jurgens affirms this in the following summation of Cyprian's practice which reflected his theory of ecclesiology:

> Although Cyprian was on excellent terms with Pope St. Cornelius...he fell out sharply with Cornelius' successor, Pope St. Stephen...on the question of the rebaptizing of converted heretics. It was the immemorial custom of the African Church to regard Baptism conferred by heretics as invalid, and in spite of Stephen's severe

The Practice of the Early Church 199

warnings, Cyprian never yielded. His attitude was simply that every bishop is responsible for his own actions, answerable to God alone.[274]

The Spanish Bishops

In 254 A.D. Cyprian wrote a letter to the bishops in Spain in response to an appeal for their help (Ep. 67, Oxford Edition). The Church in Spain had deposed two unworthy bishops, Basilides and Martialis. During the Decian persecution they had lapsed and embraced paganism. Basilides went to Rome to appeal their case and to seek reinstatment. Stephen, the bishop of Rome, judged in their favor, ruling that they should be reinstated. Upon returning to their respective congregations, the Spanish Churches wrote to Cyprian for help. Cyprian promptly called a council into session which decided in favor of the Spanish congregations. He writes them to disregard Stephen's ruling. Appealing to scripture, he states that they must adhere to their original decision and judgment, openly defying and contradicting the pope's ruling. W.H.C. Frend gives the following background to this incident:

> The bishops of Leon and Merida in Spain, Basilides and Maritalis, had lapsed and accepted testimonials to their adherence to paganism, and of the two, the conversion of Maritalis seems to have been complete. Basilides had repented and gratefully accepted the position of a layman, and both sees had been filled. Both exbishops had then had second thoughts. Basilides had gone to Rome (already therefore a place where appeals could be lodged by bishops) and persuaded Stephen to allow him and his colleague to be restored to their sees and they returned to their indignant congregations. These now acted on their own, placing their case before Cyprian who summoned a council of thirty–seven bishops to decide the issue in the autumn of 254.
>
> While Stephen may have followed Callistus' precedent and allowed ostensibly penitent clergy to resume their orders, Cyprian had made his own view of such cases clear directly after the Decian persecution. A cleric who had become apostate was in a ritually impure state. 'Flee from the pestilential contact of these men,'

Cyprian urges in *The Lapsed*. 'Their speech is a cancer, their conversation is a contagion, their persuasion more deadly and poisonous than the persecution itself.' These ideas were supported unanimously by the council and applied to the case of the Spanish bishops. Stephen's recommendation was overturned. In a remarkable letter to their congregations, the people of Leon and Merida, Cyprian gave his correspondants an insight into the thinking of the North African Christians. Their exbishops were apostates, and tested by an appeal to Scripture...they were unfit to minister...The congregations were urged to separate themselves from their abandoned clerics and choose worthy pastors in their stead.[275]

These certainly are not the actions of one who believed the bishop of Rome held supreme and universal authority in the Church. Cyprian obviously believed that the authority of a council superceded that of any bishop, including the bishop of Rome.

Augustine, the North African Church and Pope Zosimus

Pope Zosimus reigned from 417 to 418 A.D. During the Pelagian controversy, Zosimus, in an encyclical letter—therefore speaking authoritatively on a matter related to faith and morals—rebuked Augustine and the North African Church for their official condemnation of Pelagius. He declared Pelagius and his main disciple Caelestius orthodox in their teaching and demanded that the North African Church change its views towards them and submit to his judgment and authority. This was done in opposition to the opinion and authoritative judgment of Pope Innocent I, Zosimus' predecessor as bishop of Rome. The North African Church refused to submit to this 'infallible' pope, demonstrating that the early Church did not believe that the popes were infallible. This is the view, in particular, of Augustine, the premier Church father of the first four centuries and leader of the North African Church. Hefele, the Roman Catholic historian, relates the

The Practice of the Early Church 201

following background to the controversy:

> In the beginning of 417 he (Innocent) sent answers to those bishops who had assembled at Carthage and those who had met at Milve...He fully agreed with the sentence passed upon Caelestius and Pelagius by the Carthaginian bishops, praised the Africans for their discernment, confirmed the sentence of excommunication pronounced upon Caelestius, threatened with the same punishment all their adherents, and found in the work of Pelagius many blasphemies and censurable doctrines.
>
> Innocent's successor, Zosimus, who in the commencement of his reign in 417 was deceived by the ambiguous confession of faith of Pelagius and Caelestius, adopted another line. He had not long entered upon his office when Caelestius...gave him a confession of faith...Zosimus immediately assembled a Roman Synod, at which Caelestius in general terms condemned what Pope Innocent had already condemned...He so influenced the Pope in his favour, that, in a letter to the African bishops, he declared Caelestius to be orthodox, blamed their former conduct, and represented Heros and Lazarus, Caelestius' chief opponents, as very wicked men, whom he had punished with excommunication and deposition.
>
> Shortly after this Zosimus also received the confession of faith which Pelagius had already addressed, together with a letter, to Pope Innocent I. Zosimus...at once addressed a second letter to the Africans, to the effect that Pelagius, like Caelestius, had most completely justified himself, and that both recognised the necessity of grace. Heros and Lazarus, on the contrary, were bad men, and the Africans were much to blame for having suffered themselves to be influenced by such contemptible slanderers.[276]

J.E. Merdinger, who did doctoral studies under W.H.C. Frend, makes these comments:

> Augustine...could see through the entire charade. The pope had neglected to inquire rigorously into the Pelagian's (Caelestius) understanding of grace.; he had been content to accept superficial

responses...A second letter from Zosimus to the Africans, *Postquam a nobis* written in September 417, did nothing to dispel Augustine's worries. Pelagius had written to the pope once again, thoroughly convincing him of his orthodoxy, and Zosimus had ordered Pelagius' letters to be read aloud at the papal court in order that everyone could be apprised of his orthodoxy. To the Africans Zosimus ebulliently exclaimed: 'Would that some of you, dearest brethren, could have been present at the reading of the letters. What was the joy of the holy men who were present; what was the admiration of each of them! Some of them could scarcely restrain themselves from tears and weeping that such men of absolutely correct faith could have been suspected. Was there a single place in which the grace of God or his aid was omitted?' At the end of his letter, however, the pope lambasted the Africans as 'whirlwinds' and 'storms of the church' and accused them of judging Pelagius and Caelestius wholly unfairly.[277]

The African bishops warned Zosimus that he was being misled by Pelagius and Caelestius and appealed to him to uphold the official judgment rendered by his predecessor Innocent. He wrote back saying that he had given the whole affair his thorough consideration and all further consideration of the matter must cease. He demanded submission to his decree. As Merdinger observes:

> In *Quamuis patrum* written in March 418, he deliberately flaunted his apostolic authority and claimed that no one should should dispute his judgment...'So great is our authority that no decision of ours can be subjected to review.'...Such is the authority of Peter and the venerable decrees of the church that all questions concerning human and divine laws, as well as all disciplinary matters, must be referred to Rome for ultimate resolution. This was high–flown language indeed and, as far as the Africans were concerned, totally unacceptable.[278]

The North Africans then assembled a general synod of their own with some 200 bishops present in which they passed a number of canons specifically condemning the teachings of Pelagius. This was done in defiance of the express decrees of Zosimus. As a result of their

The Practice of the Early Church 203

opposition and the fact that the emperor had sided with the judgment of the North African bishops, Pope Zosimus reversed his position and rejected the Pelagian heresy. Here is how Philip Schaff describes the incident:

> The Africans were too sure of their cause, to yield submission to so weak a judgment, which, moreover, was in manifest conflict with that of Innocent. In a council at Carthage, in 417 or 418, they protested, respectfully but decidedly, against the decision of Zosimus, and gave him to understand that he was allowing himself to be greatly deceived by the indefinite explanations of Coelestius. In a general African council held at Carthage in 418, the bishops, over two hundred in number, defined their opposition to the Pelagian errors, in eight (or nine) Canons, which are entirely conformable to the Augustinian view.
>
> These things produced a change in the opinions of Zosimus, and about the middle of the year 418, he issued an encyclical letter to all the bishops of both East and West, pronouncing the anathema upon Pelagius and Coelestius...and declaring his concurrence with the decisions of the council of Carthage in the doctrine of the corruption of human nature, of baptism, and of grace. Whoever refused to subscribe the encyclical, was to be deposed, banished from his church, and deprived of his property.[279]

Robert Eno adds these thoughts:

> The one theological controversy of note that originated and ended in the West was Pelagianism. Here Pope Innocent accepted and confirmed the African condemnation issuing from the Councils of Carthage and Milevis (416). He said specifically that since all the theological points had been explained by the Africans, 'no testimony is added here by us.' Whether Innocent in fact accepted all the presuppositions of the African viewpoint is debated, but the fact that his successor Zosimus apparently was considering reversing the condemnation does not help the view that the Roman condemnation was considered infallible.[280]

The incident with Zosimus is not a case of a pope expressing a private opinion, becoming better informed, and then changing his mind. This pope not only reversed the judgment of a previous pope, but officially contradicted himself. He retracts what he had authoritatively announced in an encyclical letter on an issue of major doctrinal importance. This is an authoritative declaration addressed to all the North African bishops demanding their submission to his decrees. Did Augustine and the North African bishops comply with this papal decree? No! They withstood Zosimus to his face, resolutely refusing to submit to his error, demonstrating from their actions that they considered the pope neither infallible nor the supreme ruler of the Church. In practice, the North Africans are repudiating the assertions of Vatican I. But what about the famous statement of Augustine—in the Pelagian incident—to which Roman apologists often refer: 'Rome has spoken, the case is closed.' This statement was cited in the Introduction as used by Robert Fastiggi. He states:

> St. Augustine's recognition of the authority of the Pope is manifested by the famous words with which he welcomes the decision made by the Pope: *'Roma locuta est; causa finita est'*—Rome has spoken the case is concluded (*Sermon* 131, 6:10). Why does Augustine believe the Bishop of Rome has the final word? The answer is because the Pope is the successor of St. Peter—a fact clearly recognized by Augustine in his *Letter to Generosus* (c. 400 A.D.) in which he names all 34 of the bishops of Rome from Peter to Anastasius (*Letter* 53, 1,2).

Roman Catholic historian Robert Eno helps us to understand the proper interpretation of Augustine's statement:

> It was at this point that the famous words of Augustine were uttered (as misquoted): *Roma locuta est; causa finita est*. Actually he said (*sermo* 131): 'Already two councils on this question have been sent to the apostolic see; and replies have also come from there. The case is closed; would that the error might sometime be finished as well.' But, beyond any quibbling over precise words, the greater irony is the use of this 'quotation' in later centuries. We have all heard it used in the following sense: Rome has made its decision. All further discussions must cease.[281]

The Practice of the Early Church 205

Note that Eno gives the same quote used by Roman apologists but as Eno points out it is actually a misquote. The conclusions drawn do not reflect what Augustine really said. Eno speaks of the irony of using this misquotation. He says sarcastically: 'We have all heard it used in the following sense: Rome has made its decision. All further discussion must cease.' Employed in this way, says Eno, it is a wrong application. And this is the judgment of a Roman Catholic historian, not a Protestant.

Johann Joseph Ignaz von Döllinger was one of the most renowned historians in the Roman Catholic Church of the last century. He gives the following comments on Augustine's statement:

> The Pelagian system was in his eyes so manifestly and deadly an error (*aperta pernicies*), that there seemed to him no need even of a Synod to condemn it. The two African Synods, and the Pope's assent to their decrees, appeared to him more than enough, and so the matter might be regarded as at an end. That a Roman judgment in itself was not conclusive, but that a '*Concilium plenarium*' was necessary for that purpose, he had himself emphatically maintained: and the conduct of Pope Zosimus could only confirm his opinion.[282]

The reaction of Augustine and the North African bishops to Zosimus is proof that the all too common 'spin' put on Augustine's words was not his intent. This becomes even clearer from the letter written by Augustine and the North African bishops to Pope Celestine, the successor of Zosimus. They explicity deny that the bishop of Rome has authority in himself to be the final judge of any theological issue. As the Orthodox historian John Meyendorff explains:

> Writing to pope Celestine in 420, the Africans proclaimed what amounted to a formal denial of any 'divine' privilege of Rome. 'Who will believe,' they stated, 'that our God could inspire justice in the inquiries of one man only (i.e. the pope) and refuse it to innumerable bishops gathered in council?'[283]

Apiarius

The lack of historical precedent for the papal teachings of Vatican I is further illustrated by another incident which occurred between the North African Church and Zosimus. A certain presbyter by the name of Apiarius, had been rightly deposed by a bishop who was a friend of Augustine. Apiarius appealed to Rome over the authority of the North African Church seeking a reversal of its decision. Pope Zosimus sided with Apiarius and judged that he should be reinstated. But the North African Church resolutely refused to submit to this imposition by the bishop of Rome. Zosimus appealed to the canons of the Sardican Synod held in 342 A.D. but claimed that they were actually part of the canons of Nicaea. The North African Church could not find the canons in their copy of Nicaea. They were willing to submit to the ruling of the bishop of Rome *if* it could be proved that the canons were genuinely part of the Nicene Council. When it was finally determined that they were not from Nicaea, the North Africans rejected these canons as giving the bishop of Rome any authority to interfere in the sphere of their own jurisdiction. Significantly, in 424 A.D., at a Synod in Carthage, the Church passed decrees of its own forbidding all appeals in Church controversies to other sees apart from their own. In their thinking, there was no higher authority or court of appeal than the local bishop, except for the authority of a general Council. If papal supremacy were the common belief, teaching and practice of the Church, the North African bishops and Augustine would certainly have responded in submission and obedience and would not have prohibited appeals to any other see but their own. They were willing to obey a general Council but not the bishop of Rome. George Salmon comments:

> Apiarius...was an African presbyter, excommunicated for misconduct by his bishop. He went to Rome, and prevailed on Pope Zosimus to take up his cause with some warmth. The pope's interference and the claims on which it was founded were the subject of discussions in at least three African synods. Zosimus...founded his right to interfere

on the Sardican canons...but which he quoted as Nicene. The African prelates, in council assembled, declared that there was no such canon in their copy of the Nicene code; and they begged the pope to write to Constantinople and Alexandria, requesting that the Greek copies there might be collated, in order to ascertain whether the disputed canons had really been passed at Nicaea.

The result of the mission appears from the final letter of the African bishops. In this, after giving a short account of what had been done, they request that the pope will not in future receive persons excommunicated by their synods, this being contrary to the canons of Nicaea. They protest against appeals to foreign tribunals; they deny the pope's right to send legates to exercise jurisdiction in his name, which they say is not authorized by any canon of the Fathers, and they request that the pope will not send any agent or nuncio to interfere with them in any business for fear the Church should suffer through pride and ambition.[284]

Appeals of Eastern Fathers to Rome

An historical argument often used by Roman apologists is that of the appeals by various Eastern fathers to the bishops of Rome during times of theological or personal crisis. The argument presented is that these Church fathers appeal to Rome as the final and supreme aribiter in ecclesiastical disputes thereby demonstrating the attitude of the early Church towards the bishops of Rome. While it is true that Eastern fathers throughout Church history from time to time appealed to Rome for aid, they did not appeal to Rome exclusively as the only court of appeal. In addition to their communication with Rome they often appealed to the bishops of other important sees. One notable example of this is John Chrysostom.

John Chrysostom

When he was unlawfully deposed as bishop of Constantinople and sent into exile, Chrysostom wrote Pope Innocent I detailing the illegalities of his case and appealing for his aid. However, this letter was not addressed to Innocent alone but also to Venerius and Chromatius, the bishops of Milan and Aquileia, the two most important and influential sees in Italy next to Rome. Dom Chrysostom Baur, in his biography of Chrysostom's life, gives the following background to his appeals to Rome:

> Shortly before the last crisis had arisen, and Chrysostom had been sent from Constantinople for the second time, he and his friends had decided to set forth in detail all the events of the last months in a letter to the Pope and the Western Bishops...The note in the record which states that 'this letter was also sent to Venerius...and Chromatius,' cannot first have been added in Rome; so it cannot be that the Pope gave the order to send it to the two Bishops. It must have been thus in the original itself, since Chrysostom speaks to the recipients of the letter in the plural, in the text. That point is important for the question...as to whether this letter can be considered a formal proof of the 'primacy' of Rome.
>
> This letter has usually been classed among the great 'appeals' which apologists and dogmaticians quote in proof of the recognition of the Roman primacy. But such significance cannot be given to this 'appeal,' which Chrysostom addressed not only to Pope Innocent, but also at the same time and in the same words, to the Bishops of Milan and Aquileia. The essence of the letter is this: Chrysostom begs the Pope and the two named bishops, that they would be pleased not to let themselves be drawn to the cause of injustice by the efforts of his enemies, not to acknowledge his unjust banishment, and above all that they would not bring to an end the fellowship of the Church with him, but help according to their power, that the injustice which had been done him would be reversed, and the guilty persons judged by an impartial ecclesiastical court. He could naturally have written thus to any bishop. Actually Chrysostom demanded nothing so formal and consequential as the calling of a new impartial synod, and that was just what the Pope sought, with all his energy, to attain. So one cannot very well state that Chrysostom had appealed from the unjust judgment of a synod to the personal decision of the Pope.[285]

P.R. Coleman–Norton adds these comments:

> Though S. Chrysostom elicits the interference of Pope S. Innocent, yet he does not appeal to him as to a supreme arbitrator. That S. Chrysostom expected Pope S. Innocent to show his *Letters* to neighboring prelates is apparent from his use of the plural and from Palladius' note that the first epistle was addressed also to the bishops of Milan and Aquileia—a use and an action which can be understood only in the supposition that S. Chrysostom wrote to the Pope as a bishop to a brother-bishop.[286]

So, the mere fact that a father appeals to Rome is not evidence that he is expressing belief in papal 'primacy.' In fact, as we have seen from Chrysostom's exegesis of Matthew 16 and his overall writings, he expresses no belief in a papal primacy.

Theodore the Studite

Another example of appeals to Rome is that of Theodore the Studite, a leading Eastern theologian of the ninth century. Theodore experienced considerable conflict with the religious and political leadership of his day in the iconoclastic controversy. He found a ready ally in the see of Rome and occasionally appealed to Rome for aid. In addressing the pope he uses exalted language but this can be very misleading. It was a common Eastern practice when seeking political or ecclesiastical aid to use the language of flattery and hyperbole to try and gain the aid of a prospective ally. Karl Morrison recounts historical examples of this:

> The old challenges to Roman ecclesiology remained alive. Counter-doctrines continued to claim the adherence of some western clergy. To be sure, from the East hyberbolic affirmations came invoking the assistance of Martin I against Monothelitism, and two monks from Asia Minor addressed the pope as 'supreme and apostolic pope, head of all the priestly order beneath the sun, supreme pope truly oecumenical, apostolic pope and coryphaeus.' In 681, the Byzantine bishops wrote to the Emperor Constantine IV on concluding peace with the Roman

See, 'The supreme prince of the Apostles worked in concert with us; for we have had as patron his imitator and successor in his see, to explain in writing the mystery of the divine sacrament...Peter spoke through Agatho.' But these exalted phrases, recalling the acclamation of the Council of Chalcedon that Peter had spoken through Leo, were little more than diplomatic instruments.[287]

Meyendorff affirms this Eastern practice in these comments:

> The reformed papacy of the eleventh century used a long–standing Western tradition of exegesis when it applied systematically and legalistically the passages on the role of Peter (especially Mt. 16:18, Lk. 22:32, and Jn. 21:15-17) to the bishop of Rome. *This tradition was not shared by the East*, yet it was not totally ignored by the Byzantines, some of whom used it occasionally, especially in documents addressed to Rome and intended to win the pope's sympathy. But it was never given an ultimate theological significance.[288]

This certainly seems to be an accurate portrayal of Theodore's position, for like Chrysostom, he not only addresses his letters to the bishop of Rome but also to the patriarchs of Alexandria, Antioch and Jerusalem. He used exalted 'primatial' language in addressing all of them. The similarities between the correspondence of Theodore and Chrysostom is striking. In her biography of Theodore, Alice Gardner gives the following perspective on his correspondence:

> The most interesting part of Theodore's correspondence is that by which he sought to obtain the help of the Roman See in putting down the heresies of the East...It was...to Paschal that Theodore now appealed...He addresses the Pope as 'Master and Apostolic Father,' and acknowledges him as possessor of the keys, and as corner–stone of the church. He narrates briefly the misfortunes that have occurred, the imprisonment of the Patriarch, the insult done to the sacred images, and through them to their Prototype; the exile of the priests and monks; the great suffering inflicted on the faithful; the general terror. 'And thou when thou art converted, strengthen thy brethren'; now is

The Practice of the Early Church

the time and place; help us according to the command received from God. Stretch forth thy hand as far as thou canst; thou hast power from God in that thou art above them all...Good shepherd, lay down thy life for the sheep...Let it be heard under heaven that by thee the presumptuous ones have been synodically accursed.' At the same time, Theodore wrote to friends in Rome, begging for their co-operation, especially to the Archimandrite Basil, to whom he insisted on the essential unity of the Church. With the idea of a Synod in his mind, Theodore wrote also to the other parties whose presence was necessary for a lawful council, the Patriarchs of Alexandria and Antioch, to whom he sent an identical letter, and to the Patriarch of Jerusalem.[289]

In the following comments Meyendorff summarizes the situation with Theodore. He demonstrates that when other comments of Theodore are taken into account, it is clear he does not hold to the papal primacy espoused by Vatican I which is so contradictory to the overall view of the Eastern Church of Theodore's time:

The support given to the Orthodox party during the iconoclastic period by the Church of Rome, the friendly correspondence which Theodore was able to establish with Popes Leo III (795-816) and Paschal I (817-824), contrasted with the internal conflicts which existed with his own patriarchs, both iconoclastic and Orthodox. These factors explain the very high regard he repeatedly expressed toward the 'apostolic throne' of old Rome. For example, he addressed Pope Paschal as 'the rock of faith upon which the Catholic Church is built.' 'You are Peter,' he writes, 'adorning the throne of Peter.' The numerous passages of this kind carefully collected by modern apologists of the papacy are, however, not entirely sufficient to prove that Theodore's view of Rome is identical to that of Vatican I. In his letters, side by side with references to Peter and to the pope as leaders of the Church, one can also find him speaking of 'the five-headed body of the Church,' with reference to the Byzantine concept of a 'pentarchy' of patriarchs. Also, addressing himself to the patriarch of Jerusalem, he calls him 'first among the patriarchs' for the place where the Lord suffered presupposes 'the dignity highest of all.'

Independence of the categories of 'this world,' and therefore of the state, was the only real concern of the great Studite. The apostolic claim of Rome, but also no less real, but much less effective, claims of the other Eastern patriarchs, provided him with the arguments in his fight against the Byzantine state and Church hierarchies. Still, there is no reason to doubt that his view of the unity of the Church, which he never systematically developed, was not radically different from that of his contemporaries...In Rome, Theodore the Studite saw the foremost support of the true faith, and expressed his vision and his hope in the best tradition of Byzantine superlative style.[290]

Jaroslav Pelikan supports the comments by Meyendorff that Theodore held to the Eastern ecclesiological view of the pentarchy in the jurisdiction of the Church. He gives a quote from the writings of Theodore in which he is commenting on the meaning of Matthew 16:

Citing the words of Matthew 16:18-19, Theodore of Studios asked: 'Who are the men to whom this order is given? The apostles and their successors. And who are their successors? He who occupies the throne of Rome, which is the first; he who occupies the throne of Constantinople, which is the second; and after them those who occupy the thrones of Alexandria, Antioch and Jerusalem. This is the pentarchic authority in the church; these patriarchs have jurisdiction over divine dogmas.'[291]

The *Libellus* of Pope Hormisdas

Another historical incident often claimed as undeniable proof for the reality of papal primacy in the early Church is the *libellus* of Pope Hormisdas. The Council of Chalcedon in 451 A.D. resulted in a Monophysite rebellion leading to much political upheaval within the Eastern empire. In 476 A.D. Zeno became emperor. He attempted through political and ecclesiastical pressure to achieve unity within the borders of his empire. He issued a document known as the *Henotikon,* which was an attempt to find a unified theological common ground which all parties could accept. Zeno demanded its acceptance among the Monophysites and Chalcedonian parties within the Church. As a result of the emperor's pressure Acacius, the patriarch of Constantinople (471–489), though himself committed to Chalcedonian orthodoxy, entered into communion with the Monophysite bishop of Alexandria, Peter Mongos, whom Rome had declared excommunicated. He simply disregarded Rome's decision. This resulted in a reaction in Rome by Pope Felix III. He deposed Acasius, resulting in what has become known as the Acasian schism. During the reigns of the emperors Zeno (474—491) and Anastasius (491—518), Monophysitism gradually gained prominence, with Anastasius going so far as to expel all Chalcedonian bishops from the empire. The only sees which consistently stood against this Monophysite dominance were Constantinople in the East and Rome in the West.

With the death of Anastasius, the political and ecclesiastical situation changed dramatically. The new emperor, Justin I (518—527), was a pro–Chalcedonian ruler, who restored Chalcedonian orthodoxy to favor in the empire. He also desired to bring about ecclesiastical and political unity between the East and the West, hoping for the eventual restoration of the empire in the West. The Western Empire had collapsed in 476 A.D. and Italy was now ruled by the Goths. The Roman Church was completely independent of Eastern interference. Justin believed that if he could effect a reconciliation between the Eastern and Western Churches he could gain a political foothold and influence in Italy through the pope. He approached Hormisdas (the bishop of Rome) with plans for a restoration of communion between the Roman Church and the East. Hormisdas was receptive to these overtures but only if certain conditions were accepted by the East. He demanded that all those who had been excommunicated by Rome, including Acacius, should likewise be excommunicated by the East. He also demanded the acceptance of his *libellus*—a document which set forth a rule of faith, the condemnation of certain bishops and the teaching that the pope is the criterion of orthodoxy. Hormisdas makes the following assertion regarding the orthodoxy of the Roman Church: 'In the Apostolic See the Catholic religion has always been preserved without stain.'[292] The following is the text of the *libellus*:

> Our first safety is to guard the rule of the right faith and to deviate in no wise from the ordinances of the Fathers; because we cannot pass over the statement of our Lord Jesus Christ who said: 'Thou art Peter and upon this rock I will build my church' (Matt. 16:18). These words which were spoken, are proved by the effects of the deeds, because in the Apostolic See the Catholic religion has always been preserved without stain. Desiring not to be separated from this hope and faith and following the ordinances of the Fathers, we anathematize all heresies, especially the heretic Nestorius, who at one time was bishop of the city of Constantinople, condemned in the Council of Ephesus by the blessed Celestine, Pope of the City of Rome, and by the venerable man Cyril, high priest of the City of Alexandria. Similarly anathematizing both Eutyches and Dioscorus of Alexandria condemned in the holy Synod of Chalcedon which we follow and embrace, which following the sacred Council of Nicea proclaimed the apostolic faith, we detest both Timothy the parricide, surnamed the Cat, and likewise his disciple and follower in all things, Peter of Alexandria. We condemn too, and anathematize Acacius, formerly bishop of Constantinople, who was condemned by the Apostolic See, their confederate and follower, or those who remained in the society of their communion, because Acacius justly merited a sentence in condemnation like theirs in whose communion he mingled. No less do we condemn Peter of Antioch with his followers, and the followers of all mentioned above.
>
> Moreover, we accept and approve all the letters of blessed Leo the Pope, which he wrote regarding Christian religion, just as we said before, following the Apostolic See in all things, and extolling all its ordinances. And, therefore, I hope I may merit to be in the one communion with you, which the Apostolic See proclaims, in which there is the whole and the true and the perfect solidity of the Christian religion, promising that in the future the names of those

The Practice of the Early Church 215

separated from the communion of the Catholic Church, that is, not agreeing with the Apostolic See, shall not be read during the sacred mysteries. But if I shall attempt in any way to deviate from my profession, I confess that I am confederate in my opinion with those whom I have condemned. However, I have with my own hand signed this profession of mine, and to you, Hormisdas, the holy and venerable Pope of the City of Rome, I have directed it.[293]

Under political pressure the Eastern bishops, along with John of Constantinople, signed the *libellus* but not without qualifications. Although the Eastern bishops signed the document they did so only under pressure from the emperor and they took an essentially different view of it from that of Hormisdas. This is clear because John, the patriarch of Constantinople, changed the wording of the document before signing, significantly changing its meaning. John Meyendorff gives the following historical background to the signing of the *libellus* in the East:

> The signature implied an unprecedented recognition, by Easterners, of Roman doctrinal prestige. It would be wrong to believe, however, that both sides had suddenly acquired the same perception of authority in the Church and an identical understanding of the events which followed Chalcedon. For the Greeks, the text of the *libellus*, meant a factual recognition that the apostolic Roman church had been consistent in orthodoxy for the past seventy years and, therefore, deserved to become a rallying point for the Chalcedonians of the East. Essentially this was for them a simple acknowledgment of an historic achievement. Interestingly, patriarch John, before signing the text, added a sentence, declaring that the churches of Old and New Rome are *one church*: 'I declare,' he wrote, 'that the see of the apostle Peter and the see of this imperial city are one.' The phrase, while recognizing Rome's apostolicity and honorary priority, suggested the identity and equality of the two sees, in the sense in which they were defined in canon 28 of Chalcedon, as the churches of the first and second capitals of the one empire.[294]

Karl Morrison makes these comments:

> The reconciliation which Hormisdas and Justin effected did not, however, lead to a general conversion of eastern clergy to Roman ecclesiology. Even the letters of John of Constantinople showed how far acceptance of Roman ecclesiology was from being an integral part of the reunion...In the very letter in which he subscribed to the anathematization of Nestorius and Acacius...and affirmed that he followed in all things the Apostolic See and preached what was decreed by it, he placed a severe qualification on his oath by one sentence: 'I accept,' he wrote, 'the most holy churches of God—that is your elder and this new Rome—and I judge the see of the Apostle Peter and of this August city to be one.'
>
> John might well rejoice at reunion, 'understanding that both churches, that of the elder and that of the new Rome, are one, and judging that there is rightly one see between them both.' A synod of Constantinople under Epiphanius, John's successor, could likewise without scruple take satisfaction in the peace restored between the two Romes. For no point had been sacrificed of the ecclesiology which Acacius gave practical meaning, the doctrine which asserted that Constantinople was the peer of Rome. Epiphanius could write to Hormisdas in good conscience that he wished to be united with the pope, since nothing was more precious than the divine teachings which had been handed down from the disciples and Apostles of God, especially to the See of St. Peter, the chief of the Apostles; for to his mind the reconciliation had not changed the proper hierarchic order of the Church. Neither John nor Epiphanius were of one mind with Hormisdas in understanding Christ's commission to St. Peter...For them, St. Peter was representative and the first spokesman of the Church's true confession, not the first bishop of one particular see, and, in claiming that Constantinople and Rome were one see, John of Constantinople gave an important hierarchic cast to his thought. He undercut Hormisdas's ecclesiology with the premise that his see and Rome were, not equal, but identical.[295]

Far from demonstrating an acceptance of Roman ecclesiology the facts surrounding the *libellus* prove otherwise. There was widespread resistance to and rejection of the *libellus* throughout the East as a whole. As Meyendorff points out: 'The Easterners—as they had done already at the time of pope Damasus in the late fourth century—*de facto* disregarded papal demands.'[296] Wholesale, blatant disregard of papal demands is evidence of a mindset that is antagonistic to the doctrine of papal supremacy as formulated by Vatican I. The historical reality conclusively demonstrates that the claims of Vatican I cannot be supported by the facts of history.

One hundred fifty years after Hormisdas composed his *libellus*, Pope Agatho (678—681) made a similar assertion to that of Hormisdas, of Roman orthodoxy, which was accepted by the Sixth Ecumenical Council (III Constantinople). Agatho stated: 'This apostolic see...will never be convicted of erring from the path of apostolic tradition.'[297] Some have suggested that the Eastern acceptance of the statements of Roman consistency in orthodoxy by Hormisdas and Agatho is an implicit acceptance of the Roman interpretation that the bishops of Rome are the ultimate criterion of orthodoxy and an implicit affirmation of papal infallibility. This, it is claimed, is historical validation for the teaching of Vatican I. However, as Brian Tierney has pointed out, the same Council which acknowledged Agatho's statement also condemned a bishop of Rome, Pope Honorius, as a heretic. Tierney states:

> It is difficult for us to know exactly what men of the sixth and seventh centuries understood by formulas like those of Hormisdas and Agatho. But we do know that the general council which accepted Agatho's formula also anathematized Agatho's predecessor, Pope Honorius, on the ground that he 'followed the views of the heretic Sergius and confirmed his impious dogmas.' Agatho's successor, Pope Leo II, in confirming the decrees of the council, added that Honorius 'did not illuminate the apostolic see by teaching the apostolic tradition but, by an act of treachery strove to subvert its immaculate faith.' Whatever the council fathers may have meant by the formula they accepted concerning the unfailing faith of the apostolic see, their meaning can have had little connection with the modern doctrine of papal infallibility.[298]

The Papacy: A Process of Gradual Development

All these historical accounts reveal something of great importance. In the early Church there was no such thing as a 'pope' in the sense of a supreme ruler of the Church. That was a much later development which was restricted totally to the West, and even then under much protest as the Conciliar and Reform movements demonstrate.

In the early centuries of the Church there is a gradual development of a hierarchy and an episcopal form of government. This began with what the New Testament calls a presbyter or bishop in charge of a single congregation. This was the concept of a pastor with responsibility for his congregation ruling in concert with other elders of the same congregation. In the New Testament writings the two major offices mentioned for the oversight of the Church are those of overseer or elder and deacon. These offices relate to the functions of teaching, ruling and practical ministry. The overseer is designated as one who is called of God to teach and rule, and the deacon is called to minister in practical service. The two terms used for overseer in the New Testament—*presbuteros* and *episkopos*—which are translated elder and bishop respectively are used interchangeably in the New Testament and in the writings of the Apostolic Fathers.[299] For example, in 1 Timothy 3:1–2 Paul says, 'It is a trustworthy statement: if any man aspires to the office of overseer (*episkopos*), it is a fine work he desires to do.' The word for overseer is the Greek word *episkopos*, which is also translated bishop. In Titus 1:5–7 Paul writes: 'For this reason I left you in Crete, that you might set in order what remains, and appoint elders *(presbuteros)* in every city as I directed you, namely, if any man be above reproach, the husband of one wife, having children who believe, not accused of dissipation or rebellion. For the overseer (*episkopos*) must be above reproach as God's steward...' In this letter Paul uses the terms elder and bishop interchangeably and in the New Testament the terms overseer, bishop and elder are names for the same office with responsibility for both ruling and teaching. The New Testament exhorts believers to be submissive and obedient to the elders God

The Practice of the Early Church 219

has placed in authority over them (cf. 1 Pet. 5:5, Heb. 13:17). And as Philip Schaff points out the writings of the Apostolic Fathers use the terms elder *(presbuteros)* and bishop *(episkopos)* to speak of the same office:

> Later, at the close of the first and even in the second century, the two terms are still used in like manner for the same office. The Roman bishop Clement, in his First Epistle to the Corinthians says, that the apostles, in the newly founded churches, appointed the first fruits of the faith, i.e., the first converts, 'bishops and deacons.' Here he omits the *(presbuteroi)*, as Paul does in Phil. 1:1, for the simple reason that they are in his view identical with (episkopoi); while conversely, in c. 57, he enjoins subjection to presbyters, without mentioning bishops. The Didache mentions bishops and deacons, but no presbyters. Clement of Alexandria distinguishes, it is true, the deaconate, the presbyterate, and the episcopate; but he supposes only a two–fold official character, that of presbyters, and that of deacons—a view which found advocates so late as the middle ages, even in pope Urban II, A.D. 1091. Lastly, Irenaeus, towards the close of the second century, though himself a bishop, makes only a relative difference between *episcopi* and *presbyteri*; speaks of successions of the one in the same sense as the other; terms the office of the latter 'episcopatus'; and calls the bishops of Rome 'presbyters.'
>
> The express testimony of the learned Jerome, that the churches originally, before divisions arose through the instigation of Satan, were governed by the common council of the presbyters, and not till a later period was one of the presbyters placed at the head, to watch over the church and suppress schisms. He traces the difference of the office simply to 'ecclesiastical' custom as distinct from divine institution.[300]

So in the early Church the elder or elders would rule over a single congregation. Eventually, certain bishops or presbyters were given responsibility for several Churches in a given geographic region. This developed into the rule of Patriarchs who were located in major metropolitans of the East and West and ruled on an equal basis over a specific area of jurisdiction. Over time the most influential sees were those of Jerusalem, Alexandria, Antioch, Constantinople and Rome. And the Roman see, as we have seen, held a position of preeminence among these metropolitans due to its location in the capital city of the empire and held a primacy of honor due to its apostolic importance—both Paul and Peter were martyred in Rome. But apart from the claims of the Roman bishops, beginning in the late fourth century, the Patriarchs viewed themselves as an oligarchy; that is, elders in the Church who had responsibility for the rule of the Church over a specified geographic region within the empire, and were equal to one another in authority. No one bishop had the right to rule the entire Church. Hans Küng, in discussing the theological uncertainty of apostolic succession, gives the following description of the historical development of Church government and the rule of bishops:

> It is true that there was church leadership from the beginning, whether through the apostles or through other charismatic ministries. But it must be traced back, not to 'divine institution,' but to a long and complex historical development, (a) that the episkopoi (presbyters) prevailed against prophets, teachers and other charismatic ministries as the chief and finally sole leaders of the community...(b) that the monarchial episcopate of an individual episkopos, by contrast with the plurality of episkopoi (presbyters), increasingly penetrates the communities...(c) that, with the spread of the Church from the towns to the country, the episkopos as president of a congregation now becomes president of a whole area of the Church, of a diocese, etc., a bishop in the modern sense.
>
> On the basis of what has just been explained, it would be impossible to prove that the bishops have more advantage over the presbyters than simply the supervision (jurisdiction) of a greater area of the Church. A canonical and disciplinary demarcation is possible and reasonable; a theological–dogmatic is unjustified and impossible. Originally, episkopoi and presbyters were either otherwise or not at all distinguished from one another...The tripartite division of offices (episkopoi–presbyters–deacons) is not to be found in the New Testament, but in Ignatius of Antioch, and is therefore a development which took place first in the region of Syria.[301]

In the middle of the ninth century, a radical change began in the Western Church, which dramatically altered the Constitution of the Church, and laid the ground work for the full development of the papacy. The papacy could never have emerged without a fundamental restructuring of the Constitution of the Church and of men's perceptions of the history of that Constitution. As long as the true facts of Church history were well known, it would serve as a buffer against any unlawful ambitions. However, in the 9th century, a literary forgery occurred which completely revolutionized the ancient government of the Church in the West. It provided a legal foundation for the ascendancy of the papacy in Western Christendom. This forgery is known as the Pseudo–Isidorian Decretals, written around 845 A.D. The Decretals are a complete fabrication of Church history. They set forth precedents for the exercise of sovereign authority of the popes over the universal Church prior to the fourth century and make it appear that the popes had always exercised sovereign dominion and had ultimate authority even over Church Councils. Nicholas I (858–867) was the first to use them as the basis for advancing his claims of authority. But it was not until the 11th century with Gregory VII that the these decretals were used in a significant way to alter the government of the Western Church. It was at this time that the Decretals were combined with two other major forgeries, *The Donation of Constantine* and the *Liber Pontificalis*, along with other falsified writings, and codified into a system of Church law which elevated Gregory and all his successors as absolute monarchs over the Church in the West. These writings were then utilized by Gratian in composing his *Decretum*.[302] Through him they became the basis of all canon law in the Church and Scholastic theology. Some Roman Catholic apologists claim that though there were forgeries in the Church, these really had very little impact upon the advancement and development of the papacy, since it was already an established reality by the time the forgeries appeared. Karl Keating, for example, states that practically all the commentators, with the exception of fundamentalists, agree with this assessment. But this is totally false. We have seen from the historical facts that the papacy was never a reality. There are many eminent Roman Catholic historians who have testified to that fact as well as to the importance of the forgeries. One such historian is Döllinger who makes these important comments:

> In the middle of the ninth century—about 845—arose the huge fabrication of the Isidorian decretals...About a hundred pretended decrees of the earliest Popes, together with certain spurious writings of other Church dignitaries and acts of Synods, were then fabricated in the west of Gaul, and eagerly seized upon Pope Nicholas I at Rome, to be used as genuine documents in support of the new claims put forward by himself and his successors.
>
> That the pseudo–Isidorian principles eventually revolutionized the whole constitution of the Church, and introduced a new system in place of the old—on that point there can be no controversy among candid historians.
>
> The most potent instrument of the new Papal system was Gratian's Decretum, which issued about the middle of the twelfth century from the first school of Law in Europe, the juristic teacher of the whole of Western Christendom, Bologna. In this work the Isidorian forgeries were combined with those of the other Gregorian (Gregory VII) writers...and with Gratia's own additions. His work displaced all the older collections of canon law, and became the manual and repertory, not for canonists only, but for the scholastic theologians, who, for the most part, derived all their knowledge of Fathers and Councils from it. No book has ever come near it in its influence in the Church, although there is scarcely another so chokeful of gross errors, both intentional and unintentional.[303]

George Salmon explains the importance and influence of Pseudo–Isidore:

> In the ninth century another collection of papal letters...was published under the name of Isidore, by whom, no doubt, a celebrated Spanish bishop of much learning was intended. In these are to be found precedents for all manner of instances of the exercise of sovereign dominion by the pope over other Churches. You must take notice of this, that it was by *furnishing precedents* that these letters helped the

The Practice of the Early Church 223

growth of papal power. Thenceforth the popes could hardly claim any privilege but they would find in these letters supposed proofs that the privilege in question was no more than had been always claimed by their predecessors, and always exercised without any objection...On these spurious decretals is built the whole fabric of Canon Law. The great schoolman, Thomas Aquinas, was taken in by them, and he was induced by them to set the example of making a chapter on the prerogatives of the pope an essential part of the treatises on the Church...Yet completely successful as was this forgery, I suppose there never was a more clumsy one. These decretal epistles had undisputed authority for some seven hundred years, that is to say, down to the time of the Reformation.

If we want to know what share these letters had in the building of the Roman fabric we have only to look at the Canon Law. The 'Decretum' of Gratia quotes three hundred and twenty-four times the epistles of the popes of the first four centuries; and of these three hundred and twenty-four quotations, three hundred and thirteen are from the letters which are now universally known to be spurious.[304]

In addition to the *Pseudo Isidorian Decretals* there were other forgeries which were successfully used for the promotion of the doctrine of papal primacy. One famous instance is that of Thomas Aquinas. In 1264 A.D. Thomas authored a work entitled *Against the Errors of the Greeks*. This work deals with the issues of theological debate between the Greek and Roman Churches in that day on such subjects as the Trinity, the Procession of the Holy Spirit, Purgatory and the Papacy. In his defense of the papacy Thomas bases practically his entire argument on forged quotations of Church fathers. Under the names of the eminent Greek fathers such as Cyril of Jerusalem, John Chrysostom, Cyril of Alexandria and Maximus the Abbott, a Latin forger had compiled a catena of quotations interspersing a number that were genuine with many that were forged which was subsequently submitted to Pope Uraban IV. This work became known as the Thesaurus of Greek Fathers or *Thesaurus Graecorum Patrum*. In addition the Latin author also included spurious canons from early Ecumenical Councils. Pope Urban in turn submitted the work to Thomas Aquinas who used many of the forged passages in his work *Against the Errors of the Greeks* mistakenly thinking they were genuine. These spurious quotations had enormous influence on many Western theologians in succeeding centuries. The following is a sample of Thomas' argumentation for the papacy using the spurious quotations from the *Thesaurus*:

Chapter thirty-four

That the same (the Roman Pontiff) possesses in the Church a fullness of power.

It is also established from the texts of the aforesaid Doctors that the Roman Pontiff possesses a fullness of power in the Church. For Cyril, the Patriarch of Alexandria, says in his *Thesaurus:* "As Christ coming forth from Israel as leader and sceptre of the Church of the Gentiles was granted by the Father the fullest power over every principality and power and whatever is that all might bend the knee to him, so he entrusted most fully the fullest power to Peter and his successors." And again: "To no one else but Peter and to him alone Christ gave what is his fully." And further on: "The feet of Christ are his humanity, that is, the man himself, to whom the whole Trinity gave the fullest power, whom one of the Three assumed in the unity of his person and lifted up on high to the Father above every principality and power, so that all the angels of God might adore him (Hebr. 1:6); which whole and entire he has left in sacrament and power to Peter and to his Church.

And Chrysostom says to the Bulgarian delegation speaking in the person of Christ: "Three times I ask you whether you love me, because you denied me three times out of fear and trepidation. Now restored, however, lest the brethren believe you to have lost the grace and authority of the keys, I now confirm in you that which is fully mine, because you love me in their presence."

This is also taught on the authority of Scripture. For in Matthew 16:19 the Lord said to Peter without restriction: Whatsoever you shall bind on earth shall be bound also in heaven.

Chapter thirty-five

That he enjoys the same power conferred on Peter by Christ.

It is also shown that Peter is the Vicar of Christ and the Roman

Pontiff is Peter's successor enjoying the same power conferred on Peter by Christ. For the canon of the Council of Chalcedon says: "If any bishop is sentenced as guilty of infamy, he is free to appeal the sentence to the blessed bishop of old Rome, whom we have as Peter the rock of refuge, and to him alone, in the place of God, with unlimited power, is granted the authority to hear the appeal of a bishop accused of infamy in virtue of the keys given him by the Lord." And further on: "And whatever has been decreed by him is to be held as from the vicar of the apostolic throne."

Likewise, Cyril, the Patriarch of Jerusalem, says, speaking in the person of Christ: "You for a while, but I without end will be fully and perfectly in sacrament and authority with all those whom I shall put in your place, just as I am also with you." And Cyril of Alexandria in his *Thesaurus* says that the Apostles "in the Gospels and Epistles have affirmed in all their teaching that Peter and his Church are in the place of the Lord, granting him participation in every chapter and assembly, in every election and proclamation of doctrine." And further on: "To him, that is, to Peter, all by divine ordinance now the head, and the rulers of the world obey him as the Lord Jesus himself." And Chrysostom, speaking in the person of Christ, says: "Feed my sheep (John 21:17), that is, in my place be in charge of your brethren."[305]

With the exception of the last reference to Chrysostom all of Thomas' references cited to Cyril of Jerusalem, Cyril of Alexandria, Chrysostom and the Council of Chalcedon are forgeries. The remainder of Aquinas' treatise in defense of the papacy is similar in nature. Edward Denny gives the following historical summary of these forgeries and their use by Thomas Aquinas:

> As the *Pseudo-Isidorian Decretals* were by no means the first, so they were not the last forgeries in the interests of the advancement of the Papal system. Gratian himself, in addition to using the forged Decretals and the fabrications of others who preceded him, had incorporated also into the *Decretum* fresh corruptions of his own with that object, but amongst such forgeries a catena of spurious passages from the Greek Fathers and Councils, put forth in the thirteenth century, had probably, next to the *Pseudo-Isidorian Decretals,* the widest influence in this direction.
>
> The object of this forgery was as follows: The East had been

separated from the West since the excommunication by Pope Leo IX of Michael Cerularius, the Patriarch of Constantinople, and that of the former by the latter in July 1054, in which the other Eastern Patriarchs concurred. The Latins, especially the Dominicans, who had established themselves in the East, made strenuous efforts to induce the Easterns to submit to the Papacy. The great obstacle in the way of their success was the fact that the Orientals knew nothing of such claims as those which were advanced by the Roman Bishops. In their belief the highest rank in the Hierarchy of the Church was that of Patriarch. This was clearly expressed by the Patrician Babanes at the Council of Constantinople, 869. 'God,' he said, 'hath placed His Church in the five patriarchates, and declared in His Gospel that they should never utterly fail, because they are the heads of the Church. For that saying, "and the gates of hell shall not prevail against it," meaneth this, when two fall they run to three; when three fall they run to two; but when four perchance have fallen, one, which remains in Christ our God, the Head of all, calls back again the remaining body of the Church."

They were ignorant of any autocratic power residing *jure divino* in the Bishop of Rome. They regarded Latin authors with suspicions as the fautors of the unprimitive claims of the Bishop of Old Rome; hence if they were to be persuaded that the Papalist pretensions were Catholic, and thus induced to recognise them, the only way would be to produce evidence provided ostensibly from Greek sources. Accordingly a Latin theologian drew up a sort of *Thesaurus Graecorum Patrum*, in which, amongst genuine extracts from Greek Fathers, lie mingled spurious passages purporting to be taken from various Councils and writings of Fathers, notably St. Chrysostom, St. Cyril of Alexandria, and Maximus the Abbot.

This work was laid before Urban IV, who was deceived by it. He was thus able to use it in his correspondence with the Emperor, Michael Palaeologus, to prove that from 'the Apostolic throne of the Roman Pontiffs it was to be sought what was to be held, or what was to be believed, since it is his right to lay down, to ordain, to disprove, to command, to loose and to bind in the place of Him who appointed him, and delivered and granted to no one else but him alone what is supreme. To this throne also all Catholics bend the head by divine law, and the primates of the world confessing the true faith are obedient and turn their thoughts as if to Jesus Christ Himself, and regard

The Practice of the Early Church 227

him as the Sun, and from Him receive the light of truth to the salvation of souls according as the genuine writers of some of the Holy Fathers, both Greek and others, firmly assert."

Urban, moreover, sent this work to St. Thomas Aquinas...The testimony of these extracts was to him of great value, as he believed that he had in them irrefragable proof that the great Eastern theologians, such as St. Chrysostom, St. Cyril of Alexandria, and the Fathers of the Councils of Constantinople and Chalcedon, recognised the monarchical position of the Pope as ruling the whole Church with absolute power. Consequently he made use of these fraudulent documents in all honesty in setting forth the prerogatives of the Papacy. The grave result followed that, through his authority, the errors which he taught on the subject of the Papacy were introduced into the schools, fortified by the testimony of these fabrications, and thus were received as undoubted truth, whence resulted consequences which can hardly be fully estimated.

It was improbable that the Greeks, who had ample means of discovering the real character of these forgeries, should finally accept them and the teaching based on them; but in the West itself there were no theologians competent to expose the fraud, so that these forgeries were naturally held to be of weighty authority. The high esteem attached to the writings of St. Thomas was an additional reason why this should be the case.[306]

Döllinger elaborates on the far reaching influence of these forgeries, especially in their association with the authority of Aquinas, on succeeding generations of theologians and their extensive use as a defense of the papacy:

> In theology, from the beginning of the fourteenth century, the spurious passages of St. Cyril and forged canons of Councils maintained their ground, being guaranteed against all suspicion by the authority of St. Thomas. Since the work of Trionfo in 1320, up to 1450, it is remarkable that no single new work appeared in the interests of the Papal system. But then the contest between the Council of Basle and Pope Eugenius IV evoked the work of Cardinal Torquemada, besides some others of less importance. Torquemada's argument, which was held up to the time of Bellarmine to be the most conclusive apology of the Papal system, rests entirely on fabrications later than the

pseudo-Isidore, and chiefly on the spurious passages of St. Cyril. To ignore the authority of St. Thomas is, according to the Cardinal, bad enough, but to slight the testimony of St. Cyril is intolerable. The Pope is infallible; all authority of other bishops is borrowed or derived from his. Decisions of Councils without his assent are null and void. These fundamental principles of Torquemada are proved by spurious passages of Anacletus, Clement, the Council of Chalcedon, St. Cyril, and a mass of forged or adulterated testimonies. In the times of Leo X and Clement III, the Cardinals Thomas of Vio, or Cajetan, and Jacobazzi, followed closely in his footsteps. Melchior Canus built firmly on the authority of Cyril, attested by St. Thomas, and so did Bellarmine and the Jesuits who followed him. Those who wish to get a bird's-eye view of the extent to which the genuine tradition of Church authority was still overlaid and obliterated by the rubbish of later inventions and forgeries about 1563, when the *Loci* of Canus appeared, must read the fifth book of his work. It is indeed still worse fifty years later in this part of Bellarmine's work. The difference is that Canus was honest in his belief, which cannot be said of Bellarmine.

The Dominicans, Nicolai, Le Quien, Quetif, and Echard, were the first to avow openly that their master St. Thomas, had been deceived by an imposter, and had in turn misled the whole tribe of theologians and canonists who followed him. On the one hand, the Jesuits, including even such a scholar as Labbe, while giving up the pseudo–Isidorian decretals, manifested their resolve to still cling to St. Cyril. In Italy, as late as 1713, Professor Andruzzi of Bologna cited the most important of the interpolations of St. Cyril as a conclusive argument in his controversial treatise against the patriarch Dositheus.[307]

HISTORICAL SUMMARY

The following is a summation of the forgoing facts from leading Orthodox, Protestant and Roman Catholic historians. Their quotations provide scholarly validation of the facts and conclusions presented above. They give an overall consensus of opinion regarding the ecclesiology of the Eastern Church throughout history and its attitude toward the see of Rome. They demonstrate that the assertions of Vatican I are simply not true to the facts of history.

Aristeides Papadakis

Dr. Papadakis is an Orthodox historian and Professor of Byzantine history at the University of Maryland. He gives the following analysis of the Eastern Church's attitude towards the claims of the bishops of Rome especially as they were formulated in the 11th century Gregorian reforms. He points out that on the basis of the exegesis of scripture and the facts of history, the eastern Church has consistently rejected the papal claims of Rome:

> What was in fact being implied in the western development was the destruction of the Church's pluralistic structure of government. Papal claims to supreme spiritual and doctrinal authority quite simply, were threatening to transform the entire Church into a vast centralized diocese...Such innovations were the result of a radical reading of the Church's conciliar structure of government as revealed in the life of the historic Church. No see, regardless of its spiritual seniority, had ever been placed outside of this structure as if it were a power over or above the Church and its government...Mutual consultation among Churches—episcopal collegiality and conciliarity, in short—had been the quintessential character of Church government from the outset. It was here that the locus of supreme authority in the Church could be found. Christendom indeed was both a diversity and a unity, a family of basically equal sister-Churches, whose unity rested not on any visible juridical authority, but on conciliarity, and on a common declaration of faith and the sacramental life.
>
> The ecclesiology of communion and fraternity of the Orthodox, which was preventing them from following Rome blindly and submissively like slaves, was based on Scripture and not merely on history or tradition. Quite simply, the power to bind and loose mentioned in the New Testament had been granted during Christ's ministry to every disciple and not just to Peter alone...In sum, no one particular Church could limit the fulness of God's redeeming grace to itself, at the expense of the others. Insofar as all were essentially identical, the fulness of catholicity was present in all equally. In the event, the Petrine biblical texts, cherished by the Latins, were beside

the point as arguments for Roman ecclesiology and superiority. The close logical relationship between the papal monarchy and the New Testament texts, assumed by Rome, was quite simply undocumented. For all bishops, as successors of the apostles, claim the privilege and power granted to Peter. Differently put, the Savior's words could not be interpreted institutionally, legalistically or territorially, as the foundation of the Roman Church, as if the Roman pontiffs were alone the exclusive heirs to Christ's commission. It is important to note parenthetically that a similar or at least kindred exegesis of the triad of Matt. 16:18, Luke 22:32 and John 21:15f. was also common in the West before the reformers of the eleventh century chose to invest it with a peculiar 'Roman' significance. Until then, the three proof–texts were viewed primarily 'as the foundation of the Church, in the sense that the power of the keys was conferred on a *sacerdotalis ordo* in the person of Peter: the power granted to Peter was symbolically granted to the whole episcopate.' In sum, biblical Latin exegetes before the Gregorian reform did not view the New Testament texts unambiguously as a blueprint for papal sovereignty; their understanding overall was non–primatial.

The Byzantine indictment against Rome also had a strong historical component. A major reason why Orthodox writers were unsympathetic to the Roman restatement of primacy was precisely because it was so totally lacking in historical precedent. Granted that by the twelfth century papal theorists had become experts in their ability to circumvent the inconvenient facts of history. And yet, the Byzantines were ever ready to hammer home the theme that the historical evidence was quite different. Although the Orthodox may not have known that Gregorian teaching was in part drawn from the forged decretals of pseudo–Isidore (850's), they were quite certain that it was not based on catholic tradition in either its historical or canonical form. On this score, significantly, modern scholarship agrees with the Byzantine analysis. As it happens, contemporary historians have repeatedly argued that the universal episcopacy claimed by the eleventh–century reformers would have been rejected by earlier papal incumbents as obscenely blasphemous (to borrow the phrase of a recent scholar). The title 'universal' which was advanced formally at the time was actually explicitly rejected by earlier papal giants such as Gregory I. To be brief, modern impartial scholarship is reasonably certain that the conventional conclusion which views the Gregorians as defenders of a consistently uniform tradition is largely fiction. 'The emergence of a papal monarchy from the eleventh century onwards cannot be represented as the realization of a homogenous development, even within the relatively closed circle of the western, Latin, Church.'[308] It has been suggested that the conviction that *papatus* (a new term constructed on the analogy of *episcopatus* in the eleventh century) actually represented a rank or an order higher than that of bishop, was a radical revision of Church structure and government. The discontinuity was there and to dismiss it would be a serious oversight.[309]

Jaroslav Pelikan

Jaroslav Pelikan likewise affirms that the Eastern view of ecclesiology was not oriented towards a Roman primacy and universal jurisdiction but the sharing of jurisdiction on an equal basis between the five major patriarchal sees, a view known as pentarchy:

> The Western version of apostolic polity, by contrast with the Eastern, had definitely become a form of monarchy by the time of the collision between Old Rome and New Rome in the ninth century. The Eastern version...was not the monarchy of New Rome in the place of the monarchy of Old Rome, but the doctrine of pentarchy. This doctrine came to its focus in the schism of the eleventh century, but its basic elements had been present earlier. Pentarchy was the theory that the apostolic polity of Christendom would be maintained through the cooperation between five patriarchal sees: Rome, Constantinople, Jerusalem, Antioch, and Alexandria.[310]

Yves Congar

Yves Congar affirms the fact that the Eastern Church did not have the same view of ecclesiology as that which developed over many centuries in the Western tradition, and that in practice, as well as in theology, it never viewed the Roman Church as having authority over the Church universal:

> It must be confessed that the consciousness of the Roman primacy was not expressed in the East at the period when the primacy became classically fixed in tradition, at least not with a clarity that alone could have avoided schism. In the great councils held in the East, there had never been a formula on the universal primacy by divine right...We do not find texts in the East as strong as those in the West; the rescripts of Theodore and of Valentinian II and Valentinian III concern the West. In a number of documents Rome is merely portrayed as an ecclesiastical and canonical court of first instance. In other texts, Rome is recognized as having the right as first See, of intervening to preserve the purity of doctrinal tradition, but not to regulate the life of the churches or to settle questions of discipline in the East. Finally—and to our mind this is the most important point—although the East recognized the primacy of Rome, it did not imply by this exactly what Rome herself did, so that, even within the question on which they were in agreement, there existed the beginning of a very serious estrangement bearing upon the decisive element of the ecclesiastical constitution and the rule of communion.[311]

The East never accepted the regular jurisdiction of Rome, nor did it submit to the judgment of Western bishops. Its appeals to Rome for help were not connected with a recognition of the principle of Roman jurisdiction but were based on the view that Rome had the same truth, the same good. The East jealously protected its autonomous way of life. Rome intervened to safeguard the observation of legal rules, to maintain the orthodoxy of faith and to ensure communion between the two parts of the church, the Roman see representing and personifying the West...In according Rome a 'primacy of honour', the East avoided basing this primacy on the succession and the still living presence of the apostle Peter. A *modus vivendi* was achieved which lasted, albeit with crises, down to the middle of the eleventh century...From the perspective of an ecclesiology which is not only theoretical but is also put into practice, we are confronted by two

The Practice of the Early Church 233

logics. The East remained oriented on the logic of local or particular churches in communion with one another in the unity of faith, love and eucharist; this unity was realized by means of exchanges and communications and then, when the need made itself felt, by the holding of a council. It was a unity of communion. The West, which Islam had cut off from North Africa, accepted the authority of the Roman see, and over the course of history Rome occupied an increasingly prominent place. It is a fact that the two gravest crises between Byzantium and Rome arose in times when the papal authority was affirmed most strongly: with Photius under Nicholas I and John VIII, and with Cerularius at the time of the so-called Gregorian Reform (Nicholas II, Leo IX, Humbert, Gregory VII).[312]

John Meyendorff

John Meyendorff summarizes the views of the later Byzantine theologians towards the whole issue of apostolic succession showing how their ecclesiology was rooted in the patristic tradition. He clearly demonstrates that though the East recognized a position of primacy in the apostle Peter, in that they refer to him as chief of the apostles and first disciple of Christ, and rock of the Church, that this does not mean that they transfer this same view to the bishops of Rome, for in their minds all bishops are successors of Peter:

> The reformed papacy of the eleventh century used a long-standing Western tradition of exegesis when it applied systematically and legalistically the passages on the role of Peter (especially Mt. 16:18, Lk. 22:32, and Jn. 21:15-17) to the bishop of Rome. *This tradition was not shared by the East* (emphasis mine).[313]
>
> Eastern theologians repeat the views of the Eastern Fathers on the Petrine passages...The Eastern Churches had always recognized the particular authority of Rome in ecclesiastical affairs, and at Chalcedon had emphatically acclaimed Pope Leo as a successor of Peter, a fact which did not prevent them from condemning the monothelite Pope Honorius at the Sixth Ecumenical Council in 681...The Byzantines unanimously recognized the great *authority* of old Rome, but never

understood this authority in the sense of absolute *power*. The prestige of Rome was not due, in their eyes, only to the 'Petrine' character of this church. Indeed the famous Canon 28 of Chalcedon was for them one of the essential texts for the organization of the Church: 'It is for right reasons, that the Fathers accorded privileges to old Rome, for this city was the seat of the Emperor and Senate...' The Roman authority was thus the result of both an ecclesiastical *consensus* and of those *historical realities*, which the Church fully recognized as relevant to her own life, namely, the existence of a Christian Empire. The fact of the Pope's traditional definition as the successor of Peter was by no means denied, but it was not considered as a decisive issue. In the East there were numerous 'apostolic sees': was not Jerusalem the 'mother of all Churches'? Could not the Bishop of Antioch claim also the title of successor to Peter?...But the reason why the Roman Church had been accorded an incontestable precedence over all other apostolic Churches was that its Petrine and Pauline 'apostolicity' was in fact added to the city's position as the capital city, and only the conjunction of both these elements gave the Bishop of Rome the right to occupy the place of a primate in the Christian world with the consensus of all churches...In their (the East) conception of the nature of primacy in the Church, the idea of 'apostolicity' played a relatively unimportant role, since in itself it did not determine the real authority of a Church.

It is therefore comprehensible why, even after the schism between East and West, Orthodox ecclesiastical writers were never ashamed of praising the 'coryphaeus' and of recognizing his preeminent function in the very foundation of the Church. They simply did not consider this praise and recognition as relevant in any way to the papal claims, since any bishop, and not only the pope, derives his ministry from the ministry of Peter.

The great Patriarch Photius is the first witness to the amazing stability in Byzantium of the traditional patristic exegesis. 'On Peter,' he writes, 'repose the foundations of the faith.' 'He is the coryphaeus of the Apostles.' Even though he betrayed Christ, 'he was not deprived of being the chief of the apostolic choir, and has been established as the rock of the Church and is proclaimed by the Truth to be keybearer of the Kingdom of heaven.' One can also find expressions in which Photius aligns the foundation of the Church with the confession of Peter. 'The Lord,' he writes, 'has entrusted to Peter the keys of the Kingdom as a reward for his right confession, and on his confession he laid the foundation of the Church.'...By confessing his faith in the Divinity of the Saviour, Peter became the Rock of the Church.

All Byzantine theologians, even after the conflict with Rome, speak of Peter in the same terms as Photius...Their quiet assurance proves once more that they did not think of these texts (Mt. 16:18; Lk. 22:32; Jn. 21:15-17) as being an argument in favour of Roman ecclesiology, which they moreover ignored, and the 'logic' of which was totally alien to Eastern Christianity. The following points however seemed evident to them:

1) Peter is the 'coryphaeus' of the apostolic choir; he is the first disciple of Christ and speaks always on behalf of all. It is true that other apostles, John, James, and Paul are also called 'coryphaei' and 'primates,' but Peter alone is the 'rock of the Church.'

2) The words of Jesus on the road to Caesarea Philippi—'On this rock I will build my Church'—are bound to the confession of Peter. The Church exists in history because man believes in Christ, the Son of God; without this faith there can be no Church. Peter was the first to confess this faith, and has thus become the 'head of theologians.'

3) The Byzantine authors consider that the words of Christ to Peter (Matt. 16:18) possess a final and eternal significance. Peter is a mortal man, but the Church 'against which the gates of hell cannot prevail,' remains eternally founded on Peter.

We must note...the essential distinction made between the function of the apostles and that of the episcopal ministry in the Church; the function of Peter, as that of the other apostles, was to be a witness for the whole world, whereas the episcopal ministry is limited to a single local church...Thus the Byzantine theologians explain the New Testament texts concerning Peter within a more general ecclesiological context and more specifically in terms of a distinction between the episcopal ministry and the apostolic one. The apostles are different from the bishop in so far as the latter's function is to govern a single local church. Yet each local church has one and the same *fullness of grace*; all of them are *the Church in its totality;* the pastoral function is wholly present in every one, and all of them are established on Peter.

Faced by Roman ecclesiology, Byzantine theologians defend the ontological identity and the equality in terms of grace of all local churches. To the Roman claims to universalism, based on an institutional centre, they oppose the universalism of faith and grace.

But then why was the Church of Rome vested with primacy among other Churches, a primacy 'analogous' to the one Peter had among the Apostles? The Byzantines had a clear answer to this question: this Roman primacy came not from Peter, whose presence had been more effective and better attested in Jerusalem or in Antioch than in Rome, but from the fact that Rome was the capital of the Empire. Here all the Byzantine authors are in agreement: the 28th Canon of Chalcedon is for them an axiom.

For the whole patristic tradition, accepted also by the Byzantines, the succession of Peter depends on the confession of the true faith. The confession is entrusted to each Christian at his baptism, but a particular responsibility belongs, according to the doctrine of St. Irenaeus of Lyons, to those who occupy in each local church the very throne of Christ in apostolic succession, i.e. to the bishops. The responsibility belongs *to every one* of them, since each local church has the same fullness of grace. Thus the teaching of the Byzantine theologians agrees perfectly with the ecclesiology of St. Cyprian on the 'Cathedri Petri': there is no plurality of episcopal sees, there is but one, the chair of Peter, and all the bishops, within the communities of which they are presidents, are seated, each one for his part, on this very chair...Such is the essential notion of the succession of Peter in the Church in Orthodox ecclesiology.[314]

Conclusion

In light of the historical evidence it is clear that the Roman Catholic dogma of papal infallibility and primacy is simply not true to the facts of history. It cannot be supported by the Church fathers, the Church Councils or by the experience of the popes themselves. While it is certainly true that the bishops of Rome, beginning with the late fourth century, began to set forth an ecclesiology of papal supremacy, it is equally true that such assertions were consistently resisted and repudiated by the Eastern and the Western fathers. We have seen that the papal emphasis in the exegesis of Matthew 16, Luke 22 and John 21 was unanimously opposed by the patristic interpretation of those passages. The papal position only gradually won acceptance in the West and that on the basis of forgeries which were received as legitimate expressions of the history of the ancient Church. The Fathers in the East, though acknowledging a primacy of honor due to the great see of Rome—because it was in the capital of the empire and the place of Peter and Paul's martydom—did not in any sense hold to the Roman view of authority over the entire Church. And they almost universally interpreted the rock of Matthew 16:18 to be Peter's confession of Christ or Christ himself, rather than the person of Peter. The Eastern Church did not view the bishop of Rome as the head of the universal Church and in practice the East was not subject to Rome. Its ecclesiology was based on the shared authority of the five great patriarchates, all equal in honor and dignity. The highest authority in the Church was an ecumenical Council.

The papal teaching of Vatican I is grounded upon a misinterpretation of scripture that directly contradicts the patristic consensus and upon a misrepresentation of the facts of history. This completely undermines its claims of authority. The Roman Catholic Church has proven conclusively that it is *not* an infallible interpreter of Scripture. And if Rome can be shown to be wrong in its claims, exegetically and historically, it behooves us to seriously examine the gospel message proclaimed by this Church in the light of the ultimate authority of scripture. I would implore you to go to the scriptures and examine the official teachings of the Church of Rome. Compare its teachings to the clear teaching of the word of God.

Part III

APPENDICES

Appendix A

THE OFFICIAL ROMAN CATHOLIC TEACHING ON THE PAPACY

PAPAL PRIMACY

Vatican One

Chapter I: Of the Institution of the Apostolic Primacy in blessed Peter.

We therefore teach and declare that, according to the testimony of the Gospel, the primacy of jurisdiction over the universal Church of God was immediately and directly promised and given to blessed Peter the Apostle by Christ the Lord. For it was to Simon alone, to whom he had already said: 'Thou shalt be called Cephas,' that the Lord after the confession made by him, saying: 'Thou art the Christ, the Son of the living God,' addressed these solemn words: 'Blessed art thou, Simon Bar-Jona, because flesh and blood have not revealed it to thee, but my Father who is in heaven. And I say to thee that thou art Peter; and upon this rock I will build my Church, and the gates of hell shall not prevail against it. And I will give to thee the keys of the kingdom of heaven. And whatsoever thou shalt bind on earth, it shall be bound also in heaven; and whatsoever thou shalt loose on earth, it shall be loosed also in heaven.' And it was upon Simon alone that Jesus after his resurrection bestowed the jurisdiction of chief pastor and ruler over all his fold in the words: 'Feed my lambs; feed my sheep.' At open variance with this clear doctrine of Holy Scripture as it has been ever understood by the Catholic Church are the perverse opinions of those who, while they distort the form of government established by Christ the Lord in his Church, deny that Peter in his single person, preferably to all the other Apostles, whether taken separately or together, was endowed by Christ with a true and proper primacy of jurisdiction; or of those who assert that the same primacy was not bestowed immediately and directly upon blessed Peter himself, but upon the Church, and through the Church on Peter as her minister.

If any one, therefore, shall say that blessed Peter the Apostle was not appointed the Prince of all the Apostles and the visible Head of the whole Church militant; or that the same directly and immediately received from the same our Lord Jesus Christ a primacy of honor only, and not of true and proper jurisdiction: let him be anathema.

Chapter II: On the Perpetuity of the Primacy of blessed Peter in the Roman Pontiffs.

That which the Prince of Shepherds and great Shepherd of the sheep, Jesus Christ our Lord, established in the person of the blessed Apostle Peter to secure the perpetual welfare and lasting good of the Church, must, by the same institution, necessarily remain unceasingly in the Church; which, being founded upon the Rock, will stand firm to the end of the world. For none can doubt, and it is known to all ages, that the holy and blessed Peter, the Prince and Chief of the Apostles, the pillar of the faith and foundation of the Catholic Church, received the keys of the kingdom from our Lord Jesus Christ, the Saviour and Redeemer of mankind, and lives, presides, and judges, to this day and always, in his successors the Bishops of the Holy See of Rome, which was founded by him and consecrated by his blood. Whence, whosoever succeeds to Peter in this See, does by the institution of Christ himself obtain the Primacy of Peter over the whole Church. The disposition made by Incarnate Truth therefore remains, and blessed Peter, abiding through the strength of the Rock in the power that he received, has not abandoned the direction of the Church. Wherefore it has at all times been necessary that every particular Church—that is to say, the faithful throughout the world—should agree with the Roman Church, on account of the greater authority of the princedom which this has received; that all being associated in the unity of that See whence the rights of communion spread to all, might grow together as members of one Head in the compact unity of the body.

If, then, any should deny that it is by institution of Christ the Lord, or by divine right, that blessed Peter should have a perpetual line of successors in the Primacy over the universal Church, or that the Roman Pontiff is the successor of blessed Peter in this primacy: let him be anathema.

Chapter III: On the Power and Nature of the Primacy of the Roman Pontiff.

Wherefore, resting on plain testimonies of the Sacred Writings, and adhering to the plain and express decrees both of our predecessors, the Roman Pontiffs, and of the General Councils, we renew the definition of the ecumenical Council of Florence, in virtue of which all the faithful of Christ must believe that the holy Apostolic See and the Roman Pontiff possesses the primacy over the whole world, and that the Roman Pontiff is the successor of blessed Peter, Prince of the Apostles, and is true vicar of Christ, and head of the whole Church, and father and teacher of all Christians; and that full power was given to him in blessed Peter to rule, feed, and govern the universal Church by Jesus Christ our Lord; as is also contained in the acts of the General Councils and in the sacred Canons.

Hence we teach and declare that by the appointment of our Lord the Roman Church possesses a superiority of ordinary power over all other churches, and that this power of jurisdiction of the Roman Pontiff, which is truly episcopal, is immediate; to which all, of whatever right and dignity, both pastors and faithful, both individually and collectively, are bound, by their duty of hierarchial subordination and true obedience, to submit not only in matters which belong to faith and morals, but also in those which appertain to the discipline and government of the Church throughout the world, so that the Church of Christ may be one flock under one supreme pastor through the preservation of unity both of communion and of profession of the same faith with the Roman Pontiff. *This is the teaching of Catholic truth, from which no one can deviate without loss of faith and salvation.*

But so far is this power of the Supreme Pontiff from being any prejudice to the ordinary and immediate power of episcopal jurisdiction, by which Bishops, who have been set by the Holy Ghost to succeed and hold the place of the Apostles, feed and govern, each his own flock, as true pastors, that this their episcopal authority is really asserted, strengthened, and protected by the supreme and universal Pastor; in accordance with the words of St. Gregory the Great: 'My honor is the honor of the whole Church. My honor is the firm strength of my brethren. I am truly honored when the honor due to each and all is not withheld.'

Further, from this supreme power possessed by the Roman Pontiff of governing the universal Church, it follows that he has the right of free communication with the pastors of the whole Church, and with their flocks, that these might be taught and ruled by him in the way of salvation. Wherefore we condemn and reject the opinions of those who hold that the communication between this supreme head and the pastors and their flocks can lawfully be impeded; or who make this communication subject to the will of the secular power, so as to maintain that whatever is done by the Apostolic See, or by its authority, for the government of the Church, can not have force or value unless it be confirmed by the assent of the secular power.

And since by the divine right of Apostolic primacy the Roman Pontiff is placed over the universal Church, we further teach and declare that he is the supreme judge of the faithful, and that in all causes, the decision of which belongs to the Church, recourse may be had to his tribunal, and that none may re-open the judgment of the Apostolic See, than whose authority there is no greater, nor can any lawfully review its judgment. Wherefore they err from the right course who assert that it is lawful to appeal from the judgments of the Roman Pontiffs to an ecumenical Council, as to an authority higher than that of the Roman Pontiff.

If, then, any shall say that the Roman Pontiff has the office merely of inspection or direction, and not full and supreme power of jurisdiction over the universal Church, not only in things which belong to faith and morals, but also in those which relate to the discipline and government of the Church spread throughout the world; or assert that he possesses merely the principal part, and not all the fulness of this supreme power; or that that power which he enjoys is not ordinary and immediate, both over each and all the churches, and over each and all the pastors and the faithful: let him be anathema.[315]

Catechism of the Catholic Church

Simon Peter holds the first place in the college of the Twelve; Jesus entrusted a unique position to him. Through a revelation from the Father, Peter had confessed: 'You are the Christ, the Son of the living God.' Our Lord then declared to him: 'You are Peter, and on this rock I will build my Church, and the gates of Hades will not prevail against it.' Christ, 'the living stone,' thus assures his Church, built on Peter, of victory over the powers of death. Because of the faith he confessed Peter will remain the unshakeable rock of the Church. His mission will be to keep this faith from every lapse and to strengthen his brothers in it.

Jesus entrusted a specific authority to Peter: 'I will give you the keys of the kingdom of heaven, and whatever you bind on earth shall be bound in heaven, and whatever you loose on earth shall be loosed in heaven.' The 'power of the keys' designates authority to govern the house of God, which is the Church. Jesus, the Good Shepherd, confirmed this mandate after his Resurrection: 'Feed my sheep.' The power to 'bind and loose' connotes the authority to absolve sins, to pronounce doctrinal judgments, and to make disciplinary decisions in the Church. Jesus entrusted this authority to the Church through the ministry of the apostles and in particular through the ministry of Peter, the only one to whom he specifically entrusted the keys of the kingdom.

The words *bind and loose* mean: whomever you exclude from your communion, will be excluded from communion with God;

whomever you receive anew into your communion, God will welcome back into his. *Reconciliation with the Church is inseparable from reconciliation with God.*[316]

PAPAL INFALLIBILITY

Vatican One

Moreover, that the supreme power of teaching is also included in the Apostolic primacy, which the Roman Pontiff, as the successor of Peter, Prince of the Apostles, possesses over the whole Church, this Holy See has always held, the perpetual practice of the Church confirms, and ecumenical councils also have declared, especially those in which the East with the West met in the union of faith and charity. For the Fathers of the Fourth Council of Constantinople, following in the footsteps of their predecessors, gave forth their solemn profession: *The first condition of salvation is to keep the rule of the true faith.* And because the sentence of our Lord Jesus Christ can not be passed by, who said: 'Thou art Peter, and upon this rock I will build my Church,' these things which have been said are approved by events, because in the Apostolic See the Catholic religion and her holy and well-known doctrine has always been kept undefiled. Desiring, therefore, not to be in the least degree separated from the faith and doctrine of that See, we hope that we may deserve to be in the one communion, which the Apostolic See preaches, in which is the entire and true solidity of the Christian religion. And, with the approval of the Second Council of Lyons, the Greeks professed that the holy Roman Church enjoys supreme and full primacy and preeminence over the whole Catholic Church, which it truly and humbly acknowledges that it has received with the plentitude of power from our Lord himself in the person of the blessed Peter, Prince or Head of the Apostles, whose successor the Roman Pontiff is; and as the Apostolic See is bound before all others to defend the truth of faith, so also, if any questions regarding faith shall arise, they must be defined by its judgment. Finally, the Council of Florence defined: That the Roman Pontiff is the true vicar of Christ, and the head of the whole Church, and the father and teacher of all Christians; and that to him in blessed Peter was delivered by our Lord Jesus Christ the full power of feeding, ruling, and governing the whole Church.

To satisfy this pastoral duty, our predecessors ever made unwearied efforts that the salutary doctrine of Christ might be propagated among all the nations of the earth, and with equal care watched that it might be preserved genuine and pure where it had been received. Therefore the Bishops of the whole world, now singly, now assembled, following the long-established custom of churches, and the form of the ancient rule, sent word to this Apostolic See of those dangers especially which sprang up in matters of faith, that there the losses of faith might be most effectually repaired where the faith can not fail. And the Roman Pontiffs, according to the exigencies of times and circumstances, sometimes assembling ecumenical Councils, or asking for the mind of the Church scattered throughout the world, sometimes by particular Synods, sometimes using other helps which Divine Providence supplied, defined as to be held those things which with the help of God they had recognized as conformable with the sacred Scriptures and Apostolic traditions. For the Holy Spirit was not promised to the successors of Peter, that by his revelation they might make known new doctrine; but that by his assistance they might inviolably keep and faithfully expound the revelation or deposit of faith delivered through the Apostles. And, indeed, all the venerable Fathers have embraced, and the holy orthodox doctors have venerated and followed, their Apostolic doctrine; knowing most fully that this See of holy Peter remains ever free from all blemish of error according to the divine promise of the Lord our Saviour made to the Prince of his disciples: 'I have prayed for thee that thy faith fail not, and, when thou art converted, confirm thy brethren.'

This gift, then, of truth and never-failing faith was conferred by heaven upon Peter and his successors in his chair, that they might perform their high office for the salvation of all; that the whole flock of Christ, kept away by them from the poisonous food of error, might be nourished with the pasture of heavenly doctrine; that the occasion of schism being removed, the whole Church might be kept one, and, resting on its foundation, might stand firm against the gates of hell. But since in this very age, in which the salutary efficacy of the Apostolic office is most of all required, not a few are found who take away from its authority, we judge it altogether necessary solemnly to assert the prerogative which the only-begotten Son of God vouchsafed to join with the supreme pastoral office.

Therefore faithfully adhering to the tradition received from the beginning of the Christian faith, for the glory of God our Saviour, the exaltation of the Christian religion, and the salvation of Christian people, the sacred Council approving, we teach and define that it is a dogma divinely revealed: that the Roman Pontiff, when he speaks *ex cathedra*, that is, when in discharge of the office of pastor and doctor of all Christians, by virtue of his supreme Apostolic authority, he defines a doctrine regarding faith and morals to be held by the universal Church, by the divine assistance promised to him in blessed Peter, is possessed of that infallibility with which the divine redeemer willed that his Church should be endowed for defining doctrine regarding faith or morals; and that therefore such definitions of the Roman Pontiff are irreformable of themselves, and not from the consent of the Church. *But if any one—which may God avert—presume to contradict this our definition: let him be anathema.*[317]

Vatican II

Bishops, teaching in communion with the Roman Pontiff, are to be respected by all as witnesses to divine and Catholic truth. In matters of faith and morals, the bishops speak in the name of Christ and the faithful are to accept their teaching and adhere to it with a religious assent of soul. This religious submission of will and mind must be shown in a special way to the authentic teaching authority of the Roman Pontiff, even when he is not speaking *ex cathedra*. That is, it must be shown in such a way that his supreme magesterium is acknowledged with reverence, the judgments made by him are sincerely adhered to, according to his manifest mind and will. His mind and will in the matter may be known chiefly either from the character of the documents, from his frequent repetition of the same doctrine, or from his manner of speaking.

Although the individual bishops do not enjoy the prerogative of infallibility, they can nevertheless proclaim Christ's doctrine infallibly...This infallibility with which the divine Redeemer willed His Church to be endowed in defining a doctrine of faith and morals extends as far as extends the deposit of divine revelation, which must be religiously guarded and faithfully expounded. This is the infallibility which the Roman Pontiff, the head of the college of bishops, enjoys in virtue of his office, when, as the supreme shepherd and teacher of all the faithful, who confirms his brethren in their faith (cf. Lk. 22:32), he proclaims by a definitive act some doctrine of faith or morals. Therefore his definitions, of themselves, are not from the consent of the Church, are justly styled irreformable, for they are pronounced with the assistance of the Holy Spirit, an assistance promised to him in blessed Peter. Therefore they need no approval of others, nor do they allow an appeal to any other judgment. For then the Roman Pontiff is not pronouncing judgment as a private person. Rather, as the supreme teacher of the universal Church, as one in whom the charism of the infallibility of the Church herself is individually present, he is expounding or defending a doctrine of Catholic faith.[318]

Appendix B

Documentation From the Writings of the following Church fathers and theologians, from the third to the eighth centuries, on the meaning of the Rock and Keys of Matthew 16:18 and of Peter's relationship to the other Apostles:

Augustine	253
Ambrose	279
Ambrosiaster	282
Aphraates	284
Apostolical Constitutions	286
Asterius	286
Athanasius	288
Basil the Great	291
Basil of Seleucia	291
Bede	292
Cassiodorus	292
Cassian (John)	293
Chrysostom	295
Chrysologus (Peter)	308
Cyprian	309
Cyril of Alexandria	311
Cyril of Jerusalem	314
Didymus the Blind	314
Epiphanius	315
Ephrem Syrus	316
Eusebius	316
Firmicus Maternus	318
Firmilian	319
Fulgentius	320

Gaudentius of Brescia	320
Gregory the Great	321
Gregory Nazianzen	325
Gregory of Nyssa	325
Hilary of Poitiers	325
Ignatius	326
Isidore of Pelusium	327
Isidore of Seville	327
James of Nisbis	328
Jerome	328
John of Damascus	331
Maximus of Turin	332
Nilus of Ancyra	336
Origen	336
Pacian	339
Palladius of Helenopolis	339
Paschasius Radbertus	340
Paul of Emessa	340
Paul Orosius	341
Paulinus of Nola	341
Prosper of Aquitaine	342
Tertullian	343
Theodoret	344
Comments of 6th Century Palestinian and Syriac Clergy from a Letter to Emperor Justin	346
Comments of Chrysostom, Cyril or Origen falsely attributed to Victor of Antioch	347

Augustine

Remember, in this man *Peter, the rock*. He's the one, you see, who on being questioned by the Lord about who the disciples said he was, replied, 'You are the Christ, the Son of the living God.' On hearing this, Jesus said to him, 'Blessed are you, Simon Bar Jona, because flesh and blood did not reveal it to you, but my Father who is in heaven. And I tell you'...'*You are Peter, Rocky, and on this rock I shall build my Church*, and the gates of the underworld will not conquer her. To you shall I give the keys of the kingdom. Whatever you bind on earth shall also be bound in heaven; whatever you loose on earth shall also be loosed in heaven' (Mt 16:15–19). *In Peter, Rocky, we see our attention drawn to the rock.* Now the apostle Paul says about the former people, 'They drank from the spiritual rock that was following them; *but the rock was Christ*' (1 Cor 10:4). *So this disciple is called Rocky from the rock, like Christian from Christ.*

Why have I wanted to make this little introduction? In order to suggest to you that in Peter the Church is to be recognized. *Christ, you see, built his Church not on a man but on Peter's confession. What is Peter's confession? 'You are the Christ, the Son of the living God.' There's the rock for you, there's the foundation, there's where the Church has been built, which the gates of the underworld cannot conquer.*[319]

You see, it was by this human form that the Lord—that is, the form of a servant: he emptied himself, taking the form of a servant (Phil 2:7); so it was by this form of a servant that Peter's affection was also held captive, when he was afraid of the one whom he loved so much having to die. He loved the Lord Jesus Christ, you see, as one human being loves another; as being of flesh loves a being of flesh, not as spiritual being loves the divine majesty. How can we be sure of this? Because when the Lord had been questioning his disciples about who he was said to be by the people, and they had given the opinions of others as they recalled them, that some said he was John, others Elijah, others Jeremiah or one of the prophets, he said to them, You, though, who do you say that I am? *And Peter, one speaking for the rest of them, one for all, said, You are the Christ, the Son of the living God* (Mt 16:15–16). Excellent, couldn't be more true; rightly did he deserve to receive a reply like this: Blessed are you, Simon Bar–Jona, because it was not flesh and blood that revealed this to you, but my Father who is in heaven. And I tell you, because you have told me; you have said something; hear something; you have made a confession, receive a blessing; so: *And I tell you: you are Peter; because I am the rock, you are Rocky, Peter—I mean, rock doesn't come from Rocky, but Rocky from rock, just as Christ doesn't come from Christian, but Christian from Christ*; and *upon this rock I will build my Church* (Mt 16:17–18); *not upon Peter, or Rocky, which is what you are, but upon the rock which you have confessed.* I will build my Church though; I will build you, because in this answer of yours *you represent the Church.*[320]

In a passage in this book, I said about the Apostle Peter: 'On him as on a rock the Church was built.'…But I know that very frequently at a later time, I so explained what the Lord said: *'Thou art Peter, and upon this rock I will build my Church,'* *that it be understood as built upon Him whom Peter confessed saying: 'Thou art the Christ, the Son of the living God,' and so Peter, called after this rock, represented the person of the Church which is built upon this rock, and has received 'the keys of the kingdom of heaven.'* For, 'Thou art Peter' and not 'Thou art the rock' was said to him. *But 'the rock was Christ,' in confessing whom, as also the whole Church confesses, Simon was called Peter*. But let the reader decide which of these two opinions is the more probable.[321]

But whom say ye that I am? Peter answered, 'Thou art the Christ, The Son of the living God.' One for many gave the answer, Unity in many. Then said the Lord to him, 'Blessed art thou, Simon Barjonas: for flesh and blood hath not revealed it unto thee, but My Father which is in heaven.' Then He added, 'and I say unto thee.' As if He had said, 'Because thou hast said unto Me, "Thou art the Christ the Son of the living God;" I also say unto thee, "Thou art Peter." For before he was called Simon. *Now this name of Peter was given him by the Lord, and in a figure, that he should signify the Church. For seeing that Christ is the rock (Petra), Peter is the Christian people. For the rock (Petra) is the original name. Therefore Peter is so called from the rock; not the rock from Peter; as Christ is not called Christ from the Christian, but the Christian from Christ.* 'Therefore,' he saith, 'Thou art Peter; and upon this Rock' which Thou *hast confessed, upon this rock which Thou hast acknowledged, saying, 'Thou art the Christ, the Son of the living God, will I build My Church;' that is upon Myself, the Son of the living God, 'will I build My Church.' I will build thee upon Myself, not Myself upon Thee.*

For men who wished to be built upon men, said, 'I am of Paul; and I of Apollos; and I of Cephas,' who is Peter. *But others who did not wish to built upon Peter, but upon the Rock, said, 'But I am of Christ.'* And when the Apostle Paul ascertained that he was chosen, and Christ despised, he said, 'Is Christ divided? was Paul crucified for you? or were ye baptized in the name of Paul?' And, as not in the name of Paul, so neither in the name of Peter; *but in the name of Christ: that Peter might be built upon the Rock, not the Rock upon Peter.* This same Peter therefore who had been by the Rock pronounced 'blessed,' bearing the figure of the Church, holding the chief place in the Apostleship, a very little while after that he had heard that he was 'Peter,' a very little while after that he had heard that he was to be 'built upon the Rock,' displeased the Lord when he had heard of His future Passion, for he had foretold His disciples that it was soon to be. He feared lest he should by death, lose Him whom he had confessed as the fountain of life...Peter said to Christ, I am not willing that Thou shouldest die; but Christ far better said, I am willing to die for thee. And then He forthwith rebuked him, whom he had little before commended; and calleth him Satan, whom He had pronounced 'blessed.'...Let us, looking at ourselves in this member of the Church, distinguish what is of God and what of ourselves. For then we shall not totter, then we shall be founded on the Rock, shall be fixed and firm against the winds, and storms, and streams and temptations, I mean, of this present world. You see this Peter, who was then our figure; now he trusts, and now he totters; now he confesses the Undying, and now he fears lest he should die. Wherefore? because the Church of Christ hath both strong and weak ones; and cannot be without either strong or weak; whence the Apostle Paul says, 'Now we that are strong ought to bear the infirmities of the weak.' In that Peter said, 'Thou art the Christ, the Son of the living God,' he represents the strong: but in that he totters, and would not that Christ should suffer, in fearing death for Him, and not acknowledging the Life, he represents the weak ones of the Church. In that one Apostle then, that is, Peter, in the order of Apostles first and chiefest, in whom the Church was figured, both sorts were to be represented, that is, both the strong and weak; because the Church does not exist without them both.[322]

We recognize in heretics that baptism, which belongs not to the heretics but to Christ, in such sort as in fornicators, in unclean persons or effeminate, in idolators, in prisoners, in those who retain enmity, in those who are fond of contention, in the credulous, in the proud, given to seditions, in the envious, in drunkards, in revelers; and in men like these we hold valid the baptism which is not theirs but Christ's. For of men like these, and among them are included heretics also, none, as the apostle says, shall inherit the kingdom of heaven. Nor as they to be considered as being in the body of Christ, which is the Church, simply because they are materially partakers of the sacraments. For the sacraments indeed are holy, even in such men as these, and shall be of force in them to greater condemnation, because they handle and partake of them unworthily. But the men themselves are not within the constitution of *the Church, which increases in the increase of God in its members through connection and contact with Christ. For that Church is founded on a rock, as the Lord says, 'Upon this rock I will build my Church.'* But they build on the sand, as the same Lord says, 'Everyone that heareth these sayings of mine, and doeth them not, shall be likened unto a foolish man, which built his house upon the sand.' But that you may not suppose that *the Church which is upon a rock* is one part only of the earth, and does not extend even to its furthest boundaries, hear her voice groaning from the psalm, amid the evils of her pilgrimage. For she says, 'From the end of the earth have I cried unto Thee; when my heart was distressed *Thou didst lift me up upon the rock*; Thou hast led me, Thou, my hope, hast become a tower of courage from the face of the enemy.' See how she cries from the end of the earth. She is not therefore in Africa alone, nor only among the Africans, who send a bishop from Africa to Rome to a few Montenses, and into Spain to the houses of one lady. *See how she is exalted on a rock.* All, therefore, are not to be deemed to be in her which build upon the sand, that is, which hear the words of Christ and do them not, even though both among us and among you they have and transmit the sacrament of baptism. *See how her hope is in God the Father, the Son, and the Holy Ghost, not in Peter or in Paul, still less in Donatus or Petilianus.*[323]

But take Peter too, my brothers and sisters; from where did he get it that he could say out of love, You are the Christ, the Son of the living God? Where did he get it from? Really from his own resources? Perish the thought! Its just as well that this same passage of the gospel shows both things, what Peter got from God's, what from his own resources. You've got them both there; read; there's nothing you should be waiting to hear from me. I'll just remind you of the gospel: *You are the Christ, the Son of the living God.* And the Lord to him: Blessed are you, Simon Bar–Jona. Why? Blessed from your own resources? No. Because flesh and blood has not revealed it to you; that, after all, is what you are. Flesh and blood has not revealed it to you, but my Father who is in heaven (Mt 16:16–17). And he goes on to say more things which it would take too long to mention.

Shortly afterward, *after these words of his in which he approved of Peter's faith and showed that it was the rock,* he began there and then to show his disciples that it would be necessary for him to come to Jerusalem, and suffer many things, and be rejected by the elders and the scribes and the priests, and be killed, and on the third day rise again.[324]

So the Lord will repay his faithful followers who are so lovingly, so cheerfully, so devotedly carrying out these works, to the effect that he includes them in the construction of his own building, into which they hasten to fit as living stones (1 Pt 2:5), fashioned by faith, made solidly firm by hope, cemented together by charity. *This is the building in which that wise architect the apostle placed Christ Jesus as the foundation (1 Cor 3:10–11), also as the supreme cornerstone (Is 28:16); one which, as Peter also reminds us from the prophetic scripture, was rejected indeed by men, but chosen and honored by God (1 Pt 2:4; Ps 118:22). By adhering to this stone we are joined peaceably together; by resting on it we are fixed firmly in place. You see, he is at one and the same time the foundation stone, because he is the one who regulates us, and the cornerstone, because it is he that joins us together. He is the rock on which the wise man builds his house,* and thus continues in utter security against all the trials and temptations of this world, neither collapsing when the rain pours down, nor being swept away when the river floods, nor overthrown when the winds blow.[325]

Peter then was true; or rather was Christ true in Peter? Now when the Lord Jesus Christ would, He abandoned Peter, and Peter was found a man; but when it so pleased the Lord Jesus Christ, He filled Peter, and Peter was found true. *The Rock (Petra) made Peter true, for the Rock was Christ.*[326]

Now then seeing it hath been set forth what we ought to do, let us see what we are to receive. For he hath appointed a work, and promised a reward. What is the work? 'If ye shall continue in me.' A short work; short in description, great in execution. 'If ye shall continue.' What is, 'If ye shall continue'? *'If ye shall build on the Rock.'* O how great a thing is this, Brethren, *to build on the Rock,* how great is it! 'The floods came. The winds blew, the rain descended, and beat upon that house, and it fell not; *for it was founded upon a rock.'*[327]

This then is the sight which ravishes every rational soul with desire for it, and of which the soul is the more ardent in its desire the purer it is; and it is the purer the more it rises again to the things of the spirit; and it rises the more to the things of the spirit, the more it dies to the material things of the flesh. But while we are away from the Lord and walking by faith and not by sight (2 Cor. 5:6), we have to behold Christ's back, that is his flesh, by this same faith; *standing that is upon the solid foundation of faith, which is represented by the rock,* and gazing at his flesh from the security of the lookout on the rock, namely *the Catholic church, of which it is said, And upon this rock I will build my church (Mt. 16:18).* All the surer is our love for the face of Christ which we long to see, the more clearly we recognize in his back how much Christ first loved us.[328]

And yet, while the issue about the Church is one thing, the issue about persons another, and they are quite distinct from each other, we aren't afraid of facing the issue of persons either, whom they have accused, and been unable to convict. We know they were cleared, we have tread the documentation of their being cleared. Even if they hadn't been cleared, I would never set up a Church because of them, and build one on sand, and pull down one built on rock; *because on this rock, he said, I will build my Church, and the gates of the underworld shall not overcome it* (Mt. 16:18). *Now the rock was Christ* (1 Cor. 10:4). *Was it Paul that was crucified for you?* Hold on to these texts, love these texts, repeat them in a fraternal and peaceful manner.[329]

And this Church, symbolized in its generality, was personified in the Apostle Peter, *on account of the primacy of his apostleship.* For, as regards his proper personality, he was by nature one man, by grace one Christian, by still more abounding grace one, and yet also, *the first apostle*; but when it was said to him, 'I will give unto thee the keys of the kingdom of heaven, and whatsoever thou shalt bind on earth, shall be bound in heaven; and whatsoever thou shalt loose on earth, shall be loosed in heaven,' *he represented the universal Church,* which in this world is shaken by divers temptations, that come upon it like torrents of rain, floods and tempests, *and falleth not, because it is founded upon a rock (petra), from which Peter received his name. For petra (rock) is not derived from Peter, but Peter from petra; just as Christ is not called so from the Christian, but the Christian from Christ. For on this very account the Lord said, 'On this rock will I build my Church,' because Peter had said, 'Thou art the Christ, the Son of the living God.' On this rock, therefore, He said, which thou hast confessed, I will build my Church. For the Rock (Petra) was Christ; and on this foundation was Peter himself built. For other foundation can no man lay than that is laid, which is Christ Jesus. The Church, therefore, which is founded in Christ received from Him the keys of the kingdom of heaven in the person of Peter, that is to say, the power of binding and loosing sins. For what the Church is essentially in Christ, such representatively is Peter in the rock (petra); and in this representation Christ is to be understood as the Rock, Peter as the Church.*[330]

So what does all this symbolism mean? That receptacle signifies the Church; the four lines it was hanging from are the four quarters of the earth, through which the Catholic Church stretches, being spread out everywhere. So all those who wish to go apart into a party, and to cut themselves off from the whole, do not belong to the sacred reality signified by the four lines. But if they don't belong to Peter's vision, neither do they do so to the keys which were given to Peter. You see, God says his holy ones are to be gathered together at the end from the four winds, because now the gospel faith is being spread abroad through all those four cardinal points of the compass. So those animals are the nations. All the Gentile nations, after all, were unclean in their errors and superstitions and lusts before Christ came; but at his coming their sins were forgiven them and they were made clean. Therefore now, after the forgiveness of sins, *why should they not be received into the body of Christ, which is the Church of God, which Peter was standing for?*

Its clear, you see, from many places in scripture that Peter can stand for, or represent, the Church; above all from that place where it says, To you will I hand over the keys of the kingdom of heaven. Whatever you bind on earth shall also be bound in heaven; and whatever you loose on earth shall be loosed in heaven. (Mt. 16:19). *Did Peter receive these keys, and Paul not receive them? Did Peter receive them, and John and James and the other apostles not receive them? Or are the keys not to be found in the Church, where sins are being forgiven every day? But because Peter symbolically stood for the Church, what was given to him alone was given to the whole Church. So Peter represented the Church; the Church is the body of Christ.*[331]

The blessed Peter, the first of the apostles, the ardent lover of Christ, who was found worthy to hear, 'And I say to you, that you are Peter.' He himself, you see, had just said, 'You are the Christ, the Son of the living God.' Christ said to him, 'And I say to you that you are Peter, and upon this rock I will build my Church' (Mt. 16:16, 18). *Upon this rock I will build the faith which you have just confessed. Upon what you have just said, 'You are the Christ, the Son of the living God,' I will build my Church; because you are Peter. Peter, Rocky, from rock, not rock from Rocky. Peter comes from 'petra', rock, in exactly the same way as Christian comes from Christ.* Do you want to know what rock Peter is called after? Listen to Paul: 'I would not have you ignorant, brothers,' the apostle of Christ says; 'I would not have you ignorant, brothers, that our fathers were all under the cloud, and all passed through the sea, and all were baptized in Moses in the cloud and in the sea, and all ate the same spiritual food, and all drank the same spiritual drink. *For they drank from the rock that was following them, and the rock was Christ' (1 Cor 10:1–4). There you have* where Rocky, Peter, is from.

Before his passion the Lord Jesus, as you know, chose those disciples of his, whom he called apostles. Among these it was only Peter who almost everywhere was given the privilege of representing the whole Church. *It was in the person of the whole Church, which he alone represented, that he was privileged to hear, 'To you will I give the keys of the kingdom of heaven' (Mt 16:19). After all, it isn't just one man that received these keys, but the Church in its unity. So this is the reason for Peter's acknowledged pre–eminence, that he stood for the Church's universality and unity, when he was told, 'To you I am entrusting,' what has in fact been entrusted to all.*

I mean, to show you that it is the Church which has received the keys of the kingdom of heaven, listen to what the Lord says in another place to all his apostles: 'Receive the Holy Spirit;' and straightway, 'Whose sins you forgive, they will be forgiven them; whose sins you retain, they will be retained' (Jn 20:22-23). *This refers to the keys, about which it is said, 'whatever you loose on earth shall be loosed in heaven, and whatever you bind on earth shall be bound in heaven' (Mt 16:19). But that was said to Peter. To show you that Peter at that time stood for the universal Church,* listen to what is said to him, what is said to all the faithful, the saints: 'If your brother sins against you, correct him between you and himself alone. If he does not listen to you, bring with you one or two; for it is written, By the mouth of two or three witnesses shall every matter be settled. If he does not even listen to them, refer him to the Church; if he does not even listen to her, let him be to you as a heathen and a tax collector. Amen amen I tell you, that whatever you bind on earth shall be bound in heaven, and whatever you loose on earth shall be loosed in heaven' (Mt 16:18). *It is the dove that binds, the dove that looses, the building built upon the rock that binds and looses.*

Let those who are bound fear, those who are loosed fear. Let those who are loosed be afraid of being bound; those who are bound pray to be loosed. 'Each one is tied up in the thread of his own sins' (Prv 5:22). And apart from the Church, nothing is loosed. One four days dead is told, 'Lazarus, come forth in the open' (Jn 11:43), and he came forth from the tomb tied hand and foot with bandages. The Lord rouses him, so that the dead man may come forth from the tomb; this means he touches the heart, so that the confession of sin may come out in the open. But that's not enough, he's still bound. So after Lazarus had come out of the tomb, the Lord turned to his disciples, whom he had told, 'Whatever you bind on earth shall be bound in heaven,' and said, 'Loose him, and let him go' (Jn 11:44). He roused him by himself, he loosed him through the disciples.

Furthermore, the Church's strength and courage is supremely presented to us in Peter; because he followed the Lord as he went to his passion; and also something of its weakness is to be observed there, since when he was questioned by a maid, he repudiated the Lord.[332]

We should each of us faithfully recall, too, an example offered us in that first people. The apostle says, you see, All these things were our models (1 Cor. 10:6), when he was talking about such things. I mean, what had he just said? For I would not have you ignorant, brothers, that all our fathers were under the cloud; and all were baptized in Moses in the cloud and in the sea; and all ate the same spiritual food, and all drank the same spiritual drink. For they drank from the spiritual rock that was following them. Now the rock was Christ (1 Cor. 10:4). The one who said that these things were our models, is one whom no believer has ever contradicted. And while he mentioned many things, he only explained one of them, saying, *Now the rock was Christ. In explaining a single item, he left us the others to be inquired into; but to save inquirers from going astray by departing from Christ, and to enable them to seek surely, founded on the rock, The rock, he said, was Christ.* He said those things were our models, and they are all obscure. Who could unpack these well wrapped models? Who could open them up, who would dare to shake them out? In these densest possible thickets, so to say, and these thick shadows he has hit a light: *The rock, he says, was Christ.*

I also want to say something about the doubts the servant of God, Moses, felt...In this case too, you see, he was representative of the saints of the Old Testament. Moses had his doubts about the water; when he struck the rock with his rod, so that water flowed out, he doubted...Moses doubted when the wood came into contact with the rock; the disciples doubted, when they saw the Lord crucified. Moses figuratively stood for them; he stood for that Peter with his threefold denial. *Why did Peter doubt? Because the wood approached the rock. When the Lord himself was foretelling the kind of death he would die, that is his cross,* Peter was horrified: Far be this from you, Lord; this shall not happen. *You doubt, because you see the rod hanging over the rock.* That's why the disciples then lost the hope they had placed in the Lord; it had somehow been cut off when they saw him crucified, when they mourned him slain. He came upon them after his resurrection talking to one another about this matter, in sad conversation. He kept their eyes from recognizing him, not to remove himself from believers, but to put them off while they were still doubters, and he joined in their conversation as a third party, and asked them what they were talking about. They were astonished that he should be the only person not to know what had happened—to the very one, in fact, who was inquiring about it. Are you the only stranger, they said, in Jerusalem? And they went over all that had happened to Jesus. And straightway they proceed to open up all the depth of their despair, and albeit unwittingly they show the doctor their wounds: But we, they say, were hoping that with him there would be redemption for Israel (Lk 24:13–21). *There you are, doubt arose, because wood had come into contact with the rock. What Moses figuratively stood for was fulfilled.*

Let's take a look at this text too: Climb the mountain and die (Dt 32:49–50). The bodily death of Moses stood for the death of his doubting, but on the mountain. What marvelous mysteries! When this had been definitely explained and understood, how much sweeter it is to the taste than manna! Doubting was born at the rock, died on the mountain. *When Christ was humbled in his passion, he was like a rock lying on the ground before their eyes.* It was natural to have doubts about him; that humility was not holding out hopes for anything very great. His very humiliation naturally made him into a stone of offense (Is 8:14; 1 Pt 2:8). But once glorified by his resurrection he was seen to be great, he is now a mountain. So now let that doubt, which was born at the rock, die on the mountain. Let the disciples recognize where their salvation lies, let them summon up their hope again. Notice how that doubting dies, notice how Moses dies on the mountain. Let him not enter the promised land; we don't want any doubting there; let it die. Let Christ now show us how it dies. Peter trembled and denied three times. *The rock you see was Christ* (1 Cor. 10:4). He rose again, he became a mountain; he even gave Peter courage.[333]

By loving the sheep, *show the love you have for the shepherd*; because the very sheep themselves are members of *the shepherd*. In order that the sheep might be his members, he was prepared to be a sheep; that the sheep might be his members, like a sheep that was led to the slaughter (Is 53:7); that the sheep might be his members, it was said of him, Behold the lamb of God, behold the one who takes away the sins of the world (Jn 1:29)...

So let us *love him*, let there be nothing dearer to us than he. So do you imagine that the Lord is not questioning us? Was Peter the only one who qualified to be questioned, and didn't we? When that reading is read, every single Christian is being questioned in his heart. So when you hear the Lord saying 'Peter, do you love me?' think of it as a mirror, and observe yourself there. I mean, *what else was Peter doing but standing for the Church*? So when the Lord was questioning Peter, he was questioning us, he was questioning the Church. I mean, *to show you that Peter stood for the Church, call to mind that place in the gospel, 'You are Peter, and upon this rock I will build my Church, and the gates of the underworld shall not conquer her; to you I will give the keys of the kingdom of heaven' (Mt 16:18-19). One man receives them; you see, he explained himself what the keys of the kingdom mean: 'What you all bind on earth shall be bound in heaven; and what you all loose on earth shall be loosed in heaven' (Mt 18:18). If it was said to Peter alone, Peter alone did this; he passed away, and went away; so who binds, who looses? I make bold to say, we too have these keys. And what am I to say? That it is only we who bind, only we who loose?* No, you also bind, you also loose. Anybody who's bound, you see, is barred from your society; and when he's barred from your society, he's bound by you; and when he's reconciled he's loosed by you, because you too plead with God for him.

We all love Christ, you see, we are his members; and when he entrusts the sheep to the shepherds, the whole number of shepherds is reduced to the body of one shepherd. Just to show you that the whole number of shepherds is reduced to the one body of the one shepherd, *certainly Peter's a shepherd, undoubtedly a pastor; Paul's a shepherd, yes, clearly a pastor; John's a shepherd, James a shepherd, Andrew a shepherd, and the other apostles are shepherds. All holy bishops are shepherds, pastors, yes, clearly so.* And how can this be true: And there will be one flock and one shepherd (Jn 10:16)? Then if there will be one flock and one shepherd is true, the innumerable number of shepherds or pastors must be reduced to the body of the one shepherd or pastor.[334]

This gospel that has just been read about Christ the Lord, and how he walked over the surface of the sea, and about the apostle Peter, and how, by growing afraid as he walked, he staggered, and by losing confidence began to submerge, until by confessing he again emerged; this gospel is advising us to take the sea as meaning the present age and this world, and the apostle Peter as representing the one and only Church. Peter, you see, is first in the class of the apostles, and readiest in expressing love of Christ, and is often the one who answers for them all. Thus when the Lord Jesus Christ was inquiring who people said he was, and the disciples told him the various opinions people held, and the Lord again asked them, 'But you, who do you say that I am?'—it was Peter who answered, 'You are the Christ, the Son of the living God' (Mt 16:15–16).

Then the Lord said to him, 'Blessed are you, Simon Bar–Jona, because it is not flesh and blood that revealed it to you, but my Father who is in heaven.' Then he added, 'And I say to you.' As much as to say, Because you said to me, 'You are the Christ, the Son of the living God,' I in turn say to you, 'You are Peter' (Mt 16:7–18). Previously, of course, he was called Simon; *this name of Peter was bestowed on him by the Lord, and that with the symbolic intention of his representing the Church. Because Christ, you see, is the petra or rock; Peter, or Rocky, is the Christian people.. I mean, the basic name is 'rock.' Therefore Rocky is so called from rock, not the rock from Rocky; just as Christ is not so called from Christian, but Christian from Christ. So, 'You,' he says, 'are Peter, and on this rock,' which you have acknowledged, 'on this rock,' which you recognized when you said 'You are Christ, the Son of the living God, I will build my Church;' that is, on myself, the Son of the living God, 'I will build my Church' (Mt 16:18). I will build you on me, not me on you.*

There were people, you see, who wanted to build on human beings merely, and they would say, 'I'm Paul's man, I'm Apollo's, I'm Kephas'— that's Peter or Rocky...*And others, who didn't want to be built on Rocky, but on the rock, said, 'But I'm Christ's.'* When, however, the apostle Paul realized that he had been chosen and Christ had been ignored, he said,

'Has Christ been divided? Was Paul crucified for you, *Or were you baptized in the name of Paul?' (1 Cor 1:12-13). Not in Paul's name, nor in Rocky's either, but in the name of Christ, so that Rocky might be built up on the rock, not the rock on Rocky.*

So then, this self–same *Peter, blessed by being surnamed Rocky from the rock, representing the person of the Church, holding chief place in the apostolic ranks*, no sooner had he heard that he was blessed, no sooner had he heard that he was Rocky, *no sooner had he heard that he was to be built on the rock*, than on hearing also about the Lord's coming passion, which the Lord said was going to happen pretty quickly, he expressed his displeasure. He was afraid of losing by death the one he had confessed to be the fountain of life. He was shocked, and said, 'Far be it from you, Lord; this must not happen.' Be easy on yourself, God; I don't want you to die.

By observing this member of the Church ourselves, let us try and distinguish in our own lives what comes from God's ideas, and what from our own. Then we shan't stagger, *then we shall be founded on the rock*, then we shall be solid and steady against the winds, the storms of rain, the floods, namely the trials and temptations of this present age. However, notice that man *Peter, who was the symbolic representative of us all*; now he's trusting, now he's tottering; one moment he's acknowledging Christ to be immortal, the next he's afraid of his dying. Its because the Church of Christ in the same sort of way has strong members, and also has weak members. It can't do without its strong members, nor without its weak ones. That's why the apostle Paul says, 'But we who are strong should bear the burdens of the weak' (Rom 15:1). Now Peter, in saying 'You are the Christ, the Son of the living God' (Mt 16:15), represents the strong. But in his being filled with alarm, and his staggering, and not wanting Christ to suffer because he was afraid of death and didn't recognize life, he represents the weak members of the Church. So in that one apostle, that is, in Peter, first and chief in the ranks of the apostles, in whom the Church was symbolized, each kind of member had to be symbolized too, that is to say, the strong and the weak; because without the one or the other there is no Church.[335]

Peter had already said to him, 'You are the Christ, the Son of the living God.' He had already heard, 'Blessed are you, Simon Bar–Jona, because flesh and blood did not reveal it to you, but my Father who is in heaven.

And I tell you, that you are Peter, and upon this rock I will build my Church, and the gates of the underworld shall not conquer her' (Mt 16:16–18). Such faith was drowned when the Lord was crucified. Peter, you see, only believed he was the Son of God up to the time he saw him hanging on the tree, the time he saw him fixed there with nails, the time he saw him dead, the time he saw him buried. *Then he lost what he held. Where's the rock? Where's the immovable solidity of the rock? Christ himself was the rock, while Peter, Rocky, was only named from the rock. That's why the rock rose again, to make Peter solid and strong; because Peter would have perished, if the rock hadn't lived.*[336]

When Christ said, Who do you say that I am? *Peter answered, You are the Christ, the Son of the living God.* And the Lord said to him: Blessed are you Simon Bar–Jona, because flesh and blood has not revealed it to you, as it has to those who call me a prophet, but my Father, who is in heaven; and I say to you, you are Peter (Mt. 16:15–18). You have said to me, let me say to you; you have made your confession of faith, now hear my blessing.

You see, the Lord had said about himself what was less important, and Peter had told him what was more important. In the Lord Jesus Christ, after all, what was less important was his being the Son of man; what was more important was his being the Son of God. He mentioned the less important thing, because he humbled himself; the one whom he exalted mentioned the more important one. *Upon this rock, said the Lord, I will build my Church. Upon this confession, upon this that you said, 'You are the Christ, the Son of the living God,' I will build my Church, and the gates of hell shall not conquer her* (Mt. 16:18).[337]

For not without cause among all the Apostles doth Peter sustain the person of this Church Catholic; for unto this Church were the keys of the Kingdom of Heaven given, when they were given unto Peter: and when it is said unto him, it is said unto all, Lovest thou Me? Feed My sheep. Therefore the Church Catholic ought willingly to pardon her sons, upon their amendment, and confirmation in godliness; when we see that *Peter himself, bearing her person*, both when he had tottered on the sea, and when with carnal feeling he had sought to call back the Lord from suffering, and when he had cut off the ear of the servant with the sword, and when he had thrice denied the Lord Himself, and when afterwards he had fallen into superstitious dissembling, had pardon granted unto him, and after amendment and strengthening attained at last unto the glory of the Lord's suffering.[338]

We know what rock is; and yet a hard and obstinate person is called a rock, and a solid, immovable person is called rock. In praise you take the rock's solidity, in blame you take its hardness. *We know the solidity of the rock, and we accept Christ as the rock: Now the rock was Christ* (1 Cor. 10:4).[339]

One wicked man *represents* the whole body of the wicked; in the same way as *Peter, the whole body of the good, yea, the body of the Church*, but in respect to the good. For *if in Peter's case there were no sacramental symbol of the Church, the Lord would not have said to him, 'I will give unto thee the keys of the kingdom of heaven: whatsoever thou shalt loose on earth shall be loosed in heaven; and whatsoever thou shalt bind on earth shall be bound in heaven.' If this was said only to Peter, it gives no ground of action to the Church*. But if such is the case also in the Church, that what is bound on earth is bound in heaven, and what is loosed on earth is loosed in heaven—for when the Church excommunicates, the excommunicated person is bound in heaven; when one is reconciled by the Church, the person so reconciled is loosed in heaven—*if such, then, is the case in the Church, Peter, in receiving the keys, represented the holy Church*.[340]

Coming now to what the Lord goes on to say to Moses: 'You cannot see my face and live, for a man shall not see my face and live. And the Lord said Behold, there is a place beside me, and you shall stand upon the rock the moment my majesty passes, and I will set you at a look-out in the rock, and I will cover you with my hand until I have passed, and I will take away my hand, and then you shall see my back; for my face shall not appear to you' (Ex 33:20). This is usually understood, not inappropriately, to prefigure the person of our Lord Jesus Christ, taking his 'back' to mean his flesh, in which he was born of the virgin, died and rose again...This then is the sight which ravishes every rational soul with desire for it, and of which the soul is more ardent in its desire the purer it is; and it is the purer the more it rises again to the things of the spirit; and it rises more to the things of the spirit, the more it dies to the material things of the flesh. But while 'we are away from the Lord and walking by faith and not by sight' (2 Cor 5:6), we have to behold Christ's back, that is, his flesh, by this same faith; *standing that is upon the solid foundation of faith, which is represented by the rock*, and gazing at his flesh from the security of the lookout *on the rock, namely the Catholic Church, of which it is said, 'And upon this rock I will build my Church'* (Mt 16:18). All the surer is our love for the face of Christ which we long to see, the more clearly we recognize in his back how much Christ first loved us.

But as regards this flesh of his, it is faith in his resurrection that saves and justifies. 'If you believe in your hearts,' it says, 'that God raised him from the dead, you will be saved' (Rom 10:9); and again, 'Who delivered himself up for our transgressions and rose again for our justification' (Rom 4:25). So it is the resurrection of the Lord's body that gives value to our faith.

Even his enemies believe that the body died on the cross of pain, but they do not believe that it rose again. We however believe it absolutely, observing it so to say from the firmness of the rock, from where 'we await our adoption, the redemption of our bodies,' in the certainty of hope (Rom 8:23)...'And you shall stand,' it says, 'upon the rock the moment my majesty passes' (Ex 33:21). And in very truth, the moment the majesty of the Lord passed, in the glory of the Lord's resurrection and ascension to the Father, we were firmly established upon the rock. It was then that Peter himself was firmly established, so that he could boldly preach Christ whom he had timorously thrice denied before he was firmly established.[341]

Some one, perhaps, may inquire what is signified by the division that was made of His garments into so many parts, and of the casting of lots for the coat. The raiment of the Lord Jesus Christ parted into four, symbolized His quadripartite Church, as spread abroad over the whole world, which consists of four quarters...But the coat, on which lots were cast, signifies the unity of all the parts, which is contained in the bond of charity...And it was without seam, that its sewing might never be separated; and came into the possession of one man, because He gathereth all into one. Just as in the case of the apostles, who formed the exact number of twelve, in other words, were divisible into four parts of three each, when the question was put to all of them, *Peter was the only one that answered, 'Thou art the*

Christ, the Son of the living God;' and to whom it was said, 'I will give unto thee the keys of the kingdom of heaven,' as if he alone received the power of binding and loosing: seeing, then, that one spake in behalf of all, and received the latter along with all, as if personifying the unity itself; therefore one stands for all, because there is unity in all.[342]

The Creed of most holy martyrdom, which you received as a group and which you have recited today as individuals, *contains the truths upon which the faith of Mother Church is solidly established as on a firm foundation, which is Christ Jesus the Lord.* 'For other foundation no one can lay, but that which has been laid, which is Christ Jesus' (1 Cor. 3:11).[343]

So whoever builds him up like that is not building him on rock, but placing him on sand. 'Now the rock was Christ' (1 Cor 10:4).[344]
Well, when they had rushed for the stones, hard men for hard stones, they started hurling at him things just like themselves. He was being stoned with rocks, as *he was dying for the Rock.* Its what the apostle says: But *the rock was Christ* (1 Cor. 10:4).[345]

Peter too would walk. He as Head, Peter as Body: because, 'Upon this rock,' He saith, ' I will build My Church.' He was bidden to walk, and he was walking by the Grace of Him bidding, not by his own strength.[346]

Thus Christ is also called the cornerstone who has made both one (Eph 2:20, 14). A corner joins two walls coming from different directions. What could be more different than circumcised and uncircumcised, meaning one wall from Judea and another wall from the Gentiles? But they are joined together by the cornerstone. For the stone which the builders rejected, this has become the head of the corner (Ps 118:22).[347]

None of us lacks Christ. He is complete in all of us, and still there is more of his body waiting for him. Those disciples believed, through them many inhabitants of Jerusalem came to believe, Judea came to believe, Samaria came to believe. *Let the members join the body, the building attach itself to the foundation. For no other foundation can anyone lay, says the apostle, except what has been laid, which is Christ Jesus* (1 Cor. 3:11).[348]

That Jerusalem of ours, though, still in exile, is being built in heaven. *That's why Christ, its foundation, preceded it into heaven. That, you see, is where our foundation is, and the head of the Church, because a foundation too is also called a head*; and indeed that is what it is. Because the head of a building too is its foundation; its head isn't where it is finished, but where it starts growing upward from. The tops of earthly buildings are raised up high; yet they set their head firmly in the solid ground. In the same sort of way *the head of the Church has gone ahead into heaven*, and is seated at the right hand of the Father. Just as men go about their work, when for laying foundations they bring along suitable material to make a solid base, to ensure the security of the mass that is going to be placed on top of it in construction of the edifice to be; so in the same sort of way, by all those things that took place in Christ, being born, growing up, being arrested, enduring abuse, being scourged, crucified, killed, dying, being buried, it was like material being brought along for the heavenly foundations.

So now that our foundation has been laid in the heights, let us get ourselves built on it. Listen to the apostle: No other foundation, he says, can anyone lay, besides the one which has been laid, which is Christ Jesus (1 Cor 3:11). But what comes next? But let each of you see what you build on top of the foundation, gold, silver, precious stones, wood, grass, stubble (1 Cor:10,12). *Christ is indeed in heaven, but also in the hearts of believers. If Christ has the first place there, the foundation is rightly laid.* So if you are building on it, you may build without a qualm, if you build, to match the worth of the foundation, gold, silver, precious stones. If however, by building wood, grass, stubble, you fail to match the worth of the foundation, at least stick to the foundation, and because of the dry and fragile things you have constructed on it, prepare yourself for the fire. *But if the foundation is there, that is if Christ has obtained the first place in your heart*, while the things of this world are loved in such a way that they are not put before Christ, but the Lord Christ is put before them, so that he is the foundation, that is holding the first place in your heart, then you will suffer loss, he says, but you yourself shall be saved, in such a way, though, as is by fire (1 Cor 3:15).[349]

If in Him tempted we have been, in Him we overcome the devil... 'On the Rock Thou hast exalted me.' Now therefore here we perceive who is crying from the ends of the earth. Let us call to mind the Gospel: 'Upon this Rock I will build My Church.' *Therefore She crieth from the ends of the earth, whom He hath willed to build upon a Rock. But in order that the Church might be builded upon the Rock, who was made the Rock? Hear Paul saying: 'But the Rock was Christ.' On Him therefore builded we have been.* For this reason that Rock whereon we have been builded, first hath been smitten with winds, flood, rain, when Christ of the devil was being tempted. Behold on what firmness He hath willed to stablish thee. With reason our voice is not in vain, but is hearkened unto: for on great hope we have been set: 'On the Rock Thou hast exalted me.'[350]

For as some things are said which seem peculiarly to apply to *the Apostle Peter*, and yet are not clear in their meaning, unless when referred to *the Church, whom he is acknowledged to have figuratively represented*, on account of the primacy which he bore among the Disciples; as it is written, 'I will give unto thee the keys of the kingdom of heaven,' and other passages of like purport: so Judas doth represent those Jews who were enemies of Christ...[351]

One wicked man represents the whole body of the wicked; in the same way as Peter, the whole body of the good, yea, the body of the Church, but in respect to the good. For if *in Peter's case there were no sacramental symbol of the Church, the Lord would not have said to him, 'I will give unto thee the keys of the kingdom of heaven: whatsoever thou shalt loose on earth shall be loosed in heaven; and whatsoever thou shalt bind on earth shall be bound in heaven.' If this was said only to Peter, it gives no ground of action to the Church*. But if such is the case also in the Church, that what is bound on earth is bound in heaven, and what is loosed on earth is loosed in heaven, for when the Church excommunicates, the excommunicated person is bound in heaven; when one is reconciled by the Church, the person so reconciled is loosed in heaven: if, such, then is the case in the Church, *Peter, in receiving the keys, represented the good in the Church*, and in Judas' person were represented the bad in the Church...[352]

So my life will depend on you, and my salvation be bound up with you?

Have I forgotten my foundation all that much? *Wasn't Christ the rock?* The one who builds on the rock, isn't he the one whom neither wind nor rain nor rivers can overthrow? So come with me, if you will, onto the rock, and don't aim at replacing the rock for me.[353]

How great a house is this! But when does it sing the new song? When it is in building. When is it dedicated? At the end of the world. Its foundation has already been dedicated, because He hath ascended into heaven, and dieth no more. When we too shall have risen to die no more, then shall we be dedicated.[354]

The Church of the Jews comes from the circumcision, the Church of the Gentiles comes from the uncircumcision. Coming from different directions, they are joined together in the Lord. That is why the Lord is called the cornerstone. Thus the psalm says: The stone which the builders rejected, this very one has become the head of the corner (Ps 118:22). And the apostle says: Christ Jesus being himself the cornerstone (Eph 2:20).[355]

So was there no point in the Lord saying, What you loose on earth shall be loosed in heaven (Mt 18:18; 16:19)? So were *the keys given to the Church of God* for nothing?[356]

Luke 22:32

Listen to the Lord, when He says, 'I have prayed for thee, Peter, that thy faith fail not;' that we may never think of our faith as so lying in our free will that it has no need of the divine assistance.[357]

Faith pours out prayer, and the pouring out of prayer obtains the strengthening of faith. Faith, I say, pours out prayer, the pouring out of prayer obtains strengthening even for faith itself. For that faith might not fail in temptations, therefore did the Lord say, 'Watch and pray, lest ye enter into temptation.' What is to 'enter into temptation,' but to depart from faith? For so far temptation advances as faith gives way: and so far temptation gives way, as faith advances. For that you may know,

Beloved, more plainly, that the Lord said, 'Watch and pray, lest ye enter into temptation,' as touching faith lest it should fail and perish; He said in the same place of the Gospel, 'This night hath Satan desired to sift you as wheat, and I have prayed for thee, Peter, that thy faith fail not.'[358]

John 21:15–17

We have heard the Lord Jesus setting before us the whole office and duty of the good shepherd or pastor. In doing so, he was giving us clearly to understand that there are good shepherds. And yet, to prevent us drawing the wrong conclusions from the existence of many shepherds or pastors, I, he said, am the good shepherd. And then he went on to show what makes a good shepherd: The good shepherd, he says, lays down his life for the sheep. But the hired hand, and the one who is not the shepherd, sees the wolf coming, and runs away, because he does not care about the sheep; he is only a hired hand (Jn 10:11–13). *So Christ is the good shepherd. What about Peter? Isn't he a good shepherd? Didn't he too lay down his life for the sheep? What about Paul? What about the other apostles? What about the blessed martyr bishops who came after their times? What indeed about this saint of ours, Cyprian? Weren't they all good shepherds*, and not hired hands, of whom it says, Amen I tell you, they have received their reward (Mt 6:2)? So all these were good shepherds...

Because you see, even among the heretics, who have endured a certain amount of harassment because of their iniquities and errors, there are those who boast of being martyrs, in order to steal all the more easily under this cloak of respectability; because in fact they are wolves. But if you really want to know in what class to count them, *listen to that good shepherd the apostle Paul,* saying that not all who hand over their bodies to the flames in martyrdom are to be considered as having shed their blood for the sheep, but rather against the sheep...

But how can you have even the tiniest bit of charity, if even when you have been proved wrong, you don't love unity? When the Lord was entrusting this unity to good shepherds, he didn't wish to talk about many shepherds. As I said, it's not that Peter was not a good shepherd, or Paul, or the rest of the apostles, or the holy bishops who came after them, or blessed Cyprian. All these were good shepherds; and yet he did not draw the attention of these good shepherds to good shepherds, but to the good shepherd. I, he said, am the good shepherd (Jn 10:11)...What was Peter? Was he either not a shepherd, not a pastor, or else a bad one? Let's see if he's not a shepherd. Do you love me? You said it to him, Lord. Do you love me? And he answered, I do. And you then said to him, Feed my sheep. You, Lord, you yourself, by your very questioning of him, by the formal decree of your own lips, made a lover a pastor.

So he is a pastor, a shepherd, to whom you entrusted your sheep, with the task of feeding them. You yourself appointed him, he's a shepherd. Let's see now if he's a good one. We find out in this very exchange of question and answer. You inquired whether he loved you, he answered, I do. You saw into his heart, that he answered truthfully. So isn't he good, seeing that he loves so great a good? ...*So he was both a shepherd and a good shepherd*; nothing to compare, of course, with the authority and goodness of the shepherd of shepherds, the pastor of pastors; but all the same he too was both a pastor and a good one, and the others like him were good pastors.

So why is it that you draw the attention of good shepherds to the idea of one shepherd? For what other reason could it be, but that in the one shepherd you are teaching the lesson of unity? And the Lord explains the matter more clearly through my ministry, as he reminds your graces from the gospel and says, "Listen to what I have drawn attention to: *I am the good shepherd, I said; because all the others, all the good shepherds are my members, parts of me; one head, one body, one Christ. So both the shepherd of the shepherds, and the shepherds of the shepherd, and the sheep with the shepherds under the shepherd, are one.* All this is only what the apostle says: Just as the body is one and has many parts, but all the parts of the body, though they are many, form one body, so too is Christ (1 Cor 12:12). If, then, so too is Christ, *it was quite right for Christ, who contains all the good shepherds in himself, to draw attention to one by saying, I am the good shepherd. I am, I am one person, with me all in the unity are one.* Anyone who feeds the sheep outside me feeds them against me. Anyone who does not gather with me scatters.[359]

But first the Lord asks what He knew, and that not once, but a second and third time, whether Peter loved Him; and just as often he has the same answer, that He is loved, while just as often He gives Peter the same charge to feed His sheep. To the threefold denial there is now appended a threefold confession, that his tongue may not yield a feebler service to love than to fear, and imminent death may not appear to have elicited more from the lips than present life. Let it be the office of love to feed the Lord's flock, if it was the signal of fear to deny the Shepherd. Those who have this purpose in feeding the flock of Christ, that they may have them as their own, and not as Christ's, are convicted of loving themselves, and not Christ, from the desire either of boasting, or wielding power, or acquiring gain, and not from the love of obeying, serving and pleasing God. Against such, therefore, there stands as a wakeful sentinel this thrice inculcated utterance of Christ, of whom the apostle complains that they seek their own, not the things that are Jesus Christ's. For what else mean the words, 'Lovest thou Me? Feed My sheep,' than if it were said, If thou lovest me, think not of feeding thyself, but feed my sheep as mine, and not as thine own; seek my glory in them, and not thine own; my dominion, and not thine; my gain, and not thine; lest thou be found in the fellowship of those who belong to the perilous times, lovers of their own selves, and all else that is joined on to this beginning of evils?...With great propriety, therefore, is Peter addressed, 'Lovest thou Me:' and the command applied to him, 'Feed my lambs,' and this a second and third time...Let us, then, love not ourselves, but Him; and in feeding His sheep, let us be seeking the things which are His, not the things which are our own.[360]

But what now? The Lord asketh him as ye heard when the Gospel was being read, and saith to him, Simon, son of John, lovest thou Me more than these? He answered and said, Yea, Lord, Thou knowest that I love Thee. And again the Lord asked this question, and a third time He asked it. And when he asserted in reply his love, He commended to him the flock. For each several time the Lord Jesus said to Peter, as he said, I love Thee: Feed My lambs, feed My little sheep. *In this one Peter was figured the unity of all pastors, of good pastors,* that is, who know that they feed Christ's sheep for Christ, not for themselves.[361]

So when the Lord was speaking just now, he said he was a shepherd; he also said he was a gate. You've got each thing there; both I am the gate and

I am the shepherd (Jn 10:9,11). He's the gate in the head, the shepherd in the body. *You see, he says to Peter, whom he singles out to represent the Church, Peter, do you love me?* He answers, Lord, I do. And then a third time, Peter, do you love me? Peter was upset that he asked him a third time (Jn 21:15-17); as though the one could see his conscience when he was going to deny him could not see his faith when he wanted to confess him.[362]

Every time, though, every time, that is with each of his three questions, *as Peter answers that he loves him, the Lord Jesus entrusts him with his lambs*, and says, Feed my lambs, feed my sheep (Jn 21:15-17). What are you going to give me, since you love me? Show your love in my sheep. What are you bestowing on me by loving me, seeing that it was I who bestowed on you the ability to love me? But you do have the means of showing your love for me, you have the means of exercising it: Feed my sheep.

To what extent, though, the lambs of the Lord were to be fed, with what love the sheep bought at such a price were to be fed, he indicated in what followed. I mean, after Peter, completing the just requirement of his threefold answer, had professed himself to be a lover of the Lord, and had his sheep entrusted to him, he heard about his own future martyrdom. *Here the Lord indicated that his sheep are to be loved by those to whom he entrusts them, in such a way that they are ready to die for them*. That's what this same John writes in his letter: Just as Christ laid down his life for us, in the same way we too ought to lay down ours for the brethren (1 Jn 3:16).[363]

Here I find all the good shepherds in the one shepherd. The good shepherds are not lacking after all, but they are in the one. Those who have broken away are many. Here one is being proclaimed because unity is being commended to us. It isn't really because the Lord couldn't find shepherds to commend his sheep to that here shepherds are not mentioned and the shepherd is. In that other text he found Peter to commend them to. Yes indeed, and *in Peter himself he commended unity to us.* There were several apostles, and only one was told, Feed my sheep (Jn 21:17). It is unthinkable that good shepherds should be lacking now; far be it from us that they should be lacking, far be it from his mercy not to produce them and establish them. Of course, if there are good sheep, there are also good shepherds, because good shepherds are made out of good sheep. But all the good shepherds are in the one, they are one. They feed the sheep, Christ feeds them...And with Peter too, when he was commending his sheep to him as one man to another, he wished to make him one with himself, and to commend his sheep to him in such a way that he himself would be the head and Peter would represent the body, that is to say the Church, and like husband and wife they would be two in one flesh. Well, what did he say to him first, in order to be able to commend his sheep to him, without simply commending them to him as one man to another? Peter, do you love me? And he answered, I do. And again, Do you love me? And he answered, I do. And a third time, Do you love me? And he answered, I do (Jn 21:15–17). He makes sure of love in order to consolidate unity.[364]

Quite rightly too did the Lord after his resurrection entrust his sheep to Peter to be fed. It's not, you see, that he alone among the disciples was fit to feed the Lord's sheep; but *when Christ speaks to one man, unity is being commended* to us. And he first speaks to Peter, because *Peter is the first among the apostles.*[365]

So the Lord entrusted his sheep to us bishops, because he entrusted them to Peter; if, that is, we are worthy with any part of us, even with the tips of our toes, to tread the dust of Peter's footsteps, the Lord entrusted his sheep to us. You are his sheep, we are sheep along with you, because we are Christians. I have already said, we are fed and we feed.[366]

But when he declared his love once, and again, and a third time, *the Lord entrusted him with his sheep*. Do you love me? He said. Lord, you know that I love you. Feed my lambs. This once, and again, and a third time, as though the only way Peter could show his love for Christ would be by *being a faithful shepherd and pastor under the prince of all pastors*...Watch out, though, brothers and sisters, for men who are bad servants, who have carved out private herds for themselves out of the Lord's flock, and divided up the estate they had not bought. Some unfaithful servants have sprung up, you see, and divided the flock of

Christ, and by their thefts, as it were, from his flock have put together private herds for themselves, and you hear them saying, 'These are my sheep'...Far be it from us to call you our sheep; that's no Catholic way of speaking, it isn't brotherly, it isn't Peter's because it is against the Rock. You are sheep, but those of the one who has bought both us and you. We have one and the same Lord; he is the real shepherd, not just hired for the job. [367]

What now on this occasion? The Lord questions him, as you heard when the gospel was read, and says to him, Simon son of John, do you love me more than these? He answered and said, Yes, Lord, you know that I love you. And again the Lord asked this question, and a third time he asked this question. And every time in reply he affirmed his love, *he entrusted him with the care of his flock.* Every time, you see, that Peter said I love you, the Lord Jesus said to him, Feed my lambs, feed my sheep (Jn 21:15-17). *The one man Peter represents the unity of all the shepherds or pastors of the Church—but of the good ones, who know how to feed Christ's flock for Christ, not for themselves.*[368]

So, brothers and sisters, receive it in a spirit of obedience when you hear that you are Christ's sheep; *because we bishops too are filled with fear and trembling when we hear, Feed my sheep.*[369]

Ambrose

He, then, who before was silent, to teach us that we ought not to repeat the words of the impious, this one, I say, when he heard: 'But who do you say I am,' immediately, not unmindful of his station, *exercised his primacy, that is, the primacy of confession, not of honor; the primacy of belief, not of rank...This, then, is Peter who has replied for the rest of the Apostles; rather, before the rest of men. And so he is called the foundation, because he knows how to preserve not only his own but the common foundation.* Christ agreed with him; the Father revealed it to him. For he who speaks of the true generation of the Father, received it from the Father, did not receive it from the flesh. *Faith, then, is the foundation of the Church, for it was not said of Peter's flesh, but of his faith, that 'the gates of hell shall not prevail against it.' But his confession of faith conquered hell. And this confession did not shut out one heresy, for, since the Church like a good ship is often buffeted by many waves, the foundation of the Church should prevail against all heresies.* The day will fail me sooner than the names of heretics and the different sects, yet against all is this general faith— that Christ is the Son of God, and eternal from the Father, and born of the Virgin Mary.[370]

Jesus said to them: Who do men say that I am? Simon Peter answering said, The Christ of God (Lk. ix.20). If it is enough for Paul 'to know nothing but Christ Jesus and Him crucified,' (1 Cor. ii.2), what more is to be desired by me than to know Christ? For in this one name is the expression of His Divinity and Incarnation, and faith in His Passion. And accordingly though the other apostles knew, yet Peter answers before the rest, 'Thou art the Christ the Son of God.'...Believe, therefore, as Peter believed, that thou also mayest be blessed, and that thou also mayest deserve to hear, 'Because flesh and blood hath not revealed it to thee, but My Father who is in heaven.'...Peter therefore did not wait for the opinion of the people, but produced his own, saying, 'Thou art the Christ the Son of the living God': Who ever is, began not to be, nor ceases to be. Great is the grace of Christ, who has imparted almost all His own names to His disciples. 'I am,' said He, 'the light of the world,' and yet with that very name in which He glories, He favoured His disciples, saying, 'Ye are the light of the world.' 'I am the living bread;' and 'we all are one bread' (1 Cor. x.17)...*Christ is the rock, for 'they drank of the same spiritual rock that followed them, and the rock was Christ' (1 Cor. x.4); also He denied not to His disciple the grace of this name; that he should be Peter, because he has from the rock (petra) the solidity of constancy, the firmness of faith. Make an effort, therefore, to be a rock! Do not seek the rock outside of yourself, but within yourself! Your rock is your deed, your rock is your mind. Upon this rock your house is built. Your rock is your faith, and faith is the foundation of the Church. If you are a rock, you will be in the Church, because the Church is on a rock. If you are in the Church the gates of hell will not prevail against you*...He who has conquered the flesh is a foundation of the Church; and if he cannot equal Peter, he can imitate him.[371]

Appendix B

Which of these three different causes of impossibility, think you, which we have enumerated (setting aside the fourth) can we meetly assign to the case of the Son of God? Is He naturally insensible and immovable, like a stone? He is indeed a stone of stumbling to the wicked, a cornerstone for the faithful; but He is not insensible, upon Whom the faithful affection of sentient people are stayed. He is not an immovable rock, 'for they drank of a Rock that followed them, and that Rock was Christ.'...Moreover, that thou mayest know that it is after His Manhood that He entreats, and in virtue of His Godhead that He commands, it is written for thee in the Gospel that He said to Peter: 'I have prayed for thee, that thy faith fail not.' To the same Apostle, again, when on a former occasion he said, 'Thou art the Christ, the Son of the living God,' He made answer: 'Thou art Peter, and upon this Rock will I build My Church, and I will give thee the keys of the kingdom of heaven.' *Could He not then, strengthen the faith of the man to whom, acting on His own authority, He gave the kingdom, whom He called the Rock, thereby declaring him to be the foundation of the Church?*[372]

It was not out of confusion that Peter said: 'Depart from me Lord, for I am a sinner' (Lk. 5.8); for Peter was a wise and judicious man—a man in whom were both the foundation of the Church and the authority to discipline; and he perceived that nothing could be more useful to him than that he should be exalted as a result of Christ's ensuing act (of raising him).[373]

It is that same Peter to whom He said, 'Thou art Peter, and upon this rock I will build My Church.' Therefore, where Peter is, there the Church is, there death is not, but life eternal. And therefore did He add, 'and the gates of hell shall not prevail against it,' (or him). Blessed Peter, against whom 'the gates of hell prevailed not,' the gate of heaven closed not; but who, on the contrary, destroyed the porches of hell, and opened the heavenly vestibules; wherefore, though placed on earth, he opened heaven and closed hell.[374]

'They sucked honey out of the firm rock,' (Deut. xxxii.13): for *the flesh of*

Christ is a rock, which redeemed heaven and the whole world (1 Cor. x.4).[375]

The Lord said to Peter: on this rock I will build My Church...On this catholic confession of faith he establishes the faithful in life.[376]

Nor Paul inferior to Peter, though the latter is the foundation of the Church, and the former, a wise architect, knew how to lay a foundation for the steps of believing people; nor was Paul, I say, unworthy of the college of apostles; and is easily to be compared even with the first, and second to none. For who knows not himself unequal, makes himself equal.[377]

Ambrosiaster

By the apostles who were somewhat distinguished among their colleagues, whom also he, *Paul*, because of their constancy calls 'pillars', and who had always been intimate with the Lord, even beholding his glory on the mount, by them he (Paul) says the gift which he received from God was approved; *so that he would be worthy to have primacy in preaching to the Gentiles, even as Peter had the primacy in preaching to the circumcision.* And even as he gives colleagues to Peter, outstanding men among the apostles, so he also joins to himself Barnabas, who was associated with him by divine choice; *yet he claims the privilege of primacy granted by God for himself alone, even as it was granted to Peter alone among the apostles*, in such a way that the apostles of the circumcision stretched out their right hands to the apostles of the Gentiles to manifest a harmony of fellowship, that both parties, knowing that they had received from the Lord a spirit of completeness in the imparting of the gospel, might show that they were in no way appointing one another.[378]

(Verse 20). 'Built upon the foundation of the apostles and prophets, Christ Jesus himself being the cornerstone.' The above puts together New and Old Testaments. For the apostles proclaimed what the prophets said would be, although Paul says to the Corinthians: 'God placed the apostles first, the prophets second' (1 Cor. 12.28). But this refers to other prophets, for in 1 Cor. Paul writes about ecclesiastical orders; *here he is concerned with the foundation of the Church. The prophets prepared, the apostles laid the foundations. Wherefore the Lord says to Peter: 'Upon this rock I shall build my Church,' that is, upon this confession of the catholic faith I shall establish the faithful in life.*[379]

Paul names Peter alone and compares him to himself since he had received the privilege of founding the Church; in like manner Paul had been chosen to have the privilege of founding the Churches of the Gentiles. It did nevertheless happen that Peter preached also to the Gentiles, if he had cause, and Paul to the Jews, for each is found to have done both. *Still we find that full authority in preaching to Jews was given to Peter, and to Paul complete authority in preaching to Gentiles.* Wherefore indeed he calls himself teacher of the Gentiles in faith and truth...[380]

After the concord of fellowship and the honor which each accorded to the other in the matter of the privilege of founding churches, now, because some matter of neglect or error has intervened, the apostles seem to differ among themselves—not in a personal concern, but in a concern of the Church. 'To his face,' Paul says, '*I opposed him.*" *What does this mean, except that Paul contradicted Peter in his presence?* And Paul has added the reason: '*Because he stood condemned.*' *Condemned assuredly by evangelical truth which Peter's act (of separating himself from the circumcision) opposed. For who dared to contradict Peter, the chief apostle to whom the Lord had given the keys of the kingdom of Heaven, except such another who in the assurance of his election knew that he was not unequal, and so could firmly disavow what Peter had thoughtlessly done.*[381]

Worthy it was that Paul desired to see Peter, since Peter was chief among the apostles, to whom the Savior had entrusted the care of the Church. Not, to be sure, that Paul could learn anything from him, since he had already been taught by that same authority by whom Peter himself had been instructed: but on account of the disposition of the apostolic office, *so that Peter might know that this office which he himself had received had been given also to Paul.* Coming, therefore, to Peter, Paul was warmly received, and he remained with Peter for 15 days, as co–apostle in harmony with him. Paul makes these things known, in order to show that he possessed the agreement of the apostles and that they in no way dissented, as certain pseudo-apostles were murmuring about him.[382]

'For I am not at all inferior to these superlative apostles' (2 Cor. 12.11)...He says this because *he is inferior to his apostolic predecessors neither in preaching, nor in performing miracles, nor in worthiness*, but only in time. But if we think that things must be ranked according to time, John began to preach before Christ, and Christ did not baptize John, but John Christ. Does God judge this? Moreover, Andrew followed the Savior before Peter; and yet Andrew did not receive the privilege (of founding the Church), but Peter. Why then did Paul not seem to be an apostle to certain persons when by the grace of God he was able to do the same things which the other apostles did? Thus he grieves and under compulsion shows what, according to the estimate of the Lord, he deserves...[383]

Luke 22:32: Clearly, in Peter all are contained: praying for Peter, (Jesus) is understood to have prayed for all. It is always the people who are rebuked or praised in a leader. This is why He also says elsewhere: 'I pray for those whom you have given me' (John 17:9).[384]

Aphraates

But before all things I desire that thou wouldst write and instruct me concerning this that straitens me, namely concerning our faith; how it is, and what its foundation is, and on what structure it rises, and on what it rests, and in what way is its fulfilment and consummation, and what are the works required for it.

Faith...is like a building that is built up of many pieces of workmanship and so its edifice rises to the top. And know, my beloved, that in the foundations of the building stones are laid, and so resting upon stones the whole edifice rises until it is perfected. *Thus also the true Stone, our Lord Jesus Christ is the foundation of all faith. And on Him, on (this) Stone faith is based. And resting on faith all the structure rises until it is completed. For it is the foundation that is the beginning of all the building. For when anyone is brought nigh unto faith, it is laid for him upon the Stone, that is our Lord Jesus Christ.* And His building cannot be shaken by the waves, nor can it be injured by the winds. By the stormy blasts it does not fall, *because its structure is reared upon the rock of the true Stone. And in that I have called Christ the Stone,* I have not spoken my own thought, but the Prophets beforehand called Him the Stone.

And now hear concerning faith that is based upon the Stone, and concerning the structure that is reared up upon the Stone...So also let the man, who becomes a house, yea, a dwelling place, for Christ take heed to what is needed for the service of Christ, Who lodges in him, and with what things he may please Him. For first he builds his building on the Stone, which is Christ. On Him, on the Stone, is faith built...All these things doth the faith demand that is based on the rock of the true Stone, that is Christ.

And if perchance thou shouldest say: If Christ is set for the foundation, how does Christ also dwell in the building when it is completed? For both these things did the blessed Apostle say. For he said: 'I as a wise architect have laid the foundation.' *And there he defined the foundation and made it clear, for he said as follows:* 'No man can lay other foundation than that which is laid, which is Christ Jesus'...And therefore that word is accomplished, that Christ dwells in men, namely, in those who believe on Him, and He is the foundation on which is reared up the whole building.

But I must proceed to my former statement *that Christ is called the Stone in the Prophets.* For in ancient times David said concerning Him: 'The stone which the builders rejected has become the head of the building.' And how did the builders reject this Stone which is Christ? How else than that they so rejected Him before Pilate and said: 'This man shall not be King over us'...By these things they *rejected the Stone which is Christ.*

And furthermore Isaiah also prophesied beforehand with regard to this stone. For he said: 'Thus saith the Lord, Behold I lay in Zion a chosen stone in the precious corner, the head of the wall of the foundation.' And he said again there: 'Every one that believeth on it shall not fear. And whosoever falleth on that stone shall be broken, and everyone on whom it shall fall, it will crush. For the people of the house of Israel fell upon Him, and He became their destruction for ever.' And again: 'it shall fall on the image and crush it. And the Gentiles believed on it and do not fear.' And he shows thus with regard to that stone that it was laid as head of the wall and foundation.

And again *Daniel also spoke concerning this stone which is Christ*. For he said: 'The stone was cut out from the mountain, not by hands, and it smote the image, and the whole earth was filled with it.' This he showed beforehand with regard to Christ that the whole earth shall be filled with Him. For lo! by the faith of Christ are all the ends of the earth filled, as David said: 'The sound of the Gospel of Christ has gone forth into all the earth.' And again when He sent forth His apostles He spake thus to them: 'Go forth, make disciples of all nations and they will believe on Me.' And again the *Prophet Zechariah also prophesied about the stone which is Christ*. For he said: 'I saw a chief stone of equality and of love.'

And again the Apostle has commented for us upon this building and upon the foundation; for he said thus: 'No man can lay another foundation than that which is laid, which is Jesus Christ.'...And he showed with regard to faith that first it is laid on a sure foundation... *These then are the works of faith which is based on the true Stone which is Christ, on Whom the whole building is reared up.*[385]

The Apostolical Constitutions

Luke 22:32: For on this account the devil himself is very angry at the holy Church of God: he is removed to you, and has raised against you adversities, seditions, and reproaches, schisms and heresies. For he had before subdued that people to himself, by their slaying of Christ. But you who have left his vanities, he tempts in different ways, as he did the blessed Job. For indeed he opposed that great high priest Joshua the son of Josedek; and *he often times sought to sift us, that our faith might fail...He will say now, as He said formerly of us when we were assembled together, 'I have prayed that your faith may not fail.*[386]

Asterius

Aptly indeed Isaiah says prophetically that *the Father was laying the Son as a cornerstone, doubtless signifying that the whole structure of the world was borne upon that foundation and base*. No doubt at another time, as has been written in the holy books of the Gospel, *the only Begotten calls Peter the foundation of the Church, saying: 'You are Peter and upon this rock I shall build my Church.' Now this chief, as it were, great and hard stone, Christ*, was set into the excavated hollow of this world, into this vale of tears, as David says, *in order that he might bear all Christians founded upon him aloft into the domicile of our hope. 'For no other foundation can anyone lay than that which is laid, which is Christ Jesus.'* But our Saviour did give Peter a like appellation, thereby teaching that his chief disciple ought to be honored, calling him a *rock of faith. Through Peter*, therefore who was made a true and faithful teacher of piety, *a stable and inflexible foundation for the Church exists.* Moreover, having struck root in this foundation we stand complete, who are Christians all over the world. To be sure from the time of the announcement of the Gospel, many temptations have sprung up, and innumerable tyrants with their chief, the devil, have tried to destroy the foundations and to turn us from our moorings. Rivers have run like torrents, say the saving and holy Scriptures; the violent winds of diabolical spirits have rushed; the plentiful and harsh showers of persecution have poured down forcefully upon Christians. Yet nothing has proved more powerful than the divine ramparts, because doubtless *the foundation of faith* was raised by the holy hands of that chief apostles. These things, I think, needed to be said in response to that word of blessing from him who called the evangelist and holy preacher a rock. Moreover we may see, if we please, the method by which Peter built—not with stones and walls, or other earthly materials, but with words and deeds which he performed at the instigation of the Holy Spirit.[387]

Thus Peter calls Christ the Son of the living God. Peter and no other spoke carefully; and *he confessed the right rule of faith* which had no error in it. And having given to us all in this inviolable law a work of piety, he by no means departed without reward, since—blessed by him who is in the highest degree blessed—*he was named a rock of faith, and the foundation and basis of God's Church.* Moreover by promise he received the keys of the kingdom and was made master of its gates, so that he might open to whomever he willed and might close the gates to whomever they must rightly be closed. By these last we understand those who are defiled and profane, and those who deny that confession on account of which Peter, like a sedulous and energetic guardian of the Church's goods, was put in charge of the gates of the kingdom.[388]

Athanasius

I know moreover that not only this thing saddens you, but also the fact that while others have obtained the churches by violence, you are meanwhile cast out from your places. *For they hold the places, but you the Apostolic Faith.* They are, it is true, in the places, but outside of *the true Faith*; while you are outside the places indeed, but the Faith, within you...But ye are blessed, who by faith are in the Church, dwell upon *the foundations of the faith*, and have full satisfaction, even the highest degree of faith which remains among you unshaken. For it has come down to you from Apostolic tradition, and frequently has accursed envy wished to unsettle it, but has not been able. On the contrary, they have rather been cut off from their attempts to do so. *For thus it is written, 'Thou art the Son of the Living God,' Peter confessing it by revelation of the Father,* and being told, 'Blessed art thou Simon Barjona, for flesh and blood did not reveal it to thee, but My Father Who is in heaven,' and the rest. *No one therefore will ever prevail against your Faith, most beloved brethren.*[389]

It is written, 'The Lord in Wisdom founded the earth;' if then by Wisdom the earth is founded, how can He who founds be founded? Nay, this too is said after the manner of proverbs, and we must in like manner investigate its sense; that we may know that, while by Wisdom the Father frames and founds the earth to be firm and steadfast, *Wisdom Itself is founded for us, that It may become beginning and foundation of our new creation and renewal.* Accordingly here as before, He says not, 'Before the world He has made me Word or Son,' lest there should be as it were a beginning of His making. *For this we must seek before all things, whether He is Son, and on this point specially search the Scriptures;' for this it was, when the Apostles were questioned that Peter answered, saying, 'Thou art the Christ, the Son of the Living God.'* This also the father of the Arian heresy asked as one of his first questions; 'If Thou be *the Son of God;'* for he knew that *this is the truth and the sovereign principle of our faith*; and that, if He were Himself the Son, the tyranny of the devil would have its end; but if He were a creature, He too was one of those descended from that Adam whom he deceived, and he had no cause for anxiety. *For the same reason the Jews of the day were angered, because the Lord said that*

Appendix B 289

He was Son of God, and that God was His proper Father. For had He called Himself one of the creatures, or said, 'I am a work,' they had not been startled at the intelligence, nor thought such words blasphemy, knowing, as they did, that even Angels had come among their fathers; *but since He called Himself Son, they perceived that such was not the note of a creature, but of Godhead and of the Father's nature.* The Arians then ought, even in imitation of their own father the devil, to take some special pains on this point; and if He has said, 'He founded me to be Word or Son,' then to think as they do; but if He has not so spoken, not to invent for themselves what is not.

For He says not, 'Before the world He founded me as Word or Son,' but simply, 'He founded me,' to shew again, as I have said, *that not for His own sake but for those that are built upon Him* does He here also speak, after the way of proverbs. For this knowing, *the Apostle also writes, 'Other foundation can no man lay than that is laid, which is Jesus Christ*; but let every man take heed how he buildeth thereupon.' And it must be that the foundation should be such as the things built on it, that they may admit of being well compacted together. Being then the Word, He has not, as Word, any such as Himself, who may be compacted with Him; for He is Only-begotten; but having become man, He has the like of Him, those namely the likeness of whose flesh He has put on. *Therefore according to His manhood He is founded, that we, as precious stones, may admit of building upon Him,* and may become a temple of the Holy Ghost who dwelleth in us. *And as He is a foundation, and we stones built upon Him,* so again He is a Vine and we knit to Him as branches, not according to the essence of the Godhead; for this surely is impossible; but according to His manhood, for the branches must be like the vine, since we are like Him according to the flesh.

Thus, He saith not, 'He made me a foundation,' lest He might seem to be made and to have a beginning of being, and they might thence find a shameless occasion of irreligion; but, 'He founded Me.' *Now what is founded is founded for the sake of the stones which are raised upon it*; it is not a random process, but a stone is first transported from the mountain and set down in the depth of the earth. And while a stone is in the mountain it is not yet founded; but when need demands, and it is transported, and laid in the depth of the earth, then forthwith if the stone could speak, it would say, 'He now founded me, who brought me hither from the mountain.' Therefore the Lord also did not when founded take a beginning of existence; for He was the Word before that; but when He put on our body, which He severed and took from Mary, then He says, 'He hath founded me;' as much as to say, 'Me, being the Word, He hath enveloped in a body of earth.' *For so He is founded for our sakes, taking on Him what is ours, that we, as incorporated and compacted and bound together in Him* through the likeness of the flesh, may attain unto a perfect man, and abide immortal and incorruptible.

Wherefore also in the Judgment, when every one shall receive according to his conduct, He says, 'Come, ye blessed of My Father, inherit the kingdom prepared for you from the foundation of the world.' How then, or in whom, was it prepared before we came to be, save in *the Lord who 'before the world' was founded for this purpose; that we, as built upon Him, might partake as well-compacted stones, the life and grace which is from Him?*[390]

And so the works of the Jews are undone, for they were a shadow; *but the Church is firmly established; it is founded on the rock, and the gates of hell shall not prevail against it.* Theirs it was to say, Why dost Thou, being a man, make Thyself God? and their disciple is the Samosatene; whence to his followers with reason does he teach his heresy. But we have not so learned Christ, if so be that we have heard Him, and have learned from Him.[391]

But what is also to the point, let us note that the very tradition, teaching and *faith* of the Catholic Church from the beginning, which the Lord gave, was preached by the Apostles, and was preserved by the Fathers. *On this was the Church founded*; and if anyone departs from this, he neither is nor any longer ought to be called a Christian...And because this is *the faith of the Church*, let them somehow understand that the Lord sent out the Apostles and commanded them *to make this the foundation of the Church*...[392]

In Thy saints, who in every age have been well pleasing to Thee, is truly Thy faith; for Thou hast founded the world on Thy faith, and the gates of hell shall not prevail against it.[393]

Basil the Great

And the house of God, located on the peaks of the mountains, is the Church according to the opinion of the Apostle. For he says that one must know 'how to behave in the household of God.' *Now the foundations of this Church are on the holy mountains, since it is built upon the foundation of the apostles and prophets. One of these mountains was indeed Peter, upon which rock the Lord promised to build his Church.* Truly indeed and by highest right are sublime and elevated souls, souls which raise themselves above earthly things, called 'mountains.' *The soul of the blessed Peter was called a lofty rock because he had a strong mooring in the faith* and bore constantly and bravely the blows inflicted by temptations. All, therefore, who have acquired an understanding of the godhead—on account of the breadth of mind and of those actions which proceed from it—are the peaks of mountains, and *upon them the house of God is built*.[394]

Basil of Seleucia

'You, however, who do you say I am?' And silence held them all suspended, for not all knew. But when Jesus asked, acknowledged ignorance in some divine way suggested a response to Peter, and towards a response he was spontaneously moved, like a lyre endowed with reason and roused by action of invisible hands. In obedience the tongue of Peter sought employment and though ignorant of doctrine, supplied a response: 'You are Christ, Son of the living God.' Jesus confirmed this statement with his approbation, thereby instructing all: 'Blessed are you Simon Bar–Jonah, for flesh and blood have not revealed this to you, but my Father who is in Heaven.' He called Peter blessed, so that Peter might join faith to his statement, just as he praised the response because of its meaning...*Now Christ called this confession a rock, and he named the one who confessed it 'Peter,' perceiving the appellation which was suitable to the author of this confession. For this is the solemn rock of religion, this the basis of salvation, this the wall of faith and the foundation of truth: 'For no other foundation can anyone lay than that which is laid, which is Christ Jesus.'* To whom be glory and power forever.[395]

Peter, the Coryphaeus of the apostles, the chief of the disciples of Christ, the accurate expositor of the revelations from the Father, he who walked on the sea, &c.[396]

Bede

He commends the great perfection of faith to us (Mt. 16.16), equally he demonstrates the great strength of this perfected and completed faith against all temptation (Mt. 16.18!).[397]

You are Peter and *on this rock from which you have taken your name, that is, on myself, I will build my Church, upon that perfection of faith which you confessed I will build my Church* by whose society of confession should anyone deviate although in himself he seems to do great things he does not belong to the building of my Church...*Metaphorically it is said to him on this rock, that is, the Saviour which you confessed, the Church is to be built,* who granted participation to the faithful confessor of his name.[398]

Moreover he is called Peter because of the vigour of his mind which clung fast to *that most solid rock, Christ.*[399]

Peter, who before was called Simon, received from the Lord the name 'Peter' because of the strength of his faith and the firmness of his confession; for *Peter clung with a firm and sturdy heart to him about whom it is written: 'the rock, moreover, was Christ.'*[400]

And upon this rock, that is, upon the Lord and Saviour who gave participation in his name to the one who in faith recognized, loved, and confessed him, *so that Peter might be called by the name of the rock: upon this rock the Church is built,* so that one does not attain to eternal life and the share of the elect except by faith in and love of Christ, by partaking of Christ's sacraments, and by observing his commandments.[401]

Cassiodorus

'It will not be moved' is said about the Church to which alone that promise has been given: '*You are Peter and upon this rock I shall build my Church and the gates of Hell shall not prevail against it.*' *For the Church cannot be moved because it is known to have been founded on that most solid rock, namely, Christ the Lord...*[402]

The Church's foundation is Christ the Lord, who thus holds his Church together, so that it can by no shaking collapse, just as the Apostle says: '*For no other foundation can any one lay than that which is laid, which is Christ Jesus*' (1 Cor. 3:11)...Moreover, the words 'on the holy mountains' signify the apostles and the prophets who are called mountains because of the firmness of their faith and the excellence of their righteousness. Deservedly have they been called by such a name upon whom the true Church of God has been established.[403]

Psalm 103.5: 'Who established the earth on its foundation so that it will never be shaken.' It does not seem this verse can be construed literally; for since we have read that the earth must be changed, how can it happen that it should never be shaken? But here when we read 'established earth,' let us rather understand the strengthened Church, which can be called 'earth' insofar as it is composed of earthly men, as we read in another place: 'The earth is the Lord's and the fulness thereof.' *From this 'foundation,' Christ is rightly inferred, who is an immovable foundation and an inviolable rock. Concerning this the Apostle says: 'For no other foundation can any man lay than that which is already laid, which is Christ Jesus' (1 Cor. 3.11)*. If we abide continually upon Christ we will in no way be shaken.[404]

Cassian (John)

But if you prefer the authority of a greater person...let us interrogate no beginner or untaught schoolboy, nor a woman whose faith might appear to be rudimentary; but that greatest of disciples among disciples, and of teachers among teachers, who presided and ruled over the Roman Church, and held the chief place in the priesthood as he did in the faith. Tell us then, tell us, we pray, O Peter, thou chief of the Apostles, tell us how the Churches ought to believe in God. For it is right that you should teach us, as you were taught by the Lord, and that you should open to us the gate, of which you received the key. Shut out all those who try to overthrow the heavenly house: and those who are endeavoring to enter by secret holes and unlawful approaches: as it is clear that none can enter the gate of the kingdom save one to whom the key bestowed on the Churches is revealed by you. Tell us then how we ought to believe in Jesus Christ and to confess our common Lord. You will surely reply without hesitation: 'Why do you consult me as to the way in which the Lord should be confessed, when you have before you my own confession of Him? Read the gospel, and you will not want me myself, when you have got my confession. Nay, you have got me myself when you have my confession; for though I have no weight apart from my confession, yet the actual confession adds weight to my person.'

Tell us then, O Evangelist, tell us the confession: tell us the faith of the chief Apostle...'Thou art,' he says, 'the Christ the Son of the living God.'...Is there anything puzzling or obscure in this? It is nothing but a plain and open confession: he proclaims Christ to be the Son of God.

But what are the other words which follow that saying of the Lord's, with which He commends Peter? *'And I,' said He, 'say unto thee, that thou art Peter and upon this rock I will build My Church.' Do you see how the saying of Peter is the faith of the Church? He then must of course be outside the Church, who does not hold the faith of the Church.* 'And to thee,' saith the Lord, 'I will give the keys of the kingdom of heaven.' This faith deserved heaven: this faith received the keys of the heavenly kingdom. See what awaits you. You cannot enter the gate to which this key belongs, if you have denied the faith of this key. 'And the gate,' He adds, 'of hell shall not prevail against thee.' The gates of hell are the belief or rather the misbelief of heretics. For widely as hell is separated from heaven, so widely is he who denies from him who confessed that Christ is God. 'Whatsoever,' He proceeds, 'thou shalt bind on earth, shalt be bound in heaven, and whatsoever thou shalt loose on earth, shalt be loosed also in heaven.' *The perfect faith of the Apostle* somehow is given the power of Deity, that what it should bind or loose on earth, might be bound or loosed in heaven. For you then, who come against the Apostle's faith, as you see that already you are bound on earth, it only remains that you should know that you are bound also in heaven.[405]

Chrysostom (John)

'But whom say ye that I am?' that is, 'ye that are with me always, and see me working miracles, and have yourselves done many mighty works by me.' What then saith *the mouth of the apostles, Peter, the ever fervent, the leader of the apostolic choir?* When all are asked, he answers. And whereas when He asked the opinion of the people, all replied to the question; when He asked their own, Peter springs forward, and anticipates them, and saith, '*Thou art the Christ, the Son of the living God.*' What then saith Christ? 'Blessed art thou, Simon Barjona, for flesh and blood hath not revealed it unto thee.'...*Why then is this man blessed? Because he acknowledged Him very Son*...What then saith Christ? 'Thou art Simon, the son of Jonas; thou shalt be called Cephas.' 'Thus since thou hast proclaimed my Father, I too name him that begat thee;' all but saying, 'As thou art son of Jonas, even so am I of my Father.'

Therefore He added this, 'And I say unto thee, Thou art Peter, and *upon this rock I will build my Church; that is, on the faith of his confession.* Hereby He signifies that many were on the point of believing, and raises his spirit, and makes him a shepherd. 'And the gates of hell shall not prevail against it.' And if not against it, much more not against Me. So be not troubled because thou art shortly to hear that I shall be betrayed and crucified.' Then He mentions also another honor. 'And I also will give thee the keys of the heavens.' But what is this, 'And I also will give thee?' 'As the Father hath given thee to know Me, so I also will give thee.' And He said not, 'I will entreat the Father' (although the manifestation of his authority was great, and the largeness of the gift unspeakable), but, 'I will give thee.' What dost thou give? tell me. 'The keys of the heavens, that whatsoever thou shalt bind on earth, shall be bound in Heaven, and whatsoever thou shall loose on earth, shall be loosed in Heaven.' How then is it not 'His to give to sit on His right hand, and on His left,' when He saith, 'I will give thee?'

Seest thou how He, His own self, leads Peter on to high thoughts of Him, and reveals Himself, and implies that He is Son of God by these two promises? For those things which are peculiar to God alone, (both to absolve sins, and to make the church incapable of overthrow in such assailing waves, and to exhibit a man that is a fisher more solid than a rock, while all the world is at war with him), these He promises Himself to give;

as the Father, speaking to Jeremiah, said, He would make him as 'a brazen pillar, and as a wall;' but him to one nation only, this man in every part of the world. I fain would inquire then of those who desire to lessen the dignity of the Son, which manner of gifts were greater, those which the Father gave to Peter, or those which the Son gave him? *For the Father gave to Peter the revelation of the Son; but the Son gave him to sow that of the Father and that of Himself in every part of the world; and to mortal man He entrusted the authority over all things in Heaven, giving him the keys; who extended the church to every part of the world, and declared it to be stronger than heaven.*[406]

For Simon, saith He, 'Simon, behold Satan hath desired to have you that he may sift you as wheat;' that is, that he may trouble, confound, tempt you; but 'I have prayed for thee, that thy faith fail not.' And why, if Satan desired all, did He not say concerning all, I have prayed for you? Is it not quite plain that it is this, which I have mentioned before, that it is as reproving him, and showing that his fall was more grievous than the rest, that He directs His words to him? And wherefore said He not, But I did not suffer it, rather than, 'I have prayed?' He speaks from this time lowly things, on his way to His passion, that He might show His humanity. *For He that hath built His church upon Peter's confession*, and has so fortified it, that ten thousand dangers and deaths are not to prevail over it; He that hath given him the keys of Heaven, and hath put him in possession of so much authority, and in no manner needed a prayer for these ends (for neither did He say, I have prayed, but with His own authority, 'I will build My church, and I will give thee the keys of Heaven'), how should He need to pray, that He might brace up the shaken soul of a single man? Wherefore then did He speak in this way? For the cause which I mentioned, and because of their weakness, for they had not as yet the becoming view of Him.[407]

For when Nathaniel said, 'Thou art the Son of God,' Christ replies, 'Because I said unto thee, I saw thee under the fig-tree, believest thou? Thou shalt see greater things than these.' Now what is the question arising from this passage? It is this. *Peter*, when after so many miracles and such high doctrine he *confessed that, 'Thou art the Son of God* (Matt. Xvi.16), is called 'blessed,' as having received the revelation from the Father; while

Nathanael, though he said the very same thing before seeing or hearing either miracles or doctrine, had no such word addressed to him, but as though he had not said so much as he ought to have said, is brought to things greater still. What can be the reason for this? It is, that Peter and Nathanael both spoke the same words, but not both with the same intention. *Peter confessed Him to be 'The Son of God'* but as being very God; Nathanael, as being mere man. And whence does this appear? From what he said after these words; for after, 'Thou art the Son of God,' he adds, 'Thou art the King of Israel.' But the Son of God is not 'King of Israel' only, but of all the world. And what I say is clear, not from this only, but also from what follows. For Christ added nothing more to Peter, but as though *his faith* were perfect, said, *upon this confession He would build the Church*; but in the other case He did nothing like this, but the contrary.[408]

In speaking of S. Peter, the recollection of another Peter has come to me (St. Flavian, his bishop), the common father and teacher, who has inherited his prowess, and also obtained his chair. For this is the one great privilege of our city, Antioch, that it received the leader of the apostles as its teacher in the beginning. For it was right that she who was first adorned with the name of Christians, before the whole world, should receive the first of the apostles as her pastor. But though we received him as teacher, we did not retain him to the end, but gave him up to royal Rome. Or rather we did retain him to the end, *for though we do not retain the body of Peter, we do retain the faith of Peter, and retaining the faith of Peter we have Peter.*[409]

He saith unto him, 'Feed my sheep'. And why, having passed over the others, doth He speak with Peter on these matters? *He was the chosen one of the Apostles, the mouth of the disciples, the leader of the band*; on this account also Paul went up upon a time to enquire of him rather than the others. And at the same time to show him that he must now be of good cheer, since the denial was done away, *Jesus putteth into his hands the chief authority among the brethren*; and He bringeth not forward the denial, nor reproacheth him with what had taken place, but saith: 'If thou lovest Me, *preside over thy brethren*, and the warm love which thou didst ever manifest, and in which thou didst rejoice, show thou now; and the life which thou saidst thou wouldest lay down for Me, now give for My sheep'....*And if any should say 'How then did James receive the chair at Jerusalem?' I would make this reply, that He appointed Peter teacher not of the chair, but of the world...*'Then Peter turning about, seeth the disciple whom Jesus loved following; who also leaned on His breast at supper; and saith, Lord, and what shall this man do?' Wherefore hath he reminded us of that reclining? Not without cause or in a chance way, but to show us what boldness Peter had after the denial. For he who then did not dare to question Jesus, but committed the office to another, was even **entrusted with the chief authority over the brethren**, and not only doth not commit to another what relates to himself, but himself now puts another question to his Master concerning another. John is silent but Peter speaks. He showeth also here the love which he bare towards him; for Peter greatly loved John as is clear from what followed, and their close union is shown through the whole Gospel, and in the Acts. When therefore Christ had foretold great things to him, *and committed the world to him*, and spake beforehand of his martyrdom, and testified that his love was greater than that of the others, desiring to have John also to share with him, he said, 'And what shall this man do?' 'Shall he not come the same way with us?' And as at that other time not being able himself to ask, he puts John forward, so now desiring to make him a return, and supposing that he would desire to ask about the matters pertaining to himself, but had not courage, he himself undertook the questioning. What then saith Christ? 'If I will that he tarry till I come, what is that to thee?' Since he spake from strong affection, and wishing not to be torn away from him, Christ, to show that however much he might love, he could not go beyond his love, saith, 'If I will that he tarry—what is that to thee?'...And this He did to withdraw them (*Peter and John*) from their unseasonable sympathy for each other; *for since they were about to receive the charge of the world*, it was necessary that they should no longer be closely associated together, for assuredly this would have been a great loss to the world. Wherefore He saith unto him, 'Thou hast a work entrusted unto thee, look to it, accomplish it, labor and struggle. What if I will that he tarry here? Look thou to and care for thine own matters.'[410]

For even if all were believers, still all were not alike, but were different in their merits. Wherefore to lead them all to greater emulation, he keeps no man's ecomiums concealed. For when they who labor more, do not receive the greater reward also, many become more listless. On this ground even in the kingdom, the honors are not equal, nor among the disciples were all alike, but the three were preeminent among the rest. And among these three again there was a great difference. For this is a very exact method observed by God even to the last. Hence, 'one star differeth from another star in glory,' (1 Cor. xv.41), it says. And yet all were Apostles and all are to sit on twelve thrones, and all left their goods, and all companied with Him; still it was the three He took. And again, to these very three, He said it was possible that some might even be superior. 'For to sit,' He says, 'on My right hand and on My left, is not mine to give, save to those for whom it is prepared' (Mark x.40). *And He sets Peter before them, when He says, 'Lovest thou Me more than these' (John 21:15)? And John too was loved even above the rest.* For there shall be a strict examination of all, and if thou be but little better than thy neighbor, if it be even an atom, or anything ever so little, God will not overlook even this.[411]

On this wise again Paul saith, 'I am not meet to be called an apostle;' because of this he became even first of all. So likewise John: 'I am not meet to loose the latchet of His shoe;' because of this he was the ' friend of the Bridegroom,' and the hand which he affirmed to be unworthy to touch his shoes, this did Christ draw unto His own head. *So Peter too said, 'Depart from me, for I am a sinful man;' because of this he became a foundation of the Church.* For nothing is so acceptable to God as to number one's self with the last. This is a first principle of all practical wisdom.[412]

For the Son of thunder, the beloved of Christ, the pillar of the Churches throughout the world, who holds the keys of heaven, who drank the cup of Christ, and was baptized with His baptism, who lay upon his Master's bosom, with much confidence, this man now comes forward to us now; not as an actor of a play, not as hiding his head with a mask, (for he hath another sort of words to speak), nor mounting a platform, nor striking the stage with his foot, nor dressed out with apparel of gold, but he enters wearing a robe of inconceivable beauty.[413]

The merciful God is wont to give this honour to his servants, that by their grace others may acquire salvation; as was agreed by *the blessed Paul, that teacher of the world* who emitted the rays of his teaching everywhere.[414]

Where the Cherubim sing the glory, where the Seraphim are flying, there shall we see *Paul, with Peter, and as chief and leader of the choir of the saints*, and shall enjoy his generous love. For if when here he loved men so, that when he had the choice of departing and being with Christ, he chose to be here, much more will he there display a warmer affection. .I love Rome even for this, although indeed one has other grounds for praising it, both for its greatness, and its antiquity, and its beauty, and its populousness, and for its power and its wealth, and for its success in war. But I let all this pass, and esteem it blessed on this account, that both in his lifetime he wrote to them, and loved them so, and talked with them whiles he was with us, and brought his life to a close there. Wherefore the city is more notable upon this ground, than upon all others together. And as a body great and strong, it hath as two glistening eyes the bodies of these Saints. Not so bright is the heaven, when the sun sends forth his rays, as is the city of Rome, sending out these two lights into all parts of the world. From thence will Paul be caught up, thence Peter. Just bethink you, and shudder, at the thought of what a sight Rome will see, when Paul ariseth suddenly from that deposit, together with Peter, and is lifted up to meet the Lord. What a rose will Rome send up to Christ!...what two crowns will the city have about it! what golden chains will she be girded with! what fountains possess! Therefore I admire the city, not for the much gold, nor for the columns, not for the other display there, but for *these pillars of the Church* (1 Cor. 15:38).[415]

'For He that wrought for Peter unto the Apostleship of the Circumcision wrought for me also unto the Gentiles.' He calls the Gentiles the Uncircumcised and the Jews the Circumcision, and *declares his own rank to be equal to that of the Apostles; and, by comparing himself with their Leader not with others, he shows that the dignity of each was the same.* After he had established the proof of their unanimity, he takes courage, and proceeds confidently in his argument, not stopping at the Apostles, but advances to Christ Himself, and to the grace which He had conferred upon him...[416]

'And wherefore,' saith one, 'doth he not punish here?' That He may display that longsuffering of His, and may offer to us the salvation that cometh by repentance, and not make our race to be swept away, nor pluck away those who by an excellent change are able to be saved, before that salvation. For if He instantly punished upon the commission of sins, and destroyed, *how should Paul have been saved, how should Peter, the chief teachers of the world?* How should David have reaped the salvation that came by his repentance?[417]

This (James) was bishop, as they say, and therefore he speaks last, and herein is fulfilled that saying, 'In the mouth of two or three witnesses shall every word be established' (Deut. Xvii.6; Matt. xviii.16)...'Then all the multitude kept silence,' etc. (v. 12). There was no arrogance in the Church. After Peter Paul speaks, and none silences him: James waits patiently; not starts up (for the next word). No word speaks John here, no word the other Apostles, but held their peace, for *James was invested with the chief rule*, and think it no hardship. So clean was their soul from love of glory. Peter indeed spoke more strongly, but James here more mildly: for thus it behooves one in high authority, to leave what is unpleasant for others to say, while he himself appears in the milder part.[418]

Peter, that chief of the apostles, first in the Church, the friend of Christ who did not receive revelation from man but from the Father, as the Lord bore witness to him saying: 'Blessed are you, Simon Bar-Jonah, for flesh and blood has not revealed this to you but my Father who is in heaven': this same Peter (*when I say 'Peter,' I name an unbreakable rock, an immovable ridge, a great apostle, the first of the disciples, the first called and the first obeying*), this same Peter, I say, did not perpetrate a minor misdeed but a very great one. He denied the Lord. I say this, not accusing a just man, but offering to you the opportunity of repentance. Peter denied the Lord and governor of the world himself, the savior of all...[419]

Since then it was likely that he would be lifted up to folly by his practice of contradiction, Jesus next teacheth him not to oppose Him. This too Luke implies, when he telleth us that Christ said, 'And I have prayed for thee, that thy faith fail not' (Luke 22:32); that is, 'that thou be not finally lost.' In every way teaching him humility, and proving that human nature by itself is nothing. But, since great love made him apt for contradiction, He now so ordereth him, that he might not in after times be subject to this, *when he should have received the stewardship of the world*, but remembering what he had suffered, might know himself. And look at the violence of his fall; it did not happen to him once or twice, but he was so beside himself, that in a short time thrice did he utter the words of denial, that he might learn that he did not so love as he was loved. And yet, to one who had so fallen He saith again, 'Lovest thou Me more than these?' So that the denial was caused not by the cooling of his love, but from his having been stripped of aid from above. He accepteth then Peter's love, but cutteth off the spirit of contradiction engendered by it...For *if the leader of their band*, one so entirely fervent, was told that before the cock crew he should thrice deny his Master, it was likely that they would expect to have to undergo some great reverse, sufficient to bend even souls of the adamant. Since then it was probable that they considering these things would be astounded, see how He comforteth them, saying, 'Let not your heart be troubled.'[420]

'For other foundation can no man lay than that is laid, which is Jesus Christ.' I say, no man can lay it so long as he is a master–builder; but if he lay it...he ceases to be a master–builder. See how even from men's common notions he proves the whole of his proposition. His meaning is this: *'I have preached Christ, I have delivered unto you the foundation.* Take heed how you build thereon, lest haply it be in vainglory, lest haply so as to draw away the disciples unto men.' Let us not then give heed unto the heresies. 'For other foundation can no man lay than that which is laid.' *Upon this then let us build, and as a foundation let us cleave to it, as a branch to a vine; and let there be no interval between us and Christ*...For the branch by its adherence draws in the fatness, and the building stands because it is cemented together. Since, if it stand apart it perishes, having nothing whereon to support itself. Let us not then merely keep hold of Christ, but let us be cemented to Him, for if we stand apart, we perish...And accordingly, there are many images whereby He brings us into union. Thus, if you mark it, He is the 'Head', we are 'the body': can there be any empty interval between the head and the body? *He is a*

'Foundation', we are a 'building': He a 'Vine', we 'branches': He the 'Bridegroom', we the 'bride': He is the 'Shepherd', we the 'sheep': He is the 'Way', we 'they who walk therein.' Again, we are a 'temple,' He the 'Indweller': He the 'First–Begotten,' we the 'brethren': He the 'Heir,' we the 'heirs together with Him': He the 'Life,' we the 'living': He the 'Resurrection,' we 'those who rise again': He the 'Light,' we the 'enlightened.' All these things indicate unity; and they allow no void interval, not even the smallest.[421]

Peter, the coryphaeus of the choir of apostles, the mouth of the disciples, the foundation of the faith, the base of the confession, the fisherman of the world, who brought back our race from the depth of error to heaven, he who is everywhere fervent and full of boldness, or rather of love than boldness.[422]

He took *the coryphaei* and led them up into a high mountain apart...Why does He take these three alone? Because they excelled the others. Peter showed his excellence by his great love of Him, John by being greatly loved, James by the answer...'We are able to drink the chalice.'[423]...Do you not see that *the headship was in the hands of these three*, especially of Peter and James? This was the chief cause of their condemnation by Herod.[424]...*The coryphaei, Peter the foundation of the Church, Paul the vessel of election.*[425]

Christ foretold many things....He said, 'in the world ye shall have tribulation, but be of good cheer, I have overcome the world' (John xvi.33), that is, no man shall get the better of you. And this we see by the events has come to pass. *He said that 'the gates of hell shall not prevail against the Church'* (Matt. xvi.18), even though persecuted, and that no one shall quench the preaching of the Gospel: and the experience of events bears witness to this prediction also: and yet when He said these things it was very hard to believe Him.[426]

And besides, the prophecies are of such a kind, as that even until now time has been unable to force aside the predicted course of things...for the destruction indeed of Jerusalem took place many years ago; but there are also other predictions which extend along from that time until His coming; which examine as you please: for instance, this, 'I am with you alway, even unto the end of the world (Matt. xxviii.20) and, *'Upon this Rock I will build My Church, and the gates of hell shall not prevail against it' (Matt. xvi.18)* and, 'This Gospel shall be preached unto all nations' (Matt. xxiv.14)...[427]

He spake some things to them about Himself, and about the churches, and about the things to come; and as He spake, He wrought mighty works. By the fulfillment therefore of what He said, it is plain that both the wonders wrought were real, and the future and promised things also. But that my meaning may be plainer, let me illustrate it from the actual case. He raised up Lazarus by a single word merely, and showing him alive. Again, *He said, 'The gates of Hades shall not prevail against the Church (Matt. xvi.18)*...[428]

Yet they frequently are seen to act confidently; as when John lay upon His bosom, when they came to Him and said, 'Who is the greatest in the Kingdom of Heaven?' (Matt. xviii.1), when the sons of Zebedee entreated Him to set one of them on His right hand and the other on His left. Why then did they not here question Him? Because since all those instances related to themselves, they had need to enquire into them, while what here took place was of no such great importance to them. And indeed *John did that a long time after towards the very end, when he enjoyed greater confidence, and was bold in the love of Christ; for he it was, he saith, 'whom Jesus loved.' What could equal such blessedness*? But, beloved, let us not stop at this, the calling the Apostle blessed, but let us do all things that we also may be of the blessed, *let us imitate the Evangelist, and see what it was that caused such great love*. What then was it? He left his father, his ship, and his net, and followed Jesus. Yet this he did in common with his brother, and Peter, and Andrew, and the rest of the Apostles. What then was the special thing which caused this great love? Shall we discover it? He saith nothing of this kind about himself, but only that he was beloved; as to the righteous acts for which he was beloved he has modestly been silent. *That Jesus loved him with an especial love was clear to every one*; yet John doth not appear conversing with or questioning Jesus privately, as Peter often did, and Philip, and Judas, and Thomas, except only when he desired to show kindness and compliance to his fellow Apostle; *for when the chief of the Apostles by beckoning constrained him*, then he asked. For these two had great love each for the other. Thus, for instance, they are seen going up together into the Temple and speaking in common to the people. Yet Peter in many places is moved, and speaks more warmly than John. And at the end he hears Christ say, 'Peter, lovest thou Me more than these?' (John xxi.15). Now it is clear that he who loved 'more than these' was also beloved. But this in his case was shown by loving Jesus, in the case of the other by being beloved by Jesus. *What then was it which caused this especial love? To my thinking, it was that the man displayed great gentleness and meekness*, for which reason he doth not appear in many places speaking openly. And how great a thing this is, is plain also from the case of Moses. It was this which made him such and so great as he was. *There is nothing equal to lowliness of mind*. For which cause Jesus with this began the Beatitudes, and when about to lay as it were the foundation of a mighty building, He placed first lowliness of mind. Without this a man cannot possibly be saved; though he fast, though he pray, though he give alms, if it be with a proud spirit, these things are abominable, if humility be not there...[429]

'And when Jesus beheld him,' saith the Evangelist, *'He said, Thou art Simon, the son of Jonas; thou shalt be called Cephas, which is, by interpretation, a stone.'* He begins from this time forth to reveal things belonging to His Divinity, and to open it out by little predictions...But Peter makes no reply to these words; as yet he knew nothing clearly, but was still learning. And observe, that not even the prediction is fully set forth; for Jesus did not say, 'I will change thy name to Peter, and upon this rock I will build My Church,' but, 'Thou shalt be called Cephas.' The former speech would have expressed too great authority and power; for Christ does not immediately nor at first declare all His power, but speaks for awhile in a humbler tone; and so, when He had given the proof of His Divinity, He puts it more authoritatively, saying, *'Blessed art thou, Simon, because My Father hath revealed it to thee'; and again, 'Thou art Peter and upon this rock I will build My Church' (Matt. xvi.17,18). Him therefore He so named, and James and his brother He called 'sons of thunder' (Mark iii.17). Why then doth He this? To show that it was He who gave the old covenant, that it was He that altered names*, who called Abram 'Abraham,' and Sarai 'Sarah,' and Jacob 'Israel.' To many He assigned names even from their birth, as to Isaac, and Samson, and to those in Isaiah and Hosea (Isa. viii.3; His. I.4,6,9); but to others He gave them after they had been named by their parents, as to those we have mentioned, and to 'Joshua the son of Nun.'...But then they received each a different name, *we now have all one name, that which is greater than any, being called 'Christians,' and 'sons of God,' and (His) 'friends,' and (His) 'Body.'* For the very term itself is able more than all those others to rouse us, and make us more zealous for the practice of virtue. Let us not then act unworthily of the honor belonging to the title, considering the excess of our dignity, we who are called Christ's; for so Paul hath named us. Let us bear in mind and respect the grandeur of the appellation (1 Cor. iii.23). For if one who is said to be descended from some famous general, or one otherwise distinguished, is proud to be called this or that man's son, and deems the name a great honor, and strives in every way so as not to affix, by remissness of his own, reproach to him after whom he is called; shall not we who are called after the name, not of a general, nor any of the princes upon earth, nor Angel, nor Archangel, nor Seraphim, but of the King of these Himself, shall not we freely give our very life, so as not to insult Him who has honored us?...So let us who have been deemed worthy to be near Him, and much closer, and as much nearer than those just named, as the body is closer to the head than they, let us, I say, use every means to be imitators of Christ.[430]

And that thou mayest learn, that this denial (arose) not so much from sloth, as from his being forsaken of God, who was teaching him to know the measures of man and not to contradict the sayings of the Master, nor to be more high-minded than the rest, but to know that nothing can be done without God, and that 'Except the Lord build the house, they labor in vain who build it' (Ps. cxxvii.1): therefore also Christ said to him alone, 'Satan desired to sift thee as wheat,' and I allowed it not, 'that thy faith may not fail' (Luke xxii.31, 32). *For since it was likely that he would be high-minded*, being conscious to himself that he loved Christ more than they all, therefore 'he wept bitterly'...[431]

What sayest thou, O Peter? the prophet said, 'The sheep shall be scattered;' Christ hath confirmed the saying, and sayest thou, No? Is not what passed before enough, when Thou saidst, 'Far be it from Thee,' and thy mouth was stopped? For this then He suffers him to fall, teaching him thereby to believe Christ in all things, and to account His own declaration more trustworthy than one's own conscience. And the rest too reaped no small benefit from his denial, having come to know man's weakness, and God's truth...For where he should have prayed, and have said, Help us, that we be not cut off, *he is confident in himself* and saith, *'Though all men should be offended in Thee, yet will I never;' though all should undergo this, I shall never undergo it, which led him on little and little to self-confidence. Christ, then, out of a desire to put down this, permitted his denial. For since he neither submitted to Him nor the prophet...since he submitted not to His words, he is instructed by deeds. For in proof that for this intent He permitted it, that He might amend this in him, hear what He saith, 'I have prayed for thee, that thy faith fail not.' For this He said sharply reproving him, and showing that his fall was more grievous than the rest, and needed more help. For the matters of blame were two; both that he gainsaid; and, that he set himself before the other; or rather a third too, namely, that he attributed all to himself. To cure these things, He suffered the fall to take place...How then was it that He denied? he said not, that thou mayest not deny, but that thy faith fail not, that thou perish not utterly.* For this came from His care.[432]

Luke 22:32

And that thou mayest learn, that this denial (arose) not so much from sloth, as from his being forsaken of God, who was teaching him to know the measures of man and not to contradict the sayings of the Master, nor to be more high-minded than the rest, but to know that nothing can be done without God, and that 'Except the Lord build the house, they labor in vain who build it' (Ps. cxxvii.1): therefore also Christ said to him alone, 'Satan desired to sift thee as wheat,' and I allowed it not, 'that thy faith may not fail' (Luke xxii.31, 32). For since it was likely that he would be high-minded, being conscious to himself that he loved Christ more than they all, therefore 'he wept bitterly'...[433]

What sayest thou, O Peter? the prophet said, 'The sheep shall be scattered;' Christ hath confirmed the saying, and sayest thou, No? Is not what passed before enough, when Thou saidst, 'Far be it from Thee,' and thy mouth was stopped? For this then He suffers him to fall, teaching him thereby to believe Christ in all things, and to account His own declaration more trustworthy than one's own conscience. And the rest too reaped no small benefit from his denial, having come to know man's weakness, and God's truth...For where he should have prayed, and have said, Help us, that we be not cut off, he is confident in himself and saith, 'Though all men should be offended in Thee, yet will I never;' though all should undergo this, I shall never undergo it, which led him on little and little to self-confidence. Christ, then, out of a desire to put down this, permitted his denial. For since he neither submitted to Him nor the prophet...since he submitted not to His words, he is instructed by deeds. For in proof that for this intent He permitted it, that He might amend this in him, hear what He saith, 'I have prayed for thee, that thy faith fail not.' For this He said sharply reproving him, and showing that his fall was more grievous than the rest, and needed more help. For the matters of blame were two; both that he gainsaid; and, that he set himself before the other; or rather a third too, namely, that he attributed all to himself. To cure these things, He suffered the fall to take place...How then was it that He denied? he said not, that thou mayest not deny, but that thy faith fail not, that thou perish not utterly. For this came from His care.[434]

Chrysologus (Peter)

For though to be called Peter is elsewhere merely to receive a name, in this place (the Church) it is a sign of strength. Truly, blessed *Peter, that immovable foundation of salvation*, showed himself to be such in the priestly office as they who desire the priesthood would wish to see...*Peter is the guardian of the faith, the rock of the Church*, and the gate keeper of heaven. He was chosen to be an apostolic fisher and with the hook of sanctity he brought to himself crowds submerged in waves of error, while by the nets of his teaching he brought from the multitude an abundance of men. Moreover, he was a most blessed and apostolic bird catcher, who reached the souls of youths flying through the air with the rod of the divine word.[435]

Just as Peter received his name from the rock, because he was the first to deserve to establish the Church, by reason of his steadfastness of faith, so also Stephen was named from a crown...the first who deserved to bear witness with his blood. *Let Peter hold his ancient primacy of the apostolic choir. Let him open to those who enter the kingdom of heaven.* Let him bind the guilty with his power and absolve the penitent in kindness.[436]

Cyprian

The Lord saith unto Peter, I say unto thee, (saith He,) that thou art Peter, and upon this rock I will build My Church, and the gates of Hell shall not prevail against it. And I will give unto thee the keys of the kingdom of heaven, and whatsoever thou shalt bind on earth, shall be bound in heaven, and whatsoever thou shalt loose on earth, shall be loosed in heaven (Matt. 16:18-19). To him again, after His resurrection, He says, Feed My sheep. Upon him being one He builds His Church; and although He gives to all the Apostles an equal power, and says, As My Father sent Me, even so I send you; receive ye the Holy Ghost: whosoever sins ye remit, they shall be remitted to him, and whosoever sins ye shall retain, they shall be retained (John 20:21);—yet in order to manifest unity, He has by His own authority so placed the source of the same unity, as to begin from one. *Certainly the other Apostles also were what Peter was, endued with an equal fellowship both of honour and power; but a commencement is made from unity, that the Church may be set before as one*; which one Church, in the Son of Songs, doth the Holy Spirit design and name in the Person of our Lord: My dove, My spotless one, is but one; she is the only one of her mother, elect of her that bare her (Cant. 9:6).

He who holds not this unity of the Church, does he think that he holds the faith? He who strives against and resists the Church, is he assured that he is in the Church? For the blessed Apostle Paul teaches this same thing, and manifests the sacrament of unity thus speaking, There is One Body, and One Spirit, even as ye are called in One Hope of your calling; One Lord, One Faith, One Baptism, One God (Eph. 4:4). This unity firmly should we hold and maintain, especially we Bishops, presiding in the Church, in order that we may approve the Episcopate itself to be one and undivided. Let no one deceive the Brotherhood by falsehood; no one corrupt the truth of our faith, by a faithless treachery. The Episcopate is one; it is a whole, in which each enjoys full possession. The Church is likewise one, though she be spread abroad, and multiplies with the increase of her progeny: even as the sun has rays many yet one light; and the tree boughs many, yet its strength is one, seated in the deep–lodged root; and as, when many streams flow down from one source, though a multiplicity of waters seems to be diffused from the bountifulness of the overflowing abundance, *unity is preserved in the source itself. Part a ray of the sun from its orb, and its unity forbids this division of light; break a branch from the tree, once broken it can bud no more; cut the stream from its fountain, the remnant will be dried up. Thus the Church, flooded with the light of the Lord, puts forth her rays through the whole world, with yet one light, which is spread upon all places, while its unity of body is not infringed.* She stretches forth her branches over the universal earth, in the riches of plenty, and pours abroad her bountiful and onward streams; *yet is there one head, one source*, one Mother, abundant in the results of her fruitfulness.

It is of her womb that we are born; our nourishing is from her milk, our quickening from her breath. The spouse of Christ cannot become adulterate, she is undefiled and chaste; owning but one home, and guarding with virtuous modesty the sanctity of one chamber. She it is who keeps for God, and appoints unto the kingdom the sons she has borne. Whosoever parts company with the Church, and joins himself to an adulteress, is estranged from the promises of the Church. He who leaves the Church of Christ, attains not to Christ's rewards. He can no longer have God for a Father, who has not the Church for a Mother. If any man was able to escape, who remained without the ark of Noah, then will that man escape who is out of doors beyond the Church. The Lord warns us and says, He who is not with Me is against Me, and he who gathereth not with Me, scattereth. He who breaks the peace and concord of Christ, sets himself against Christ. He who gathers elsewhere but in the Church, scatters the Church of Christ.[437]

Our Lord, whose precepts and warnings we ought to observe, determining the honour of a Bishop and to the ordering of His own Church, speaks in the Gospel, and says to Peter, I say unto thee, That thou art Peter, and on this rock will I build My Church; and the gates of hell shall not prevail against it. And I will give unto thee the keys of the kingdom of heaven: and whatsoever thou shalt bind on earth shall be bound in heaven; and whatsoever thou shalt loose on earth shall be loosed in heaven (Matt. 16:18-19). *Thence the ordination of Bishops, and the ordering of the Church, runs down along the course of time and line of succession, so that the Church is settled upon her Bishops; and every act of the Church is regulated by these same Prelates.*[438]

Luke 22:31-32

For Apostolic men also ceased not to pray day and night; and our Lord Himself also, the Author of our rule of life, and the Way of our example, prayed often and with watching, as we read in the Gospel, He went out into a mountain to pray, and continued all night in prayer to God: and we may be assured that when he prayed, *He prayed for us*, since He Himself was not a sinner, but bore the sins of others. *But so truly did He pray for us, that we read in another place, And the Lord said to Peter, Behold, Satan hath desired to have you, that he might sift you as wheat, but I have prayed for thee that thy faith fail not.*[439]

The Lord offered petition, not for Himself (for what should He, the Innocent, ask for on His own account?) But for our sins, as Himself makes known when He says to Peter, Behold, Satan hath desired that he might sift you as wheat, but I have prayed for thee, that thy faith fail not. And afterwards He entreats the Father for all, saying, Neither pray I for these alone, but for them also that shall believe on Me, through their word; that they all may be one, as Thou, Father, art in Me, and I in Thee, that they also may be one in us.[440]

Cyril of Alexandria

But why do we say that they are 'foundations of the earth'? *For Christ is the foundation and unshakable base of all things*—Christ who restrains and holds together all things, that they may be very firm. Upon him also we all are built, a spiritual household, put together by the Holy Spirit into a holy temple in which he himself dwells; for by our faith he lives in our hearts. *But the next foundations, those nearer to us, can be understood to be the apostles and evangelists, those eyewitnesses and ministers of the word who have arisen for the strengthening of the faith.* For when we recognize that their own traditions must be followed, we serve a faith which is true and does not deviate from Christ. For when he wisely and blamelessly confessed his faith to Jesus saying, 'You are Christ, Son of the living God,' Jesus said to divine Peter: 'You are Peter and upon this rock I will build my Church.' *Now by the word 'rock', Jesus indicated, I think, the immoveable faith of the disciple.* Likewise, the psalmist says: 'Its foundations are the holy mountains.' Very truly should the holy apostles and evangelists be compared to holy mountains for their understanding was laid down like a foundation for posterity, so that those who had been caught in their nets would not fall into a false faith.[441]

'Upon this rock I shall build my Church. And I shall give you the keys of the kingdom of heaven.' Observe how he declares himself to be Lord of both heaven and earth. For he promises things which are beyond the capacity of our nature, nay, even beyond the condition of angels—things which all should fittingly ascribe to a unique and surpassing nature and majesty. In the first place he says that the Church is under his own authority, but Scripture elsewhere affirms that the Church is subject to God rather than to any man. For Paul says that *Christ has prepared the Church for himself* to be without any wrinkle or blemish—the Church which he has founded, *the foundation itself being predicated of him,* since he is the Lord of strength. And of this Church he puts Peter the shepherd in charge. Then he adds: 'And to you I shall give the keys of the kingdom of heaven.' This word no angel nor any other rational power can speak. It is proper only to God, Lord of all, who holds power in heaven and earth. Moreover the time of the gift was the hour of the resurrection when he said: 'Receive the Holy Spirit. If you forgive the sins of any they are forgiven; if you retain the sins of any they are retained.'[442]

For that reason divine Scripture says that Peter, that exceptional figure among the apostles, was called blessed. For when the Savior was in that part of Caesarea which is called Philippi, he asked who the people thought he was, or what rumor about him had been spread throughout Judea and the town bordering Judea. And in response Peter, having abandoned the childish and abused opinions of the people, wisely and expertly exclaimed:

'You are Christ, Son of the living God.' Now when Christ heard this true opinion of him, he repaid Peter by saying: 'Blessed are you Simon Bar-Jonah, for flesh and blood have not revealed this to you but my Father who is in heaven. And I tell you, you are Peter, and upon this rock I will build my Church, and the gates of hell shall not prevail against it.' *The surname, I believe, calls nothing other than the unshakable and very firm faith of the disciple 'a rock,' upon which the Church was founded and made firm and remains continually impregnable even with respect to the very gates of Hell.* But Peter's faith in the Son was not easily attained, nor did it flow from human apprehension; rather it was derived from the ineffable instruction from above; since God the Father clearly shows his own Son and causes a sure persuasion of him in the minds of his people. For Christ was in no way deceptive when he said, 'Flesh and blood has not revealed this to you, but my Father in heaven.' If, therefore, blessed Peter, having confessed Christ to be the Son of the living God, are those not very wretched and abandoned who rashly rail at the will and undoubtedly true teaching of God, who drag down the one who proceeds from God's own substance and make him a creature, who foolishly reckon the coeternal author of life to be among those things which have derived their life from another source? Are such people not at any rate very ignorant?[443]

But allusively to the name from the rock (petra), He changes his name to Peter (petros), for on him was He about to found His Church.[444]

The Church is unshaken, and 'the gates of hell shall not prevail against it,' according to the voice of the Saviour, for *it has Him for a foundation.*[445]

It is likely that by these words (Is. 33:16) our Lord Jesus *Christ is called a rock, in Whom,* as some cave or sheepfold, *the Church is conceived as having a safe and unshaken abiding place* for its well-being; 'For thou art Peter,' the Saviour says, 'and *upon this rock I will build My Church.*'[446]

There is then one Christ and Son and Lord, not as though he were a man connected with God simply by a unity of dignity or authority, for equality of honour does not unite natures: Peter and John are equal in honour in that they are apostles and holy disciples, but the two are not one.[447]

John 21:15–17

If anyone asks for what cause he asked Simon only, though the other disciples were present, and what he means by 'Feed my lambs,' and the like, we answer that St. Peter, with the other disciples, had been already chosen to the Apostleship, but because meanwhile Peter had fallen (for under great fear he had thrice denied the Lord), he now heals him that was sick, and exacts a threefold confession in place of triple denial, contrasting the former with the latter, and compensating the fault with the correction...By the triple confession Peter abrogates the sin contracted in his triple denial. For from what our Lord says, 'Feed my lambs,' a renewal of the Apostolate already delivered to him is considered to have been made which presently absolves the disgrace of his sin and blots out the perplexity of his human infirmity.'[448]

Cyril of Jerusalem

As the delusion was extending, *Peter and Paul*, a noble pair, *chief rulers of the Church*, arrived and set the error right...[449]

Didymus the Blind

How powerful is Peter's faith and his confession that Christ is the only-begotten God, the word, the true Son of God, and not merely a creature. Though he saw God on earth clothed in flesh and blood, Peter did not doubt, for he was willing to receive what 'flesh and blood have not revealed to you.' Moreover he recognized the consubstantial and coeternal branch of God, thereby glorifying that uncreated root, that root without beginning which had revealed the truth to him. Peter believed that Christ was one and the same deity with the Father; and so he was called blessed by him who alone is the blessed Lord. *Upon this rock the Church was built, the Church which the gates of hell—that is, the arguments of heretics—will not overcome.* The keys to the kingdom of heaven were given to Peter in order that, 'baptizing them in the name of the Father, and Son, and the Holy Spirit,' he might open the gates of

God's kingdom to those whose faith agreed both with his own confession and with those things which he and the other apostles heard from Christ. To those, however, who do not, *by like confession*, offer a hymn of praise, Peter shuts the most blessed and hoped for entrance.[450]

Epiphanius

Those too who have fallen away through persecution, if they show full repentance, sit in sackcloth and ashes and weep before the Lord - the Benefactor has the power to show mercy even to them. No ill can come of repentance. Thus the Lord and his church accept the penitent, as Manasseh the son of Hezekiah returned and was accepted by the Lord—and the chief of the apostles, St. Peter, who denied for a time and still became our truly solid rock which supports the Lord's faith, and on which the church is in every way founded. This is, forst of all, because he confessed that 'Christ' is 'the Son of the living God,' and was told, '*On this rock of sure faith will I build my church*'—for he plainly confessed that Christ is true Son. For when he said, 'Son of the living God,' with the additional phrase, 'the living,' he showed that Christ is God's true Son, as I have said in nearly every Sect. Peter also makes us certain of the Holy Spirit by saying to Ananias, 'Why hast Satan tempted you to lie to the holy Ghost? Ye have not lied unto man, but unto God,' for the Spirit is of God and not different from God. And Peter also became the solid rock of the building and foundation of God's house, because, after denying, turning again, and being found by the Lord, he was privileged to hear, 'Feed my lambs and feed my sheep.' For with these words Christ led us to the turning of repentance, so that our well founded faith might be rebuilt in him—a faith that forbids the salvation of no one alive who truly repents, and amends his faults in this world.[451]

The first of the Apostles, that firm rock upon which the church of God is built, so that the gates of hell, that is to say the heresies and heresiarchs, will not prevail against it. For in every way was the faith confirmed in him who received the key of heaven, in him who looses on earth and binds in heaven. For in him are found all the subtle questions of faith.[452]

Ephrem Syrus

In the tenth year let Mount Sinai give glory, which melted—before its Lord! It saw against its Lord—stones taken up: but He took stones—to build the Church upon the Rock; blessed be His building!⁴⁵³

Shadowed forth in thy beauty is *the beauty of the Son*, Who clothed Himself with suffering when the nails passed through Him. The awl passed in thee since they handled thee roughly, as they did His hands; and because He suffered He reigned, as by thy sufferings thy beauty increased. And if they showed no pity upon thee, neither did they love thee: still suffer as thou mightest, thou hast come to reign! *Simon Peter showed pity on the Rock*; whoso hath smitten it, is himself thereby overcome; it is by reason of Its suffering that Its beauty hath adorned the height and the depth.⁴⁵⁴

Hail, O Peter: gate of sinners, firm trust of penitents, encouragement of converts, recalling those who deny, consolation of the lapsed. Hail, O Peter: tongue of the disciples, voice of the heralds, eye of the apostles, keeper of the heavens, firstborn of the key–bearers. Hail, O Peter: who plays out the devil's contest, and after injury brings back victory with violence, who overthrows the greatest enemy, who after being wounded brought back honour and after a fall erected a trophy and ripped off the crown from the head of the adversary.⁴⁵⁵

Eusebius

'And he sent out arrows, and scattered them; he flashed forth lightnings, and routed them. Then the channels of the sea were seen, and the foundations of the world were laid bear, at thy rebuke, O Lord, at the blast of thy nostrils' (Ps. 18.14)...By 'the foundations of the world,' we shall understand the strength of God's wisdom, by which, first, the order of the universe was established, and then, the world itself was founded—a world which will not be shaken. Yet you will not in any way err from the scope of the truth if you suppose that 'the world' is actually *the Church of God, and that its 'foundation' is in the first place, that unspeakably solid rock on which it is founded, as Scripture says: 'Upon this rock I will build my Church, and the gates of hell shall not prevail against it'; and elsewhere: 'The rock, moreover, was Christ.' For, as the Apostle indicates with these words: 'No other foundation can anyone lay than that which is laid, which is Christ Jesus.' Then, too, after the Savior himself, you may rightly judge the foundations of the Church to be the words of the prophets and apostles, in accordance with the statement of the Apostle: 'Built upon the foundation of the apostles and the prophets, Christ Jesus himself being the cornerstone.'* These foundations of the world have been laid bare because the enemies of God, who once darkened the eyes of our mind, lest we gaze upon divine things, have been routed and put to flight— scattered by the arrows sent from God and put to flight by the rebuke of the Lord and by the blast from his nostrils. As a result, having been saved from these enemies and having received the use of our eyes, we have seen the channels of the sea and have looked upon the foundations of the world. This has happened in our lifetime in many parts of the world.[456]

The Savior prophesied that His doctrine would be preached over the whole world, wherever man was, as a testimony to all nations; and, by a divine foreknowledge predicted that the Church, too, which, during the years of His sojourning amongst men, was not seen nor established, should be invincible, incapable of being overthrown, and never to be overcome by death; but should, according to His declaration, stand and continue immoveable, as being, by His power, firmly established and embedded on a rock that could not be moved, nor broken. Better than all reasoning, with good cause should the accomplishment of this prophecy put to silence the unbridled tongues of all who, unchecked by shame, are ever ready to give proof of their audacity. For the fame of His Gospel has filled every country which the sun illumines. Nor has it in any way yielded to its enemies, or even to the gates of death; and this because of that word which He uttered, 'I will build My Church upon a rock, and the gates of hell shall not prevail against it.'[457]

Peter, on whom is built Christ's Church, against which (Church) the gates of hell shall not prevail...[458]

Firmicus Maternus

Another pagan sacrament has the key word, *theos ek patras*, 'god from a rock.' Why do you adulterate the faith and transfer this holy and worshipful mystery to pagan doings? Different is the stone which God promised He would lay in making strong the foundations of the promised Jerusalem. What the symbol of the worshipful stone means to us is Christ. Why do you with the knavery of a thief transfer to foul superstitions the dignity of a worshipful name? Your stone is one that ruin follows and the disastrous collapse of tumbling towers; but our stone, laid by the hand of God, builds up, strengthens, lifts, fortifies, and adorns the grace of the restored work with the splendor of everlasting immortality.

For Isaias says of this at the behest of the Holy Spirit: Thus saith the Lord: Behold, I lay a stone for the foundations of Sion, a precious stone, elect, a chief cornerstone, honored, and he that shall believe in it shall not be confounded. Also in the Psalms there is a similar declaration, for the Holy Spirit says in the 117th Psalm: The stone which the builders rejected: the same is become the head of the corner. This is the Lord's doing: and it is wonderful in our eyes. Through many prophets the Holy Spirit shows us the meaning of that name, for the prophet Zacharias says: Behold, I bring my servant, the Orient is his name; for the stone that I have laid before the face of Jesus; upon the stone there are seven eyes.

Now that through this 'stone,' that is, through our Lord Jesus Christ, both these gods will fall and the multitudinous temples with them, is clearly explained by Daniel in worshipful prophesies...What oracular utterance of the prophets issues any statement concerning the stone of the idolaters, whereof people say 'god from a rock'? And for whom has the stone been an obstacle, for whom a help? But this holy stone (that is, Christ) either supports the foundations of faith or, being set in the corner, unites with balanced control the two lines of the wall (that is, it gathers into one the strength of the Old and New Testament), or at any rate brings into accord the disparity of body and soul by conferring immortality upon man, or promulgates the law, or gives testimony against sinners, or, what is better, smites the statue of the devil, so that when he is overcome and prostrate and turned into ashes and cinders, Christ may lift up His sublime head and attain the pure realm of His sovereignty.[459]

Firmilian

But how great his error, how exceeding his blindness, who says, that remission of sins can be given in the synagogues of heretics, and *abideth not on the foundation of the one Church which was once fixed by Christ on a rock, may be hence learnt, that Christ said to Peter alone, Whatsoever thou shalt bind on earth shall be bound in heaven; and whatsoever thou shalt loose on earth shall be loosed in heaven* (Matt. 16:18–19): and again in the Gospel, when Christ breathed on the Apostles only, saying, Receive ye the Holy Ghost: whose soever sins ye remit, they are remitted unto them; and whoso ever sins ye retain, they are retained (John 20:22–23). *The power then of remitting sins was given to the Apostles, and to the Churches which they, sent by Christ, established, and to the Bishops who succeeded them vicarious ordination.*

And herein I am justly indignant at such open and manifest folly in Stephen, that *he who boasts of the seat of his episcopate, and contends that he holds the succession from Peter, on whom the foundations of the Church were laid*, introduces many other rocks, and buildeth anew many Churches, in that by his authority he maintains baptism among them. For they who are baptized, without doubt fill up the number of the Church. But whoso approves their baptism, must needs also maintain of those baptized, that the Church also is with them. Nor *does he perceive that he who thus betrays and abandons unity, casts into the shade, and in a manner effaces, the truth of the Christian Rock...Stephen, who proclaims that he occupies by succession the chair of Peter*, is roused by no zeal against heretics, conceding to them no small but the very greatest power of grace, so far as to say and assert that through the Sacrament of Baptism they wash off the defilement of the old man, pardon the old deadly sins, make sons to God by heavenly regeneration, renew to eternal life by the sanctification of the Divine laver. He who concedes and assigns heretics such great and heavenly privileges of the Church, what else does he than hold communion with them, for whom he maintains and claims so much grace.[460]

Fulgentius

For the Saviour and judge of men has ordained, that only in this life would anyone's sins be remitted by him...Wherefore human vanity should not pointlessly hope to hear (at some future time after death) what divine truth has or has not promised. It is for this reason that *Christ has assigned on earth the power of binding and loosing to Peter—that is, to his Church—* in order that we may recognise during this life the free mercy offered in the forgiveness of sins and in the future the just wages which are repaid to all for the quality of their deeds.[461]

Supplication for the pardon of one's sins would never have been ordained for the sinner, if forgiveness were not truly offered to the suppliant. But repentance will indeed benefit the sinner, provided the catholic Church oversees it. *For God ascribed to the Church in the person of blessed Peter the power to bind and to loose, saying: 'Whatever you bind on earth shall be bound in heaven, and whatever you loose on earth shall be loosed in heaven' (Mt. 16.19).* At whatever age, therefore, a man should make true repentance of his sins and by the direction of God should correct his life, he will not be deprived of the reward of forgiveness, since God, as he says through the prophet, does not wish the death of a sinner; but let the sinner turn from his way and let his soul live (Ez. 33.11).[462]

Gaudentius of Brescia

I beseech our common father *Ambrose*, that, after the scanty dew of my discourse, he may pour abundantly into your hearts the mysteries of the divine writings. Let him speak from that Holy Spirit with which he is filled, and 'from his belly shall flow rivers of living water;' and, *as a successor of Peter*, he shall be the mouth of all the surrounding priests. For when the Lord Jesus asked of the apostles, 'Whom do you say that I am?' Peter alone replies, with the mouth of all believers, 'Thou art the Christ, the Son of the living God.' What reward did that confession at once receive? Blessedness indeed, and the most glorious power of the heavenly kingdom. *Now when Peter alone speaks, the faith of the other belivers is not excluded*; but a fitting order is observed; whilst to the prince of the apostles the first place of speaking is justly deferred, lest there might seem to be confusion rather than reply, if all emulously and together had answered on that occasion. And it is to be considered how that Judas Iscariot could not have confessed with the mouth and with the heart he believed not...But later, when Judas had been condemned for the crime that he had committed; *all the apostles, when Christ had risen, receive the keys in Peter; yea, rather, with Peter* receive the keys of the heavenly kingdom from the Lord Himself, when He says, 'Receive ye the Holy Ghost, whose sins you shall forgive, they are forgiven;' and again, 'Going,' He says, 'teach all nations and baptize them in the name of the Father, and of the Son, and of the Holy Ghost.' For the gate of the kingdom of heaven is not opened save by this key of the spiritual sacraments.[463]

Gregory the Great

For since the truth shines forth from the Church Catholic alone, the Lord says that there is a place by Him, from which He is to be seen. Moses is placed on a rock, to behold the form of God, because if any one maintains not *the firmness of Faith,* he discerns not the Divine presence. *Of which firmness* the Lord says, *'Upon this rock I shall build my Church.'*[464]

Gregory to John, Bishop of Constantinople: At the time when your Fraternity was advanced to Sacredotal dignity, you remember what peace and concord of the churches you found. But, with what daring or with what swelling of pride I know not, you have attempted to seize upon a new name, whereby the hearts of all your brethren might have come to take offence. I wonder exceedingly at this, since I remember how thou wouldest fain have fled from the episcopal office rather than attain it. And yet, now that thou hast got it, thou desirest so to exercise it as if thou hadst run to it with ambitious intent. For, having confessed thyself unworthy to be called a bishop, thou hast at length been brought to such a pass as, despising thy brethren, to covet to be named the only bishop...I have taken care to address your Fraternity, not indeed in writing, but by word of mouth, desiring you to restrain yourself from such presumption...I beg you, I beseech you, and with all the sweetness in my power demand of you, that your Fraternity gainsay all who flatter you and offer you this name of error, nor foolishly consent to be called by the proud title. Consider, I pray thee, that in this rash presumption the peace of the whole Church is disturbed, and that it is in contradiction to the grace that is poured out on all in common...And thou wilt become by so much the greater as thou restrainest thyself from the usurpation of a proud and foolish title: and thou wilt make advance in proportion as thou art not bent on arrogation by derogation of thy brethren. Wherefore, dearest brother, with all thy heart love humility, through which the concord of all the brethren and the unity of the holy universal Church may be preserved.

Certainly the apostle Paul, when he heard some say, I am of Paul, I of Apollos, but I of Christ (1 Cor. 1:13), regarded with the utmost horror such dilaceration of the Lord's body, whereby they were joining themselves, as it were, to other heads, and exclaimed, saying, Was Paul crucified for you? or were ye baptized in the name of Paul (ib.)? If then he shunned the subjecting of the members of Christ partially to certain heads, as if beside Christ, though this were to the apostles themselves, *what wilt thou say to Christ, who is the Head of the universal Church, in the scrutiny of the last judgment, having attempted to put all his members under thyself by the appellation of Universal?* Who, I ask, is proposed for imitation in his wrongful title but he who, despising the legions of angels constituted socially with himself, attempted to start up to an eminence of singularity, that he might seem to be under none and to be alone above all? Who even said, I will ascend into heaven, I will exalt my throne above the stars of heaven; I will sit upon the mount of the testament, in the sides of the North: I will ascend above the heights of the clouds; I will be like the most High (Isai. xiv.13).

For what are all thy brethren, the bishops of the universal Church, but stars of heaven, whose life and discourse shine together amid the sins and errors of men, as if amid the shades of night? *And when thou desirest to put thyself above them by this proud title, and to tread down their name in comparison with thine, what else dost thou say but I will ascend into heaven; I will exalt my throne above the stars of heaven? Are not all the bishops together clouds, who both rain in the words of preaching, and glitter in the light of good works? And when your Fraternity despises them, and you would fain press them down under yourself, what else say you but what is said by the ancient foe, I will ascend above the heights of the clouds?*

This most holy man the lord John, of so great abstinence and humility, has, through the seduction of familiar tongues, broken out into such a pitch of pride as to attempt, in his coveting of that wrongful name, to be like him who, while proudly wishing to be like God, lost even the grace of the likeness granted him, and because he sought false glory, thereby forfeited true blessedness.

Certainly Peter, the first of the apostles, himself a member of the holy and universal Church, Paul, Andrew, John—what were they but heads of particular communities? And yet all were members under one Head. And (to bind all together in a short girth of speech) the saints before the law, the saints under the law, the saints under grace, all these making up the Lord's Body, were constituted as members of the Church, and not one of them has wished himself to be called universal. Now let your Holiness acknowledge to what extent you swell within yourself in desiring to be called by that name by which no one presumed to be called who was truly holy.

Was it not the case, as your Fraternity knows, that the prelates of this Apostolic See, which by the providence of God I serve, had the honour offered them of being called universal by the venerable Council of Chalcedon. But yet not one of them has ever wished to be called by such a title, or seized upon this ill-advised name, lest if, in virtue of the rank of the pontificate, he took to himself the glory of singularity, he might seem to have denied it to all his brethren...What, then, can we bishops say for ourselves, who have received a place of honour from the humility of our Redeemer, and yet imitate the pride of the enemy himself?...What, then, dearest brother, wilt thou say in that terrible scrutiny of the coming judgment, if thou covetest to be called in the world not only father, but even general father?...Lo, by reason of this execrable title of pride the Church is rent asunder, the hearts of all the brethren are provoked to offence...And thou attemptest to take the honour away from all which thou desirest unlawfully to usurp to thyself singularly.

I therefore have once and again through my representatives taken care to reprove in humble words this sin against the whole Church; and now I write myself.[465]

To Eulogius, Bishop of Alexandria: In position you are my brethren...and lo, in the preface of the epistle which you have addressed to myself who forbade it, you have thought it fit to make use of a proud appellation, calling me Universal Pope. But I beg your most sweet Holiness to do this no more, since what is given to another beyond what reason demands is subtracted from yourself. For as for me, I do not seek to be prospered by words but by my conduct. Nor do I regard that as an honour whereby I know that my brethren lose their honour. For my honour is the honour of the universal Church...Then am I truly honoured when the honour due to all and each is not denied them. For if your Holiness calls me Universal Pope, you deny that you are yourself what you call me universally. But far be this from us. Away with words that inflate vanity and wound charity.[466]

To Eulogius, Bishop of Alexandria: Your most sweet Holiness has spoken much in your letter to me about the chair of Saint Peter, Prince of the apostles, saying that he himself now sits on it in the persons of his successors...*He has spoken to me about Peter's chair who occupies Peter's chair*...I greatly rejoiced because you, most holy ones, have given to yourselves what you have bestowed upon me. For who can be ignorant that holy Church has been made firm in the solidity of the Prince of the apostles, who derived his name from the firmness of his mind, so as *to be called Petrus from petra*. And to him it is said by the voice of Truth, To thee I will give the keys of the kingdom of heaven (Matt. xvi.19). And again it is said to him, And when thou art converted, strengthen thy brethren (xxii.32). And once more, Simon, son of Jonas, lovest thou Me? Feed My sheep (Joh. xxi.17). Wherefore though there are many apostles, yet with regard to the principality itself of *the See of the Prince of the apostles alone has grown strong in authority, which in three places is the See of one*. For he himself exalted the See in which he deigned even to rest and end the present life. He himself adorned the See to which he sent his disciple as evangelist. He himself stablished the See in which, though he was to leave it, he sat for seven years. *Since then it is the See of one, and one See, over which by divine authority three bishops now preside, whatever good I hear of you, this I impute to myself...We are one in Him...*[467]

Gregory Nazianzen

Shall I bring forth another and laudable example of order and discipline—one great and laudable, especially worthy of our present commemoration and calling to mind? Notice how out of the disciples of Christ—all great and lofty, all worthy of Christ's selection—*only one is called a rock and receives for his faith the founding of the Church*. And another is loved more earnestly, and rests upon the breast of Jesus; yet the other disciples accept it with a calm spirit that these should be preferred to themselves. Now when Christ made his ascent up the mountain to be transfigured and to lay open his divinity and to lay that bare which was covered by the flesh, who, pray, went up together with him—for not all were admitted to the sight of this miracle? Peter, James and John who were esteemed above the others.[468]

Gregory of Nyssa

These men (i.e., Peter, James, & John) are the foundations of the Church, and the pillars and mainstays of truth. They are the perpetual founts of salvation, from whom the copious waters of divine doctrine flow. The prophet bids us go to them when he writes: 'With joy you will draw water from the founts of the Saviour.' We celebrate the memory of *Peter, who is the chief of the apostles*, and together with him the other members of the Church are glorified; for upon him the Church of God is established. Indeed *this man*, in accordance with the title conferred upon him by the Lord, *is the firm and very solid rock upon which the Saviour has built his Church*. Finally we celebrate the memory of James and John.

But what effort is required of us to exert ourselves in such a way that our commemoration may be worthy of the virtue of the apostles? *The warmth of our praises does not extend to Simon insofar as he was a catcher of fish; rather it extends to his firm faith, which is at the same time the foundation of the whole Church.*[469]

Hilary of Poitiers

A belief that the Son of God is Son in name only, and not in nature, is not the faith of the Gospels and of the Apostles...whence I ask, was it that the blessed Simon Bar–Jona confessed to Him, Thou art the Christ, the Son of the living God?...*And this is the rock of confession whereon the Church is built*...that Christ must be not only named, but believed, the Son of God.

This faith is that which is the foundation of the Church; through this faith the gates of hell cannot prevail against her. This is the faith which has the keys of the kingdom of heaven. Whatsoever this faith shall have loosed or bound on earth shall be loosed or bound in heaven...The very reason why he is blessed is that he confessed the Son of God. This is the Father's revelation, *this the foundation of the Church*, this the assurance of her permanence. Hence has she the keys of the kingdom of heaven, hence judgment in heaven and judgment on earth....*Thus our one immovable foundation, our one blissful rock of faith, is the confession from Peter's mouth, Thou art the Son of the living God.*[470]

Matthew also, chosen to proclaim the whole mystery of the Gospel, first a publican, then an Apostle, and John, the Lord's familiar friend, and therefore worthy to reveal the deepest secrets of heaven, and *blessed Simon, who after his confession of the mystery was set to be the foundation–stone of the Church*, and received the keys of the kingdom of heaven, and all his companions who spoke by the Holy Ghost, and Paul, the chosen vessel, changed from persecutor into Apostle, who, as a living man, abode under the deep sea and ascended into the third heaven, who was in paradise before his martyrdom, whose martyrdom was the perfect offering of a flawless faith...[471]

Ignatius

Luke 22:32: They are ashamed of the cross; they mock at the passion; they make a jest of the resurrection. *They are the offspring of that spirit who is the author of all evil*, who led Adam, by means of his wife, to transgress the commandment, who slew Abel by the hands of Cain, who fought against Job, who was the accuser of Joshua, the son of Josedech, *who sought to 'sift the faith' of the apostles*, who stirred up the multitude of the Jews against the Lord, who also now 'worketh in the children of disobedience;' from whom *the Lord Jesus Christ will deliver us, who prayed that the faith of the apostles might not fail*, not because He was not able of Himself to preserve it, but because He rejoiced in the pre-eminence of the Father.[472]

Isidore of Pelusium

Christ, who searcheth the hearts, did not ask His disciples, 'Whom do men say that I, the Son of Man, am?' Because He did not know the varying opinion of men concerning Himself, but was desirous, of teaching all that same *confession which Peter*, inspired by Him, *laid as the basis and foundation, on which the Lord built His Church.*[473]

Christ is the Rock, abiding unshaken, when He was incarnate.[474]

Isidore of Seville

Peter bears the character of the Church, which has the power to forgive sins and to lead men from Hades to the heavenly kingdom...All the apostles also bear the type of the whole Church, since they also have received a like power of forgiving sins. They bear also the character of the patriarchs, who by the word of preaching spiritually brought forth God's people in the whole world...*The wise man who built his house upon the rock signifies the faithful teacher, who has established the foundations of his doctrine and life upon Christ.*[475]

Moreover, *Christ is called a 'foundation' because faith is established in him, and because the catholic Church is built upon him.*[476]

Thus far we have spoken of priestly origins in the Old Testament. But in the New Testament after Christ the priestly order arises from Peter; for to him the first priestly office in the Church of Christ was given. Thus the Lord says to him: 'You are Peter and upon this rock I shall build my Church, and the gates of Hell shall not prevail against it; and I shall give you the keys of the kingdom of Heaven.' *So Peter first received the power of binding and loosing, and he first led people to faith by the power of his preaching. Still, the other apostles have been made equal with Peter in a fellowship of honor and power. They also, having been sent out into all the world, preached the Gospel. Having descended from these apostles, the* bishops have succeeded them, and through all the world they have been established in the seats of the apostles.[477]

James of Nisbis

Faith is composed and compacted of many things. It is like a building, because it is constructed and completed in much hope. You are not ignorant that large stones are placed in the foundations of a building, and then all that is built thereon has the stones joined together, and so raised till the completion of the work. *So, of all our faith, our Lord Jesus Christ is the firm and true foundation; and upon this rock our faith is established. Therefore, when any one has come to faith, he is set upon a firm rock, which is our Lord Jesus Christ. And, calling Christ a rock, I say nothing of my own, for the prophets have before called Him a rock*...And our Lord, the bestower of life, to all those who come to Him to be healed, said, 'Be it done unto thee according to thy faith.' Thus, when the blind man came to Jesus, He says to him, 'Dost thou believe that I can cure thee?' And he answered, 'Yea, Lord, I believe.' (Matt. ix.28)...*And Simon, who was called a rock, was deservedly called a rock because of his faith*.[478]

And *Simon, the head of the apostles*, who denied Christ, saying, 'I saw Him not,' and cursed and swore that 'he knew Him not,' as soon as he offered unto God contrition and penitence, and washed his sins in the tears of his sorrow, *our Lord received him, and made him the foundation, and called him a rock, of the building of His Church*.[479]

Josue arranged and set stones as a testimony to Israel; and *Jesus, our Saviour, called Simon the rock of faith, and placed him as a faithful testimony amongst the Gentiles*.[480]

Jerome

The one foundation which the apostolic architect laid is our Lord Jesus Christ. Upon this stable and firm foundation, which has itself been laid on solid ground, the Church of Christ is built...For the Church was founded upon a rock...upon this rock the Lord established his Church; and the apostle Peter received his name from this rock (Mt. 16.18).[481]

She, that with a firm root is founded upon the rock, Christ, the Catholic Church, is the one dove; she stands the perfect one, and near to His right hand, and has nothing sinister in her.[482]

This mountain is in the house of the Lord, which the prophet sighs after, saying, 'One thing I have asked of the Lord, this will I seek after, that I may dwell in the house of the Lord all the days of my life,' (Ps. xxvii.4), and concerning which Paul writes to Timothy, 'But if I tarry long, that thou mayest know how thou oughtest to behave thyself in the house of God, which is the Church of the living God, the pillar and ground of the truth' (1 Tim. iii.15). *This house is built upon the foundation of the apostles and prophets*, as imitators of Christ. Of this house, Jerusalem, the Psalmist cries out saying, 'They that trust in the Lord shall be as Mount Sion; he shall not be moved for ever that dwelleth in Jerusalem. Mountains are round about it; and the Lord is round about His people' (Ps. cxxiv.1). *Whence also upon one of the mountains Christ founds the Church, and says to him, 'Thou art Peter, and upon this rock I will build My Church, and the gates of hell shall not prevail against it.*[483]

The rock is Christ, Who gave to His apostles, that they also should be called rocks, 'Thou art Peter, and upon this rock I will build My Church.'[484]

'You are Peter and upon this rock I shall build my Church.' Just as Christ himself gave light to the apostles, in order that they might be called the light of the world, so other names were derived from the Lord: for example, *Simon, who believed in the rock, Christ, was given the name 'Peter.'* And in accordance with the metaphor of the rock, Jesus rightly said to him: 'I shall build my Church upon you. And the gates of hell shall not prevail against it.'[485]

'Built upon the foundation of the apostles and prophets.'...For if those who are no longer strangers and sojourners, but fellow citizens with the saints and *members of God's household have been built upon the foundation of the apostles and the prophets, Christ himself being the cornerstone*—in whom the whole building has been joined together into a temple holy in the Lord, in whom the Ephesians are built into a temple of God in the spirit: if this is so, then there is one God of one building and temple which is built upon the foundation of the apostles and prophets. Now if a universal building is joined together and is growing into a temple holy in the Lord, then we must strive with every effort to become the sorts of stones about which it is written: 'holy stones are rolled upon the earth.'[486]

Though, he says, the Lord had with Him the apostles Peter and John; and they saw Him transfigured on the mount, and upon them the foundation of the Church is placed...[487]

Was there no other province in the whole world to receive the gospel of pleasure, and into which the serpent might insinuate itself, except *that which was founded by the teaching of Peter upon the rock Christ.*[488]

When subsequently one presbyter was chosen to preside over the rest, this was done to remedy schism and to prevent each individual from rending the church of Christ by drawing it to himself. For even at Alexandria from the time of Mark the Evangelist until the episcopates of Heraclas and Dionysius the presbyters always named as bishop one of their own number chosen by themselves...For what function, excepting ordination, belongs to a bishop that does not also belong to a presbyter? *It is not the case that there is one church at Rome and another in all the world beside. Gaul and Britain, Africac and Persia, India and the East all worship one Christ and observe one rule of truth. If you ask for authority, the world outweighs its capital. Wherever there is a bishop, whether it be at Rome or at Engubium, whether it be at Constantinople or at Rhegium, whether it be at Alexandria or at Zoan, his dignity is one and his priesthood is one. Neither the command of wealth nor the lowliness of poverty makes him more of a bishop or less a bishop. All alike are successors of the apostles.*[489]

But you say, the Church was founded upon Peter: although elsewhere the same is attributed to all the Apostles, and they all receive the keys of the kingdom of heaven, and the strength of the Church depends upon them all alike, yet one among the twelve is chosen so that when a head has been appointed, there may be no occasion for schism.[490]

I have all but passed over the most important point of all. While you were still quite small, bishop Anastasius of holy and blessed memory ruled the *Roman* church.[491]

Away with all that is overweening; let the state of Roman majesty withdraw. My words are spoken to the successor of the fisherman, to the disciple of the cross. As I follow no leader save Christ, so I communicate with none but your blessedness, that is, with the chair of Peter. For this I know, is the rock on which the church is built![492]

John of Damascus

At Caeserea Philippi...where his disciples were assembled, on the spur of the moment *the Rock of Life himself* excavated a seat from a certain rock. Then he asked his disciples who the people were saying the Son of Man was. He did not seek this information because he was unaware of the ignorance of men; for Jesus requires no investigation. But he wanted to dispel by the light of knowledge the fog which lay upon the disciple's spiritual eyes. The disciples responded that some called Jesus John the Baptist, others Elijah, still others Jeremiah or one of the prophets...In order to erase this suspicion and to give to the ignorant the most excellent gift possible, namely, a true confession, what did Jesus do, he for whom nothing was impossible? As a man he posed a probing question, but as God he brought him out of the dark who first had been called and first had followed. This was the man whom Christ in his foreknowledge had predestined to be a worthy overseer of the Church. As God, Jesus inspired this man and spoke through him. What was the question? 'But who do you say I am?' And Peter, fired by a burning zeal and prompted by the Holy Spirit replied: 'You are Christ, Son of the living God.' Oh blessed mouth! Perfectly, blessed lips! Oh theological soul! Mind filled by God and made worthy by divine instruction! Oh divine organ through which Peter spoke! Rightly are you blessed, Simon son of Jonah...because neither flesh nor blood nor human mind, but my Father in heaven has revealed this divine and mysterious truth to you. For no one knows the Son, save he who is known by him...*This is that firm and immovable faith upon which, as upon the rock whose surname you bear, the Church is founded.*

Against this the gates of hell, the mouths of heretics, the machines of demons—for they will attack—will not prevail. They will take up arms but they will not conquer.[493]

This rock was Christ, the incarnate Word of God, the Lord, for Paul clearly teaches us: 'The rock was Christ' (1 Cor. 10.4).[494]

Moreover, that Christ is one—one person and hypostasis—is evident. He asks: 'Who do people say that I am?'...Peter replied, saying: '*You are Christ, Son of the living God.*'...Wherefore, indeed, he heard: 'Blessed are you Simon Bar-Jonah since neither flesh nor blood has revealed this to you, but my Father who is in heaven. You are Peter'—*and upon this rock the Church was firmly established*—'*and the gates of hell*'—*that is, the mouths of heretics*—'*shall not prevail against it.*'[495]

Maximus of Turin

This is Peter to whom Christ the Lord freely conceded participation in his name. For as the Apostle teaches, *Christ is the rock; and by Christ Peter was made a rock when the Lord said to him: 'You are Peter and upon this rock I shall build my Church.'* For just as water flowed from the rock when God's people were thirsting in the desert, so when the whole world was languishing in drought the *spring of a saving confession flowed from the mouth of Peter*. This is Peter to whom Christ entrusted the feeding of his sheep and lambs just before he ascended to the Father. As Christ had redeemed these by the compassion of his obedient service, so Peter served them by virtue of his faith. And rightly did that witness of mysteries, the Son of God, commit the feeding and tending of sheep to Peter whom he knew would not desist in his enthusiasm and faithfulness in nourishing the Lord's flock...[496]

It is necessary, however, to inquire how closed heavens are to be opened. I think that they cannot be opened otherwise than by taking up the keys of the apostle Peter—the keys which the Lord bestowed on him when he said: 'To you I give the keys of the kingdom of heaven.' Indeed let us ask Peter, that as a good gate keeper of the heavenly palace, he may open to us.

Moreover, let us diligently ask what these keys may be. I say that Peter's key is Peter's faith, by which he opened heaven, by which, secure, he penetrated hades, by which, fearless, he walked on water. For so great is the power of apostolic faith, that all elements lie open to it: the angelic gates are not closed to it, nor do the gates of Hell prevail against it, nor do floods of water sink it. That key itself, which we call faith, let us see how firm and solid it is. I judge that it was produced by the work of 12 artisans; for the holy faith was comprehended in the creed of the 12 apostles, who, like skilled artisans working in concert, produced the key by their understanding. For *I call the creed itself the key*, which causes the shades of the devil to draw back, that the light of Christ may come. The hidden sins of conscience are brought into the open so that the clear works of justification may shine. Therefore this key must be shown to our brothers in order that they also as followers of Peter may learn to unlock hades and to open heaven.[497]

We have frequently said that Peter was called a rock by the Lord. Thus: 'You are Peter, and upon this rock I will build my Church.' *If, then, Peter is the rock upon whom the Church is built, rightly does he first heal feet, so that as he maintains the foundations of the Church's faith he also strengthens the foundations of a person's limbs.* Rightly, I say, does he first heal a Christian's feet so that he can walk upon the rock of the Church not as one who is fearful and weak but as one who is robust and strong. And where are the words of Paul the apostle not read? Where are they not written down, kept in the heart, and preserved in speech? This *Paul was called a vessel of election by the Lord.* A good vessel, in which the precious precepts of Christ's commandments are treasured! A good vessel, from whose fulness the substance of life is always poured forth for the peoples, and still it is full. *Rock and vessel—most appropriate names for the apostles, and necessary instruments for the house of the Savior! For a strong house is built of rock and rendered useful by vessels. A rock provides the peoples with something firm lest they waver, while a vessel shelters Christians lest they be tempted.*[498]

Last Sunday we showed that Saint Peter proceeded along his erring ways during the Savior's suffering and that after he denied the Lord he was better. For he became more faithful after he wept over the faith that he had lost, and for that reason he gained back a greater grace than he lost: like a good shepherd he accepted the charge of protecting the sheep, so that he who had previously been weak to himself would now become the foundation for all, and the very person who had faltered when tested by questioning would strengthen others with the unwavering character of his faith. *On account of the firmness of his faithfulness he is called the rock of the churches, as the Lord says: You are Peter, and upon this rock I will build my Church. He is called a rock because he will be the first to lay the foundations of faith among the nations and so that, like an immovable stone, he might hold fast the fabric and structure of the whole Christian endeavor. Because of his faithfulness, therefore, Peter is called a rock, as the apostle says: And they drank from the spiritual rock, and the rock was Christ. Rightly does he who merits fellowship in deed merit fellowship also in name, for in the same house Peter laid the foundation and Peter does the planting, and the Lord gives the increase and the Lord provides the watering.*[499]

On account of his faithfulness Peter is told: Blessed are you, Simon bar Jonah, because flesh and blood have not revealed this to you but my Father who is in heaven. And I say to you: You are Peter, and upon this rock I will build my Church. Although he used to be called Simon, then, he is named Peter on account of his faithfulness. We read what the Apostle says of the Lord Himself: *They drank from the spiritual rock, but the rock was Christ. Rightly, then, inasmuch as Christ is a rock, is Simon named Peter, in order that he who shared with the Lord in faith might be at one with the Lord as well in the Lord's name—that just as a Christian is so called from Christ, the apostle Peter would similarly receive his name from Christ the rock.*[500]

But let us see what Simon Peter's boat is, which the Lord judged the more fitting of the two to teach from and which keeps the Savior safe from harm and brings the words of faith to the people. For we have discovered that the Lord previously set sail in another boat and was provoked by serious wrongs. For He sailed with Moses in the Red Sea when he led the people of Israel through the waters, but He was hurt by serious wrongs, as He himself says to the Jews in the Gospel: If you believe Moses you would also believe Me. The wrong inflicted upon the Savior is the Synagogue's disbelief. Therefore He chooses Pater's boat and forsakes Moses'; that is to say, He spurns the faithless Synagogue and takes the faithful Church. For the two were appointed by God as boats, so to speak, which would fish for the salvation of humankind in this world as in a sea, as the Lord says to the apostles: Come, I will make you fishers of men.

Of these two boats, then, one is left useless and empty on the shore, while the other is led out heavily laden and full to the deep. It is the Synagogue that is left empty at the shore because it has rejected Christ as well as the oracles of the prophets, but it is the Church that is taken heavily laden out to the deep because it has received Christ with the teaching of the apostles. The Synagogue, I say, stays close to the land as if clinging to earthly deeds. The Church, however, is called out into the deep, delving, as it were, into the profound mysteries of the heavens, into that depth concerning which the Apostle says: O the depth of the riches of the wisdom and knowledge of God. For this reason it is said to Peter: Put out into the deep - that is to say, into the depths of reflection upon the divine generation. For what is so profound as what Peter said to the Lord: You are the Christ, the Son of the living God? What is so trivial as what the Jews said about the Lord: Is this not the son of Joseph the carpenter? For the one, by a higher counsel, assented in divine fashion to the birth of Christ, while the others, with a viper's mind, considered His heavenly generation in fleshly wise. Hence the Savior says to Peter: because flesh and blood has not revealed this to you but my Father who is in heaven. But to the Pharisees he says: How are you able to speak good things when you are evil?

The Lord, then, gets only into this boat of the Church, in which Peter has been proclaimed pilot by the Lord's own words: Upon this rock I will build my Church. This boat so sails upon the deeps of this world that, when the earth is destroyed, it will preserve unharmed all whom it has taken in. Its forshadowing we see already in the Old Testament. For as Noah's ark preserved alive everyone whom it had taken in when the world was going under, so also Peter's Church will bring back unhurt everyone whom it embraces when the world goes up in flames. And as a dove brought the sign of peace to Noah's ark when the flood was over, so also Christ will bring the joy of peace to Peter's Church when the judgment is over, since He Himself is dove and peace, as He promised when He said: I shall see you again and your heart will rejoice.

But since we read in Matthew that this same boat of Peter, from which the Lord is now drawing forth the sacraments of His heavenly teaching, was so shaken about by violent winds as the Lord was sleeping in it that all the apostles feared for their lives, let us see why in one and the same boat at one time He teaches the people in tranquility and at another He inflicts the fear of death upon the disciples in stormy weather, especially inasmuch as Simon Peter was there with the other apostles. This was the reason for the danger: Simon Peter was there, but the betrayer Judas was also there. *For although the faith of the one was the foundation of the boat*, still the faithlessness of the other shook it. *Tranquility exists when Peter alone pilots*, stormy weather when Judas comes aboard.[501]

Nilus of Ancyra

If, moreover, a man of the Lord is meant, the first to be compared to gold would be *Cephas, whose name is interpreted 'rock.' This is the highest of the apostles, Peter, also called Cephas, who furnished in his confession of faith the foundation for the building of the Church.*[502]

Origen

And if we too have said like Peter, 'Thou art the Christ, the Son of the living God,' not as if flesh and blood had revealed it unto us, but by light from the Father in heaven having shone in our heart, *we become a Peter, and to us there might be said by the Word, 'Thou art Peter,' etc. For a rock is every disciple of Christ of whom those drank who drank of the spiritual rock which followed them, and upon every such rock is built every word of the church*, and the polity in accordance with it; *for in each of the perfect*, who have the combination of words and deeds and thoughts which fill up the blessedness, *is the church built by God.*

But if you suppose that upon the one Peter only the whole church is built by God, what would you say about John the son of thunder or each one of the Apostles? Shall we otherwise dare to say, that against Peter in particular the gates of Hades shall not prevail, but that they shall prevail against the other Apostles and the perfect? Does not the saying previously made, 'The gates of Hades shall not prevail against it,' hold in regard to all and in the case of each of them? And also the saying, 'Upon this rock I will build My church'? Are the keys of the kingdom of heaven given by the Lord to Peter only, and will no other of the blessed receive them? But if this promise, 'I will give unto thee the keys of the kingdom of heaven,' be common to others, how shall not all things previously spoken of, and the things which are subjoined as having been addressed to Peter, be common to them?

'Thou art the Christ, the Son of the living God.' *If any one says this to Him...he will obtain the things that were spoken according to the letter of the Gospel to that Peter, but, as the spirit of the Gospel teaches, to every one who becomes such as that Peter was. For all bear the surname of 'rock' who are the imitators of Christ, that is, of the spiritual rock which followed those who are being saved, that they may drink from it the spiritual draught. But these bear the surname of the rock just as Christ does. But also as members of Christ deriving their surname from Him they are called Christians, and from the rock, Peters...And to all such the saying of the Saviour might be spoken, 'Thou art Peter' etc., down to the words, 'prevail against it.' But what is the 'it'? Is it the rock upon which Christ builds the church, or is it the church? For the phrase is ambiguous. Or is it as if the rock and the church were one and the same? This I think to be true; for neither against the rock on which Christ builds the church, nor against the church will the gates of Hades prevail.* Now, if the gates of Hades prevail against any one, such an one cannot be a rock upon which Christ builds the church, nor the church built by Jesus upon the rock.[503]

Look at the great foundation of that Church and at the very solid rock upon which Christ has founded the Church. Wherefore the Lord says: 'Ye of little faith, why have you doubted?'[504]

Moreover in the law this (love) is said to be the first commandment, and in the Gospels one is taught above all other things about love. Although the highest calling of feeding the sheep was communicated to Peter, and though the Church was established upon him as upon a solid ground, the confession of no other virtue is required of him, save that of love...[505]

But if she (the soul) does contrive to get through these unscathed, then the winter is past, and spring has come to her. For spring for her is when repose is given to her soul and calmness to her mind. Then the Word of God comes to her, then He calls her to Himself, and bids her come forth, not only from the house, but from the city itself—in other words, she must forsake not only fleshly vices, but also everything bodily and visible that the world contains. For we have already demonstrated plainly that the city is a figure for the world. The soul, therefore, is summoned forth outside the wall, and is brought to the outwork, when, forsaking and leaving things seen and temporal, she hastens towards those that are unseen and eternal. She is shown, however, that the way thereto must be followed beneath the cover of the rock, and not out in the open. And that she may not suffer the sun's heat and perhaps become tanned again and say once more: 'The sun hath looked askance at me,' therefore she takes the way beneath the cover of the rock.

But He will not have this covering made for her of branches, or canvas, or skins; *He will have her covering made of rock—that is, the firm and solid teachings of Christ. For Him St. Paul declares to be a rock when he says: And the rock was Christ.*

If, then, the soul be shielded and covered with the doctrine and the faith of Christ, she can come safely to that secret place wherein she may behold the glory of the Lord with open face. We may well believe that covering of the rock is safe, since Solomon also says of it in Proverbs that the tracks of the serpent cannot be detected on the rock...For no tracks of the serpent—that is, no marks of sin—can be found in this rock which is Christ, for it is He alone who did no sin. Having therefore availed herself of the covering of this rock, the soul comes safely to the place on the outwork—that is, to the contemplation of things incorporeal and eternal. David speaks of this same rock under another metaphor in Psalm Seventeen: And He set my feet upon a rock and ordered my paths. Do not be surprised if with David this rock is as it were the ground and basis upon which a soul goes to God, while with Solomon it is the covering of the soul that is set upon reaching the mystical secrets of wisdom; seeing that Christ Himself is at one time called the Way by which believers go, and again the Forerunner, as when Paul says: Into which the forerunner Jesus entered for us.

Like to these is the saying of God to Moses: Lo, I have set thee in a cleft of the rock, and thou shalt see my back parts. That Rock which is Christ is, therefore, not completely closed, but has clefts. But the cleft of the rock is He who reveals God to men, and makes Him known to them; for no one knoweth the Father, save the Son. So no one sees the back parts of God— that is to say, the things that are come to pass in the latter times, unless he be placed in the cleft of the rock, that is to say, when he is taught them by Christ's own revealing.[506]

But who is thus blessed, who so throws off the burden of temptations that no thought of ambiguity creeps up on his mind? See what was said by the Lord to the great foundation of the church and very solid rock, upon which Christ founded the church: 'O you of little faith he says, why have you doubted?'[507]

Pacian

All you seek then, you have in Matthew. Why did not you, who teach a bishop, read it all? Look at the opening words of that precept. As Matthew himself reports, *the Lord spoke to Peter a little earlier; he spoke to one, that from one he might found unity, soon delivering the same to all.* Yet he still begins just as to Peter: 'And I say also unto thee', he says 'that thou art Peter...'[508]

Palladius of Helenopolis

'You, however, who do you say I am?' Not all responded, but Peter only, interpreting the mind of all: 'You are Christ, Son of the living God.' The Saviour, approving the correctness of this response, spoke, saying: '*You are Peter, and upon this rock*'—that is, upon this confession—'*I shall build my Church, and the gates of Hell shall not prevail against it.*' Now with respect to this confession you will find...among all men both censure and praise. Thus at one time the Ephesians spoke ill of Christ and the apostles, crying: 'They turn the world upside down' (Acts 17.6). Now, however, they have ceased speaking ill, they themselves having been glorified...They are swine and dogs who say, 'He deceived the world'; but they are disciples who seek after him, saying: 'You are Christ, the Son of the living God.'[509]

By the permission of the Lord, these things were in the beginning for the discipline of the saints, the devil seeking to have them, as the saving Word says, 'Simon, Simon, Satan hath desired to have you, that he may sift you as wheat. But I have prayed for thee, that thy faith fail not.' And not solely did Jesus pray for Peter, but for all who have the faith of Peter.[510]

Paschasius Radbertus

There is one response of all upon which the Church is founded and against which the gates of hell will not prevail...Such a great faith does not arise except from the revelation of God the Father and inspiration of the Holy Spirit so that anyone that has faith, like firm stone, is called Peter...It should be noted that anyone of the faithful is rock as far as he is an imitator of Christ and is light as far as he is illuminated by light and by this the Church of Christ is founded upon those as far as they are strengthened by Christ. So not on Peter alone but on all the apostles and the successors of the apostles the Church of God is built. But these mountains are first built on the mountain Christ is elevated above all mountains and hills.[511]

One heavenly house in the heavens has been established, through the foundation of faith, upon him who is rightly called 'a rock.'[512]

For the name, derived equally in Latin from the 'rock' (petra) which is Christ, designates the firmness of his faith.[513]

This is indeed the true and inviolable faith given to Peter from God the Father, which affirms that if there had not always been a son there would not always have been a Father, upon which faith the whole Church is both founded and remains firm, believing that God is the Son of God.[514]

Paul of Emessa

Upon this faith the Church of God has been founded. With this expectation, upon this rock the Lord God placed the foundations of the Church. When then the Lord Christ was going to Jerusalem, He asked the disciples, saying, 'Whom do men say that the Son of Man is?' The apostles say, 'Some Elias, others Jeremias, or one of the prophets.' And He says, but you, that is, My elect, you who have followed Me for three years, and have seen My power, and miracles, and beheld Me walking on the sea, who have shared My table, '*Whom do you say that I am?*' *Instantly, the Coryphaeus of the apostles, the mouth of the disciples, Peter, 'Thou art the Christ, the Son of the living God.'*[515]

Paul Orosius

Oh Peter, upon whom Christ founded his Church, and oh Paul, who laid a foundation besides which no one can place another, namely, Christ: blessed apostles, pillars and mainstays of the truth...[516]

Peter loved Christ and he never departed from that love; and as a testimony of his love for the Lord, *he is at one moment established as the rock of the Church's foundation*; yet in the next moment he is seduced by the word of Satan.[517]

Paulinus of Nola

Likewise He shares His glory with His people, giving us a participation in almost everything, even in His names. Just as He is called the Strength of God, so He deigns to be our strength, too: God is our Refuge and our Strength. As we are His heirs, so He is ours, for you read in the book of Moses: The people of Jacob are become the Lord's portion; and again in the Psalms: The Lord is my portion. Just as He called Himself the Light of this world, so He said to His own: You are the light of this world. Again, He says: I am the living bread; and: We are all one bread. Elsewhere He states: I am the true Vine; and to you He says: I planted thee a fruitful vine, all true. Christ is the mountain of God, in which God is well pleased to dwell, and His saints are the mountains of God, fruitful mountains, from which He enlighteneth us wonderfully from the everlasting mountains. *Christ is the rock, for they drank of the spiritual Rock that followed them, and the Rock was Christ. The favour of this name, too, He did not refuse to His disciple; He says to him: Upon this rock I will build My church, and the gates of hell shall not prevail against it. But why are we surprised that*

He granted His names to His servants, when He shares even His Father and His kingship with them? For to those who received Him, He gave them power to be made the sons of God.[518]

Prosper of Aquitaine

In the same sense He said: Simon, Simon, behold Satan hath desired to have you, that he may sift you as wheat. But I have prayed for thee, that thy faith fail not; and thou, being converted in the end, confirm thy brethren. And pray lest ye enter into temptation. When the faith of so great an Apostle was going to give way unless Christ prayed for him, this was a sure sign that he, too, was subject to unsteadiness which could falter in temptation; and he was not so confirmed with the strength to persevere, that he was not liable to any weakness. For, indeed, even after all this, trepidation was to shake him so badly that in the house of Caiaphas, frightened by the questions of some servant girl, his constancy was to give way, and that to the extent of disowning Christ three times, after he had promised to die for Him...The Lord could also have given the chief of His disciples such firmness of soul that, as He Himself was not to be deterred from the resolve to undergo His Passion, so Saint Peter also on that occasion would not have been overcome by fear. But such steadfastness belonged only to Him who alone could say in truth and reality, I have power to lay down my life, and I have power to take it up again. In all other men, as long as the flesh lusteth against the spirit, and the spirit against the flesh, and as long as the spirit indeed is willing, but the flesh is weak, immovable strength of soul is not to be found, because the perfect and undisturbed happiness of peace is not our lot in this life, but in the next only. But in the uncertainty of the present struggle, when the whole of life is a trial and when victory itself is not shielded from the Waylayer's pride, the danger of inconstancy is ever present...The most blessed Peter himself passed through this conflict at the very moment when he was about to crown all his victories...Who, then, would doubt, who would fail to see that this strongest of rocks, who shared in the strength and the name of the first Rock, had always nourished the wish to be given the strength of dying for Christ?[519]

Tertullian

Again, He changes the name of Simon to Peter, inasmuch as the Creator also altered the names of Abram, Sarai, and Oshea, by calling the latter Joshua, and adding a syllable to each of the former. *But why Peter? If it was because of the vigour of his faith, there were many solid materials which might lend a name from their strength. Was it because Christ was both a rock and a stone?* For we read of his being placed 'for a stone of stumbling and for a rock of offence.' I omit the rest of the passage. Therefore He would fain impart to the dearest of His disciples a name which was suggested by one of His own especial designations in figure; because it was, I suppose, more peculiarly fit than a name which might have been derived from no figurative description of Himself.[520]

For though you think heaven still shut, remember that the Lord left here to Peter and through him to the Church, the keys of it, which every one who has been here put to the question, and also made confession, will carry with him.[521]

If, because the Lord has said to Peter, 'Upon this rock I will build My Church,' 'to thee have I given the keys of the heavenly kingdom;' or, 'Whatsoever thou shalt have bound or loosed in earth, shall be bound or loosed in the heavens,' you therefore presume that the power of binding and loosing has derived to you, that is, to every Church akin to Peter, what sort of man are you, subverting and wholly changing the manifest intention of the Lord, conferring (as that intention did) this (gift) personally upon Peter? *'On thee,' He says, 'will I build My Church;' and, 'I will give to thee the keys,' not to the Church; and, 'Whatsoever thou shalt have loosed or bound,' not what 'they shall have loosed or bound.' For so withal the result teaches. In (Peter) himself the Church was reared; that is, through (Peter) himself; (Peter) himself essayed the key; you see what (key): 'Men of Israel, let what I say sink into your ears: Jesus the Nazarene, a man destined by God for you,' and so forth. (Peter) himself, therefore, was the first to unbar, in Christ's baptism, the entrance to the heavenly kingdom, in which (kingdom) are 'loosed' the sins that were beforetime 'bound;' and those which have not been 'loosed' are 'bound,' in accordance with true salvation...*[522]

Was anything withheld from the knowledge of Peter, who is called 'the rock on which the church should be built, 'who also obtained 'the keys of the kingdom of heaven,' with the power of 'loosing and binding in heaven and on earth?'[523]

For because Jesus Christ was to introduce the second people (which is composed of us nations, lingering deserted in the world aforetime)into the land of promise, 'flowing with milk and honey' (that is, into the possession of eternal life, than which nought is sweeter); this had to come about, not through Moses (that is, not through the Law's discipline), but through Joshua (that is, through the new law's grace), *after our circumcision with 'a knife of rock' (that is, with Christ's precepts, for Christ is in many ways and figures predicted as a rock*); therefore the man who was being prepared to act as images of this sacrament was inaugurated under the figure of the Lord's name, even so as to be named Jesus.[524]

Theodoret

Let no one then foolishly suppose that the Christ is any other than the only begotten Son. Let us not imagine ourselves wiser than the gift of the Spirit. Let us hear the words of the great Peter, 'Thou art the Christ, the Son of the living God.' *Let us hear the Lord Christ confirming this confession, for 'On this rock,' He says, 'I will build my church and the gates of Hell shall not prevail against it.' Wherefore too the wise Paul, most excellent master builder of the churches, fixed no other foundation than this. 'I,' he says, 'as a wise master builder have laid the foundation, and another buildeth thereon. But let every man take heed how he buildeth thereon. For other foundation can no man lay than that is laid, which is Jesus Christ.'* How then can they think of any other foundation, when they are bidden not to fix a foundation, but to build on that which is laid? The divine writer *recognises Christ as the foundation*, and glories in this title.[525]

Other foundation no man can lay but that which is laid, which is Christ Jesus (1 Cor. iii.11). It is necessary to build upon, not to lay foundations. For it is impossible for him who wishes to build wisely to lay another foundation. The blessed Peter also laid this foundation, or rather the Lord

Himself. *For Peter having said, 'Thou art the Christ, the Son of the living God;' the Lord said, 'Upon this rock I will build My Church.' Therefore call not yourselves after men's names, for Christ is the foundation.*[526] Wherefore our Lord Jesus Christ permitted *the first of the apostles, whose confession He had fixed as a kind of groundwork and foundation of the Church*, to waver to and fro, and to deny Him, and then raised him up again.[527]

Surely he is calling pious faith and true confession a 'rock.' For when the Lord asked his disciples who the people said he was, blessed Peter spoke up, saying 'You are Christ, the Son of the living God.' To which the Lord answered: 'Truly, truly I say to you, you are Peter and *upon this rock I shall build my Church, and the gates of hell shall not prevail against it.*'[528]

'Its foundations are on the holy mountains.' The 'foundations' of piety are divine precepts, while the 'holy mountains' upon which these foundations are laid are the apostles of our Saviour. Blessed Paul says concerning these foundations: 'You have been built upon the foundation of the apostles and prophets whose cornerstone is Christ Jesus.' And again he says: 'Peter, James and John who are perceived to be pillars.' And after Peter had made that true and divine confession, Christ said to him: 'You are Peter, and upon this rock I shall build my Church; and the gates of hell shall not prevail against it.' And elsewhere Christ says: 'You are the light of the world, and a city set on a hill cannot be hid.' *Upon these holy mountains Christ the Lord laid the foundations of piety.*[529]

Dioscurus, however, refuses to abide by these decisions; he is turning the see of the blessed Mark upside down; and these things he does though he perfectly well knows that the *Antiochean metropolis possesses the throne of the great Peter, who was the teacher of the blessed Mark, and first and coryphaeus of the apostles.*[530]

Let us inquire who is he that is called a stone; and at which appearing small, later became very great, and covered the earth. Let us, therefore, hearken to God Himself saying by the prophet Isaias, 'Behold I lay in Sion a stone costly, a corner stone, precious, elect, into the foundations thereof, and everyone that believeth in it shall not be confounded' (Is.

xxviii.16)...Let us also listen to the blessed David prophecying and crying out, 'The stone which the builders rejected, the same is become the head of the corner?' (Matt. xxi.42). *And the blessed apostle Peter teaching among the Jews, and bringing before them the prophecy of the Lord, says, 'This is the stone which, rejected by you the builders, is become the head of the corner' (Acts iv.11). And the blessed apostle says, 'Built upon the foundation of the apostles and prophets, Jesus Christ Himself being the chief corner stone' (Eph. ii.20); and elsewhere he says, 'Other foundation no man can lay but that which is laid, which is Christ Jesus,' (1 Cor. iii.11); and again, 'They drank,' he says, 'of the spiritual rock which followed them, but the rock was Christ'(1 Cor. x.4). Wherefore we are taught by the Old and New Testament, that our Lord Jesus Christ is called a stone.*[531]

For if they say that these things happened before baptism, let them learn that *the great foundation of the Church was shaken, and confirmed by divine grace.* For the great Peter, having denied thrice, remained first; cured by his own tears. And the Lord commanded him to apply the same cure to the brethren, 'And thou,' He says, 'converted, confirm thy brethren' (Luke xxii.32).[532]

The Comments of 6th Century Palestinian and Syriac Clergy from a Letter to the Emperor Justin

With joy you will draw water from the springs of salvation (Isa. 12). Springs of salvation, says the prophet, meaning obviously *the preaching of evangelical truth*, from which spring the blessed apostles and their followers who were disciples through ordination and the wise teachers of the Church drew the saving water of faith, then irrigated the holy Church of God which, *fixed on the rock of that greatest of apostles, defends the true and inflexible confession, and faithfully in every age exclaims with him (i.e. Peter) to the only Son of God: You are the Christ, the Son of the living God.* Receiving this saving confession from the four holy synods which are honored for their evangelical teachings, we have never, by the grace of Christ, deviated from the true **dogmas** handed down to us; as an examination of the matter proves and as the constancy of our faith in times of necessity demonstrates. Since, therefore, as Christians we share in the doctrines of faith, and since, most reverend lord (i.e. Justin), we press for common peace and unity, we hereby make the faith, which we have acknowledged, from the beginning, open to your goodness through this our apology.[533]

The Comments of Origen, Chrysostom or Cyril of Alexandria Falsely Attributed to Victor of Antioch

And to Simon He gave the name Peter (Mark iii.16). Lest any may think the apostles were chosen by chance or at random, the Evangelist gives the names of each in order. And he says that 'to Simon He gave the name Peter,' that the name may anticipate the event itself; because as *Christ the Lord was about to build His Church on Peter, that is, on the unbroken and sound doctrine of Peter, and his unshaken faith*, therefore in prophetic spirit does He call him Peter.[534]

Endnotes

[1] Pat Robertson in the foreword to Keith A. Fournier, *A House Divided* (Colorodo Springs: Navpress, 1994), p. 8.

[2] Pat Robertson in the foreword to Keith A. Fournier, *A House Divided* (Colorodo Springs: Navpress, 1994), p. 7.

[3] Keith A. Fournier, *A House Divided* (Colorodo Springs: Navpress, 1994), pp. 29-30.

[4] Keith A. Fournier, *A House Divided* (Colorodo Springs: Navpress, 1994), p. 32.

[5] Catechism of the Catholic Church (Chicago: Loyola University Press, 1994), p. 235.

[6] Catechism of the Catholic Church (Chicago: Loyola University Press, 1994), p. 235f.

[7] Catechism of the Catholic Church (Chicago: Loyola University Press, 1994), p. 142.

[8] Catechism of the Catholic Church (Chicago: Loyola University Press, 1994), p. 234.

[9] For an authoritative statement of the decrees of Vatican One on Papal Jurisdiction please refer to Appendix A.

[10] *Dogmatic Decrees of the Vatican Council* as found in Philip Schaff, *The Creeds of Christendom* (New York: Harper, 1877), Chapters I, II, III.

[11] *Dogmatic Decrees of the Vatican Council*, On Faith, Chapter III as found in Philip Schaff, *The Creeds of Christendom* (New York:Harper, 1877), Volume II, pp. 244-245.

[12] Letter (October 1994) from Robert Fastiggi to James Ross critiquing the booklet *Roman Catholic Tradition: Claims and Contradictions* by William Webster. The letter was subsequently mailed to the author.

[13] Oscar Cullmann, *Peter:Disciple-Apostle-Martyr* (Philadelphia: Westminster, 1953), p. 162

[14] Alexander Roberts and James Donaldson, *The Ante-Nicene Fathers* (Grand Rapids: Eerdmans, 1951), Volume III, Tertullian, *Prescription Against Heretics* 22.

[15] Alexander Roberts and James Donaldson, *The Ante-Nicene Fathers* (Grand Rapids: Eerdmans, 1951), Volume IV, Tertullian, *On Modesty* 21, p. 99.

[16] Karlfried Froehlich, *Saint Peter, Papal Primacy, and Exegetical Tradition, 1150-1300*, pp. 13. Taken from *The Religious Roles of the Papacy: Ideals and Realities, 1150-1300*, ed. Christopher Ryan, Papers in Medieval Studies 8 (Toronto: Pontifical Institute of Medieval Studies, 1989).

[17] Scott Butler, Norman Dahlgren, David Hess, *Jesus, Peter and the Keys* (Santa Barbara: Queenship, 1996), pp. 216-217.

[18] *Ancient Christian Writers* (New York: Newman, 1989), *The Sermons of St. Maximus of Turin*, Sermon 77.1, p. 187

[19] *Exodus, Homily 5.4.* Cited by Karlfried Froehlich, *Formen der Auslegung von Matthaus 16,13-18 im lateinischen Mittelaiter*, Dissertation (Tubingen, 1963), p. 100.

[20] Allan Menzies, *The Ante-Nicene Fathers* (Grand Rapids: Eerdmans, 1951), Origen, *Commentary on Matthew*, Chapters 10-11.

[21] John Meyendorff, *Byzantine Theology* (New York: Fordham, 1974), pp. 97-98.

[22] Paul Empie and Austin Murphy, Ed., *Papal Primacy in the Universal Church* (Minneapolis: Augsburg, 1974), Lutherans and Catholics in Dialogue V, pp. 60-61.

[23] *A Library of the Fathers of the Holy Catholic Church* (Oxford: Parker, 1844), Cyprian, *On The Unity of the Church* 3-4, pp. 133-135.

[24] *A Library of the Fathers of the Holy Catholic Church* (Oxford: Parker, 1844), Cyprian, *On The Unity of the Church* 3, p. 133.

[25] *A Library of the Fathers of the Holy Catholic Church* (Oxford: Parker, 1844), *The Epistles of S. Cyprian*, Ep. 33.1.

[26] Robert Eno, *The Rise of the Papacy* (Wilmington: Michael Glazier, 1990), pp. 57-60.

[27] *Papal Primacy and the Universal Church*, Edited by Paul Empie and Austin Murphy (Minneapolis: Augsburg, 1974), Lutherans and Catholics in Dialogue V, pp. 68-69.27

[28] Michael Winter, *St. Peter and the Popes* (Baltimore: Helikon, 1960), pp. 47-48.

[29] Karlfried Froehlich, *Saint Peter, Papal Primacy, and the Exegetical Tradition, 1150-1300*, p. 36, 13, n. 28 p. 13. Taken from *The Religious Roles of the Papacy: Ideals and Realities, 1150-1300*, ed. Christopher Ryan, Papers in Medieval Studies 8 (Toronto: Pontifical Institute of Medieval Studies, 1989).

[30] John Meyendorff, *Byzantine Theology* (New York: Fordham University, 1974), p. 98.

[31] John Meyendorff, *Imperial Unity and Christian Divisions* (Crestwood: St. Vladimir's, 1989), pp. 61, 152.

[32] Reinhold Seeberg, *Text-Book of the History of Doctrines* (Grand Rapids: Baker, 1952), Volume I, p. 182-183.

[33] *De Schismate Donatistorum*, Book I.10; Book 2,3,4,6; C.S.E.L. 26. 12, 36. Cited by E. Giles, *Documents Illustrating Papal Authority* (London: SPCK, 1952), pp. 118-119.

Endnotes 351

[34] Robert Eno, *The Rise of the Papacy* (Wilmington: Michael Glazier, 1990), pp. 67-69.

[35] *A Library of the Fathers of the Holy Catholic Church* (Oxford: Parker, 1844), The Epistles of St. Cyprian, *Epistle* LXX. 17, 18, 20, pp. 279-281.

[36] *Commentary on the Psalms*, M.P.G., Vol. 23, Col. 173, 176.

[37] *Ecclesiastical History* II.XXV (Grand Rapids: Baker, 1977), p. 246.

[38] Michael Winter, *St. Peter and the Popes* (Baltimore: Helikon, 1960), p. 53.

[39] Philip Schaff, *Nicene and Post Nicene Fathers* (Grand Rapids: Eerdmans, 1953), *Letters of Athanasius*, Letter 29, p. 551.

[40] Philip Schaff, *Nicene and Post Nicene Fathers* (Grand Rapids: Eerdmans, 1953), Volume IV, St. Athanasius, *Four Discourses Against the Arians*, Discourse II, Chapter XXII.73, 74, 76; pp. 388-389.

[41] *A Library of the Fathers of the Holy Catholic Church* (Oxford: Parker, 1844), Select Treatises of S. Athanasius, *Discourse* IV, Subject IX.11.

[42] *Psalm 11.* Cited by J. Waterworth S.J., *A Commentary* (London:Thomas Richardson, 1871), p. 50.

[43] *Four Letters to Serapion of Thmuis* 1.28. Cited by William Jurgens, *The Faith of the Early Fathers* (Collegeville: Liturgical Press, 1970), Volume I, p. 336.

[44] *De Trinitate Liber Primus* I.30, M.P.G., Vol. 39, col. 416.

[45] William Jurgens, *The Faith of the Early Fathers* (Collegeville: Liturgical, 1979), Vol. 3, p. 1.

[46] *The Fathers of the Church* (Washington D.C., Catholic University, 1968), Saint Augustine, *The Retractations* Chapter 20.1.

[47] John Rotelle, Ed., *The Works of Saint Augustine* (New Rochelle: New City Press, 1993), *Sermons,* Vol. 6, Sermon 229P.1, p. 327.

[48] Philip Schaff, *Nicene and Post-Nicene Fathers* (Grand Rapids: Eerdmans, 1956), Volume VI, St. Augustin, *Sermon* XXVI.1-4, pp. 340-341.

[49] Philip Schaff, *Nicene and Post-Nicene Fathers* (Grand Rapids: Eerdmans, 1956), Volume VII, St. Augustin, *On the Gospel of John,* Tractate 124.5.

[50] John Rotelle, Ed., *The Works of Saint Augustine* (Hyde Park: New City, 1994), *Sermons,* III/8 (273-305A), On the Saints, Sermon 295.1-3, pp. 197-198.

[51] John Rotelle, Ed., *The Works of Saint Augustine* (New Rochelle: New City, 1993), *Sermons,* Sermon 265D.6, p. 258-259, n. 9.

[52] Karlfried Froehlich, *Saint Peter, Papal Primacy, and Exegetical Tradition, 1150-1300,* pp. 3, 8-14. Taken from *The Religious Roles of the Papacy: Ideals and Realities, 1150-1300,* ed. Christopher Ryan, Papers in Medieval Studies 8 (Toronto: Pontifical Institute of Medieval Studies, 1989).

[53]Karl Morrison, *Tradition and Authority in the Western Church 300-1140* (Princeton: Princeton University, 1969), p. 162.

[54]Reinhold Seeberg, *Text-Book of the History of Doctrines* (Grand Rapids: Baker, 1952), Volume I, p. 318-319.

[55]W.H.C. Frend, *The Early Church* (Philadelphia: Fortress, 1965), p. 222.

[56]Scott Butler, Norman Dahlgren, David Hess, *Jesus, Peter and the Keys* (Santa Barbara: Queenship, 1996), p. 252.

[57]W.A. Jurgens, *The Faith of the Early Fathers* (Collegeville: Liturgical, 1979), Volume 2, St. Ambrose, *On Twelve Psalms* 440,30, p. 150.

[58]*The Fathers of the Church* (Washington D.C., Catholic University, 1963), Saint Ambrose, Theological and Dogmatic Works, *The Sacrament of the Incarnation of Our Lord* IV.32-V.34, pp. 230-231.

[59]*Commentary in Luke* VI.98, CSEL 32.4.

[60]Robert Eno, *The Rise of the Papacy* (Wilmington: Michael Glazier, 1990), pp. 83-84.

[61]*On the Inscription of Acts*, II. Taken from E. Giles, *Documents Illustrating Papal Authority* (London: SPCK, 1952), p.168.

[62]Karlfried Froehlich, *Saint Peter, Papal Primacy, and Exegetical Tradition, 1150-1300*, p. 12. Taken from *The Religious Roles of the Papacy: Ideals and Realities, 1150-1300*, ed. Christopher Ryan, Papers in Medieval Studies 8 (Toronto: Pontifical Institute of Medieval Studies, 1989).

[63]*Epistle* 43.9. Cited by J. Waterworth S.J., *A Commentary* (London: Thomas Richardson, 1871), p. 76.

[64]Unde dicit Dominus ad Petrum: Super istam petram aedificabo Ecclesiam meam, hoc est, in hac catholicae fidei confessione statuam fideles ad vitam (*Commentary on Ephesians 2:20*. P.L. 17.380D).

[65]Philip Schaff and Henry Wace, *Nicene and Post-Nicene Fathers* (Grand Rapids: Eerdmans, 1955), *On The Trinity*, Book VI.36,37; Book II.23; Book VI.20.

[66]Philip Schaff and Henry Wace, *Nicene and Post-Nicene Fathers* (Grand Rapids: Eerdmans, 1954), Volume VI, St. Jerome, Epistle 15.2, *To Pope Damasus*, p. 18.

[67]*Commentary on Matthew* 7.25, M.P.L., Vol. 26, Col. 51. Cited by Karlfried Froehlich, *Formen der Auslegung von Matthaus 16,13-18 im lateinischen Mittelalter*, Dissertation (Tubingen, 1963), Footnote #200, p. 49.

[68]*Epistle 65.15, Ad Principiam*. Cited by J. Waterworth S.J., *A Commentary* (London: Thomas Richardson, 1871), p. 109.

[69]*Commentary on Amos* vi.12-13. Cited by J. Waterworth S.J., *A Commentary* (London: Thomas Richardson, 1871), pp. 112-113.

Endnotes 353

[70] Philip Schaff and Henry Wace, *Nicene and Post-Nicene Fathers* (Grand Rapids: Eerdmans, 1954), Volume VI, St. Jerome, *Against Jovinanius*, Book 2.37.

[71] *Commentary on Isaiah* ii.2. Cited by J. Waterworth S.J., *A Commentary* (London: Thomas Richardson, 1871), pp. 111-112.

[72] *Commentary on Matthew* III, 16:18, M.P.L., Vol. 26, Col. 121-122.

[73] *Commentary on Ephesians* II.20, M.P.L., Vol. 26, Col. 506-507.

[74] *Commentary on Galatians* I.11. Cited by J. Waterworth S.J., *A Commentary* (London: Thomas Richardson, 1871), pp. 116-117.

[75] Epistle 146.1, *To Evangel us*. Cited by J. Waterworthy S.J., *A Commentary* (London: Thomas Richardson, 1871), pp. 288-289.

[76] *Against Jovinianus* 1.26. Cited by J. Waterworthy S.J., *A Commentary* (London: Thomas Richardson, 1871), p. 366.

[77] *Epistle* 130.16. Cited by J. Waterworthy S.J., *A Commentary* (London: Thomas Richardson, 1871), p. 269.

[78] *Commentaria in XIII Epistolas Beati Pauli*, on Gal. 2.9,10. Cited by E. Giles, *Documents Illustrating Papal Authority* (London: SPCK, 1952), pp. 122-123.

[79] *Commentary on Ephesians*, M.P.L., Vol. 17, Col. 380.

[80] *Commentary on Ephesians*, M.P.L., Vol. 17, Col. 350.

[81] *Commentary on Ephesians*, M.P.L., Vol. 17, Col. 344.

[82] Michael Winter, *St. Peter and the Popes* (Baltimore: Helikon, 1960), p. 62.

[83] William Jurgens, *The Faith of the Early Fathers* (Collegeville: Liturgical Press, 1979), Volume 2, pp. 84-86.

[84] *De Eleemos* III.4, M.P.G., Vol. 49, Col. 298.

[85] *Hom. de decem mille talentis 3*, PG III, 20. Cited by Dom Chapman, *Studies in the Early Papacy* (London: Sheed & Ward, 1928), p. 74.

[86] Philip Schaff, *Nicene and Post-Nicene Fathers* (Grand Rapids: Eerdmans, 1956), Volume X, Saint Chrysostom, *Homilies on the Gospel of Saint Matthew*, Homily 56.2; p. 345.

[87] Dom John Chapman, *Studies on the Early Papacy* (London: Sheed & Ward, 1928), John Chrysostom, *Homilies on the Acts of the Apostles*, Homily XXVI, Footnote #5, p. 75.

[88] *Contra ludos et theatra 1*, PG VI, 265. Cited by Chapman, *Studies on the Early Papacy* (London: Sheed & Ward, 1928), p. 76.

[89] Philip Schaff, *Nicene and Post-Nicene Fathers* (Grand Rapids: Eerdmans, 1956), Volume XIV, Saint Chrysostom, *Homilies on the Gospel of John*, Homily 88.1-2, pp. 331-332.

[90] Philip Schaff, *Nicene and Post-Nicene Fathers* (Grand Rapids: Eerdmans, 1956), Volume XIV, Saint Chrysostom, *Homilies on the Gospel of John*, Homily 1.1, p. 1.

⁹¹*Homily 24, On Genesis.*.Cited by E. Giles, *Documents Illustrating Papal Authority* (London: SPCK, 1952), p. 165.

⁹²Philip Schaff, *Nicene and Post-Nicene Fathers*(Grand Rapids: Eerdmans, 1956), Volume XIV, Saint Chrysostom, *Homilies on the Gospel of John*, Homily 88.1-2, pp. 331-332.

⁹³Philip Schaff, *Nicene and Post-Nicene Fathers* (Grand Rapids: Eerdmans, 1956), Volume XIV, Saint Chrysostom, *Homilies on the Gospel of John*, Homily 88.1-2, pp. 331-332.

⁹⁴Philip Schaff, *Nicene and Post-Nicene Fathers* (Grand Rapids: Eerdmans, 1956), Volume XIV, Saint Chrysostom, *Homilies on the Gospel of John*, Homily 1.1, p. 1.

⁹⁵Philip Schaff, *Nicene and Post-Nicene Fathers* (Grand Rapids: Eerdmans, 1956), Volume XI, Saint Chrysostom, *Homilies on the Epistle to the Romans*, Homily 32, Ver. 24, pp. 561-562.

⁹⁶Philip Schaff, *Nicene and Post-Nicene Fathers* (Grand Rapids: Eerdmans, 1956), Volume XI, Saint Chrysostom, *Homilies on the Acts of the Apostles*, Homily 33, pp. 205, 207.

⁹⁷Dom John Chapman, *Studies on the Early Papacy* (London: Sheed & Ward, 1928), p. 90.

⁹⁸Philip Schaff, *Nicene and Post-Nicene Fathers* (Grand Rapids: Eerdmans, 1956), Volume XIV, Saint Chrysostom, *Homilies on the Gospel of John*, Homily 88.1-2, pp. 331-332..

⁹⁹*A Library of Fathers of the Holy Catholic Church* (Oxford, Parker, 1844), *Homilies of S. John Chrysostom on the Gospel of St. Matthew*, Homily 54.3.

¹⁰⁰Philip Schaff, *Nicene and Post-Nicene Fathers* (Grand Rapids: Eerdmans, 1956), Volume XIV, Saint Chrysostom, *Homilies on the Gospel of John*, Homily 1.1, p. 1.

¹⁰¹Philip Schaff, *Nicene and Post-Nicene Fathers* (Grand Rapids: Eerdmans, 1956), Volume X, Saint Chrysostom, *Homilies on the Gospel of Saint Matthew*, Homily 54.2-3; pp. 332-334..

¹⁰²Philip Schaff, *Nicene and Post-Nicene Fathers* (Grand Rapids: Eerdmans, 1956), Volume X, Chrysostom, On Matthew, Homily 82.3, p. 494.

¹⁰³Philip Schaff, Nicene and Post-Nicene Fathers (Grand Rapids: Eerdmans, 1956), Volume XII, Saint Chrysostom, Homilies on the Epistles of Paul to the Corinthians, Homily VIII.7, p. 47.

¹⁰⁴Dom John Chapman, *Studies on the Early Papacy* (London: Sheed & Ward, 1928), p. 77.

¹⁰⁵*A Library of Fathers of the Holy Catholic Church* (Oxford, Parker, 1844), *Homilies of S. John Chrysostom on the Gospel of St. Matthew*, Homily 54.3.

Endnotes 355

[106] Dom John Chapman, *Studies on the Early Papacy* (London: Sheed & Ward, 1928), p. 79.

[107] John Rotelle, *The Works of Saint Augustine* (Brooklyn: New City, 1992), *Sermons*, Sermon 147.3, p. 449.

[108] *On the Inscription of the Acts*, II. Cited by E. Giles, *Documents Illustrating Papal Authority* (London: SPCK, 1952), p. 168. Cf. Chapman, *Studies on the Early Papacy*, p. 96.

[109] *On the Inscription of the Acts*, II. Cited by E. Giles, *Documents Illustrating Papal Authority* (London: SPCK, 1952), p. 168. Cf. Chapman, *Studies on the Early Papacy*, p. 96.

[110] S. Herbert Scott, *The Eastern Churches and the Papacy* (London: Sheed & Ward, 1928), p. 133.

[111] S. Herbert Scott, *The Eastern Churches and the Papacy* (London: Sheed & Ward, 1928), p. 133.

[112] *On the Inscription of the Acts*, II. Cited by E. Giles, *Documents Illustrating Papal Authority* (London: SPCK, 1952), p. 168. Cf. Chapman, *Studies on the Early Papacy*, p. 96.

[113] S. Herbert Scott, *The Eastern Churches and the Papacy* (London: Sheed & Ward, 1928), p. 133.

[114] Dom Chrysostumus Baur, O.S.B., *John Chrysostom and His Time* (Westminster: Newman, 1959), Vol. I, pp. 348-349.

[115] Michael Winter, *St. Peter and the Popes* (Baltimore: Helikon, 1960), p. 73.

[116] Philip Schaff, *Nicene and Post-Nicene Fathers* (Grand Rapids: Eerdmans, 1953), Volume III, Theodoret, Epistle 146, *To John the Economus*, p. 318.

[117] *Commentary on 1 Corinthians* 1,12. Cited by J. Waterworth S.J., *A Commentary* (London: Thomas Richardson, 1871), p. 149.

[118] *Commentary on Canticle of Canticles* II.14, M.P.G., Vol. 81, Col. 108.

[119] *Commentary on Psalms* 86.1, M.P.G., Vol. 80, Col. 1561.

[120] Philip Schaff, *Nicene and Post-Nicene Fathers* (Grand Rapids: Eerdmans, 1956), Volume III, Theodoret, Epistle 77, *To Eulalius*, p. 273.

[121] *Haeret. Fab.* Book 5, Chapter 28. Cited by J. Waterworth S.J., *A Commentary* (London: Thomas Richardson, 1871), p. 152.

[122] Philip Schaff, *Nicene and Post-Nicene Fathers* (Grand Rapids: Eerdmans, 1956), Volume III, Theodoret, Epistle 86, *To Flavianus, bishop of Constantinople*, p. 281.

[123] Michael Winter, *St. Peter and the Popes* (Baltimore: Helikon, 1960), p. 74.

[124] *Dialogue on the Trinity* IV, M.P.G., Vol. 75, Col. 866.

[125] *Commentary on Isaiah* IV.2, M.P.G., Vol. 70, Col. 940.

[126] *Commentary on Zacharias.* Cited by J. Waterworth S.J., *A Commentary* (London: Thomas Richardson, 1871), p. 143.

[127] *Commentary on Isaiah* 3.iii, on Isaiah 28:16. Cited by J. Waterworth S.J., *A Commentary* (London: Thomas Richardson, 1871), p. 142.

[128] Michael Winter, *St. Peter and the Popes* (Baltimore: Helikon, 1960), pp. 74-76.

[129] William Jurgens, *The Faith of the Early Fathers* (Collegeville: Liturgical Press, 1979), Volume II, p. 3.

[130] *Commentary on the Prophet Isaias,* Cap. II.66; M.P.G., Vol. 30, Col. 233; Cited by Michael Winter, *St. Peter and the Popes* (Baltimore: Helikon, 1960), p. 55.

[131] *Adversus Eunomius II.4;* M.P.G., Vol. 29, Col. 577.

[132] *Commentary on the Prophet Isaiah*, Cap. II.66, M.P.G., Vol. 30, Col. 233.

[133] George Salmon, *The Infallibility of the Church* (London: John Murray, 1914), p. 338.

[134] *Panegyric on St. Stephen,* M.P.G., Vol. 46, Col. 733.

[135] *Sermon 1 de Fide* I.13. Cited by J. Waterworth, *A Commentary* (London: Thomas Richardson, 1871), pp. 39-40.

[136] *Sermon vii. de Poeniten.* 6. Cited by J. Waterworth S.J., *A Commentary* (London: Thomas Richardson, 1871), p. 40.

[137] *Sermon* xi. Cited by J. Waterworth S.J., *A Commentary* (London: Thomas Richardson, 1871), p. 40.

[138] *A Library of the Fathers of the Holy Catholic Church* (London: Oxford, 1842), *The Catechetical Lectures of S. Cyril,* Lecture XI.3, p. 111.

[139] Philip Schaff and Henry Wace, *Nicene and Post-Nicene Fathers* (Grand Rapids: Eerdmans, 1955), Volume VII, *The Catechetical Lectures* 6.15.

[140] Philip Schaff and Henry Wace, *Nicene and Post-Nicene Fathers* (Grand Rapids: Eerdmans, 1955), Volume XI, *The Seven Books of John Cassian,* Book III, Chapter 12, 14.

[141] Michael Winter, *Saint Peter and the Popes* (Baltimore: Helikon, 1960), p. 61.

[142] *The Panarion of Epiphanius of Salamis* (Leiden: Brill, 1994), Books II and III, *Haer.* 59.7, 6-8,3, pp. 108-109.

[143] *Ancoratus* 9.6. G.C.S., Epiphanius, Vol. I, p. 16.

[144] Michael Winter, *St. Peter and the Popes* (Baltimore: Helikon, 1960), p. 57.

[145] Philip Schaff, *Nicene and Post-Nicene Fathers* (Grand Rapids: Eerdmans, 1956), Vol XIII, Aphrahat, *Select Demonstrations,* Demonstration I.2-6,13,19.

[146] Philip Schaff, *Nicene and Post-Nicene Fathers* (Grand Rapids: Eerdmans, 1956), Volume XIII, *Hymns for the Feast of the Epiphany* II.14, p. 267.

[147] Philip Schaff, *Nicene and Post-Nicene Fathers* (Grand Rapids: Eerdmans, 1956), Volume XIII, *The Pearl,* Hymn 2.2.

Endnotes 357

[148] *Dialogue on the Life of John Chrysostom*, M.P.G., Vol. 47, Col. 68.

[147] Michael Winter, *St. Peter and the Popes* (Baltimore: Helikon, 1960), p. 73.

[150] *Oratio* XXV.4, M.P.G., Vol. 85, Col. 296-297.

[151] *Oratio* 16. Cited by J. Waterworth S.J., *A Commentary* (London: Thomas Richardson, 1871), p. 168.

[152] *Commentary in Canticle of Canticles*, M.P.G., Vol. 87 (ii), Col. 1693.

[153] *The Encyclopedia of the Early Church* (New York: Oxford University, 1992), Volume II, p. 868.

[154] Cited by J. Waterworth S.J., *A Commentary* (London: Thomas Richardson, 1871), pp. 133-134.

[155] *Homily VIII, On Saints Peter and Paul*, M.P.G., Vol. 40, Col. 268-269.

[156] *Homily of the Nativity*. Cited by J. Waterworth S.J., *A Commentary* (London: Thomas Richardson, 1871), p. 148.

[157] *Epistle 235*. Cited by C. DeLisle Shortt, *Who Was the First Bishop of Rome* (Edinburgh: T&T Clark, 1935), p. 110.

[158] *Epistle 416*. Cited by C. DeLisle Shortt, *Who Was the First Bishop of Rome* (Edinburgh: T&T Clark, 1935), p. 110.

[159] *Expositions in the Psalms*, Psalm 45.5, M.P.L., Vol. 70, Col. 330.

[160] *Expositions in the Psalms*, Psalm 86.1, M.P.L., Vol. 70, Col. 618.

[161] *Exposition of the Psalms.*, Psalm 103.5, M.P.L., Vol. 70, Col. 729-730.

[162] *De Remissione Peccatorum* II.20, M.P.L., Vol. 65, Col. 571.

[163] *De Fide* III.37, M.P.L., Vol. 65, Col. 690.

[164] *A Library of the Fathers of the Holy Catholic Church* (Oxford: Parker, 1850), Volume 31, S. Gregory the Great, *Morals on the Book of Job*, Book XXXV.13, p. 670. M.S.L., Vol. 94, Col. 222.

[165] Philip Schaff and Henry Wace, *The Nicene and Post-Nicene Fathers* (Grand Rapids: Eerdmans, 1956), Volume XII, *Epistles of Gregory the Great*, Book V, Epistle XVIII.

[166] Philip Schaff and Henry Wace, *The Nicene and Post-Nicene Fathers* (Grand Rapids: Eerdmans, 1956), Volume XII, *Epistles of Gregory the Great*, Book VIII, Epistle 30, p. 241.

[167] Philip Schaff and Henry Wace, *The Nicene and Post-Nicene Fathers* (Grand Rapids: Eerdmans, 1956), Volume XII, *Epistles of Gregory the Great*, Book VII, Epistle 40, pp. 228-229.

[168] John Meyendorff, *Imperial Unity and Christian Divisions* (Crestwood: St. Vladmir's, 1989), pp. 305-307.

[169] Karl Morrison, *Tradition and Authority in the Western Church* (Princetion: Princeton University, 1969), pp. 132-135.

[170] R.A. Markus, *From Augustine to Gregory the Great* (London: Vaorium Reprints, 1983), Chapter XV, pp. 32-33.

[171] Homily LXVIII, *In Nativitate Petri et Pauli*, M.P.L., Vol. 57, Col. 394.

[172] *Ancient Christian Writers* (New York: Newman, 1989), *The Sermons of St. Maximus of Turin*, Sermon 9.1, p. 27. M.S.L., Vol. 39, Col. 2119.

[173] *Ancient Christian Writers* (New York: Newman, 1989), *The Sermons of St. Maximus of Turin*, Sermon 77.1, p. 187.

[174] *Ancient Christian Writers* (New York: Newman, 1989) *The Sermons of St. Maximus of Turin*, Sermon 80.3, p. 193.

[175] Sermon XXVIII, M.P.L., Vol. 57, Col. 587-588.

[176] *Ancient Christian Writers* (New York: Newman, 1989), *The Sermons of St. Maximus of Turin*, Sermon 49.2-3, pp. 115-117.

[177] Sermon 107, M.P.L., Vol. 57, Col. 498.

[178] Sermon 154, P.L., Vol. 52, Col. 608. Cited by E. Giles, *Documents Illustrating Papal Authority* (London: SPCK, 1952), p. 283.

[179] Epistle of Justin to Pope Hormisdas, M.P.L., Vol. 63, Col. 503.

[180] Karl Morrison, *Tradition and Authority in the Western Church* (Princeton: Princeton University, 1969), p. 116.

[181] William Jurgens, *The Faith of the Early Fathers* (Collegeville: Liturgical Press, 1979), Volume III, p. 328.

[182] *Allegories in the New Testament*, M.P.L., Vol. 83, Col. 117-118, Numbers 135, 136, 148.

[183] *Etymologies* VII.2, M.P.L., Vol. 82, Col. 267.41.

[184] *De Ecclesiasticus* II.5, M.P.L., Vol. 83, Col. 781-782.5-6.

[185] Michael Winter, *St. Peter and the Popes* (Baltimore: Helikon, 1960), p. 71.

[186] *Homily on the Transfiguration*, M.P.G., Vol. 96, Col. 554-555.

[187] *Homily on the Transfiguration*, M.P.G., Vol. 96, Col. 548.

[188] *Liber de Recta Sententia*, M.P.G., Vol. 94, Col. 1429.

[189] Scott Butler, Norman Dahlgren, David Hess, *Jesus, Peter and the Keys* (Santa Barbara: Queenship, 1996), p. 275.

[190] Cited by John Bigane, *Faith, Christ or Peter* (Washington D.C.: University, 1981), p. 311, 57-58.

[191] Homily 2.16, M.P.L., Vol. 94, Col. 94. Cited by Karlfried Froehlich, *Formen der Auslegung von Matthaus 16,13-18 im lateinischen Mittelalter*, Dissertation (Tubingen, 1963), Footnote #140, p. 134.

[192] Homily 23, M.P.L., Vol. 94, Col. 260. Cited by Karlfried Froehlich, *Formen der Auslegung von Matthaus 16,13-18 im lateinischen Mittelalter*, Dissertation

Endnotes

(Tubingen, 1963), Footnote # 204, p. 156.

[193]Homily 23, M.S.L., Vol. 186, Col. 108. Cited by Karlfried Froehlich, *Formen der Auslegung von Matthaus 16,13-18 im lateinischen Mittelalter*, Dissertation (Tubingen, 1963), Footnote #124

[194]Homily 16, M.S.L., Vol. 94, Col. 222. Cited by Karlfried Froehlich, *Formen der Auslegung von Matthaus 16,13-18 im lateinischen Mittelalter*, Dissertation (Tubingen, 1963), Footnote #125.

[195]Homily 16, M.S.L., Vol. 94, Col. 222. Cited by Karlfried Froehlich, *Formen der Auslegung von Matthaus 16,13-18 im lateinischen Mittelalter*, Dissertation (Tubingen, 1963), Footnote #138.

[196]Jaroslav Pelikan, *The Christian Tradition: A History of the Development of Doctrine* (Chicago: University of Chicago, 1974), Volume III, pp. 46-47.

[197]Commentary on Matthew, M.P.L., Vol. 120, Col. 561. Cited by Karlfried Froehlich, *Formen der Auslegung von Matthaus 16,13-18 im lateinischen Mittelalter*, Dissertation (Tubingen, 1963), Footnote #141-142, p. 134.

[198]Commentary on Matthew, M.S.L., Vol. 120, Col. 329. Cited by Karlfried Froehlich, *Formen der Auslegung von Matthaus 16,13-18 im lateinischen Mittelalter*, Dissertation (Tubingen, 1963), Footnote #211.

[199]Commentary on Matthew 10.4, M.S.L., Vol. 120, Col. 404. Cited by Karlfried Froehlich, *Formen der Auslegung von Matthaus 16,13-18 im lateinischen Mittelalter*, Dissertation (Tubingen, 1963), Footnote #129.

[200]Commentary on Matthew, M.S. L., Vol. 120, Col. 555f. Cited by Karlfried Froehlich, *Formen der Auslegung von Matthaus 16,13-18 im lateinischen Mittelalter*, Dissertation (Tubingen, 1963), Footnote #162.

[201]Alexander Roberts and James Donaldson, Ed., *The Ante-Nicene Fathers* (Buffalo: Christian Literature, 1885), Volume I, *Epistle of Ignatius to the Smyraeans*, Chapter VII, p. 89.

[202]*A Library of the Fathers of the Holy Catholic Church* (Oxford: Parker, 1844), *The Epistles of S. Cyprian*, Epistle, XI.5, p. 27.

[203]*A Library of the Fathers of the Holy Catholic Church* (Oxford: Parker, 1839), *The Treatises of S. Caecilius Cyprian*, Treatise VII, *On the Lord's Prayer* 19, pp. 193-194.

[204]John Rotelle, Ed., *The Works of Saint Augustine* (Hyde Park: New City Press, 1995), *Sermons*, Volume III/10, Sermon 392.3, p. 422.

[205]Philip Schaff, *Nicene and Post-Nicene Fathers* (Grand Rapids: Eerdmans, 1956), Volume XIV, Saint Chrysostom, *The Epistle to the Hebrews*, Homily XXXI.4, p. 507.

[206]Ambrosiaster, *Quaestiones in Novum Testamentum*, no. 75 (PL 35:2273A). Cited by Karlfreid Froehlich, *St. Peter, Papal Primacy, and the Exegetical Tradition*, 1150-

1300, in *The Religious Roles of the Papacy; Ideals and Realities* 1150-1300 (Toronto: Pontifical Institute, 1989), Christopher Ryan, Ed., p. 22.

[207] Alexander Roberts and James Donaldson, Ed., *The Ante–Nicene Fathers* (Buffalo: Christian Literature, 1885), Volume VII, *Apostolic Teaching and Constitutions*, Book VI, Chapter V, p. 452.

[208] *Quaestiones in Novum Testamentum*, no. 75.

[209] Karlfried Froehlich, *Saint Peter, Papal Primacy and the Exegetical Tradition, 1150-1300.* pp. 19-23.

[210] Karlfried Froehlich, *Saint Peter, Papal Primacy and the Exegetical Tradition, 1150-1300.*, pp. 24-25.

[211] Brian Tierney, *Origins of Papal Infallibility* (Leiden: Brill, 1972), pp. 11-13.

[212] Luis Bermejo, *Infallibility on Trial* (Westminster: Christian Classics, 1992), pp. 164-165.

[213] *A Library of the Fathers of the Holy Catholic Church* (Oxford: Parker, 1845), Volume 20, Sermon 99.7, p. 691.

[214] *A Library of the Fathers of the Holy Catholic Church* (Oxford: Parker, 1845), Volume 20, Sermon 97.2, p. 685.

[215] Philip Schaff, *Nicene and Post-Nicene Fathers*, Volume VII, St. Augustine, *On The Gospel of St. John*, Tractate 50.12, p. 282.

[216] *The Canons and Decrees of the Council of Trent*, Fourth Session, Decree Concerning the Canonical Scriptures. Cited by Philip Schaff, *The Creeds of Christendom* (New York: Harper, 1877), Volume II, p. 83.

[217] *Dogmatic Decrees of the Vatican Council.* Cited by Philip Schaff, *The Creeds of Christendom* (New York: Harper, 1877), Volume II, p. 207.

[218] Jaroslav Pelikan, *The Christian Tradition: A History of the Development of Doctrine* (Chicago: University of Chicago, 1974), Volume Two, pp. 160-161.

[219] Janus (Johann Joseph Ignaz von Dollinger), *The Pope and the Council* (Boston: Roberts, 1869), pp. 70-74.

[220] Michael Winter, *St. Peter and the Popes* (Baltimore: Helicon, 1960), p. 53.

[221] Michael Winter, *St. Peter and the Popes* (Baltimore: Helicon, 1960), p. 76.

[222] Karlfried Froehlich, *Saint Peter, Papal Primacy, and Exegetical Tradition, 1150-1300*, pp. 3, 8-14, 42. Taken from *The Religious Roles of the Papacy: Ideals and Realities, 1150-1300*, ed. Christopher Ryan, Papers in Medieval Studies 8 (Toronto: Pontifical Institute of Medieval Studies, 1989).

[223] Yves Congar, *After Nine Hundred Years* (New York: Fordham University, 1959), pp. 61-62.

[224] Yves Congar, *Tradition and Traditions* (New York: Macmillan, 1966), p. 398.

Endnotes

[225] Cited by Yves Congar, *After Nine Hundred Years* (New York: Fordham University, 1959), pp. 61-62.

[226] John Meyendorff, *Byzantine Theology* (New York: Fordham University, 1974), p. 97.

[227] John Meyendorff, *St. Peter in Byzantine Theology*. Taken from *The Primacy of Peter* (London: Faith, 1963), pp. 7-29.

[228] Janus (Johann Joseph Ignaz von Dollinger), *The Pope and the Council* (Boston: Roberts Brothers, 1870), pp. 63-64.

[229] Norman Tanner S.J., Ed., *Decrees of the Ecumenical Councils* (Washington D.C.: Georgetown University, 1990), Volume I, First Council of Nicaea, Canon 6, pp. 8-9.

[230] George Salmon, *The Infallibility of the Church* (London: Murray, 1914), p. 420, 421-422.

[231] John Meyendorff, *Imperial Unity and Christian Division* (Crestwood: St. Vladimir's, 1989), p. 328.

[232] Paul Empie and Austin Murphy, Ed., *Papal Primacy and the Universal Church* (Augsburg: Minneapolis, 1974), Lutherans and Catholics in Dialogue V, pp. 72, 77.

[233] Peter, L'Huillier, *The Church of the Ancient Councils* (Crestwood: St. Vladimir's, 1996), p. 46, 47.

[234] Robert Eno, *The Rise of the Papacy* (Wilmington: Michael Glazier, 1990), p. 123.

[235] Karl Morrison, *Tradition and Authority in the Western Church* (Princeton: Princeton University, 1969), p. 67.

[236] *The New Catholic Encyclopedia* (New York: McGraw Hill, 1967), Volume X, *Nicaea I, Council Of*, p. 433.

[237] Philip Schaff, *Nicene and Post-Nicene Fathers* (Grand Rapids: Eerdmans, 1956), Series II, Volume VII, *The Seven Ecumenical Councils*, pp. 43-45.

[238] Norman Tanner S.J., Ed., *Decrees of the Ecumenical Councils* (Washington D.C.: Georgetown University, 1990), Volume I, First Council of Constantinople, Canons 2 and 3, pp. 31-32.

[239] Charles Joseph Hefele, *A History of the Councils of the Church* (Edinburgh: T&T Clark, 1895), Volume II, I Constantinople, Canon 3, p. 357.

[240] W.H.C. Frend, Reprinted from *The Rise of Christianity* (Philadelphia: Fortress, 1984), pp. 629, 639. Used by permission of Augsburg Fortress.

[241] Francis Dvornik, *Byzantium and the Roman Primacy* (New York: Fordham University, 1966), pp. 43-44.

[242] George Salmon, *The Infallibility of the Church* (London: Murray, 1914), p. 420, 421-422.

[243] John Meyendorff, *Imperial Unity and Christian Division* (Crestwood: St. Vladimir's, 1989), pp. 61-62.

[244] Paul Empie and Austin Murphy, Ed., *Papal Primacy and the Universal Church* (Minneapolis: Augsburg, 1974), pp. 82-83.

[245] Norman Tanner S.J., Ed., *Decrees of the Ecumenical Councils* (Washington D.C.: Georgetown University, 1990), Volume I, Council of Chalcedon, Canon 28, pp. 99-100.

[246] John Meyendorff, *Imperial Unity and Christian Division* (Crestwood: St. Vladimir's, 1989), pp. 175, 183.

[247] W.H.C. Frend, *The Rise of Christianity* (Philadelphia: Fortress, 1984), pp. 772-773.

[248] Karl Morrison, *Tradition and Authority in the Western Church* (Princeton: Princeton University, 1969), p. 95.

[249] John Meyendorff, *Orthodoxy and Catholicity* (New York: Sheed & Ward, 1966), pp. 55-56.

[250] John Meyendorff, *Byzantine Theology* (New York: Fordham University, 1974), pp. 99-100.

[251] John Meyendorff, *Imperial Unity and Christian Division* (Crestwood: St. Vladimir's, 1989), p. 183.

[252] W.H.C. Frend, *The Early Church* (Philadelphia: Fortress, 1965), p. 232.

[253] Robert Eno, *The Rise of the Papacy* (Wilmington: Michael Glazier, 1990), p. 117.

[254] W.H.C. Frend, *The Early Church* (Philadelphia: Fortress, 1965), p. 232.

[255] S. Herbert Scott, *The Eastern Churches and the Papacy* (London: Sheed & Ward, 1928), p. 199.

[256] Paul Empie and Austin Murphy, Ed., *Teaching Authority & Infallibility in the Church* (Minneapolis: Augsburg, 1978). Robert Eno, *Some Elements in the Pre-History of Papal Infallibility*, p. 249.

[257] John Meyendorff, *Imperial Unity and Christian Division* (Crestwood: St. Vladimir's, 1989), p. 155-156.

[258] *The Councils of the Church* (Philadelphia: Fortress, 1966), The Councils of the Ancient Church, p. 78.

[259] W.J. Sparrow Simpson, *Roman Catholic Opposition to Papal Infallibility* (London: John Murray, 1909), p. 28.

[260] Charles Joseph Hefele, *A History of the Councils of the Church* (Edinburgh: Clark, 1895), Volume IV, pp. 322-23.

[261] Charles Joseph Hefele, *A History of the Councils of the Church* (Edinburgh: Clark, 1895), Volume IV, pp. 347-48.

Endnotes 363

[262] Jaroslav Pelikan, *The Christian Tradition: A History of the Development of Doctrine* (Chicago: University of Chicago, 1974), Volume Two, pp. 150-151.

[263] Karl Keating, *Catholicism and Fundamentalism* (San Francisco: Ignatius, 1988), p. 229.

[264] Charles Joseph Hefele, *A History of the Councils of the Church* (Edinburgh: Clark, 1896), Volume V, pp. 181-187.

[265] Janus (Johann Joseph Ignaz von Dollinger), *The Pope and the Council* (Boston: Roberts, 1870), p. 61.

[266] Philip Schaff and Henry Wace, *Nicene and Post-Nicene Fathers* (Grand Rapids: Eerdmans, 1956), Volume XIV, The Seven Ecumenical Councils, pp. 342-344.

[267] John Meyendorff, *Imperial Unity and Christian Division* (Crestwood:St. Vladimir's, 1989), p. 353.

[268] W.J. Sparrow Simpson, *Roman Catholic Opposition to Papal Infallibility* (London: John Murray, 1909), p. 35.

[269] W.J. Sparrow Simpson, *Roman Catholic Opposition to Papal Infallibility* (London: John Murray, 1909), p. 33.

[270] W.H.C. Frend, *The Early Church* (Philadelphia: Fortress, 1965), pp. 221, 223.

[271] *A Library of the Fathers of the Holy Catholic Church* (Oxford: Parker, 1844), The Epistles of St. Cyprian, The Judgments of Eighty-Seven Bishops in the Council of Carthage on the Question of Baptizing Heretics, pp. 286-287.

[272] *A Library of the Fathers of the Holy Catholic Church* (Oxford: Parker, 1844), The Epistles of St. Cyprian, *Epistle* LXXV. 17, 18, 20, pp. 279-281.

[273] Karl Morrison, *Tradition and Authority in the Western Church* (Princeton: Princeton University, 1969), pp. 31-32.

[274] William Jurgens, *The Faith of the Early Fathers* (Collegeville: Liturgical, 1970), Volume I, p. 216-217.

[275] W.H.C. Frend, *The Rise of Christianity* (Philadelphia: Fortress, 1984), pp. 353-354.

[276] Charles Joseph Hefele, *A History of the Councils of the Church* (Edinburgh: Clark, 1895), Volume II, pp. 456-457.

[277] J.E. Merdinger, *Rome and the African Church in the Time of Augustine* (New Haven: Yale University, 1997), p. 128.

[278] J.E. Merdinger, *Rome and the African Church in the Time of Augustine* (New Haven: Yale University, 1997), p. 129.

[279] Philip Schaff, *History of the Christian Church* (Grand Rapids: Eerdmans, 1910), Volume Three, p. 798-799.

[280] Paul Empie and Austin Murphy, Ed., *Teaching Authority & Infallibility in the*

Church (Minneapolis: Augsburg, 1978). Robert Eno, *Some Elements in the Pre-History of Papal Infallibility*, p. 249.

[281] Robert Eno, *The Rise of the Papacy* (Wilmington: Glazier, 1990), p. 73.

[282] Janus (Johann Joseph Ignaz von Dollinger), *The Pope and the Council* (Boston: Roberts Brothers, 1870), p. 58.

[283] John Meyendorff, *Imperial Unity and Christian Division* (Crestwood: St. Vladimir's, 1989), p. 65.

[284] George Salmon, *The Infallibility of the Church* (London: John Murray, 1914), pp. 414-415.

[285] Dom Chrysostumus Baur, O.S.B., *John Chrysostom and His Time* (Westminster: Newman, 1959), Volume II, pp. 299, 301-302; Vol. I, pp. 349-350.

[286] P.R. Coleman-Norton, *The Correspondence of John Chrysostom (With Special Reference to His Epistles to Pope S. Innocent I)*. Found in *Classical Philology*, Volume 24, 1929, p. 284.

[287] Karl Morrison, *Tradition and Authority in the Western Church* (Princeton: Princeton University, 1969), p. 141.

[288] John Meyendorff, *Byzantine Theology* (New York: Fordham University, 1974), p. 97.

[289] Alice Gardner, *Theodore of Studium* (New York: Burt Franklin, 1974), p. 82-183.

[290] John Meyendorff, *Byzantine Theology* (New York: Fordham University, 1974), pp. 57-58.

[291] Jaroslav Pelikan, *The Christian Tradition: A History of the Development of Doctrine* (Chicago: University of Chicago, 1974), Volume II, p. 164.

[292] *Libellus professionis fidei*. Cited by H. Denzinger, *The Sources of Catholic Dogma* (London: Herder, 1954), St. Hormisdas, p. 73.

[293] *Libellus professionis fidei*. Cited by H. Denzinger, *The Sources of Catholic Dogma* (London: Herder, 1954), St. Hormisdas, p. 73-74.

[294] John Meyendorff, *Imperial Unity and Christian Divisions* (Crestwood: St. Vladimir's, 1989), p. 213-214.

[295] Karl Morrison, *Tradition and Authority in the Western Church* (Princeton: Princeton University, 1969), pp. 115-116.

[296] John Meyendorff, *Imperial Unity and Christian Divisions* (Crestwood: St. Vladimir's, 1989), p. 215.

[297] Cited by Brian Tierney, *The Origins of Papal Infallibility* (Leiden: Brill, 1972), p. 9.

[298] Brian Tierney, *The Origins of Papal Infallibility* (Leiden: Brill, 1972), p. 11.

[299] The Apostolic Fathers is a collection of late first and early second century post–apostolic writings.

Endnotes 365

[300] Philip Schaff, *History of the Christian Church* (Grand Rapids: Eerdmans, 1910), Volume Two, pp. 139-140.

[301] Hans Küng, *Infallible? An Inquiry* (Garden City: Doubleday, 1971), pp. 82-83.

[302] This work, published in 1151, was intended as a collection of everything that Gratian could find having the force of law in the Church; and it had such success that it became the standard work of the law of the Roman Church (Salmon, p. 453).

[303] Johann Joseph Ignaz von Dollinger, *The Pope and the Council* (Boston: Roberts, 1870), pp. 76-77, 79, 115-116.

[304] George Salmon, *The Infallibility of the Church* (London: John Murray, 1914), pp. 449, 451, 453.

[305] James Likoudis, *Ending the Byzantine Greek Schism* (New Rochelle: Catholics United for the Faith, 1992), St. Thomas Aquinas, *Against the Errors of the Greeks*, pp. 182-184.

[306] Edward Denny, *Papalism* (London: Rivingtons, 1912), pp. 114-117.

[307] (Janus) Johan Joseph Ignaz von Dollinger, *The Pope and the Council* (Boston: Roberts, 1870), pp. 233-234.

[308] R.A. Marcus, *From Augustine to Gregory the Great* (London: Variorum Reprints, 1983), p. 355.

[309] Aristeides Papadakis, *The Christian East and the Rise of the Papacy* (Crestwood: St. Vladimir's, 1994), pp. 158-160, 166-167.

[310] Jaroslav Pelikan, *The Christian Tradition: A History of the Development of Doctrine* (Chicago: University of Chicago, 1974), Volume II, p. 164.

[311] Yves Congar, *After Nine Hundred Years* (New York: Fordham University, 1959), pp. 61-62.

[312] Yves Congar, *Diversity and Communion* (Mystic: Twenty-Third, 1982), pp. 26-27.

[313] John Meyendorff, *Byzantine Theology* (New York: Fordham University, 1974), p. 97.

[314] John Meyendorff, *St. Peter in Byzantine Theology*. Taken from *The Primacy of Peter* (London: Faith, 1963), pp. 7-29.

Appendix A

[315] *Dogmatic Decrees of the Vatican Council* as found in *The Creeds of Christendom* by Philip Schaff, Chapters I,II, III.

[316] *Cathechism of the Catholic Church* (New Hope: Urbi et Orbi, 1994), Paragraphs 552-553, 1445, pp. 141-142, 363.

[317] Philip Schaff, *The Creeds of Christendom* (New York: Harper, 1877), Dogmatic Decrees of the Vatican Council, Chp. 4, pp. 266-71
[318] *The Documents of Vatican II* (Chicago: Follett, 1966), Walter M. Abbott, S.J., General Editor, pp. 47-49.

Appendix B

[319] John Rotelle, O.S.A., Ed., *The Works of Saint Augustine* (New Rochelle: New City Press, 1993), *Sermons*, Volume III/6, Sermon 229P.1, p. 327.

[320] John Rotelle, Ed., *The Works of Saint Augustine* (New Rochelle: New City Press, 1993), *Sermons*, Volume III/7, Sermon 270.2, p. 289.

[321] *The Fathers of the Church* (Washington D.C., Catholic University, 1968), Saint Augustine, *The Retractations* Chapter 20.1.

[322] Philip Schaff, *Nicene and Post-Nicene Fathers* (Grand Rapids: Eerdmans, 1956), Volume VI, St. Augustin, *Sermon* 26.1-4, pp. 340-341.

[323] Philip Schaff, *Nicene and Post-Nicene Fathers* (Buffalo: Christian Literature, 1887), Volume IV, St. Augustin, *Against the Donatists*, Book II, Chap. 109, p. 595.

[324] John Rotelle, Ed., *The Works of Saint Augustine* (New Rochelle: New City Press, 1993), *Sermons*, Volume III/5, Sermon 183.14, p. 343.

[325] John Rotelle, Ed., *The Works of Saint Augustine* (Hyde Park: New City Press, 1994), *Sermons*, Volume III/9, Sermon 337.1, p. 271.

[326] *A Library of the Fathers of the Holy Catholic Church* (Oxford: Parker, 1845), Volume 20, Sermon 97.3, p. 686, (Sermon 147, Benedictine Edition).

[327] Philip Schaff, *Nicene and Post-Nicene Fathers* (Grand Rapids: Eerdmans, 1956), Volume VI, St. Augustin, *Sermons on New-Testament Lessons,* Sermon LXXXIV.2, p. 510.

[328] John Rotelle, Ed., *The Works of Saint Augustine* (Brooklyn: New City Press, 1991), Volume I/5, *The Trinity*, Book II.28, p. 119.

[329] John Rotelle, Ed., *The Works of Saint Augustine* (New Rochelle: New City Press, 1995), *Sermons*, Volume III/10, Sermon 358.5, p. 193.

[330] Philip Schaff, *Nicene and Post-Nicene Fathers* (Grand Rapids: Eerdmans, 1956), Volume VII, St. Augustin, *On the Gospel of John,* Tractate 124.5.

[331] John Rotelle, Ed., *The Works of Saint Augustine* (New Rochelle: New City, 1992), *Sermons*, III/5, Sermon 149.6-7, p. 21.

[332] John Rotelle, Ed., *The Works of Saint Augustine* (Hyde Park: New City, 1994), *Sermons*, III/8 (273-305A), On the Saints, Sermon 295.1-3, pp. 197-198.

[333] John Rotelle, Ed., *The Works of Saint Augustine* (Hyde Park: New City, 1995), *Sermons*, Volume III/10, Sermon 352.3-5, pp. 138-143.

Endnotes 367

[334] John Rotelle, Ed., *The Works of Saint Augustine* (New Rochelle: New City, 1993), *Sermons*, Volume III/6, Sermon 229N.1-3, pp. 320-321.

[335] John Rotelle, Ed., *The Works of Saint Augustine* (New City: Brooklyn, 1991), *Sermons*, Volume III/3, Sermon 76.1-4, pp. 311-313.

[336] John Rotelle, Ed., *The Works of Saint Augustine* (New Rochelle: New City, 1993) *Sermons*, Volume III/7, Sermon 244.1, pp. 95-96.

[337] John Rotelle, Ed., *The Works of Saint Augustine* (New Rochelle: New City, 1993) *Sermons*, Volume III/7, Sermon 236A.3, p. 48.

[338] *A Library of the Fathers of the Holy Catholic Church* (Oxford: Parker, 1847), Seventeen Short Treatises of S. Augustine, *De Agone Christiano* (The Christian Conflict) 32, p. 184.

[339] John Rotelle, Ed., *The Works of Saint Augustine* (Brooklyn: New City, 1990), *Sermons*, Volume III/1, Sermon 4.22, p. 197.

[340] Philip Schaff, *Nicene and Post-Nicene Fathers* (Grand Rapids: Eerdmans, 1956), Volume VII, St. Augustine, *On The Gospel of St. John*, Tractate 50.12, p. 282.

[341] John Rotelle, Ed., *The Works of Saint Augustine* (Brooklyn: New City, 1991), Part I - Books, Volume V, *The Trinity*, Book II.6.28-30, pp. 117-119.

[342] Philip Schaff, *Nicene and Post-Nicene Fathers* (Grand Rapids: Eerdmans, 1956), Volume VII, St. Augustin, *Homilies on the Gospel of St. John*, Tractate 118.4, p. 431.

[343] *The Fathers of the Church* (New York: Fathers of the Church, 1959), Volume 38, Saint Augustine, *Sermons on the Liturgical Seasons*, Sermon 215.1, p. 142.

[344] John Rotelle, Ed., *The Works of Saint Augustine* (Brooklyn: New City, 1990), *Sermons*, Volume III/2, Sermon 46.10, p. 269.

[345] John Rotelle, Ed., *The Works of Saint Augustine* (Hyde Park: New City, 1994), *Sermons*, Volume III/9, Sermon 317.5, p. 144.

[346] Philip Schaff, *Nicene and Post-Nicene Fathers* (Grand Rapids: Eerdmans, 1956), Volume VIII, Saint Augustin, *Exposition on the Book of Psalms*, Psalm LV.5, p. 211.

[347] John Rotelle, Ed., *The Works of Saint Augustine* (Brooklyn: New City, 1991), *Sermons*, Volume III/3, Sermon 88.10, p. 426.

[348] John Rotelle, Ed., *The Works of Saint Augustine* (Brooklyn: New City, 1992), *Sermons*, Volume III/4, Sermon 116.6, p. 206.

[349] John Rotelle, Ed., *The Works of Saint Augustine* (Hyde Park: New City Press, 1993), *Sermons*, Volume III/10, Sermon 362.8-9, p. 246.

[340] Philip Schaff, *Nicene and Post-Nicene Fathers* (Grand Rapids: Eerdmans, 1956), Volume VIII, Saint Augustin, *Exposition on the Book of Psalms*, Psalm LXI.3, p. 249.

[351] Philip Schaff, *Nicene and Post-Nicene Fathers* (Grand Rapids: Eerdmans, 1956), Volume VIII, Saint Augustin, *Exposition on the Book of Psalms*, Psalm CIX.1, p. 536.

352 Philip Schaff, *Nicene and Post-Nicene Fathers* (Grand Rapids: Eerdmans, 1956), Volume VII, St. Augustin, *Homilies on the Gospel of John*, Tractate 50.12, p. 282.

353 John Rotelle, Ed., *The Works of Saint Augustine* (Brooklyn: New City Press, 1992), *Sermons*, Volume III/4, Sermon 129.8, p. 307.

354 *A Library of the Fathers of the Holy Catholic Church* (Oxford: Parker, 1845), Volume 16, Sermon 66.7, p. 485, (Sermon 116, Benedictine Edition).

355 John Rotelle, Ed., *The Works of Saint Augustine* (Brooklyn: New City Press, 1990), *Sermons*, Volume III/1, Sermon 4.18, p. 195.

356 John Rotelle, Ed., *The Works of Saint Augustine* (Hyde Park: New City Press, 1995), *Sermons*, Volume III/10, Sermon 392.3, p. 422.

357 Philip Schaff, *Nicene and Post-Nicene Fathers* (Grand Rapids: Eerdmans, 1956), Volume VII, St. Augustin: *Homilies on the Gospel of John*, Tractate 53.8, p. 294.

358 Philip Schaff, *Nicene and Post-Nicene Fathers* (Grand Rapids: Eerdmans, 1956), Volume VI, St. Augustin, *Sermon* LXV. 1, p. 454.

359 John Rotelle, Ed., *The Works of Saint Augustine* (Brooklyn: New City Press, 1992), *Sermons*, Volume III/4, Sermon 138.2-5, pp. 385-387.

360 Philip Schaff, *Nicene and Post-Nicene Fathers* (Grand Rapids: Eerdmans, 1956), Volume VII, St. Augustin, *Homilies on the Gospel of John*, Tractate 123.5, pp. 445-446.

361 *A Library of the Fathers of the Holy Catholic Church* (Oxford: Parker, 1845), Volume 20, Sermon 97.2, p. 685, (Sermon 147, Benedictine Edition).

362 John Rotelle, Ed., *The Works of Saint Augustine* (Brooklyn: New City Press, 1992), *Sermons*, Volume III/4, Sermon 137.3, p. 373.

363 John Rotelle, Ed., *The Works of Saint Augustine* (New Rochelle: New City Press, 1993), *Sermons*, Volume III/7, Sermon 253.2, pp. 148-149.

364 John Rotelle, Ed., *The Works of Saint Augustine* (New Rochelle: New City Press, 1990), *Sermons*, Volume III/2, Sermon 46.30, pp. 282-283.

365 John Rotelle, Ed., *The Works of Saint Augustine* (New Rochelle: New City Press, 1994), *Sermons*, Volume III/8, Sermon 295.4, p. 199.

366 John Rotelle, Ed., *The Works of Saint Augustine* (New Rochelle: New City Press, 1994), *Sermons*, Volume III/8, Sermon 296.13, p. 211.

367 John Rotelle, Ed., *The Works of Saint Augustine* (Brooklyn: New City Press, 1992), *Sermons*, Volume III/4, Sermon 147A.1-2, pp. 451-452.

368 John Rotelle, Ed., *The Works of Saint Augustine* (Brooklyn: New City Press, 1992), *Sermons*, Volume III/4, Sermon 147.2, p. 448.

369 John Rotelle, Ed., *The Works of Saint Augustine* (Brooklyn: New City Press, 1992), *Sermons*, Volume III/4, Sermon 146.1, p. 445.

Endnotes 369

[370] *The Fathers of the Church* (Washington D.C.: Catholic University, 1963), Saint Ambrose, *The Sacrament of the Incarnation of Our Lord* 4.32-5.35, pp. 230-1.

[371] *Commentary in Luke* VI.98, CSEL 32.4, Cited by Karlfreid Froehlich, *Formen der Auslegung von Matthaus 16:13-18 im lateinischen Mittelater*, Dissertation, Tubingen, 1963.

[372] Philip Schaff and Henry Wace, *The Nicene and Post-Nicene Fathers* (Grand Rapids: Eerdmans, 1955), Volume X, St. Ambrose, *On Christian Faith* 4.5.53, p. 268-9.

[373] *De Virginitate* XVI.105, M.P.L. Vol 16, Col 292.

[374] *Commentary on Psalm* 40.30. Cited by J. Waterworth S.J., *A Commentary* (London: Thomas Richardson, 1871), p. 69.

[375] *Epistle* 43.9. Cited by J. Waterworth S.J., *A Commentary* (London: Thomas Richardson, 1871), p. 76.

[376] Unde dicit Dominus ad Petrum: Super istam petram aedificabo Ecclesiam meam, hoc est, in hac catholicae fidei confessione statuam fideles ad vitam (*Commentary on Ephesians 2:20*. P.L. 17.380D).

[377] De S. *Sancto*, Book 2, Chapter 13. Cited by J. Waterworth S.J., *A Commentary* (London: Thomas Richardson, 1871), p. 75.

[378] *Commentaria in XIII Epistolas Beati Pauli*, on Gal. 2.9,10. Taken from *Documents Illustrating Papal Authority* by E. Giles, pp. 122-123.

[379] *Commentary on Ephesians*, M.P.L., Vol. 17, Col. 380.

[380] *Commentary on Galatians*, M.P.L., Vol. 17, Col. 349.

[381] *Commentary on Galatians*, M.P.L., Vol. 17, Col. 350.

[382] *Commentary on Galatians*, M.P.L., Vol. 17, Col. 344.

[383] *Commentary on 2 Corinthians*, M.P.L., Vol. 17, Col. 332.

[384] Ambrosiaster, *Quaestiones in Novum Testamentum*, no. 75 (PL 35:2273A). Cited by Karlfreid Froehlich, *St. Peter, Papal Primacy, and the Exegetical Tradition*, 1150-1300, in *The Religious Roles of the Papacy; Ideals and Realities* 1150-1300 (Toronto: Pontifical Institute, 1989), Christopher Ryan, Ed., p. 22.

[385] Philip Schaff, *Nicene and Post-Nicene Fathers* (Grand Rapids: Eerdmans, 1956), Vol XIII, Aphrahat, *Select Demonstrations*, Demonstration I.2-6,13,19.

[386] Alexander Roberts and James Donaldson, Ed., *The Ante–Nicene Fathers* (Buffalo: Christian Literature, 1885), Volume VII, *Apostolic Teaching and Constitutions*, Book VI, Chapter V, p. 452.

[387] Homily VIII, *On Saints Peter and Paul*, M.P.G., Vol. 40, Col. 268-269.

[388] Homily VIII, *On Saints Peter and Paul*, M.P.G., Vol. 40, Col. 280-281.

[389] Philip Schaff, *Nicene and Post Nicene Fathers* (Grand Rapids: Eerdmans, 1953), Volume IV, St. Athanasius, *Letters of Athanasius*, Letter 29, p. 551.

[390]Philip Schaff, *Nicene and Post Nicene Fathers* (Grand Rapids: Eerdmans, 1953), Volume IV, St. Athanasius, *Four Discources Against the Arians*, Discourse II, Chapter XXII.73, 74, 76; pp. 388-389.

[391]*A Library of the Fathers of the Holy Catholic Church* (Oxford: Parker, 1844), Select Treatises of S. Athanasius, *Discourse* IV, Subject IX.11.

[392]*Four Letters to Serapion of Thmuis* 1.28. Cited by William Jurgens, *The faith of the Early Fathers* (Collegeville: Liturgical Press, 1970), Volume I, p. 336.

[393]*Psalm 11*. Cited by J. Waterworth S.J., *A Commentary* (London:Thomas Richardson, 1871), p. 50.

[394]*Commentary on the Prophet Isaiah*, Cap. II.66, M.P.G., Vol. 30, Col. 233.

[395]*Oratio* XXV.4, M.P.G., Vol. 85, Col. 296-297.

[396]*Or*. 16. Cited by J. Waterworth S.J., *A Commentary* (London: Thomas Richardson, 1871), p. 168.

[397]Homily 2.16, M.P.L., Vol. 94, Col. 94. Cited by Karlfried Froehlich, *Formen*, Footnote #140, p. 134.

[398]Homily 23, M.P.L., Vol. 94, Col. 260. Cited by Karlfried Froehlich, *Formen*, Footnote #204, p. 156.

[399]Homily 23, M.S.L., Vol. 186, Col. 108. Cited by Karlfried Froehlich, *Formen*, Footnote #124.

[400]Homily 16, M.S.L., Vol. 94, Col. 222. Cited by Karlfried Froehlich, *Formen*, Footnote #125.

[401]Homily 16, M.S.L., Vol. 94, Col. 222. Cited by Karlfried Froehlich, *Formen*, Footnote #138.

[402]*Expositions in the Psalms*, Psalm 45.5, M.P.L., Vol. 70, Col. 330.

[403]*Expositions in the Psalms*, Psalm 86.1, M.P.L., Vol. 70, Col. 618.

[404]*Expositions in the Psalms*, Psalm 103.5, M.P.L., Vol. 70, Col. 729-730.

[405]Philip Schaff, *Nicene and Post-Nicene Fathers* (Grand Rapids: Eerdmans, 1956), Volume XI, *The Seven Books of John Cassian*, Book III, Chapter 12, 14.

[406]Philip Schaff, *Nicene and Post-Nicene Fathers* (Grand Rapids: Eerdmans, 1956), Volume X, Saint Chrysostom, *Homilies on the Gospel of Saint Matthew*, Homily 54.2-3; pp. 332-334..

[407]Philip Schaff, *Nicene and Post-Nicene Fathers* (Grand Rapids: Eerdmans, 1956), Volume X, Chrysostom, *Homilies on the Gospel of Saint Matthew*, Homily 82.3, p. 494.

[408]Philip Schaff, *Nicene and Post-Nicene Fathers* (Grand Rapids: Eerdmans, 1956), Volume XIV, Saint Chrysostom, *Homilies on the Gospel of John*, Homily XXI.1, pp. 72-73.

Endnotes 371

[409] *On the Inscription of the Acts*, II. Taken from *Documents Illustrating Papal Authority* (London: SPCK, 1952), E. Giles, Ed., p. 168. Cf. Chapman, *Studies on the Early Papacy*, p. 96.

[410] Philip Schaff, *Nicene and Post-Nicene Fathers* (Grand Rapids: Eerdmans, 1956), Volume XIV, Saint Chrysostom, *Homilies on the Gospel of John*, Homily 88.1-2, pp. 331-332.

[411] Philip Schaff, *Nicene and Post-Nicene Fathers* (Grand Rapids: Eerdmans, 1956), Volume XI, Saint Chrysostom, *Homilies on the Acts of the Apostles*, Homily 31, ver. 16, p. 557.

[412] Philip Schaff, *Nicene and Post-Nicene Fathers* (Grand Rapids: Eerdmans, 1956), Volume X, Saint Chrysostom, *Homilies on the Gospel of Saint Matthew*, Homily III.8, p. 19.

[413] Philip Schaff, *Nicene and Post-Nicene Fathers* (Grand Rapids: Eerdmans, 1956), Volume XIV, Saint Chrysostom, *Homilies on the Gospel of John*, Homily 1.1, p. 1.

[414] *Homily 24, On Genesis.* Taken from *Documents Illustrating Papal Authority* (London: SPCK, 1952), E. Giles, Ed.; p. 165.

[415] Philip Schaff, *Nicene and Post-Nicene Fathers* (Grand Rapids: Eerdmans, 1956), Volume XI, Saint Chrysostom, *Homilies on the Epistle to the Romans*, Homily 32, Ver. 24, pp. 561-562.

[416] Philip Schaff, *Nicene and Post-Nicene Fathers* (Grand Rapids: Eerdmans, 1956), Volume XIII, Saint Chrysostom, *Homilies on the Epistle to the Galatians,* Chapter II, ver. 8, p. 17.

[417] Philip Schaff, *Nicene and Post-Nicene Fathers* (Grand Rapids: Eerdmans, 1956), Volume XIII, Saint Chrysostom, *Homilies on the Epistle to the Corinthians*, 2 Corinthians, Homily IX.4, p. 324.

[418] Philip Schaff, *Nicene and Post-Nicene Fathers* (Grand Rapids: Eerdmans, 1956), Volume XI, Saint Chrysostom, *Homilies on the Acts of the Apostles*, Homily 33, pp. 205, 207.

[419] *De Eleemos* III.4, M.P.G., Vol. 49, Col. 298.

[420] Philip Schaff, *Nicene and Post-Nicene Fathers* (Grand Rapids: Eerdmans, 1956), Volume XIV, Saint Chrysostom, *Homilies on the Gospel of John*, Homily LXXIII.1, pp. 267-268.

[421] Philip Schaff, *Nicene and Post-Nicene Fathers* (Grand Rapids: Eerdmans, 1956), Volume XII, Saint Chrysostom, *Homilies on the Epistles of Paul to the Corinthians*, 1 Corinthians, Homily VIII.7, p. 47.

[422] *Hom. de decem mille talentis 3,* PG III, 20. Cited by Dom Chapman, *Studies in the Early Papacy* (London: Sheed & Ward, 1928), p. 74.

[423] Philip Schaff, *Nicene and Post-Nicene Fathers* (Grand Rapids: Eerdmans, 1956), Volume X, Saint Chrysostom, *Homilies on the Gospel of Saint Matthew*, Homily 56.2; p. 345.

[424] Dom John Chapman, *Studies on the Early Papacy* (London: Sheed & Ward, 1928), John Chrysostom, *Homilies on the Acts of the Apostles*, Homily XXVI, Footnote #5, p. 75.

[425] *Contra ludos et theatra 1*, PG VI, 265. Cited by Dom Chapman, *Studies on the Early Papacy* (London: Sheed & Ward, 1928), p. 76.

[426] Philip Schaff, *Nicene and Post-Nicene Fathers* (Grand Rapids: Eerdmans, 1956), Volume XIV, Saint Chrysostom, *Homilies on the Epistle to the Hebrews*, Homily XXI.5, p. 463.

[427] Philip Schaff, *Nicene and Post-Nicene Fathers* (Grand Rapids: Eerdmans, 1956), Volume XII, Saint Chrysostom, *Homilies on the Epistles of Paul to the Corinthians*, 1 Corinthians, Homily VI.7, p. 32.

[428] Philip Schaff, *Nicene and Post-Nicene Fathers* (Grand Rapids: Eerdmans, 1956), Volume XII, Saint Chrysostom, *Homilies on the Epistles of Paul to the Corinthians*, 1 Corinthians, Homily VII.19, p. 42.

[429] Philip Schaff, *Nicene and Post-Nicene Fathers* (Grand Rapids: Eerdmans, 1956), Volume XIV, Saint Chrysostom, *Homilies on the Gospel of John*, Homily XXXIII.3, p. 117.

[430] Philip Schaff, *Nicene and Post-Nicene Fathers* (Grand Rapids: Eerdmans, 1956), Volume XIV, Saint Chrysostom, *Homilies on the Gospel of John*, Homily IX.1-3, pp. 67-69.

[431] Philip Schaff, *Nicene and Post-Nicene Fathers* (Grand Rapids: Eerdmans, 1956), Volume XIV, Saint Chrysostom, *Homilies on the Epistle to the Hebrews*, Homily XXXI.4, p. 507.

[432] Philip Schaff, *Nicene and Post-Nicene Fathers* (Grand Rapids: Eerdmans, 1956), Volume X, Saint Chrysostom, *Homilies on the Gospel of Saint Matthew*, Homily LXXXII.3, pp. 493-494.

[433] Philip Schaff, *Nicene and Post-Nicene Fathers* (Grand Rapids: Eerdmans, 1956), Volume XIV, Saint Chrysostom, *The Epistle to the Hebrews*, Homily XXXI.4, p. 507.

[434] Philip Schaff, *Nicene and Post-Nicene Fathers* (Grand Rapids: Eerdmans, 1956), Volume X, Saint Chrysostom, *The Gospel of St. Matthew*, Homily LXXXII.3, pp. 493-494.

[435] *Sermon* 107, M.P.L., Vol. 57, Col. 498.

[436] *Sermon* 154, P.L., Vol. 52, Col. 608. Cited by E. Giles, p. 283.

[437] *A Library of the Fathers of the Holy Catholic Church* (Oxford: Parker, 1842), Cyprian, *On the Unity of the Church* 3-4, pp. 133-135.

Endnotes 373

[438] *A Library of the Fathers of the Holy Catholic Church* (Oxford: Parker, 1842), *The Epistles of S. Cyprian*, Ep. 33.1.

[439] *A Library of the Fathers of the Holy Catholic Church* (Oxford: Parker, 1844), *The Epistles of S. Cyprian*, Epistle, XI.5, p. 27.

[440] *A Library of the Fathers of the Holy Catholic Church* (Oxford: Parker, 1839), *The Treatises of S. Caecilius Cyprian*, Treatise VII, *On the Lord's Prayer* 19, pp. 193-194.

[441] *Commentary on Isaiah* IV.2, M.P.G., Vol. 70, Col. 940.

[442] *Commentary on Matthew*, M.P.G., Vol. 72, Col. 421, 424.

[443] *Dialogue on the Trinity* IV, M.P.G., Vol. 75, Col. 866.

[444] *Commentary on John*. Cited by J. Waterworth S.J., *A Commentary* (London: Thomas Richardson, 1871), p. 145.

[445] *Commentary on Zacharias*. Cited by J. Waterworth S.J., *A Commentary* (London: Thomas Richardson, 1871), p. 143.

[446] *Commentary on Isaiah* 3.iii, on Isaiah 28:16. Cited by J. Waterworth S.J., *A Commentary* (London: Thomas Richardson, 1871), p. 142.

[447] *Epistle* 17.5, P.G., Vol. 77, Col. 108. Cited by E. Giles, *Documents Illustrating Papal Authority* (London: SPCK, 1952), pp. 242-243.

[448] Cited by George Salmon, *The Infallibility of the Church* (London: John Murray, 1914), pp. 345-346.

[449] Philip Schaff and Henry Wace, *Nicene and Post-Nicene Fathers* (Grand Rapids: Eerdmans, 1955), Volume VII, *The Catechetical Lectures* 6.15.

[450] *De Trinitate Liber Primus* I.30, M.P.G., Vol. 39, col. 416.

[451] *The Panarion of Epiphanius of Salamis* (Leiden: Brill, 1994), Books II and III, *Haer.* 59.7,6-8,3, p. 108-109.

[452] *Ancoratus* 9.6. G.C.S., Epiphanius, Vol. I, p. 16.

[453] Philip Schaff, *Nicene and Post-Nicene Fathers* (Grand Rapids: Eerdmans, 1956), Volume XIII, *Hymns for the Feast of the Epiphany* II.14, p. 267.

[454] Philip Schaff, *Nicene and Post-Nicene Fathers* (Grand Rapids: Eerdmans, 1956), Volume XIII, *The Pearl*, Hymn 2.2.

[455] *Eulogy on Peter, Paul, Andrew, etc.*, Works, Class 5, Sermon 11. Collectio Ecclesiae Patrum 37.446. Cited by E. Giles, *Documents Illustrating Papal Authority* (London: SPCK, 1952), p. 116.

[456] *Commentary on the Psalms*, M.P.G., Vol. 23, Col. 173, 176.

[457] *Prep. Ev.* I.3. Cited by J. Waterworth, *A Commentary* (London: Thomas Richardson, 1871), pp. 34-35.

[458] *Ecclesiastical History* vi.25.

[459] Johannes Quasten, *Ancient Christian Writers* (New York: Newman, 1970), Firmicus Maternus, *The Error of the Pagan Religions* Chapter 20.1-2, 4-6, pp. 87-89.

[460] *A Library of the Fathers of the Holy Catholic Church* (Oxford: Parker, 1844), *The Epistles of S. Cyprian*, Epistle 75.17-18.

[461] *De Remissione Peccatorum* II.20, M.P.L., Vol. 65, Col. 571.

[462] *De Fide* III.37, M.P.L., Vol. 65, Col. 690.

[463] Tract. 16, *De Ordin. Ipsius*. Cited by J. Waterworth S.J., *A Commentary* (London: Thomas Richardson, 1871), pp. 105-107.

[464] *A Library of the Fathers of the Holy Catholic Church* (Oxford: Parker, 1850), Volume 31, S. Gregory the Great, *Morals on the Book of Job*, Book XXXV.13, p. 670. M.S.L., Vol. 94, Col. 222.

[465] Philip Schaff and Henry Wace, *The Nicene and Post-Nicene Fathers* (Grand Rapids: Eerdmans, 1956), Volume XII, *Epistles of Gregory the Great*, Book V, Epistle XVIII.

[466] Philip Schaff and Henry Wace, *The Nicene and Post-Nicene Fathers* (Grand Rapids: Eerdmans, 1956), Volume XII, *Epistles of Gregory the Great*, Book VIII, Epistle 30, p. 241.

[467] Philip Schaff and Henry Wace, *The Nicene and Post-Nicene Fathers* (Grand Rapids: Eerdmans, 1956), Volume XII, *Epistles of Gregory the Great*, Book VII, Epistle 40, p. 228-229.

[468] *Discourse* 32.18, M.P.G., Vol. 36, Col. 193-194.

[469] *Panegyric on St. Stephen*, M.P.G., Vol. 46, Col. 733.

[470] Philip Schaff and Henry Wace, *Nicene and Post-Nicene Fathers* (Grand Rapids: Eerdmans, 1955), *On The Trinity*, Book VI.36,37; Book II.23.

[471] Philip Schaff and Henry Wace, *Nicene and Post-Nicene Fathers* (Grand Rapids: Eerdmans, 1955), *On The Trinity*, Book VI.20, p. 105.

[472] Alexander Roberts and James Donaldson, Ed., *The Ante–Nicene Fathers* (Buffalo: Christian Literature, 1885), Volume I, *Epistle of Ignatius to the Smyraeans*, Chapter VII, p. 89.

[473] *Epistle 235*. Cited by C. DeLisle Shortt, *Who Was the First Bishop of Rome* (Edinburgh: T&T Clark, 1935), p. 110.

[474] *Epistle 416*. Cited by C. DeLisle Shortt, *Who Was the First Bishop of Rome* (Edinburgh: T&T Clark, 1935), p. 110.

[475] *Allegories in the New Testament*, M.P.L., Vol. 83, Col. 117-118, Numbers 135, 136, 148.

[476] *Etym.* VII.2, M.P.L., Vol. 82, Col. 267.41.

[477] *De Ecclesiasticus* II.5, M.P.L., Vol. 83, Col. 781-782.5-6.

[478] *Sermon 1 de Fide* i.13. Cited by J. Waterworth, *A Commentary* (London: Thomas Richardson, 1871), pp. 39-40.

[479] *Sermon vii., de Poeniten.* 6, Cited by J. Waterworth, *A Commentary* (London: Thomas Richardson, 1871), p. 40.

Endnotes

[480] *Sermon* xi, Cited by J. Waterworth, *A Commentary* (London: Thomas Richardson, 1871), p. 40.

[481] *Commentary on Matthew* 7.25, M.P.L., Vol. 26, Col. 51. Cited by Karlfried Froehlich, *Formen der Auslegung von Matthaus 16,13-18 im lateinischen Mittelalter*, Dissertation (Tubingen, 1963), Footnote #200, p. 49.

[482] *Epistle 65.15, Ad Principiam*. Cited by J. Waterworth S.J., *A Comentary* (London: Thomas Richardson, 1871), p. 109.

[483] *Commentary on Isaiah* ii.2. Cited by J. Waterworth S.J., *A Comentary* (London: Thomas Richardson, 1871), p. 111-112.

[484] *Commentary on Amos* vi.12-13. Cited by J. Waterworth S.J., *A Comentary* (London: Thomas Richardson, 1871), p. 112-113.

[485] *Commentary on Matthew* III, 16:18, M.P.L., Vol. 26, Col. 121-122.

[486] *Commentary on Ephesians* II.20, M.P.L., Vol. 26, Col. 506-507.

[487] *Commentary on Galatians* I.11. Cited by J. Waterworth S.J., *A Commentary* (London: Thomas Richardson, 1871), pp. 116-117.

[488] Philip Schaff and Henry Wace, *Nicene and Post-Nicene Fathers* (Grand Rapids: Eerdmans, 1954), Volume VI, St. Jerome, *Against Jovinanius*, Book 2.37.

[489] Philip Schaff and Henry Wace, *Nicene and Post-Nicene Fathers* (Grand Rapids: Eerdmans, 1954), Volume VI, St. Jerome, Epistle 146.1, *To Evangelus*, pp. 288-289.

[490] Philip Schaff and Henry Wace, *Nicene and Post-Nicene Fathers* (Grand Rapids: Eerdmans, 1954), Volume VI, St. Jerome, *Against Jovinianus* 1.26, p. 366.

[491] Philip Schaff and Henry Wace, *Nicene and Post-Nicene Fathers* (Grand Rapids: Eerdmans, 1954), Volume VI, St. Jerome, *Epistle* 130.16, p. 269.

[492] Philip Schaff and Henry Wace, *Nicene and Post-Nicene Fathers* (Grand Rapids: Eerdmans, 1954), Volume VI, St. Jerome, Epistle 15.2, *To Pope Damasus*, p. 18.

[493] *Homily on the Transfiguration*, M.P.G., Vol. 96, Col. 554-555.

[494] *Homily on the Transfiguration*, M.P.G., Vol. 96, Col. 548.

[495] *Liber de Recta Sententia*, M.P.G., Vol. 94, Col. 1429.

[496] Homily LXVIII, *In Nativitate Petri et Pauli*, M.P.L., Vol. 57, Col. 394.

[497] Sermon XXVIII, M.P.L., Vol. 57, Col. 587-588.

[498] *Ancient Christian Writers* (New York: Newman, 1989), *The Sermons of St. Maximus of Turin*, Sermon 9.1, p. 27. M.S.L., Vol. 39, Col. 2119.

[499] *Ancient Christian Writers* (New York: Newman, 1989), *The Sermons of St. Maximus of Turin*, Sermon 77.1, p. 187.

[500] *Ancient Christian Writers* (New York: Newman, 1989) *The Sermons of St. Maximus of Turin*, Sermon 80.3, p. 193.

[501] *Ancient Christian Writers* (New York: Newman, 1989), *The Sermons of St. Maximus of Turin*, Sermon 49.2-3, pp. 115-117.

[502] *Commentary in Canticle of Canticles*, M.P.G., Vol. 87 (ii), Col. 1693.

[503] Allan Menzies, *The Ante-Nicene Fathers* (Grand Rapids: Eerdmans, 1951), Origen's Commentary on Matthew, Chapters 10-11.

[504] *Exodus, Homily 5.4*. Cited by Karlfried Froehlich, *Formen der Auslegung von Matthaus 16,13-18 im lateinischen Mittelaiter*, Dissertation (Tubingen, 1963), p. 100.

[505] *Commentary on Romans*, Romans 5:10, M.P.G., Vol. 14, Col. 1053. Cited by Karlfried Froehlich, *Formen*, p. 100.

[506] Johannes Quasten, Ed., *Ancient Christian Writers* (London: Longmans, Green, 1957), Origen, *The Song of Songs*, Book Three, pp. 248-250.

[507] *Homily V on Exodus* 14:11-12, PG Volume 12, Column 329. Cited by John Bigane, *Faith, Christ or Peter* (Washington D.C.: University Press, 1981), p. 26, 54.

[508] Epistle 3, *to Sympronianus*. Cited by J. Waterworth S.J., *A Commentary* (London: Thomas Richardson, 1871), p. 123.

[509] *Dialogue on the Life of John Chrysostom*, M.P.G., Vol. 47, Col. 68.

[510] *Dialogue on the Life of John Chrysostom*, Ch. 20.

[511] Commentary on Matthew, M.P.L., Vol. 120, Col. 561. Froehlich, *Formen*, Footnote #141-142, p. 134.

[512] Commentary on Matthew, M.S.L., Vol. 120, Col. 329. Cited by Froehlich, *Formen*, Footnote #211.

[513] Commentary on Matthew 10.4, M.S.L., Vol. 120, Col. 404. Cited by Froehlich, *Formen*, Footnote #129.

[514] Commentary on Matthew, M.S. L., Vol. 120, Col. 555f. Cited by Froehlich, *Formen*, Footnote #162.

[515] *Homily of the Nativity*. Cited by J. Waterworth S.J., *A Commentary* (London: Thomas Richardson, 1871), p. 148.

[516] *Liber Apologeticus Contra Pelagium* 27.3, CSEL, Vol. 5, p. 647.

[517] *Liber Apologeticus Contra Pelagium* 23.5, CSEL, Vol. 5, p. 641.

[518] Johannes Quasten, Ed., *Ancient Christian Writers* (London: Longmans, Green, 1968), *Letters of St. Paulinus of Nola*, Volume II, Letter 23.43-44, p. 46.

[519] Johannes Quasten, Ed., *Ancient Christian Writers* (London: Longmans, Green, 1952), St. Prosper of Aquitaine, *The Call of All Nations*, Book II, Chapter 28, pp. 138-140.

[520] Alexander Roberts and James Donaldson, *The Ante-Nicene Fathers* (Grand Rapids: Eerdmans, 1951), Volume III, Tertullian, *Against Marcion* IV.13, p. 365.

[521] Alexander Roberts and James Donaldson, *The Ante-Nicene Fathers* (Grand Rapids: Eerdmans, 1951), Volume III, Tertullian, *Scorpiace X.*, p. 643.

[522] Alexander Roberts and James Donaldson, *The Ante-Nicene Fathers* (Grand Rapids: Eerdmans, 1951), Volume IV, Tertullian, *On Modesty* 21, p. 99.

[523] Alexander Roberts and James Donaldson, *The Ante-Nicene Fathers* (Grand Rapids: Eerdmans, 1951), Vol. III, Tertullian, *Prescription Against Heretics* 22.

[524] Alexander Roberts and James Donaldson, *The Ante-Nicene Fathers* (Grand Rapids: Eerdmans, 1951), Volume III, Tertullian, *An Answer to the Jews*, Chapter ix, p. 163.

[525] Philip Schaff, *Nicene and Post-Nicene Fathers* (Grand Rapids: Eerdmans, 1956), Volume III, Theodoret, Epistle 146, *To John the Economus*, p. 318.

[526] *Commentary on 1 Corinthians* 1,12. Cited by J. Waterworth S.J., *A Commentary* (London: Thomas Richardson, 1871), p. 149.

[527] Philip Schaff, *Nicene and Post-Nicene Fathers* (Grand Rapids: Eerdmans, 1956), Volume III, Theodoret, Epistle 77, *To Eulalius,* p. 273.

[528] *Commentary on Canticle of Canticles* II.14, M.P.G., Vol. 81, Col. 108.

[529] *Commentary on Psalms* 86.1, M.P.G., Vol. 80, Col. 1561.

[530] Philip Schaff, *Nicene and Post-Nicene Fathers* (Grand Rapids: Eerdmans, 1956), Volume III, Theodoret, Epistle 86, *To Flavianus, bishop of Constantinople*, p. 281.

[531] *Commentary on Daniel ii.34.* Cited by J. Waterworth S.J., *A Commentary* (London: Thomas Richardson, 1871), p. 153.

[532] *Haeret. Fab.* Book 5, Chapter 28. Cited by J. Waterworth S.J., *A Commentary* (London: Thomas Richardson, 1871), p. 152

[533] Epistle of Justin to Pope Hormisdas, M.P.L., Vol. 63, Col. 503.

[534] *In Ev. Marc.* chap. 3. Cited by J. Waterworth S.J., *A Commentary* (London: Thomas Richardson, 1871), pp. 133-134.

INDEX

Acasian Schism *213*
Against the Errors of the Greeks 223-225
Agatho (pope) *217*
Ambrose, *15, 20, 62-67, 279-82*
Ambrosiaster *72-75, 138, 282-84*
Anastasius (Emperor) *213*
Aphraates *103-05, 284-86*
Apiarius *206-07*
Apostles: *All Equal to Peter*
   Ambrosiaster *72-75, 282-84*
   Augustine *56-57, 253-82*
   Basil the Great *94-95, 291*
   Chrysostom *78-71, 295-309*
   Cyprian *33-34, 309-11*
   Cyril of Alexandria *92, 311-14*
   Cyril of Jerusalem *98-99, 314*
   Firmilian *43-45, 319*
   Gregory the Great, *321-25*
   Gregory of Nyssa *96-97, 325*
   Isidore of Seville *129-30, 327-28*
   Jerome *69-70, 328-331*
   Origen *30-32, 336-38*
   Paschasius Radbertus *136, 340*
   Theodoret *88, 344-46*
Apostolical Constitutions 138-39, 286
Appeals to Rome
   Chrysostom *207-09*
   Theodore the Studite *209-12*
Aquinas, Thomas *223-228*
Arabic Canons of Nicaea *167-70*
Asterius *109-10, 286-87*
Athanasius, *15, 48-51, 288-90*
Augustine, *15, 20, 52-62, 75, 98, 138-40, 200-05, 253-82*
Authority, Roman Catholic Teaching *12-13*

Baptism (Heretical)
   Conflict between Cyprian and Pope Stephen *194-99*

Basil of Seleucia *107-08, 291-92*
Basil the Great *93-96, 291*
Batiffol, P. *154*
Bauer, Chrysostomus *84-85*
Bede *133-35, 292*
Burmejo, Luis *141*
Canons of Councils:
   6 of Nicaea *163-67*
   2, 3 of Constantinople I *170-73*
   28 of Chalcedon *173-81*
Cassian, John *99-100, 293-94*
Cassiodorus *111-13, 292-93*
Celestine (pope) *205*
Chair of Peter, *34-43, 196*
   and Cyprian, *20, 34-40*
   and Optatus, *40-42*
   and Firmilian, *196*
   and Gregory the Great *324*
Chapman, Dom John *78-82*
Chrysologus, Peter *126-27, 308-09*
Chrysostom, *15, 74-86, 138, 207-209, 295-309*
Coleman-Norton, P.R. *209*
Comments of 6th Century Eastern Clergy from a Letter to Emperor Justin *128-29, 346-47*
Comments of Either Chrysostom, Cyril of Alexandria or Origen on Matthew 16 Falsely Attributed to Victor of Antioch *347*
Congar, Yves *153-54, 231-33*
Constantine (Emperor) *164*
Constantinople III (Council)
   Decree Condemning pope Honorius for Heresy *184-93*
Council of
   Carthage (256 A.D.) *195*
   Carthage (424 A.D.) *206*
   Chalcedon *173-81*
   Constantinople I *170-73*

Constantinople II *181-84*
Constantinople III *184-93*
Nicaea I *163-70*
Sardica *206*
Cullmann, Oscar *26*
Cyprian *20, 32-40, 137, 194-200 309-11*
Cyril of Alexandria *88-93, 180-81 311-14*
Cyril of Jerusalem *98-99, 314*

Denny, Edward *225-227*
Didymus the Blind *50-51, 314-15*
Dollinger, Johann Joseph Ignaz von *147-48, 162, 188-89, 205 227-28*
Dvornik, Francis *171-72*

Ecumenism *10-11*
Eno, Robert *34-36, 42-43, 65,177, 179-180*
Ephrem Syrus *105-06, 316*
Epiphanius *101-04, 315*
Eusebius *45-48, 316-17*

Fastiggi, Robert *20-21, 35, 36, 204*
Firmicus Maternus *318-19*
Firmilian *43-45, 195-98, 319*
Fournier, Keith *12-13*
Frend, WHC *61, 170-71, 175, 177- 178, 193, 199-200*
Froehlich, Karlfried *27, 38, 59-60, 66, 139-40, 150-53*
Fulgentius of Ruspe *113-14, 320*

Gardner, Alice *210*
Gaudentius of Brescia *320-21*
Gospel (the)
  and Roman Catholic Claims *9-18*
Gratian (Emperor) *170*
Gregory the Great *114-21, 321-25*
Gregory Nazianzen *325*
Gregory of Nyssa *96-97, 325*

Hefele, Charles Joseph *183-84, 185- 188, 200-201*

Hilary of Poitiers *68-69, 341-42*
Honorius (pope) *192-201*
Hormisdas (pope) *212-217*

Ignatius *136, 326-27*
Infallibility (Papal)
  Catechism of Catholic Church *13-14*
  Council of Constantinople III *184-193*
  Vatican I *246-249*
Isidore of Pelusium *111, 327*
Isidore of Seville *129-30, 327-28*

James of Nisbis *97-98, 328*
Jerome *68-71, 328-31*
Jesus, Peter and the Keys 28, 31, 47, 62, 89,93
John 21:15-17:
  Augustine *142-43, 274-79*
  Chrysostom *295-309*
  Cyril of Alexandria *92, 311-14*
John of Constantinople *114-21, 214-15*
John of Damascus *130-33, 331-32*
Jurgens, William *51, 74, 93, 129, 198-99*
Justification, *11-12*
Justin I (Emperor) *213*
Justinian (Emperor) *181*

Keating, Karl *26, 185, 191*
Keys (The) *156-57*
  Entrusted to All Apostles Equally
  Augustine *56-57, 253-82*
  Cassian *293-94*
  Chrysostom *295-309*
  Cyprian *309-11*
  Didymus the Blind *314-15*
  Firmilian *319*
  Gaudentius *320-21*
  Jerome *328-31*
  Maximus of Turin *332-36*
  Origen *337-39*
  Pacian *339*
Kretchmar, Georg *181*
Kung, Hans *220*

Leo I (pope) *175-81*
Leo II (pope) *188-89, 192*

Index

L'Huiller, Peter *165-66*
Libellus of Pope Hormisdas *213-17*
Liber Pontificalis 221
Luke 22:32 *136-42*
   Ambrosiaster *144*
   Apostolical Constitutions 144-45
   Augustine *139-40, 273-74*
   Chrysosotm *138, 307-08*
   Cyprian *137, 309-11*
   Ignatius *136-37*

Markus, R.A. *120-21*
Maximus of Turin *121-26, 348-52*
McCue, James *31-32, 37, 165*
Meletius *173*
Merdinger, J.E. *201, 202*
Meyendorff, John *30, 38-39, 119-20, 155-56, 164-65, 172-73, 176-77, 180-81, 191-92, 205-06, 210, 215, 216-17, 233-36*
Monophysitism *212*
Monotheletism *184-93*
Morrison, Karl *60, 120, 129, 166-67, 175-76, 197-98, 209-210, 215-16*

Nilus of Ancyra *108-09, 336*

Origen *29-32, 336-39*

Pacian *339*
Palladius of Helenopolis *106-07, 339-340*
Papadakis, Aristeides *229-31*
Paschasius Radbertus *141-42, 340*
Paul of Emessa *110-11, 340*
Paul Orosius *341*
Paulinus of Nola *341-42*
Pelikan, Jaroslav *134-35, 146-47, 184-85, 231*
Pelagius *200-04*
Peter (Apostle)
   Figurative Representative of the Church
      Augustine *53-54, 59-62, 253-82*
      Cyprian *33-34, 309-11*

Fulgentius *113-14, 320*
Gregory the Great *117-18, 321-325*
Isidore of Seville *129-30, 327-28*
Origen *29-32, 336-39*
Tertullian *28, 343-44*
Church Not Built on His Person but on His Faith
   Ambrose *62-67, 297-282*
   Augustine *52-62, 253*
   Tertullian *26-28, 343-44*
Primacy: Meaning of:
   Ambrose *62-67*
   Augustine *52-62*
   Chrysostom *74-86*
Petrine Succession
   Not Exclusive to Rome *171-72, 176-177*
Piepkorn, Arthur *173*
Prosper of Aquitaine *342-43*
Pseudo Isidorian Decretals *221-23*

Rock (The): Various Interpretations
   Peter:
      Asterius *109-10, 286-87*
      Chrysologus (Peter) *126-27, 308-309*
      Cyprian *32-40, 309-11*
      Gregory Nazianzen *325*
      James of Nisbis *97-98, 328*
      Maximus of Turin *121-26, 332-36*
      Origen *29-32, 336-39*
      Paul Orosius *341*
      Paulinus of Nola *341-42*
      Tertullian *26-28, 343-44*
   Peter's Confession of Faith:
      Ambrose *62-67, 279-82*
      Athanasius *48-51, 288-90*
      Augustine *52-62, 252-82*
      Basil of Seleucia *107-08, 291-92*
      Bede *133-35, 292*
      Cassian (John), *99-100, 293-94*
      Chrysostom *74-86, 295-309*
      Cyril of Alexandria *88-93, 311-14*
      Didymus the Blind *50-51, 314-15*
      Epiphanius *101-04, 315*

Gregory the Great *114-21, 321-325*
Gregory of Nyssa *96-97, 325*
Hilary of Poitiers *67-68, 325-26*
Isidore of Pelusium *111, 327*
James of Nisbis *97-98, 328*
John of Damascus *130-33, 331-332*
Maximus of Turin *121-26, 332-336*
Nilus of Ancyra *108-09, 336*
Palladius of Helenopolis *106-07 339-40*
Paschasius Radbertus *135-36 340*
Paul of Emessa *110-11, 340*
Theodoret *86-89, 344-46*
Theophylact *132-33*
6th Century Eastern Clergy *346-47*

Christ:
Ambrose *62-67, 279-82*
Aphraates *103-05, 284-86*
Asterius *113-14, 286-87*
Augustine *52-62, 253-282*
Bede *133-35, 292*
Cassiodorus *111-13, 292-93*
Chrysologus (Peter) *126-27 308-09*
Cyril of Alexandria *88-93 311-14*
Ephrem Syrus *105-06, 316*
Eusebius *45-48, 316-17*
Firmicus Maternus *318-19*
Fulgentius *113-14, 320*
Isidore of Pelusium *111, 327*
Isidore of Seville *129-30, 327-328*
James of Nisbis *97-98, 328*
Jerome *68-71, 328-31*
John of Damascus *130-33, 331-332*
Paschasius Radbertus *135-36, 340*
Paulinus of Nola *341-42*
Theodoret *86-89, 344-46*

All True Believers
Ambrose *288-90*
Basil the Great *291*
Origen *29-32, 336-39*

Robertson, Pat *10*
Roman See,
 Limited Jurisdiction *163-67*
 Primacy of Honor *163, 173-75*
Rotelle, John *59*

Salmon, George *95-96, 164, 172, 206-207, 222-23*
Schaff, Philip *166-70, 203, 219*
Scott, Herbert *83-84, 178*
Seeburg, Reinhold *39-60-61*
Sparrow-Simpson, W.J. *181*
Stephen (pope)
 and Firmilian, *43-45, 195-98*
 and Cyprian, *194-99*

Tertullian *26-28, 343-44*
Theodore the Studite *209-13*
Theodoret *86-89, 344-46*
Theophylact of Bulgaria *132-33*
Tierney, Brian *140-41, 217*

Unanimous Consent, *18, 25, 143-46*
Vatican I, *9*
 Papal Rule, *17-18, 241-46*
 Papal Infallibility, *17-18, 246-49*
Vigilius (pope) *181-84*

Winter, Michael *37, 72-73, 85-86, 89 93-94, 102, 106-07 149-50*

Zeno (Emperor) *213*
Zosimus (pope)
 and Pelagius *200-04*
 and Apiarius *206-07*